Albrecht Classen
Freedom, Imprisonment, and Slavery in the Pre-Modern World

Fundamentals of Medieval and Early Modern Culture

Edited by
Albrecht Classen and Marilyn Sandidge

Volume 25

Albrecht Classen

Freedom, Imprisonment, and Slavery in the Pre-Modern World

Cultural-Historical, Social-Literary, and Theoretical Reflections

DE GRUYTER

ISBN 978-3-11-073712-7
e-ISBN (PDF) 978-3-11-073179-8
e-ISBN (EPUB) 978-3-11-073185-9
ISSN 1864-3396

Library of Congress Control Number: 2021932115

Bibliographic information published by the Deutsche Nationalbibliothek
The Deutsche Nationalbibliothek lists this publication in the Deutsche Nationalbibliografie; detailed bibliographic data are available on the Internet at http://dnb.dnb.de.

© 2021 Walter de Gruyter GmbH, Berlin/Boston
Printing and binding: CPI books GmbH, Leck

www.degruyter.com

Fig. 1: Vincent de Beauvais, *Speculum historiale*. St. Leonard between two prisoners; ca. 1370–1380; Bibliothèque nationale de France, manuscript NAF 15944, fol. 37v.

Contents

Introduction —— 1
1   Harsh Realities: Lack of Freedom – Desire for Freedom —— 1
         Extremes of Human Existence Past and Present —— 1
2   Modern Phenomena and Pre-Modern Conditions —— 4

A   Imprisonment —— 19
1   Medieval Comments on Imprisonment and Prisons —— 19
2   The Exemplary Case of Hans Ulrich Krafft: An Early Modern Prisoner Reflects on His Experiences —— 26
3   The Philosopher in the Prison (Boethius and Thomas More) —— 29
4   The Exile: Literary Reflections from Antiquity to the Late Middle Ages —— 32
5   The Prisoner —— 37
6   The Slave —— 39

B   Freedom —— 40
1   Freedom – A Complex Topic Throughout Time —— 40
2   Hugo von Trimberg: The Social Discourse in the High and Late Middle Ages —— 48
3   Eike von Repgow, *Sachsenspiegel* —— 53
4   The Quest for Freedom in Medieval Fables —— 55
4.1   Marie de France —— 60
4.2   Ulrich Bonerius —— 61

C   Imprisonment and Slavery Through Many Different Lenses —— 66
1   Former Slaves as Authors —— 70
1.1   Johann Schiltberger —— 71
1.2   The Slave Georgius of Hungary —— 74
1.3   The Slave Harck Olufs —— 84
2   Dante Alighieri and Boethius, Again —— 86
3   Freedom and Imprisonment since Antiquity —— 93
4   *The Magna Carta* —— 100
5   *Waltharius*: An Early Medieval Heroic Poem in Latin —— 103
6   Marie de France: Marriage as Prison? —— 110

D	**Literary Treatment of Imprisonment and Slavery — 120**
1	Boccaccio's *Decameron* — 120
2	Heinrich Kaufringer: Further Examples in Late Medieval *mæren* — 121
3	Interim – Slavery in Historical Terms: A Few Examples in Support of the Literary Evidence — 124
4	Slavery in Icelandic Sagas – Fleeting but Revealing References — 125
5	*Aucassin and Nicolette:* The Female Slave as the Beloved — 133
6	*Floire et Blanchefleur* — 138
7	Konrad Fleck: The Middle High German Version — 141
8	Wolfram von Eschenbach, *Willehalm* — 143
9	The Literary and the Historical Dimension Intertwined — 147
10	*Apollonius of Tyre* — 148
11	*Kudrun:* A Thirteenth-Century Heroic Epic — 152
12	*Das Lied vom Hürnen Seyfrid* — 156
13	Rudolf von Ems: *Der guote Gêrhart* — 160
14	Geoffrey de Villehardouin's *Conquête de Constantinople* — 166
15	Boccaccio's *Decameron* in a New Context — 168
16	Don Juan Manuel, *El Conde Lucanor* – Medieval Spanish Reflections — 171

E	**Famous Historical Prisoners — 174**
1	Richard I: The English King as Prisoner — 174
2	The French King Louis IX as Prisoner of the Mamluks of Egypt — 180
3	Charles d'Orléans: The French Dauphin as Royal Prisoner in England — 182
4	King James I of Scotland: Another Royal Prisoner and Poet — 190
5	Oswald von Wolkenstein: A Tyrolean Poet and His Prison Experience — 194

F	**Crime and Imprisonment in Literary Terms — 199**
1	Wolfram von Eschenbach's *Parzival* — 199
2	Geoffrey Chaucer and Rape — 201
2.1	Imprisonment and Punishment of the Evil Knight — 201
2.2	Chaucer's Knights in the Prison — 201
3	Ulrich von Zatzikhoven and His Version of the *Lancelot* Romance — 204

4		Other Literary Reflections of Imprisonment —— **207**
5		Dante Alighieri, the Allegorical Prison —— **211**
6		Christine de Pizan: A Late Medieval Female Writer's —— **217**
7		*Fortunatus* (anonymous, 1509) —— **219**
G		**Freedom, the Protestant Reformation, and Slavery in the New World —— 227**
1		Martin Luther's Concept of Freedom —— **227**
2		Bartolomé de las Casas —— **232**
3		Marguerite de Navarre: Life as a Prison. Allegorical Reflections —— **240**

Conclusions —— 242

Acknowledgment —— 252

Bibliography —— 257

Index —— 307

Introduction

Biskop Tomas frihetssång.

Frihet är det ädlaste ting
Som sökas må all verlden kring,
Den frihet väl kan bära.
Vill du dig sjelfvan vara huld,
Du älske frihet mer än guld,
Ty frihet följer ära.

1 Harsh Realities: Lack of Freedom – Desire for Freedom

Extremes of Human Existence Past and Present

Most of medieval and early modern literature seems to ignore some of the darkest moments in human life, but it also abstains, at least at first sight, from discussing the issue of freedom. Although there have always been imprisonment or enslavement in human culture and civilization, not to mention executions or other forms of gruesome penalties, those seem to be addressed less commonly in poetic or fictional form because pre-modern literature hardly catered to sadistic pleasures. The reason for this phenomenon might perhaps have been that those experiences would have been too shocking for the various (courtly or urban) audiences looking for entertainment and uplifting material within their banal, trivial, and uneventful lives. The vast world of courtly romance, of short verse narratives (*fabliaux, mæren, novelli*), of religious plays, of heroic epics, and of love poetry normally turns its attention away from the sordid, miserable, painful, and horrifying moments in a person's life when everything suddenly comes to a screeching halt because external forces impose themselves on the individual and remove him/her from the ordinary course of events, creating a terrible hiatus, or an absolute or final change from freedom to imprisonment or, even worse, to slavery.

What is meant here is not death, which represents a total closure and end of all existence, but the temporary or a life-long loss of freedom experienced by the slave which often amounted nearly to a form of 'death' while the person was still alive and held in captivity or bondage. By the same token, the desire for freedom seems to be a fundamental aspect and need of human culture, although, considering world history, it has been more often an evanescent and ephemeral experience than a stable and guaranteed form of existence. It was never enough simply to say, following René Descartes, *cogito, ergo sum* (1637; *Discours de la*

Méthode Pour bien conduire sa raison, et chercher la vérité dans les sciences, translated into Latin in 1656). The human being also needs freedom, space to breathe, to act according to his/her own will, and independence from a dictatorial, tyrannical, hence repressive ruler – a notion which gained primary shape since the eighteenth century, as we commonly hear. Hence, to adapt Descartes's adage, the real message would be: 'libero, ergo sum,' a concept which has resonated throughout time and so also in the works of many recent philosophers, economists, and sociologists, such as Amartya Sen, Daron Acemoglu, and James A. Robinson, and which has been enshrined in many western constitutions.[1]

There is, unfortunately, very valid concern in many modern countries, both in the East and the West, that the hard-fought victories of democracy and free-

---

[1] Amartya Sen, *Development as Freedom* (Oxford: Oxford University Press, 1999); Shahram Jafarzadeh and Mohhamad Bagher Beheshti, "Importance of Freedom in Humanities Developing," *Procedia: Social and Behavioral Sciences* 31 (2012): 323–32 (despite a somewhat faulty English, certainly a useful study). As Peter Augustine Lawler and Richard Reinsch, "Freedom and the Human Person," *National Affairs* 44 (2020), online at: https://www.nationalaffairs.com/publications/detail/freedom-and-the-human-person (last accessed on Jan. 15, 2021), state: "The American, constitutional mean between abstract universalism and tribal secessionism, according to Brownson, is a limited political unity of citizens who know they are also more than and less than citizens. All of us equally are shaped by natural, personal imperatives having to do with flourishing as material, political, and spiritual beings. When we forget any of the three, we fall into trouble. The material being is concerned with the personal subsistence of himself and his family. The political being is concerned with the common good shared by citizens in a 'territorial democracy' in a particular part of the world. The spiritual being is concerned with discovering his relational duties to his loving personal Creator and sharing that personal news with his fellow creatures through the church" (no pagination). See now also the serious warning by Larry M. Bartels about the possible destruction of fundamental democratic principles and ethical norms by the radical right in the United States in the 2020 presidential elections, dangerously inflamed because of the perceived threat to their traditional white male, Christian, and straight American culture: "Ethnic Antagonism Erodes Republicans' Commitment to Democracy," *Proceedings of the National Academy of Sciences of the United States of America (PNSA)* 117.37 (2020): 22752–22759; online at: https://doi.org/10.1073/pnas.2007747117. There is a whole legion of relevant research on this huge, and probably also very ideological topic. Consequently, I accept, of course, that this entire aspect could be viewed quite differently from the other side of the political spectrum. See, for instance, the contributions to *Culture Wars: An Encyclopedia of Issues, Viewpoints, and Voices*, ed. Roger Chapman (Armonk, NY, and London: M. E. Sharpe, 2010); Bradley Campbell and Jason Manning, *The Rise of Victimhood Culture: Microaggressions, Safe Spaces, and the New Culture Wars* (Cham: Springer International Publishing, 2018). As to the danger which all democratic countries today face especially from within, see Daron Acemoglu and James A. Robinson, *Economic Origins of Dictatorship and Democracy* (Cambridge: Cambridge University Press, 2009); id., *The Narrow Corridor: States, Societies, and the Fate of Liberty* (New York: Penguin, 2019).

dom might be at risk again because neo-fascist, radically militarized, and in fact repressive forces are gaining greatly in influence all over the world at an alarming rate, using the legal system, the military might, and the police force to their own advantages, attempting to manipulate public opinions against the fundamental concepts of individual freedom in the name of an elusive notion of 'the nation' run by the 'great leader' allegedly protecting the people from external and internal forces. Charisma is thus replacing democracy, and a cult-culture replacing a freedom-based society.

We seem to understand the meaning of freedom fully only when it is in danger of being lost or already taken away from us, as many historical examples from ancient Greece to imperial Rome, and throughout the Middle Ages and beyond have demonstrated. Freedom is hardly ever discussed when all members of a society enjoy it and do not perceive any danger that they might lose it. History teaches us, however, that human societies have always struggled against dictators, tyrants, oligarchs, and even against the tyranny of the very people who rallied against their aristocratic oppressors and then turned against wide swaths of the population perceived to be not on their side (French Revolution, Russian Revolution). Thus, probing the meaning of freedom and its potential loss opens many significant perspectives regarding the fundamental structures and value systems of any society throughout time.

These preliminary, maybe subjective reflections serve here only as a springboard for cultural-historical investigations concerning the pre-modern discourse on freedom, imprisonment, and slavery. But, examining past comments on those three fundamental aspects and investigating how medieval and early modern authors thought and argued about them in philosophical, spiritual, ethical, and political terms, promises to provide us with valuable tools in the current situation because historical experiences serve exceedingly well as mirrors or models for our own discourse. If we do not know of and about the struggles in the past, we would simply not be prepared enough for our modern challenges. The cry for freedom, for instance, resonates throughout history, and medieval poets also and very meaningfully emerge as powerful contributors to the global efforts in the twenty-first century to fight against injustice, political subjugation, dictatorship, and in support of public and private efforts to maintain or to gain our freedom. The number of relevant voices from that time period might not be very large, but we can be certain that those existed as well. Bringing those to light here constitutes, I dare say, the opening-up of a new page in our history books of the Middle Ages and the early modern age.

By the same token, many medieval cultural texts, such as sacred, religious works, or heroic epics, contain references to imprisonment, often brought about by monstrous creatures, such as dragons or griffins. Only the intervention of the hero or the growth of the young protagonist into a hero makes possible the liberation from the prison. There are even cases of self-imposed imprisonment for religious reasons. I will provide examples for these phenomena in the discussions further below. We will also observe that neither gender nor social class matters in terms of imprisonment, and even members of a royal family could become victims of slavery. The issue that will be addressed below thus proves to be, from the start, extremely complex and challenging, and hence of fundamental relevance also, if not particularly, for pre-modern society.

2 Modern Phenomena and Pre-Modern Conditions

Certainly, the western world today seems to enjoy a high level of individual freedom, guaranteed through constitutions or other basic laws, but we also know that slavery continues to exist, in the very same world, mostly hidden, but not eradicated at all. Enormous economic progress is noticeable at current times, but personal freedom, justice, and inclusivity are alarmingly on a steady decline, and this now for some decades, so it seems. As we can clearly observe, all over the world increasingly autocratic governments have claimed absolute power over their citizens, and the post-modern world faces the surprising development that freedom for the individual within a democratic system is suddenly at stake, once again.[2] Kidnapping happens in many countries today at an alarming rate, and in many countries,[3] and, not necessarily related to that, there are more prisons than

---

[2] Julia O'Connell Davidson, *Modern Slavery: The Margins of Freedom* (Basingstoke, Hampshire, and New York: Palgrave Mcmillan, 2015); Norbert Campagna, *Staatliche Macht und menschliche Freiheit: Das Staatsdenken Bertrand de Jouvenels*. Staatsdiskurse, 35 (Stuttgart: Franz Steiner Verlag, 2020); see also the contributions to *Die Wirklichkeit der konkreten Freiheit: G. W. F. Hegels Lehre vom Staat als ausgeführter Idee der Sittlichkeit*, ed. Michael Städtler. Staatsdiskurse, 37 (Stuttgart: Franz Steiner Verlag, 2020); *Digitalisierung und Demokratie: Ethische Perspektiven*, ed. Petra Grimm and Oliver Zöllner. Medienethik, 18 (Stuttgart: Franz Steiner Verlag, 2020); Laura DeNardis, *The Internet in Everything: Freedom and Security in a World With No Off Switch* (New Haven, CT: Yale University Press, 2020).

[3] Wolf Middendorf, *Menschenraub, Flugzeugentführungen, Geiselnahme, Kidnapping: historische und moderne Erscheinungsformen* (Bielefeld: Gieseking, 1972); *La sottrazione internazionale di minori da parte di un genitore: studi e documenti sul "kidnapping" internazionale*, ed. Franco Mosconi. Pubblicazioni della Università di Pavia: Studi nelle scienze giuridiche e sociali. Nuova serie, 53 (Padua: CEDAM, 1988); Rolando Ochoa, *Intimate Crimes: Kidnapping, Gangs, and Trust in Mexico City*. Clarendon Studies in Criminology (Oxford: Oxford University Press, 2019); Stephen Morewitz, *Kidnapping and Violence: New Research and Clinical Perspectives*. SpringerNature, 4116 (New York: Springer New York, 2019). There is much literature on this topic, unfortunately, because the issue is so complex and the practice so widespread. For the

ever before because they have become big business in the hands of certain corporations.[4] Freedom of expression, assembly, religion, movement, activities, and so forth are tenuous ideals, and considering the growth of repressive regimes in many countries even in the twenty-first century, those of us who still enjoy those freedoms can count them as our blessing and hope they are not goig to be lost to a growing authoritarianism in many different countries.

It amounts to a grotesque irony of the twenty-first century that the United States, above all, while being predicated on the supposed pursuit of and commitment to freedom, as reflected, for instance, in its constitution and the national anthem, yet proves to be the one country in the world ranked first in terms of the number of imprisoned people. This fact cannot be simply explained away by claiming that there exists an extreme form of a criminal mind-set among certain sections of the American population. Instead, here we observe the insidious results of racism and, at the same time, a war against the class of poor people, and this amazingly, if not shockingly, in the post-modern world. Are we really progressing, or are we in regression? Or is racism a global and timeless issue that remains stubbornly with us because people throughout the ages and all over the globe have always looked for hermeneutic instruments to differentiate themselves from 'the others,' the perfect recipe for racism, both then and today. Studying the global discourse on these issues already in the pre-modern world thus empowers us to understand much better than before the constructive, hence tenuous, nature of freedom and subsequently also the loss of freedom.

---

latest statistics, see https://socialprogress.blog/2020/09/10/announcing-the-2020-social-progress-index/ (last accessed on Jan. 15, 2021).

4 According to Wendy Sawyer and Peter Wagner, "Mass Incarceration: The Whole Pie 2020," online report at: https://www.prisonpolicy.org/reports/pie2020.html (last accessed on Jan. 15, 2021), "The American criminal justice system holds almost 2.3 million people in 1,833 state prisons, 110 federal prisons, 1,772 juvenile correctional facilities, 3,134 local jails, 218 immigration detention facilities, and 80 Indian Country jails as well as in military prisons, civil commitment centers, state psychiatric hospitals, and prisons in the U.S. territories." See also Byron Eugene Price and John Charles Morris, *Prison Privatization: The Many Facets of a Controversial Industry* (Westport, CT: ABC-CLIO, 2012); Shane Bauer, *American Prison: A Reporter's Undercover Journey Into the Business of Punishment* (New York: Penguin, 2018); see also the report by Kara Gotsch and Vinay Basti about the vast changes in the US imprisonment policies and the consequences of the privatization of prisons, "Capitalizing on Mass Incarceration: U.S. Growth in Private Prisons," online at: https://www.sentencingproject.org/wp-content/uploads/2018/07/Capitalizing-on-Mass-Incarceration.pdf; https://worldpopulationreview.com/country-rankings/incarceration-rates-by-country (both last accessed on Jan. 15, 2021). For the British prison system, see *Handbook on Prisons*, ed. Yvonne Jewkes, Ben Crewe, and Jamie Bennett. Sec. ed. (London and New York: Routledge, 2016).

To re-emphasize this, freedom and imprisonment, and so also slavery, are cultural phenomena, the results of public discourses and of individual and collective efforts and power struggles, and while we can study them critically through sociological, legal, political, or psychological lenses, we have also great opportunities to come to terms with them through the medium of literature and historical and artistic documents and objects. Insofar as we are today the heirs of centuries of struggles for freedom and a fair and transparent prison system, it would be a logical and necessary step to look backwards and trace the origin of those discourses also in earlier times, here especially the Middle Ages and the early modern age.[5]

If we consider, for instance, the extent to which early medieval Icelandic society handled crimes by means of payments, settlements, temporary expulsions, and virtually not by means of prisons and executions (cf. *Njál's Saga*), we realize how much the current situation in the United States is the result of specific economic, political, social, and racial conditions created by the majority in direct clash with some minorities. A country that can look back to publicly approved lynching perpetrated by the Ku Klux Klan and other groups of white people, a country that suffers from horrifying police brutality and murder primarily of Black Americans, and a country where the prison complex is a major economic factor, apparently seems to be deeply interested in perpetuating conditions of inequality and unfreedom of marginalized groups that originated in the days of slavery and that continue to provide huge capitalistic incentives.

A vast majority of the American prison population consists of poor and particularly Black Americans, a statistic which certainly reflects the huge disadvantages which this section of the American population suffers from and which has been widely reported on (see the reports issued by the Brennan Center for Justice). Instead of the Statue of Liberty in the New York harbor, now the American prisons, along with the border wall between the United States and Mexico, have become the central icons of a certain portion of a population deliberately contra-

---

5 Donald W. Treadgold, *Freedom: A History* (New York: New York University Press, 1990); *Freedom: A Philosophical Anthology*, ed. Ian Carter, Matthew H. Kramer, and Hillel Steiner (Malden, MA: Blackwell Publishing, 2007); *The Liberty Reader*, ed. and intro. David Miller (1991; Edinburgh: Edinburgh University Press, 2006); *Race and Liberty in America*, ed. Jonathan J. Bean (Lexington, KY: Kentucky University Press, 2009); for historical perspectives, see Luca Scholz, *Borders and Freedom of Movement in the Holy Roman Empire* (Oxford: Oxford University Press, 2020). See also the contributions to *Slavery's Capitalism: A New History of American Economic Development*, ed. Sven Beckert and Seth Rockman. Early American Studies (Philadelphia: University of Pennsylvania Press, 2016). The literature on this topic is vast, and rightly so because the topic itself quickly proves to be highly complex, full of conflict, determined by deep divides regarding group identities, racial relationships, gender issues, and so forth.

dicting its own constitutional values and ideals, as contested as this notion might be among certain political circles. Is this modern country really under siege, threatened by dangerous criminal elements everywhere? Of course, there are major organizations, groups, and political units that see all this very differently, and if this book were about current politics, they would deserve to be listened to as well.

To be sure, the term 'freedom' quickly proves to be highly complex since it could be understood in philosophical, political, theological, spiritual, physical, and sociological terms. It could imply freedom from political suppression, from the constrictions of one's material existence, from bodily limitations and worldly temptations, or from being bound to one's social class. Freedom has also been discussed in many respects as 'freedom of will' and intellectual independence. The same challenges apply to the other two terms, 'imprisonment' and 'enslavement,' each containing a kaleidoscope of meanings that can only be unearthed and explored by means of a sensitive, flexible, and discriminating approach. The following investigations try to take a wide range of concepts into consideration, especially because each textual source mirrors or evokes a different level or context, which needs to be probed carefully in order to come to a solid understanding of the various types of discourses involved here, bringing many diverse cases to the table.

Let us hence take a quick look at some of those studies where we might expect that the topics to be addressed here already to be addressed. However, most cultural historians focused on the Middle Ages and beyond have surprisingly little to say about imprisonment, if this issue is even mentioned in the first place. The contributors to the *Revelations of the Medieval World*, for example, edited by famous Georges Duby, offer valuable insights into aristocratic households, the life of Tuscan notables, the emergence of self-reflections in literature, the role of private space, and the development of individuality, but nothing about questions about freedom or the loss thereof.[6] There are excellent studies on medieval civilization, but we would not need to consult them in search of material about freedom and its opposite.[7] Scholars interested in the history of mentality have

---

6 *Revelations of the Medieval World*, ed. Georges Duby, trans. Arthur Goldhammer. A History of Private Life, II (1985; Cambridge, MA, and London: The Belknap Press of Harvard University Press, 1988).

7 See, for instance, Kay Slocum, *Medieval Civilization* (Belmont, CA: Thomson Wadsworth, 2005); Clifford R. Backman, *The Worlds of Medieval Europe* (New York and Oxford: Oxford University Press, 2003), 125, refers to slaves at least once (Carolingian era). The anthology *Reading the Middle Ages: Sources from Europe, Byzantium, and the Islamic World*, ed. Barbara H. Rosenwein (Peterborough, Ont.: Broadview Press, 2006), 141–42, includes a map of the slave trade

opened many new windows toward the fundamental make-up of medieval society and culture on a deeper level, but the desire for freedom, for instance, or the fear of enslavement, does not seem to matter there.[8] The same applies to the field of investigation generally called 'everyday life,' maybe because the world of crime, violence, imprisonment, and, even worse, of slavery was assumed to be an oddity or something unusual.[9] Others have certainly addressed the topics of law, punishment, and also execution, especially when those took place in public, but the extreme issue of freedom and slavery does not figure there either, and we hear really little about what the situation in pre-modern prisons was really like, whether they even existed in the first place, and for what purposes.

Fortunately, the prison itself, as a public institution, as it had emerged already in the thirteenth century (if not much earlier), has recently attraced some significant interest, especially if we think of Guy Geltner's study on the medieval prison, particularly in Venice, Florence, and Bologna (2008). As he observes, the medieval prison was not a completely isolating location; instead, it was situated in the middle of medieval cities; prisoners very commonly had regular contacts with the outside world, and were normally allowed to conduct their own lives as before, though in a more coercive and restricted manner (see the case of Hans Ulrich Krafft, below).[10] This is not to say at all that prisons were

---

across Europe and the Middle East, and a text excerpt from 724 C.E. concerning the sale of a slave in Italy.

8 See, for instance, *Europäische Mentalitätsgeschichte: Hauptthemen in Einzeldarstellungen*, ed. Peter Dinzelbacher. Sec. rev. and expanded ed. Kröner's Taschenausgabe, 469 (1993; Stuttgart: Alfred Kröner, 2008). Cf. also Peter Dinzelbacher, *Lebenswelten des Mittelalters 1000–1500*. Bachmanns Basiswissen, 1 (Badenweiler: Wissenschaftlicher Verlag Bachmann, 2010). For an important exception, see Marc Bloch's chapter "Servitude and Freedom" in his *Feudal Society* (Chicago: University of Chicago Press, 1961), 255–74 (first volume appeared originally in 1939); see now also the contributions to *The Work of Work: Servitude, Slavery, and Labor in Medieval England*, ed. Allen J. Frantzen (Glasgow: Cruithne Press, 1994); Carl I. Hammer, *A Large-Scale Slave Society of the Early Middle Ages: Slaves and Their Families in Early Medieval Bavaria* (Aldershot: Ashgate, 2002); *Forms of Servitude in Northern and Central Europe: Decline, Resistance, and Expansion*, ed. Paul H. Freedman. Medieval Texts and Cultures of Northern Europe, 9 (Turnhout: Brepols, 2005).

9 See the contributions to *Alltag im Spätmittelalter*, ed. Harry Kühnel. 3rd ed. (1984; Graz, Vienna, and Cologne: Verlag Styria, 1984).

10 Gerd Althoff, Hans-Werner Goetz, Ernst Schubert, *Menschen im Schatten der Kathedrale: Neuigkeiten aus dem Mittelalter* (Darmstadt: Primus Verlag, 1998). For the history of public executions in early modern England, see the extensive research compiled in *Public Execution in England, 1573 – 1868*, ed. Leigh Yetter. 10 vols. (London: Pickering & Chatto, 2009–2010). See also the contributions to *Crime and Punishment in the Middle Ages and Early Modern Age: Mental-Historical Investigations of Basic Human Problems and Social Responses*, ed. Albrecht Classen and

pleasant institutions; on the contrary, but it would be misleading to identify them, as Geltner emphasizes, as representative icons of a 'persecuting society.'

Curiously, however, many of the major encyclopedias on the Middle Ages have not even included those three important concepts among their lemmata; others, however, such as the famous *Lexikon des Mittelalters*, do, but then mostly in a more laconic fashion without giving us a full understanding of the many profound implications, especially with regard to reflections on those terms in literary, philosophical, and theological context.[11] The topic of slavery, by contrast, has attracted much interest, but mostly with regard to the respective trade in the eastern Mediterranean, as if there had not been any slaves or slave markets in other parts of medieval Europe. Slavery was also not limited to Europe, but has, unfortunately, always been in existence in many other parts of the world throughout time.[12] Could we thus assume that medieval writers (chroniclers, poets, theologians, philosophers, and others) did not bother much with issues such as freedom, or the lack thereof?

At first sight, that impression might hold true, especially because medieval literary scholarship has not dealt with those topics in-depth, maybe out of a lack

---

Connie Scarborough. Fundamentals of Medieval and Early Modern Culture, 11 (Berlin and Boston: Walter de Gruyter, 2012); Guy Geltner, *The Medieval Prison: A Social History* (Princeton, NJ: Princeton University Press, 2008); see also Patricia Turning, *Municipal Officials, Their Public, and the Negotiation of Justice in Medieval Languedoc: Fear not the Madness of the Raging Mob*. Later Medieval Europe, 10 (Leiden and Boston: Brill, 2012).

11 For negative examples, reference works with no relevant entries, see Aryeh Grabois, *The Illustrated Encyclopedia of Medieval Civilization* (Jerusalem: The Jerusalem Publishing, 1980); *The Oxford Dictionary of the Middle Ages*, ed. Robert E. Bjork (Oxford: Oxford University Press, 2010). For the opposite, see C. Schott, "Freiheit, Freie (Rechtsgesch[ichte])," *Lexikon des Mittelalters*, ed. Robert-Henri Bautie, vol. 4 (Munich and Zürich: Artemis, 1988), 896–99. The information provided still proves to be rather vague. See also O. Pesch, "Freiheit, Freie: Philosophische und Theologische," ibid., 899–901; and there are several entries on slavery, in vol. 5 (1995), 1977–1987. I must admit that when I conceived of the *Handbook of Medieval Culture: Fundamental Aspects and Conditions of the European Middle Ages*, ed. Albrecht Classen. 3 vols. (Berlin and Boston: Walter de Gruyter, 2015), I did not consider freedom, imprisonment, or slavery either because it did not figure prominently on my cultural-historical horizon at that time. For some early efforts, however, see the contributions to *Mantik, Schicksal und Freiheit im Mittelalter*, ed. Loris Sturlese. Technical ed. Katrin Bauer. Archiv für Kulturgeschichte, Beihefte zum Archiv für Kulturgeschichte, 70 (Cologne, Weimar, and Vienna: Böhlau, 2011); for collective concepts of freedom in the early modern period, see *Kollektive Freiheitsvorstellungen im frühneuzeitlichen Europa: (1400–1850)*, ed. Georg Schmidt, Martin van Gelderen, and Christopher Snigula. Jenaer Beiträge zur Geschichte, 8 (Frankfurt a.M., Berlin, Bern, et al.: Peter Lang, 2006).

12 See the contributions to *Sklaverei in der Vormoderne: Beispiele aus außereuropäischen Gesellschaften*, ed. Stephan Conermann. Dhau, 2 (St. Ingbert: Röhrig Universitätsverlag, 2017). This is, of course, a huge, if not a global topic, which I cannot cover here any further.

of interest or simply out of ignorance. But the history of the crusades, for instance, always involved also the tragic development that Christian knights were taken prisoners and had to be freed by way of a ransom, if they were allowed to live. Not by accident, this task was the primary objective of the Order of the Trinitarians, founded in 1198,[13] operating mostly in the eastern Mediterranean supporting the crusaders, and of the Order of Merced, whose focal point was the western Mediterranean (Kingdom of Aragon, Al-Andalus, Morocco, etc.). We can assume that high-ranking Muslim lords who were taken prisoner also had to pay high ransom to be freed, whereas the masses of ordinary soldiers were commonly massacred, and this on both sides.[14]

Of course, if we turn to modern and contemporary history and consider the terrible consequences for massive numbers of people who were treated as terrorists or simply as threats to the government, including the Holocaust and the Soviet Gulag, but also the vast system of internment camps for Japanese-Americans during the Second World War (1942–1945), then we hear more often about literature produced in prisons or internment and concentration camps. But recent research has also demonstrated that many of the major intellectuals from the early modern age and also the Middle Ages had to suffer from imprisonment and worse because they became victims of jealous or fearful colleagues, neighbors,

---

[13] J. J. Gross, "Trinitarier, -innen," *Lexikon des Mittelalters*. Vol. VIII (Munich: Lexma Verlag, 1997), 1009–11; see also the current website of the modern order at: https://trinitarians.org/pages/about (last accessed on Jan. 15, 2021).

[14] James William Brodman, *Ransoming Captives in Crusader Spain: The Order of Merced on the Christian-Islamic Frontier*. The Middle Ages Series (Philadelphia, PA: University of Pennsylvania Press, 1986); see also http://libro.uca.edu/rc/captives.htm (last accessed on Jan. 15, 2021). Consult also J. L. Perez, "Mercedarier," *Lexikon für Theologie und Kirche*, ed. Josef Höfer and Karl Rahner. Vol. 7 (Feiburg i. Br.: Herder, 1962), 304–05; older research can be found there. For the opposite situation, of Muslim nobles in Christian imprisonment, see Sonja Zöller, *Kaiser, Kaufmann und die Macht des Geldes: Gerhard Unmaze von Köln als Finanzier der Reichspolitik und der "Gute Gerhard" des Rudolf von Ems*. Forschungen zur Geschichte der älteren deutschen Literatur, 16 (Munich: Wilhelm Fink Verlag, 1993), 299. For the efforts on both sides to organize the payment of ransom, see now Gottfried Liedl, *Granada. Ein europäisches Emirat an der Schwelle zur Neuzeit. Islamische Renaissancen*, 2. Die Levante – frühe Ansätze der Globalisierung. Vom 5. Jahrhundert bis zur Neuzeit, 3 (Vienna: LIT Verlag, 2020), 74. For relevant documents, see id., *Dokumente der Araber in Spanien: Zur Geschichte der spanisch-arabischen Renaissance in Granada*. Vol. 2 (Vienna: Turia and Kant, 1993), 244–45 (document no. 8); Nikolas Jaspert, "Gefangenenloskauf in der Krone Aragón und die Anfänge des Mercedarierordens: Institutionelle Diversität, religiöse Kontexte, mediterrane Verflechtungen," *Gefangenenloskauf im Mittelmeerraum: Ein interreligiöser Vergleich: Akten der Tagung vom 19. bis 21. September 2013 an der Universität Paderborn*, Heike Grieser and Nicole Priesching. Sklaverei – Knechtschaft – Zwangsarbeit, 13 (Hildesheim, Zürich, and New York: Georg Olms Verlag, 2015), 99–121.

superiors, or authority figures, such as the Swedish historian, professor, diplomat, and scholar Johannes Messenius (1579–1636), not to speak of famous Galileo Galilei (1564–1642).[15]

Widening our perspective, we would then easily discover the full extent to which also eighteenth-century poets kept in prisons continued to be active, if the time in prison did not even turn individuals previously untouched by literature into poets for the first time in their lives.[16]

Spending time in prison has apparently always represented a significant hiatus in one's life, unwanted, imposed, forced upon, and dangerous for one's well-being because of lack of food, exercise, fresh air, and intellectual stimulation. Worst, however, might be the absence of freedom, the inability to move at one's wishes, and being under the order of prison guards and the legal system. As early as in the tenth century, Hrotsvit of Gandersheim, famous for her Latin

---

15 As to the issues of freedom as explored by poets from the Renaissance to the modern age in French literature, see the contributions to *Liberté e(s)t choix: Verhandlungen von Freiheit in der französischen Literatur*, ed. Sieglinde Borvitz and Yasmin Temelli. Studienreihe Romania (StR), 34 (Berlin: Erich Schmidt Verlag, 2019). For a variety of other approaches, see Horst Brandstätter, *Asperg: ein deutsches Gefängnis; der schwäbische Demokratenbuckel und seine Insassen: Pfarrer, Schreiber, Kaufleute, Lehrer, gemeines Volk und andere republikanische Brut, mit Abschweifungen über Denunzianten und Sympathisanten in alter und neuer Zeit*. Wagenbachs Taschenbücher, 46 (Berlin: Wagenbach, 1976); Uta Klein, *Gefangenenliteratur: Sprechen, Schreiben, Lesen in deutschen Gefängnissen* (Hagen: Padligur, 1988); *Captivating Subjects: Writing Confinement, Citizenship, and Nationhood in the Nineteenth Century*, ed. Julia M. Wright and Jason Haslam (Toronto: University of Toronto Press, 2005); Andrew Sobanet, *Jail Sentences: Representing Prison in Twentieth-Century French Fiction*. Stages (Lincoln, NE: University of Nebraska Press, 2008); Simonetta Sanna, *Nazi-Täterinnen in der deutschen Literatur: die Herausforderung des Bösen*. Signaturen der Gewalt, 1 (Frankfurt a. M., Bern, Brussels, et al.: Peter Lang, 2017); Rachel Knighton, *Writing the Prison in African Literature*. Race and Resistance Across Borders in the Long Twentieth Century, 5 (Oxford, Bern, Berlin, et al.: Peter Lang, 2019). See also Susanna Niiranen, "From Prison to Print: Johannes Messenius' *Scondia illustrata* as a Co-Product of Early Modern Prison Writing," *Transmission of Knowledge in the Late Middle Ages and the Renaissance*, ed. Outi Merisalo, Miika Kuha, and Susanna Niiranen. Bibliologia, 53 (Turnhout: Brepols, 2019), 153–65; cf. also Simone Giese, "Johannes Messenius, ein schwedischer Gelehrter im Konflikt mit überkommenen Traditionen," *Frühneuzeitliche Universitätskulturen: Kulturhistorische Perspektiven auf die Hochschulen in Europa*, ed. Barbara Krug-Richter and Ruth E. Mohrmann. Beihefte zum Archiv für Kulturgeschichte (Cologne: Böhlau, 2009), 223–44; Bernard Faidutti, *Copernic, Kepler et Galilée face aux pouvoirs: les scientifiques et la politique*. Acteurs de la science, 363 (Paris: L'Harmattan, 2010); Alberto A. Martínez, *Burned Alive: Giordano Bruno, Galileo and the Inquisition* (London: Reaktion Books, 2018). The literature on these topics has grown manifold by now.
16 *Friedrichs Freyherrn von der Trenck Kaiserl. Königl. Obristwachtmeisters Samlung vermischter Gedichte, welche in seinem zehnjährigen Gefängnis in Magdeburg geschrieben wurden* (Frankfurt a.M. and Leipzig: n.p., 1767); online at: https://digital.staatsbibliothek-berlin.de/werkansicht?PPN=PPN662301161&PHYSID=PHYS_0005&DMDID= (last accessed on Jan. 15, 2021).

plays and religious narratives, included various references to prisons, such as in *Pelagius* (to hold military prisoners or their proxies), or in *Abraham* (to put away a rueful and repenting prostitute, Maria).[17] Once young Pelagius has volunteered to serve in his father's place, the duke of Galicia who was defeated by the Arab forces, he is led to a miserable dark dungeon in Córdoba, Andalusia. There the king, Caliph Abd al-Rahmān III (889/91–961)

> instantly ordered   that Christ's illustrious friend
> Be bound and then thrown   into a dark prison
> And be fed but little food   he who was used to plenitude.
> Cordoba has a place,   foul and under vaults
> Oblivious to light,   consigned to deep darkness,
> Souce of great suffering,   they say, to poor wretches. (p. 34)

He is only released when the king has learned that Pelagius is a physically highly attractive young man of great rhetorical skills who might become his 'prostitute' or lover. However, this does not happen because he fights him violently in order to maintain his chastity and innocence, whereupon Pelagius is martyred, though it takes extra efforts by the executioner to carry out the death penalty. Granted, the poet was probably not familiar with actual prisons, and she drew here from legendary accounts she had learned from representatives of a diplomatic mission to Emperor Otto I in Frankfurt at any rate, but her account still offers noteworthy details of the misery in such a dungeon by which she wants to evoke her audience's empathy and pity.

Imprisonment has a huge, dramatic and traumatic impact on people, whether in the Middle Ages or in the nineteenth century, in antiquity or in the present age. By the same token, gaining freedom, either from slavery or from imprisonment, either as an individual or as an entire people, has always been regarded as a major transformation in life, in history, as a glorious triumph, such as when we think of the liberation of the Dutch Republic from Spanish control in 1581 by the

---

17 Here quoted from Hrotsvit of Gandersheim, *A Florilegium of Her Works*. The Library of Medieval Women (Woodbridge, Suffolk: S. S. Brewer, 1998); for the critical edition, see Hrotsvit von Gandersheim, *Opera omnia*, ed. Walter Berschin. Bibliotheca scriptorum Graecorum et Romanorum Teubneriana (Leipzig: B. G. Teubner, 2013); for recent studies, see *A Companion to Hrotsvit of Gandersheim: Contextual and Interpretive Approaches*, ed. Phyllis R. Brown and Stephen L. Wailes (Leiden and Boston: Brill, 2012). As to the Caliph, see Maribel Fierro, *'Abd al-Rahman III: The First Cordoban Caliph* (Oxford: Oneworld, 2005). Concerning the way how Hrotsvit learned about the religious legend of Pelagius, see Albrecht Classen, "Die iberische Halbinsel im frühen Mittelalter: Ausgangspunkt für interkulturelle Kontakte zwischen den Ottonen und den andalusischen Muslimen. Kulturhistorische Betrachtungen aus literarischer (Hrotsvit von Gandersheim) und chronikalischer Sicht (Johannes von Gorze)," *arcadia* 53.2 (2018): 397–418.

Act of Abjuration, the declaration of independence of the provinces from Philip II, which was finally concluded in 1648 with the Peace Treaty of Münster and Osnabrück (end of the Thirty Years' War). Another highly dramatic case of self-liberation was the peaceful revolution in East Germany which led to the collapse of the Socialist regime, the opening of the border (fall of the Berlin Wall), and the country's freedom in 1989, which then reunified with West Germany on October 3, 1990.

Significantly, there is a vast amount of data that confirms the huge role which slave trade played also throughout the entire pre-modern world, and also the deep impact of imprisonment on many people, high and low, whether for valid reasons or unjustly.[18] Both experiences, certainly very distinct from each other, and yet often creating the same experience for the victim, have always been profoundly traumatic, and maybe for that very reason most literary entertainers, musicians, and artists have shied away from addressing these topics, unless they were driven by religious, moral, or ethical motives to address them, such as warning their audiences about this sudden, shocking downfall always possible in human life. Modern journalism has certainly changed all that.

To cite just one of many examples from the late Middle Ages, though one which has hardly ever been considered in this context, the Bernese Dominican priest Ulrich Bonerius formulates in his fable "Of an Emperor's Gemstone" (no. 87), contained in his collection *Der Edelstein* (ca. 1350), warning them:

> Think of that, young and old,
> how quickly the world's power disappears,
> and so also wisdom, nobility, and wealth.
> Who can be of a joyful mind
> and live happily in this world,
> when no one can resist death?[19]

---

[18] Jürgen Misch, *Das christliche Sklavenland: Menschenhandel im frühen Mittelalter bis zur Neuzeit* (Berlin: Rhombos-Verlag, 2015); Heike Grieser, *Sklaverei im spätantiken und frühmittelalterlichen Gallien: (5.–7. Jh.): das Zeugnis der christlichen Quellen*. Forschungen zur antiken Sklaverei, 28 (Stuttgart: Steiner, 1997); David Wyatt, *Slaves and Warriors in Medieval Britain and Ireland, 800–1200*. The Northern World, 45 (Leiden and Boston: Brill, 2009); William D. Phillips, *Slavery in Medieval and Early Modern Iberia*. The Middle Ages Series (Philadelphia, PA: University of Pennsylvania Press, 2014); Tomás Petrácek, *Power and Exploitation in the Czech Lands in the 10th–12th Centuries: A Central European Perspective*. East Central and Eastern Europe in the Middle Ages, 40 (Leiden: Brill, 2017). Every time scholars turn to the archives for specific areas of medieval Europe, whether during the early, the high, or the late Middle Ages, they can stumble upon voluminous material confirming the existence of slavery.

[19] Ulrich Bonerius, *Der Edelstein: Eine mittelalterliche Fabelsammlung. Zweisprachige Ausgabe: Mittelhochdeutsch – Neuhochdeutsch*, ed. Manfred Stange (Bielefeld: verlag regionalkultur,

Loss of freedom would be just one step away from loss of life. We can thus firmly claim, as the starting point of this investigation, that the desire for freedom and the deep fear of its disappearance (prison or slavery) constitutes one of the fundamental human needs and concerns. Further below, I will return to Bonerius because he has quite a bit more to say about the high value of freedom on a very individual level.

Undoubtedly, it has always been more entertaining to relate stories of humorous erotic encounters than to talk of the dark time when a person had to suffer in prison for a very long and a very lonely period.[20] However, a close examination of a large variety of medieval and early modern texts, both literary and philosophical, both historical and theological, easily confirms that those existentially negative experiences were dealt with more often than we might have assumed, as mirrored impressively and extensively by the fifteenth-century French poet François Villon (ca. 1431–1463), or his contemporary, the German (Tyrolean) Oswald von Wolkenstein (ca. 1376/77–1445), to whom I will return below.

This also implies, of course, that imprisonment and enslavement were probably much more common phenomena during the pre-modern era than we normally might expect, maybe because official records were rather hesitant to offer many details in that regard. Numerous historians have actually tackled this large issue, certainly more than mainstream research seems to indicate, although these issues have still not fully attracted central attention, maybe because prisons and prisoners, and so also slaves, were commonly kept out of public site, which is still the case today. What our discussion of slavery and freedom in the Middle Ages then can achieve is to provide a socio-historical and economic-political foundation for the much larger issue of both topics in the modern era especially since the eighteenth century, when the demand for freedom and subsequently also the fight against slavery became explosive issues. This book, however, can only refer to those and must limit itself to the pre-modern evidence, that is, roughly speaking, up to the seventeenth century.

But addressing those two topics all by themselves without keeping the broader context in mind would not be sufficient if we want to do justice to them. We also have to include the issue of freedom, both in personal and collec-

---

2016), vv. 49–55. See now my English translation, *The Fables of Ulrich Bonerius (ca. 1350): Masterwork of Late Medieval Didactic* Literature, trans. Albrecht Classen (Newcastle Upon Tyne: Cambridge Scholars Publishing, 2020).

20 See, for instance, *Erotic Tales of Medieval Germany*, selected and trans. by Albrecht Classen. Medieval and Renaissance Texts and Studies, 328. 2nd ed. (2007; Tempe, AZ: Arizona Center for Medieval and Renaissance Studies, 2009); *The Fabliaux: A New Verse Translation*, trans. Nathaniel E. Dubin. Intro. R. Howard Bloch (New York and London: W. W. Norton, 2013).

tive terms, both spiritually and politically, and at a closer examination, we can observe that the discourse on freedom, surprisingly close to the one that has determined modernity, was pursued quite energetically, both by poets and philosophers, among other intellectuals.

Additionally, we can also observe that there were quite a number of peoples and societies in pre-modern Europe and elsewhere who enjoyed a considerable degree of political freedom or energetically fought against outside attempts to subjugate them, such as Iceland, Switzerland, Bohemia, Pommerania, and others.[21] As Hermann Pálsson underscored regarding Iceland: "the society that was created in Iceland by the original settlers and their immediate descendants early in the tenth century was more democratic than any other communiyy in medieval Europe."[22] Granted, the Althing, a kind of rudimentary parliament, often consisted of less than forty men, yet their decision-making process reflected a broader distribution of power than anywhere else in the Middle Ages. To study this phenomenon would also require, by contrast, to acknowledge unique forms of pre-modern colonization, which certainly happened in many parts of Europe, such as in the lands east of the Elbe river, in the Baltic countries, and in the Holy Land, but here I limit myself to more personal experiences as reflected both in historical and literary sources from the pre-modern world, such as epigrams by the humanist Sebastian Brant.[23]

---

21 Donald W. Treadgold, *Freedom* (see note 5); see also the contributions to *Die abendländische Freiheit vom 10. zum 14. Jahrhundert: der Wirkungszusammenhang von Idee und Wirklichkeit im europäischen Vergleich*, ed. Johannes Fried. Vorträge und Forschungen / Konstanzer Arbeitskreis für Mittelalterliche Geschichte, 39 (Sigmaringen: Thorbecke, 1991).
22 Herrman Pálsson, *Oral Tradition and Saga Writing* (Vienna: Fassbaender, 1999), 67.
23 See the classical studies by Charles Verlinden, *The Beginnings of Modern Colonization: Eleven Essays with an Introduction* (Ithaca, NY, and London: Cornell University Press, 1970); Elspeth Jane Carruthers, "Christianization and Colonization on the Medieval South Baltic Frontier," Ph.D. diss., Princeton University, 1999; cf. also Felipe Fernández-Armesto, *Before Columbus: Exploration and Colonisation from the Mediterranean to the Atlantic 1229–1492*. New Studies in Medieval History (Basingstoke: Macmillan, 1987); see also the contributions to *Internal Colonization in Medieval Europe*, ed. Felipe Fernández-Armesto. The Expansion of Latin Europe, 1000–1500, 2 (Aldershot: Ashgate, 2008). As an example of lack of insightfulness and an absent awareness of recent and new approaches to this critical issue, see, for example, the remarkably well researched and comprehensive website https://en.wikipedia.org/wiki/History_of_colonialism (last accessed on Jan. 15, 2021). For more appropriate comments, however, see now John Dagenais and Margaret R. Greer in their introductory article to a guest-edited volume, "Decolonizing the Middle Ages: Introduction," *Journal of Medieval and Early Modern Studies* 30.3 (Fall 2000): 431–48. They emphasize, "As we seek to decolonize The Middle Ages, then, postcolonial studies provide a rich variety of resources for understanding the colonization process itself and the ways in which we might challenge and transform it. It is that concrete variety, rather than any partic-

This actually aligns well with recent scholarship on the emergence of a clearly marked form of individualism during the twelfth century, both in political and in religfious terms, which then gained in intensity especially in the fourteenth and fifteenth centuries (*Devotio moderna*). With individuals such as Peter Abe-

---

ular abstract model of colonial or postcolonial relations which is the true value of postcolonial discourse for medievalists" (448). The entire issue is hotly debated in current research and cannot be easily addressed here. See, above all, Kim M. Phillips, *Before Orientalism: Asian Peoples and Cultures in European Travel Writing, 1245–1510*. The Middle Ages Series (Philadelphia, PA: University of Pennsylvania Press, 2013); this has been critically commented by Jeffrey Jerome Cohen and Karl Steel, "Race, Travel, Time, Heritage," *Postmedieval: A Journal of Medieval Cultural Studies* 6.1 (2015): 98–110; see also Sharon Kinoshita's review in *The American Historical Review* 120.1 (February, 2015): 202–03. Whether we can really talk about colonialism in the Middle Ages remains problematic; see Shirin Azizeh Khanmohamadi, *In Light of Another's Word: European Ethnography in the Middle Ages*. The Middle Ages Series (Philadelphia, PA: University of Pennsylvania Press, 2013); cf. also Carol Symes, "The Middle Ages Between Nationalism and Colonialism," *French Historical Studies* 34.1 (2011): 37–46. We also need to keep in mind that the pre-modern era was already deeply determined by racism, although the available sources often do not address racial differences as clearly as modern writers do. See, for instance, Geraldine Heng, *The Invention of Race in the European Middle Ages* (New York and Cambridge: Cambridge University Press, 2018); Cord J. Whitaker, *Black Metaphors: How Modern Racism Emerged from Medieval Race-Thinking*. The Middle Ages Series (Philadelphia, PA: University of Pennsylvania Press, 2019); M. Lindsay Kaplan, *Figuring Racism in Medieval Christianity* (New York: Oxford University Press, 2019). As she rightly claims: "The growing critical consensus on the centrality of religion for the historical – as well as the contemporary –construction of racism additionally challenges the claim that true racism imagines the inferior status as permanent. Although Yerushalmi and Balibar have respectively argued that biological as well as cultural formations of religious status give rise to an immutable racist identity, scholars have subsequently contended that premodern as well as later racist discourses rely on ideas of both fluidity and fixity" (8). I would also like to refer to Frantz Fanon's famous study *Peau noire, masques blancs*. Collection points, 26 (Paris: Éd. du Seuil, 1975), in which he deeply reflects on the psychology of racism as it impacts both the Black person and white people, each in a different way mirroring the different power distribution, which finds significant expression in the use of 'white' language versus 'black' language. See the recent studies in *Frantz Fanon's 'Black Skin, White Masks': New Interdisciplinary Essays*, ed. Maxim Silverman (Baltimore, MD: Project Muse, 2018). The question to what extent racism existed already in the Middle Ages cannot be addressed here and anyway amounts to a highly politicized issue hotly debated at current times. See, for instance, Dorothy Kim, "Introduction to Literature Compass Special Cluster: Critical Race and the Middle Ages," *Literature Compass* 16.9–10 (2019): 1–16. Provocatively, she argues: "Race is political. Race matters now and race matters in the premodern past" (13). For a critical response, warning us about naively equating modern-day racism with medieval racism, whatever that might mean, see Vanita Seth, "The Origins of Racism: A Critique of the History of Ideas," *History & Theory* 59.3 (2020): 343–68; online at: DOI: 10.1111/hith.12163. However, all this is a very complicated and very important issue that I cannot touch here much further if I do not want to deviate radically from the historical emphasis of the present book.

lard (1079–1142), Bernard of Clairvaux (1090–1153), or William of St. Thierry (1075/80–1148), then also mystically inspired women such as Elisabeth of Schönau (ca. 1129–1164) and Hildegard of Bingen (1098–1179), European intellectuals increasingly carved out a space for themselves, free of external influence, even though that did not yet necessarily have an impact on the political conditions at that time.[24] Spiritual freedom, based on a personal quest for God, created noteworthy separation lines between individuals and the official Church, which, in the long run, contributed to the rise of the Protestant Reformation and the development of the notion of personal freedom.

Altogether, with respect to 'freedom,' we face, of course, a highly complex phenomenon that has always been subject to countless interpretations and definitions, deeply dependent on the semantic framework of that term and the socio-historical conditions. While the Vikings settling in Iceland and elsewhere found their personal freedom in concretely political and material terms, European mystics and philosophers such as Meister Eckhart (ca. 1260–1328) and later Geert Groote (1340–1384) discovered freedom in their spiritual transformation, exploring what we would call 'negative theology' today.[25] Of course, we quickly face a critical problem if we view all those religious and philosophical notions of 'freedom' in the very same light as political and military freedom.

The purpose of the subsequent investigations, however, is not to reach a narrowly defined concept of freedom versus imprisonment or slavery because they all belong to complex discourses that intersect with each other and yet also represent individual dimensions. Those are relevant, by contrast, and the more diverse the approaches prove to be, the better can we perceive the broad spectrum in the discussion of those terms and notions.

---

24 See the contributions to *Inwardness, Individualization, and Religious Agency in the Late Medieval Low Countries: Studies in the* Devotio Moderna *and Its Contexts*, ed. Rijcklof Hofman, Charles Caspers, Peter Nissen, et al. Medieval Church Studies, 43 (Turnhout: Brepols, 2020). Rijcklof Hofman, in his article "Inwardness and Individualization in the Late Medieval Low Countries: An Introduction" (1–34), emphasizes the impact of individuality as it developed in the twelfth century (7–14). To what extent the notion of freedom would thus have evolved from this individualization remains to be probed, as I will attempt to do below.
25 *Meister Eckhart und die Freiheit*, ed. Christine Büchner and Freimut Löser, together with Janina Franzke. Meister-Eckhart-Jahrbuch, 12 (Stuttgart: Verlag W. Kohlhammer, 2018). See also Rachel Elior, *Jewish Mysticism: The Infinite Expression of Freedom*, trans. Yudith Nave and Arthur B. Millman. The Littman Library of Jewish Civilization (Oxford and Portland, OR: Littman Library of Jewish Civilization, 2007); *Mystik, Recht und Freiheit: religiöse Erfahrung und kirchliche Institutionen im Spätmittelalter*, ed. Dietmar Mieth and Britta Müller-Schauenburg (Stuttgart: Kohlhammer, 2012).

The intention of this study thus consists of providing a kaleidoscope of diverse insights into the social, historical, legal, but also mental-historical conditions in the pre-modern world, bringing together much material both from medieval and early modern literature, religion, philosophy, and also history. I will consult numerous cases of imprisonment and slavery from the twelfth through the seventeenth century, thereby widening considerably our historical frame of reference. While there are many specialized studies on the institution of the prison and on the practice of slavery in the Middle Ages, there are much less investigations of the theme of freedom, although all three are closely interrelated.[26] The reader can thus expect to be confronted with a wide range of sources reflecting the experiences of prisoners and slaves, and the desire to gain or maintain freedom from a very individualistic perspective, and this already in the time of pre-modernity. The political, philosophical, religious, military, and also economic discourses on personal freedom, the role of the authorities versus the individual, on individual spirituality, and then even on personal freedom versus slavery thus are bundled together here to gain a new understanding of this huge and highly influential complex of ideas which all speak to each other in one way or the other.

---

[26] For a more specialized approach, highlighting the wide range of criminal and 'authorized' killing, leading to executions, see Peter Schuster, *Verbrecher, Opfer, Heilige: eine Geschichte des Tötens 1200–1700* (Stuttgart: Klett-Cotta, 2015).

A Imprisonment

1 Medieval Comments on Imprisonment and Prisons

The introduction has laid some foundations and staked the wide field of this broad topic, but it easily proves to be a complex task to examine the interrelated and yet separate topics of freedom, imprisonment, and slavery. Fortunately, many scholars have turned their attention at least to the institution of the prison and the personal experiences of prisoners, and given us thereby an important perspective regarding the dark side of early to modern society.[27]

We know considerably less about those issues in the pre-modern world, though there are, as Sonja Kerth has recently claimed, countless examples of references to imprisonment in medieval German literature, and this both in concrete, physical and in metaphorical terms (love as a prison, e. g.) – not to forget such a famous prisoner as Marco Polo (1254–1324) who spent considerable time in a cell together with the poet Rustichello da Pisa after he had been made a captive following the war between Geno and Venice and to whom he told his many travel experiences. Both then composed together, as far as we can tell, Polo's famous *Travels* sometime around 1298/1299.[28] Significantly, many fictional ac-

---

[27] *The Oxford History of the Prison: The Practice of Punishment in Western Society*, ed. Norval Morris and David J. Rothman (New York: Oxford University Press, 1995); Brian Jarvis, *Cruel and Unusual: Punishment and US Culture* (London and Sterling, VA: Pluto Press, 2004); Guy Geltner, "Medieval Prisons: Between Myth and Reality, Hell and Purgatory," *History Compass* 4 (2006): 10.1111/j.1478-0542.2006.00319.x, p. 1–2; id., "Coping in Medieval Prisons," *Continuity and Change* 23.1 (2008): 151–72; Christine Winter, "Prisons and Punishments in Late Medieval London," Ph.D. diss., Royal Holloway, University of London, 2012 (https://repository.royalholloway.ac.uk/file/66be0e74-3911-4bf7-b32e-17597027f1bf/1/2013WinterCLPhD.pdf.pdf); last accessed on Jan. 15, 2021); see also much older, but still valuable research by R. von Hippel, "Beiträge zur Geschichte der Freiheitsstrafe," *Zeitschrift für die gesamte Strafrechtswissenschaften* 18 (1898): 419–94, 609–66; Roger Grand, "La prison et la notion d'emprisonnement dans l'ancien droit," *Revue historique de droit français et étranger*, 4th ser., 19–20/1–2 (1940–1941): 58–87; and A. Bertolotti, "Prigioni e prigionieri in Mantova dal secolo XIII al secolo XIX," *Bullettino ufficiale della Direzione Generale delle Carceri* 17 (1887): 51–70, 163–82, which subsequently appeared as a monograph in 1888.

[28] Sonja Kerth, "Gefängnis, Orte der Gefangenschaft," *Literarische Orte in deutschsprachigen Erzählungen des Mittelalters: ein Handbuch*, ed. Tilo Renz, Monika Hanauska, and Mathias Herweg (Berlin and Boston: Walter de Gruyter, 2018), 190–98; see also the contributions to *Réalités, images, écritures de la prison au Moyen Âge*, ed. Jean-Marie Fritz. Écritures (Dijon: Éd. Univ. de Dijon, 2012). The contributors focus on the motif of the prison and prisoner mostly in medieval French literature, such as *La Prison d'Amour* by Baudouin de Conde (Silvère Menegaldo), *La Prison amoureuse* by Froissart (Fabienne Pomel), and *Fortunes et Advertizer* by Jean Regnier (Gerard

counts (romances) about military conflicts conclude with the winner taking the defeated opponent as a prisoner (not killing him), sending him to the court of his overlord (King Arthur) to submit himself, on the pledge of honor to carry this out, such as in Wolfram von Eschenbach's *Parzival* (ca. 1205). When the young protagonist fights against the knights besieging the lady Condwiramurs, he succeeds in defeating them all, gaining control over their freedom of movement, so to speak, which allows him to send them by force to King Arthur where they are to submit themselves under his command. As the defeated King Clamide of Isaterre, Condwiramur's suitor, announces, once he has arrived there and addresses Lady Cunneware de Lalant:

> "… It is in pure distress that compels me to this. The Red Knight sent you his homage, wanting to take entire responsibility for any disgrace that has been inflicted upon you. He also asks that the case be brought before Arthur. I believe you were beaten for his sake. Lady, I bring you my oath of surrender, as he who fought with me commanded. Now I'll willingly carry this out, whenever you wish. My life was forfeit to death!"[29]

Prisons are also mentioned at the end of a devastating battle, such as in the *Nibelungenlied*, with Gunther and Hagen being kept in dark rooms somewhere in the castle before they are executed – probably the differences in genres (heroic versus courtly) being responsible for the difference in the treatment of prisoners. Many times, also women are kidnapped and sold as sex slaves, such as in Konrad Fleck's *Flore und Blanscheflur* (ca. 1220), or they are adopted by their owners and, after they have converted to Christianity and have been baptized, treated like members of the family, such as in the anonymous *Aucassin et Nicolette* (ca. 1240). Marie de France (fl. ca. 1170–1200) includes spatial settings of some the ladies in her *lais* which can only described as prisons, but none of those examples lend much weight to the topic itself, the suffering in a prison, not to talk about the normally expected preconditon, a crime with subsequent apprehension, court trial, and then the punishment.

Gros). Marco Polo has been discussed already at length; but see John Larne, *Marco Polo and the Discovery of the World* (New Haven, CT: Yale University Press, 1999).

29 For convenience sake, here I simply draw from the English translation: Wolfram von Eschenbach, *Parzival* and *Titurel*, trans. with Notes by Cyril Edwards (Oxford: Oxford University Press, 2006), Book IV, ch. 218, p. 92. The issue involved here has much to do with ritual, ceremony, habit, public negotiations, agonal performance, and gestures. The knights are certainly taken prisoners, but this cannot be equated with the imprisonment of a criminal or violent offender. See Gert Althoff, *Spielregeln der Politik im Mittelalter: Kommunikation in Frieden und Fehde* (Darmstadt: Primus Verlag, 1997); id., *Die Macht der Rituale: Symbolik und Herrschaft im Mittelalter* (Darmstadt: Primus Verlag, 2003).

Many times, however, knights are imprisoned and badly mistreated not because of any wrongdoing on their part, but because they have become the victim of an evil magician, such as in Ulrich von Zazikhoven's *Lanzelet* (early thirteenth century). In his castle 'Schatel le Mort,' the magician Mâbûz the Craven has created a prison for scores of knights who suffer there without any fault on their own and are completely subject to arbitrary executions whenever Mâbûz feels irritated about something, though they have nothing to do with it:

> Whomever he captured was led into a vast prison, where at this very time lay a hundred knights and more, whose hearts were constantly tormented by the fear of death. Whenever Mabuz became angry or anything unpleasant happened to him, he ordered a man killed. That is how he slaked his wrath. (68–69; vv. 3554–62).[30]

The magic spell placed on this castle transforms anyone who has not been invited in and makes him, if he was a bold and courageous before, into a complete coward, and vice versa. This also happens to the protagonist Walwein, which makes his beloved lady think extremely lowly of him. The prison itself, however, is not simply a dungeon, as we would expect; instead there are regular mealtimes with food served at dinner tables. Walwein, however, although he is such a bold knight once outside of the castle and freed from the spell, performs most miserably in the prison, as if he were out of his mind:

> Whenever the captives sat down at the table in proper fashion and ate, he took bread in his hand and huddled against a wall, where he chewed and gnawed; he never washed his hands, and showed the manners of a contemptible knave. He was the vilest man who ever lived, without courage and without strength. (70)

Sonja Kerth also identifies numerous other literary genres where we hear of prisons, some of which are rather loosely described, keeping the individuals simply away from the rest of society, while others are rocky caves or inaccessible mountain tops. Not to forget the major castle built by the magician Clinschor in Wolfram's *Parzival* where he keeps scores of noble ladies as prisoners until Gawan, the protagonist's famous friend, succeeds in liberating them all by defeating the spell through his most courageous and knightly bravery (Book X).

---

30 Ulrich von Zatzikhoven, *Lanzelet: Mittelhochdeutsch/Neuhochdeutsch* von Wolfgang Spiewok. Wodan, 71. Texte des Mittelalters, 16 (Greifswald: Reineke-Verlag, 1997); for a reliable and very readable English translation, from which I quote here, see Ulrich von Zatzikhoven, *Lanzelet*, trans. by Thomas Kerth, with additional notes by Kenneth G. T. Webster and Roger Sherman Loomis. Records of Western Civilization (New York: Columbia University Press, 2004).

One extreme case, determined by utmost misogyny and male brutality beyond all measure, especially because it takes place within the private sphere, is the verse narrative (*mære*) by Der Stricker, "Die eingemauerte Frau" (ca. 1220–1230; The Walled-in Woman), in which a knight badly suffers from what he considers to be his evil wife whom he cannot bring to reason, i.e., to complete subordination, even when he beats her so badly that he himself is utterly exhausted and worn out, while she is completely bloody with her skin terribly lacerated. In his desperation over having failed to change her uppityness, the knight then creates a private prison and locks her in it for such a long time that she finally changes her mind, gives up her urge for independence, and utterly submits under him. Basically, he breaks her will, not granting her any chance to be released from this prison until she finally abandons her 'evil' character and accepts his utter mastership over her.

The knight goes so far as to manipulate all of her relatives who might have considered intervening on her behalf, threatening them with taking over their properties if their own promises regarding her changed character would prove to be a failure. Only once she realizes that she is completely isolated and cannot get any outside help, does she abandon all hope and her own will and turns into a 'holy' woman who subsequently, once she has been freed, teaches all other 'evil' women about the danger if they might ever dare to stand up to their husbands.[31] The deeply misogynist and extremely patriarchal worldview in this verse narratives would not need to be commented on any further.

---

31 Der Stricker, *Erzählungen, Fabeln, Reden. Mittelhochdeutsch / Neuhochdeutsch*, ed., trans., and commentary by Otfrid Ehrismann (Stuttgart: Philipp Reclam jun., 1992), no. 17, pp. 120–42. See Sandra Lindemann Summers, *Ogling Ladies: Scopophilia in Medieval German Literature* (Gainesville, Tallahassee, et al.: University Press of Florida, 2013), 41–46. The parallels to medieval anchorite women are striking, such as Julian of Norwich (1343–after 1416), but the critical difference is, of course, that the anchorites voluntarily entered such a 'cell,' often close to the altar in a church, whereas Der Stricker projects a private prison built on behalf of the knight to punish his wife. This prison has no door, and only one small window. The miserable woman receives only hard and dark bread to eat; her husband does not talk to her, and he acts out scenes of pleasure with other women and festive dinners right next to her prison to torture her further. For detailed comments, see Stephen L. Wailes, *Studien zur Kleindichtung des Stricker*. Philologische Studien und Quellen, 104 (Berlin: Erich Schmidt Verlag, 1981). As to anchorites, who deliberately chose the prison as the site of their spiritual transformation, see the contributions to *Medieval Anchorites in Their Communities*, ed. Cate Gunn and Liz Herbert McAvoy. Studies in the History of Medieval Religion (Woodbridge, Suffolk: D. S. Brewer, 2017); *Hermits and Anchorites in England, 1200–1550*, selected sources trans. and annotated by E. A. Jones (Manchester: Manchester University Press, 2019).

Sir Thomas Malory: The Inventive Prisoner

In Sir Thomas Malory's *Le Morte d'Arthur* (first printed in 1485, but originally composed several decades earlier), we hear of the imprisonment of knights as well, worst, perhaps, in the case of Sir Ector following his terrible joust with the knight Turquin: "And then he gart to unarm him, and beat him with thorns all naked, and sithen put him down in a deep dungeon, where he knew many of his fellows" (VI.2, p. 197). Not only was he defeated in the combat, but then taken prisoner and tortured. Launcelot, however, later overcomes Turquin and kills him, which makes it possible for Launcelot to liberate all the prisoners: "hastily he opened the prison door, and there he let out all the prisoners, and every man loosed other of their bond" (VI.9, p. 209–10).[32]

Malory certainly reflected on his own experiences as a prisoner, whether for simply criminal, political, or other reasons. Whether true or not, he was charged with many different petty crimes and also serious transgressions, including ambush, rape, burglary, and violent robbery. He was first tried in Nuneaton on August 23, 1451 and imprisoned in London, but he escaped, yet he was captured and convicted again, imprisoned thereafter several times again in Marshalsea Prison, where he remained until 1461, when he was pardoned by King Edward IV. But he ended in prison yet another time, from 1468 to 1470, then because of his participation in a conspiracy with Richard Neville, the new Earl of Warwick, to overthrow King Edward IV, and it was during that time when he probably composed his *Mort d'Arthur*. To be sure a rather turbulent series of events, but the glorious outcome was this masterpiece of late medieval English literature.

---

[32] I would like to express my gratitude to Fidel Fajardo-Acosta for alerting me to this important textual example. Sir Thomas Malory, *Le Morte d'Arthur*, ed. Janet Cowen. 2 vols. (1969; Harmondsworth, Middlesex: Penguin, 1979). For relevant research, see the contributions to *A Companion to Malory*, ed. Elizabeth Archibald. Arthurian Studies, 37 (Cambridge: D. S. Brewer, 1996); and to *A New Companion to Malory*, ed. Megan G. Leitch and Cory James Rushton. Arthurian Studies, 87 (Cambridge: D. S. Brewer, 2019). In particular, see Davidson Roberta, "Prison and Knightly Identity in Sir Thomas Malory's Morte Darthur," *Arthuriana* 14.2 (2004): 54–63; and Molly A. Martin, *Castles and Space in Malory's Morte Darthur*. Arthurian Studies, 89 (Cambridge: D. S. Brewer, 2019). For biographical information, particularly Malory's life as a criminal and prisoner, see Gweneth Whitteridge, "The Identity of Sir Thomas Malory, Knight-Prisoner," *The Review of English Studies* 24.95 (1973): 257–65; cf. also P. J. C. Field, *The Life and Times of Sir Thomas Malory*. Arthurian Studies, 29 (Cambridge: D. S. Brewer, 1993); Christina Hardyment, *Malory: The Life and Times of King Arthur's Chronicler* (London: HarperCollins, 2005). For other contemporary prison writing, see Susanna Niiranen, "From Prison to Print" (see note 15).

Late Medieval Prisons and Prisoners as Fictional Characters

Although there are many other examples listed by Sonja Kerth in her excellent survey study illustrating how many times, after all, medieval German poets addressed prisons and imprisonment, which often involved particularly the high-ranking protagonists, we do not detect therefore a specific discourse on the personal suffering in the prison – for some exceptions, see the anonymous *Salman und Morolf* (second half of the twelfth century), *Wolfdietrich D* (ca. 1230), or *Sigenot* (before 1300).

Both the most unusual prisoner and also most unusual prison appear in the very popular late medieval prose narrative *Melusine*, first composed by Jean d'Arras (1393), then in the verse version by Couldrette (ca. 1400), which then was followed by the prose version in early New High German by Thüring von Ringoltingen (1456), not to forget numerous translations into other languages. According to Thüring, King Helmas of Albania had married the fairy Persina after he had promised to obey the taboo never to sleep with her during her being in childbed. Helmas, however, did not observe this taboo, so his wife and her three daughters left him for good. Once Melusine, the oldest of them, had learned about his breaking of his promise, she and her sisters kidnapped their father and took him to a mountain cave which was to become his prison for the rest of his life.[33] At the same time, a giant arrived to guard that prison, and he also began to ravage the country, causing endless suffering for the people which continued over generations without anyone capable of protecting the innocent victims.

However, the situation with the originally married couple proved to complex because Persina explicitly stated later in an epitaph attached to Helmas's grave that she had dearly love her husband, so, she could not help him when his daughters punished him (138).[34] Fifteen years later, Melusine and her sisters were informed by Presine about the situation with their father whom she had abandoned for good, and, Melusine as the youngest, riled up her sisters against Helmas, kidnapped him and imprisoned him in the mountain (139). We are not informed what happened subsequently, and only learn that after his death, Presine buried him there and attached an epitaph with the entire story, which Geff-

---

33 *Romane des 15. und 16. Jahrhunderts*, ed. Jan-Dirk Müller. Bibliothek der frühen Neuzeit, 1 (Frankfurt a. M.: Deutscher Klassiker Verein, 1990), 135. Müller provides an excellent and detailed commentary, 1012–87.
34 As to the epitaph and its epistemological function, see Albrecht Classen, "Objects of Memory as Hermeneutic Media in Medieval German Literature: Hartmann von Aue's *Gregorius*, Wolfram von Eschenbach's Parzival, Thüring von Ringoltingen's *Melusine*, and *Fortunatus*," *Amsterdamer Beiträge zur älteren Germanistik* 65 (2009): 159–82.

roy, one of Melusine's sons, gets to read before he manages to kill the giant protecting the mountain from intruders. But, as the epitaph also reveals, the giant was appointed by Presine to ensure that no one would be able to make his way into the cave unless he were a descendent of herself or of her daughters, as is the case with Geffroy.

Much of this account remains mythical and leaves much unexplained, especially because the epitaph finally even reveals: "Dann wiewol er sich ser an mir übergriffen hette, dennoch was ich im von herczen günstig / das ich die rach so mein tochter vorgenant von meinen wegen an im begiengen nit mocht noch wolt vngerochen lassen" (140–41; Even though he transgressed badly with me, I still loved him with all my heart; hence, I could not avoid avenging the revenge which my daughters had done with him for my sake).

In Jean d'Arras's version, some of the details are different, but the imprisonment of King Elinas of Scotland, as Presina's (sic) husband is called here, is recounted similarly.[35] And in both narratives, once the young hero has found the grave of his imprisoned grandfather, he also discovers a prison in which the giant keeps a large number of people who warn Geffroy to hide from the giant, otherwise he would suffer badly (Thüring von Ringoltingen, 141; Jean d'Arras, 199).

In the German version, this prison is located underneath a tower; in the French version, it is an iron cage holding a hundred men, who are deeply grateful for the hero's accomplishment against the giant and for their own liberation. Thüring included a short conversation between Geffroy and the prisoners who explain that the giant had placed them in the cage because they had not been able to pay the tribute to him (143), whereas Jean has them explain only that their liberator was the first man in four hundred years to succeed in making his way through the cavern (199).

In short, at closer analysis we discover many more references to imprisonment in medieval literature than we might have assumed. This also encourages us to search for more material concerning the other two major issues, freedom and slavery. Undoubtedly, the early modern age knows of scores of prisoners as well, some of whom left very detailed accounts. One early modern case, certainly somewhat different from what we found out in Thüring's prose novel, deserves to be discussed briefly, before we turn to more philosophical issues in-

---

[35] Jean d'Arras, *Melusine; or, the Noble History of Lusignan*, trans. and with an intro. by Donald Maddox and Sara Sturm-Maddox (University Park, PA: The Pennsylvania State University Press, 2012), 198.

volved in this huge complex because it also illustrates the dramatic, if not traumatic, consequences of losing one's freedom, maybe for the rest of one's life.

2 The Exemplary Case of Hans Ulrich Krafft: An Early Modern Prisoner Reflects on His Experiences

The South-German merchant Hans Ulrich Krafft (1550–1621) went to the Levant in 1573 on behalf of his company back home, the Melchior Manlich Trade Company (Augsburg), spending most of his time in Aleppo and especially Tripoli (today Lebanon). He developed a close network of business partners, especially with Turks and Jews, the latter proving to be particularly helpful to him because of their linguistic abilities and friendliness. In the late summer of 1574, news reached the city that Manlich had become bankrupt, which put Krafft into a very uncomfortable situation because he was quickly taken to court over many credits which he had received on behalf of his company to carry out his business. He was only twenty-four years of age at that point and then had to spend three years in prison, from August 24 1574 to August 24, 1577, often under rather difficult, if not unpleasant conditions, although he obviously coped very well.

While incarcerated, he struck a friendship with a Jew, whose name is never mentioned, who taught him how to produce buttons to make money which would help him to pay off debts and to alleviate his life in prison. The Jew even assisted him in selling the buttons on the market, and when Krafft was transferred to the Tripoli citadel, where he was no longer allowed to do his work because knives and scissors were not permitted there, his friend intervened and managed to get him back to the previous prison.

On May 23, 1575, Krafft was visited by a Jew, Mayer Winterbach, who originated from near-by his own home town, who had heard about Krafft's misery and tried to provide him with some assistance. Although Krafft was rather apprehensive of this Jew, the latter demonstrated considerable loyalty to this prisoner, visited him regularly after he had returned from Safed in Galilee, and could eventually convince the various creditors that the young man was not really involved in the credit scheme by the Manlich Trade Company. He was released from prison in 1577 and soon after left Tripoli, obviously as a result of Mayer Winterbach's intervention on his behalf. Krafft reached Marseille on October 19, 1577, then moved to Genoa, from where he finally made his way back to Germany in 1578. He returned to Ulm permanently only in 1585. Much later, shortly before his death, he composed his memoirs from 1614 to 1616.

As bitter as his experiences in the prison must have been, he was not charged for any real crime and was kept there only because of the failed credit business which he had carried out on behalf of his company. The three years he seemed to have spent fairly comfortably, working on producing buttons and similar objects, receiving visitors, and communicating with the world outside quite openly. He learned to speak some Arabic, enjoyed the food brought in from the outside, and lived under not so terrible conditions.

Krafft's memoirs serve us well today to gain insight into a prison situation under the Ottomans, and it sheds important light on the global exchanges and trade in the eastern Mediterranean, with Turks, Jews, Italians, Germans, and many others operating together on the local markets.[36] He himself described his imprisonment as his personal purgatory, and he was greatly relieved when he was released and thus regained his freedom.

One of his main arguments in self-defense was that his previous masters were responsible for the bankruptcy, and that the creditors could not expect anything to come out of his imprisonment (273–74). Nevertheless, he was released from prison only after lengthy negotiations, pleadings, meetings, and appeals. The extensive report which he composed later was based on copious notes which he put down during his travels and the long period of his imprisonment (327–28), and it reveals most impressively how the Ottomans treated foreigners who had failed to deliver on their credit promises and how this German prisoner handled the many language barriers, the differences in culture, and foodstuff.

Significantly, we find parallel cases also in eastern Europe, such as the merchant (?) Bogdan (Aswadur) from Lemberg/Lviv (today Ukraine, straight east of Cracow), perhaps an Armenian, but more likely a Latvian, whose parents, both of aristocratic rank, had been killed by Russian solders, whereupon the boy was sold into slavery. An Armenian named Migerditz had bought him and taught him many different languages, as one of his later students, the Danzig merchant Martin Gruneweg (1562–ca. 1618), reports in his memoirs:

---

[36] The original manuscript is located in the Stadtarchiv Ulm, Bestand H (Handschriften / Nachlässe: Krafft, Hans Ulrich; for editions, see *Reisen und Gefangenschaft Hans Ulrich Kraffts, aus der Originalhandschrift herausgegeben* von Dr. L. D. Haszlett. Bibliothek des Litterarischen Vereins, LXI (Stuttgart: Litterarischer Verein, 1861); for the online version, see https://ia800307. us.archive.org/4/items/bub_gb_ii-6c_stmuwC/bub_gb_ii-6c_stmuwC.pdf (last accessed on Jan. 15, 2021); a condensed version was published more recently: *H. U. Krafft: Ein schwäbischer Kaufmann in türkischer Gefangenschaft: Reisen und Gefangenschaft Hans Ulrich Kraffts*, ed. Klaus Schubring. Schwäbische Lebensläufe (Heidenheim: Heidenheimer Verlags-Anstalt, 1970). See now Daniel Jütte, "Interfaith Encounters between Jews and Christians in the Early Modern Period and Beyond: Toward a Framework," *American Historical Review* 118.2 (2013): 378–400; cf. also the valuable database of 'ego-documents,' including an entry on Krafft: http://www.geschkult. fu-berlin.de/e/jancke-quellenkunde/verzeichnis/k/hu_krafft/index.html (last accessed on Jan. 15, 2021).

Bey diesem Migerditz lernete er diese sprachen, Armenisch, Tatterss, Polnisch unde Reusisch, welche er alle so perfect kontte, als were er dainne geboeren, von seines vatters sprache aber, gedachte er nicht ein wortt... . was er nun angrieff, ging im so von handen, das sichs idermenniglich wundern muste, dennoch fehlte ihm die schuele, wiewol er einwenig auf Armenisch buchstabierte... .[37]

[With this Migerditz he learned the following languages: Armenian, Tartar, Polnish, and Russian, which he could all speak perfectly as if he had been born in them, but he never said a word about his father's language... . Whatever he took upon him he managed to do so well that everyone was amazed, and yet he lacked the school training, though he knew a little how to spell in Armenian ...]

Despite the fact that he was a slave, he obviously enjoyed high respect as a language teacher, though he deliberately left out German, which might have been his mother tongue. We may surmise that the traumatic experience of being sold into slavery made him deliberately stay away from that language so that he could avoid remembering that physical and psychological suffering during his childhood.

Once this Bogdan had reached young adulthood, Migerditz set him free and began to pay him for all of his services as all of his other normal employees. Gruneweg traces his subsequent life to some extent, but he has no particular comments as to his previous status as a slave. For this Dominican author, Bogdan was a most impressive personality, whom he regarded both like a father figure and like an angel helping him in his need – certainly a reflection of Gruneweg's strongly homosexual tendency (637). The entire text passage reads as if it was not out of the ordinary that young orphans could be sold into slavery; that way, at least, they found people who took care of them. Bogdan is introduced to us as a magnificent and wealthy merchant, and his past as a slave does not cast any negative shadow on him, at least in the way how Gruneweg descirbes him.

---

37 *Die Aufzeichnungen des Dominikaners Martin Gruneweg (1562 – ca. 1618) über seine Familie in Danzig, seine Handelsreisen in Osteuropa und sein Klosterleben in Polen*, ed. Almut Bues. 4 vols. Quellen und Studien / Deutsches Historisches Institut Warschau, 19.1–4 (Wiesbaden: Harrassowitz, 2008), vol. 2, 627. The edition consists of one complete pagination system across all volumes. Cf. Bogusłse Dybaś, "Probleme der Mehrsprachigkeit bei Martin Gruneweg," *Mehrsprachigkeit in Ostmitteleuropa (1400–1700): Kommunikative Praktiken und Verfahren in gemischtsprachigen Städten und* Verbänden, ed. Hans-Jürgen Bömelburg and Norbert Kersken. Tagungen zur Ostmitteleuropaforschung, 37 (Marburg: Verlag Herder-Institut, 2020), 207–19; here 211–12.

3 The Philosopher in the Prison (Boethius and Thomas More)

Like Boethius in the early sixth century, Thomas More (1478–1535), famous author of *Utopia* (1516), faced his execution while being imprisoned in the Tower of London. Having refused to swear an Oath of Supremacy to King Henry VIII and to sign the parliamentary Act of Succession (1534) in favor of Queen Anne Boleyn, he was condemned to death for state treason. Significantly, during his time in prison he had Boethius's *De consolatione philosophiae* (ca. 524) with him and gained considerable comfort from this treatise, in which the late antique author outlined a fundamental philosophical approach to the workings of Fortune and the search for true happiness.[38] Boethius had found himself also in prison, charged with state treason without any justification, according to his own statement, and wrote about the consolation of philosophy in order to come to terms with this situation of injustice and imminent execution.

Similar to his famous predecessor, More composed his own philosophical reflections on his personal suffering and how to come to terms with it as an absolute injustice done to him in his *A Dialogue of Coumfort agaynst Tribulacion*. Here, the narrative figure of Anthony is visited in prison by his nephew, Vincent, who, though not a prisoner himself, seeks consolation from the older man because he is deeply worried about the military advances of the Ottoman forces on the eastern flank of Europe threatening the Christian heartland. Anthony offers in response a detailed reflection on the need to accept one's tribulation as having been imposed by God, and to embrace faith in God as the only possible remedy.

In contrast to Boethius, More uses this dialogic framework to develop an extensive meditation on human sinfulness, failure, and weakness, and correlates those with God's will and punishment. Altogether, his treatise served More exceedingly well to transcend his own suffering in prison and to find his way to God despite his miserable situation awaiting his execution despite his obvious innocence, a destiny that has been shared by countless other victims throughout time who were subjects of dictatorial or tyrannical systems.[39] Deeply inspired by

---

[38] Guy Bayley Dolson, "Imprisoned English Authors and the Consolation of Philosophy of Boethius," *The American Journal of Philology* 43.2 (1922): 168–69; Philip Edward Phillips, "Boethius, the Prisoner, and *The Consolation of Philosophy*," *Prison Narratives from Boethius to Zana*, ed. id. (New York: Palgrave Macmillan, 2014), 11–33. See also Jamie S. Scott, *Christians and Tyrants: The Prison Testimonies of Boethius, Thomas More, and Dietrich Bonhoeffer*. Toronto Studies in Religion, 19 (New York, Washington, DC, Baltimore, MD, et al.: Peter Lang, 1995).
[39] For the 1565 edition, see https://thomasmorestudies.org/wp-content/uploads/2020/12/TM_s-1565-Omnia-Opera-Utopiae-Libri-Duo.-1-18.pdf (last accessed on Jan. 15, 2021). For the most re-

his late antique source, he gained the inner strength to transform the terrible loss of freedom into a medium to discover the freedom of his spirit.⁴⁰ More was, however, not at all the first and certainly not the last to respond so intensely to Boethius's teachings, which laid the groundwork of the entire western discourse on happiness, individual liberty, and on the tension between temporary and universal goods and ideals.

We could also think of Pietro della Vigna (ca. 1190–1249), who similarly composed a Boethian-style *Consolatio* while in prison on possibly trumped-up charges of treason (as a "proditor") and corruption because he had been Emperor Frederick II's trusted legal advisor (protonotary and chancellor) for many years. Frederick ordered him to be blinded as punishment for his alleged crimes in 1249, and he died shortly thereafter, very similar to Boethius having been the victim of an intrigue against him at court, as he claimed himself. Because he committed suicide while in prison in San Miniato near Pisa, suffering deeply from the false charges against him, Dante later eternalized him in his *Inferno*, Circle VII, Ring II, Canto XIII, verses 58–78.⁴¹

Another significant example, several hundreds of years later, would be the famous Walter Raleigh (1552/1554–1618), who had to spend a long period of time as a prisoner in the Tower of London for political reasons. Having lost the royal favor after Elizabeth I had died on March 24 in 1603, Raleigh was arrested on 19 July 1603, charged with treason because of his alleged involvement in the so-called Main Plot against the queen's successor, James I, to remove him from the throne and to replace him with Arabella Stuart, a plot headed by

---

cent new edition, see Thomas More, *A Dialogue of Comfort Against Tribulation* (New York: Dover Publications, 2016). It has been translated into a variety of European languages. For the latest English translation by Gerlad Malsbary, 2020, see https://thomasmorestudies.org/wp-content/uploads/2020/12/Utopia-Selected-Epigram-Notes-11-23-2020-compressed.pdf

40 See the contributions to *The Cambridge Companion to Thomas More*, ed. George M. Logan. Cambridge Companions to Religion (Cambridge and New York: Cambridge University Press, 2011). For the broader context, see *Christian Spirituality: The Essential Guide to the Most Influential Spiritual Writings of the Christian Tradition*, ed. Frank N. Magill and Ian P. McGreal (San Francisco, CA: Harper & Row, 1988). See also Paul Strauss, *In Hope of Heaven: English Recusant Prison Writings of the Sixteenth Century*. American University Studies. Series IV, English Language and Literature, 166 (New York: Peter Lang, 1995).

41 H. M. Schaller, "Petrus de Vinea," *Lexikon des* Mittelalters, Vol. VI (Munich: Artemis, 1993), 1987–88. For more comments, see Dante, *The Divine Comedy:* Vol. I: *Inferno*, trans. with an intro., notes, and commentary by Mark Musa (London: Penguin, 1971), 192–93. See also Benoît Grévin, *Rhétorique du pouvoir médiéval: les lettres de Pierre de la Vigne et la formation du langage politique européen, XIIIe–XVe siècle*. Bibliothèque des écoles françaises d'Athènes et de Rome, 339 (Rome: École française de Rome, 2008).

Henry Brooke and Lord Cobham and allegedly funded by the Spanish government.

Whether Raleigh was truly involved in this sedition attempt, cannot be easily determined, but we know for sure that he was convicted and had to spend the next thirteen years in prison, during which he wrote extensively, such as his *Historie of the World*, published in 1614. He was pardoned in 1617, and then even allowed to embark on an extensive expedition to Venezuala and Guyana (in modern terms) to find gold. Unfortunately, some of his men engaged, maybe without Raleigh's knowledge and against all political agreements between England and Spain, with a Spanish outpost, Santo Tomé de Guayana on the Orinoco River, resulting in scores of dead. This scandal created an enormous public outcry and resulted in the Spanish ambassador in London demanding the reinstitution of Raleigh's death penalty. King James had no alternative but to oblige – and probably it also satisfied his own plans with his political opponent – so Raleigh, after his return, was re-apprehended and executed on October 29, 1618.[42]

During his long imprisonment before the second condemnation, to reiterate the same point, he was highly productive in writing and composing poetry, meaning that he must have enjoyed the considerable privilege of being put in a rather comfortable prison, appropriate for his social class. The Newgate prison was for the ordinary felons, whereas the Ludgate prison was for white collar crime.[43] The Tower, on the other hand, was reserved primarily for high-ranking and particularly political prisoners, and we would have to pursue its history all by itself because it housed so many famous and important inmates throughout history.[44]

---

[42] There is much literature on Raleigh; see, for instance, Andrew Hiscock, "Walter Ralegh and the Arts of Memory," *Literature Compass* 4.4 (2007): 1030–58; Anna Beer, *Patriot or Traitor: The Life and Death of Sir Walter Raleg* (London: Oneworld, 2018); and for a comparison between him and other famous prisoners-poets, see *The Great Prisoners: The First Anthology of Literature Written in Prison*, selected and ed. Isidore Abramowitz (New York: Dutton, 1946). See now Cyril L. Caspar, "New Perspectives of the Early Modern Afterlife: The Last Pilgrimage in the Poetry of John Donne and Sir Walter Raleigh," *Death in the Middle Ages and Early Modern Times: The Material and Spiritual Conditions of the Culture of Death*, ed. A. Classen. Fundamentals of Medieval and Early Modern Culture, 16 (Berlin and Boston: Walter de Gruyter, 2016), 433–56.

[43] Caroline Jowett, *The History of Newgate Prison* (Bamsley: Pen & Sword History, 2017); for the period starting in the eighteenth century, see Gary Kelly, *Newgate Narratives: General Introduction and Newgate Documents*. Newgate Narratives, 1 (London: Routledge, 2017).

[44] Nigel H Jones, *Tower: An Epic History of the Tower of London* (London: Hutchinson, 2011); Geoffrey Parnell, *The Tower of London: Past and Present* (Stroud, Gloucestershire: Sutton Publishing, 2009); David Wilson, *Pain and Retribution: A Short History of British Prisons 1066 to the Present* (London: Reaktion Books, 2014); see also the older, but still valuable study by William L. L. F. de Ros, *Memorials of the Tower of London* (1866; Norderstedt: Hansebooks GmbH,

In fact, world history all by itself could be viewed through the lens of crime, criminals, prisons, court proceedings, convictions, imprisonments, and executions, such as in the case of the Augsburg patrician, merchant, and city councilman, Friedrich Endorfer (1569–1628), who was charged with having embezzled a huge amount of money from the city budget. He died in prison while still being investigated, but the way how the authorities dealt with his corpse indicates that he would certainly have received the death penalty. He was denied a Christian burial and was treated most dishonorable, finding his final resting place outside of the official cemetery.[45] As we will observe below, a surprisingly large number of major philosophical and religious treatises, but then also poems, epics, travelogues, letters, and journals were composed by significant and influential writers throughout time, probably because the imprisonment imposed silence, isolation, and a deep sense of unjust treatment on the individual victim, especially when this imprisonment was the result of political persecution.

4 The Exile: Literary Reflections from Antiquity to the Late Middle Ages

A Metaphorical Prison

Writing has regularly assumed a critical function for many different prisoners throughout time in many cultures all over the world, but Boethius can be identified as one of the first to create this genre through which the author could transcend the prison walls and find his/her way toward spiritual freedom. Of course, we could also refer to famous Ovid who was exiled from Rome for some obscure reasons, being forced to live in Tomis (now Constanța, Romania) by decree of the emperor Augustus in 8 C.E., and he bitterly lamented about his destiny in his two

---

2018). For an excellent list of famous prisoners in the Tower, divided by centuries, see the certainly valuable article online at: https://en.wikipedia.org/wiki/List_of_prisoners_of_the_Tower_of_London (last accessed on Jan. 15, 2021).

45 See the introduction to *Die Korrespondenz der Augsburger Patrizierfamilie Endorfer, 1621–1627: Briefe aus Italien und Frankreich im Zeitalter des Dreißigjährigen Krieges*, ed. Mark Häberlein, Hans-Jörg Künast, and Irmgard Schwanke. Documenta Augustana, 21 (Augsburg: Wißner, 2011). For an excellent treatment of dishonorable executions and burials (or lack thereof), see Romedio Schmitz-Esser, *Der Leichnam im Mittelalter: Einbalsamierung, Verbrennung und die kulturelle Konstruktion des toten Körpers*. Mittelalter-Forschungen, 48 (2014; Ostfildern: Jan Thorbecke Verlag, 2016), 592–94. An English translation is soon to appear, prepared by Albrecht Classen and Carolin Radtke (Turnhout: Brepols, 2021).

major works, *Tristia* and *Epistulae ex Ponto*, but this was not a prison as such, although he died in his exile in 17 or 18 C.E.[46]

Many medieval poets refer to their protagonists' exile, such as the Count of Antwerp in the eighth story told on the second day in Boccaccio's *Decameron* (ca. 1350), but again, this experience is far removed from the suffering in a prison or on death row.[47] We could continue from here and create an almost infinite list of individuals, high and low, who were not allowed to stay within their social and political community, hence were forced into exile, and this both in the Middle Ages and until today.[48] And we could also include the extensive genre of late medieval German heroic poems dealing with Dietrich, such as *Dietrichs Flucht*, *Ortnit*, *Alpharts Tod*, and *Rabenschlacht* (thirteenth century), all treating in one way or the other the protagonist's traumatic experience of being forced to go into exile because of military and political constraints, evil opponents, and personal misfortune.[49]

The history of medieval German literature begins, to draw from yet another example, with a short, heroic poem, "Hildebrandslied" (ca. 820, copied down in the monastery of Fulda; it survived only as a fragment), in which the protagonist reveals that as a young man he had been forced to accompany his lord, Theoderic, on his escape from Odoacre, fleeing into exile, which he spent many years under the Hunnish ruler Attila. Although he had to leave behind his family and tribe, feudal bonds forced him to abandon all and follow his destiny.[50]

---

46 Ovid was not the first and by far not the last exile to suffer this destiny; see Gordon P. Kelly, *A History of Exile in the Roman Republic* (Cambridge: Cambridge University Press, 2006); Adrian Rădulescu, *Ovid in Exile: Ovidiu la Pontul Euxin* (Las Vegas, NV: Vita Histria, 2019); *Two Thousand Years of Solitude: Exile After Ovid*, ed. Jennifer Ingleheart. Classical Presences (Oxford: Oxford University Press, 2011).
47 Giovanni Boccaccio, *The Decameron*, trans. with an intro. and notes by G. H. McWilliam. Sec. ed. (1972; London: Penguin, 1995), 148–64.
48 *Exile in the Middle Ages: Selected Proceedings from the International Medieval Congress, University of Leeds, 8–11 July 2002*, ed. Laura Napran and E. van Houts. International Medieval Research, 13 (Turnhout: Brepols, 2004).
49 *Dietrichs Flucht*, ed. Elisabeth Lienert and Gertrud Beck. Texte und Studien zur mittelhochdeutschen Heldenepik, 1 (Tübingen: Max Niemeyer, 2003). For critical investigations, see Joachim Heinzle, *Einführung in die mittelhochdeutsche Dietrichepik*. de Gruyter Studienbuch (Berlin and New York: Walter de Gruyter, 1999); Elisabeth Lienert, *Die ›historische‹ Dietrichepik: Untersuchungen zu ›Dietrichs Flucht‹, ›Rabenschlacht‹ und ›Alpharts Tod‹*. Texte und Studien zur mittelhochdeutschen Heldenepik, 5 (Berlin and New York: Walter de Gruyter, 2010).
50 *Althochdeutsche Literatur: Mit altniederdeutschen Textbeispielen. Auswahl mit Übertragungen und Kommentar*, ed. Horst Dieter Schlosser. 2nd, rev. and expanded ed. (1998; Berlin: Erich Schmidt, 2004), 68–71. For further discussion of this poem, but in a different context, see below.

This individual did not have the freedom to decide his own life, even though he then lived far away from his kith and kin for thirty years.

Then there was the idea of self-imposed exile, such as the crusade, or pilgrimage, to repent for one's sins. And, even more abstract, monasticism was often equated with exile, an exile from this world, in the continuous quest for spiritual enlightenment and for the union with the Godhead. However, in order to stay on target, following I will explore more specifically the experience of imprisonment, the desire for freedom, and the fear of slavery as we can find it in a vast corpus of literary and historical text, but then also in visual documents. The struggle for individual and communal freedom, such as in the case of the Dutch against the Spaniards (1596–1648), illustrates this phenomenon most dramatically.[51] The entire history of religion, whether Jewish, Christian, Muslim, Hindu, or Buddhist, has been either deeply or at least to some extent impacted by expulsions, ostracism, persecutions, imprisonment, and pogroms, since in the name of any kind of god all kinds of injustices, crimes, many forms of violence and hostilities have been committed throughout time. We only need to think of the Jewish diaspora, the crusades to liberate the Holy Land as well as those targeting the Cathars or Albigensians, the wars between Catholics and Protestants, the expulsions of Jews from various countries throughout the late Middle Ages (at last, 1492, from Spain, 1496, from Portugal), the expulsion of the Huguenots from France first following the St. Bartholomew's Day massacre in 1572, and then in 1685 according to Louis XIV's Edict of Fontainebleau., and so forth. Many times, the history of Renaissance Italy was shaped by deep divides between rival groups, dynasties, city states, and between the various

---

51 Lisa Di-Crescenzo and Sally Fisher, "Exile and Imprisonment in Medieval and Early Modern Europe," *Parergon* 34.2 (2017): 1–23; Ole Peter Grell, *Calvinist Exiles in Tudor and Stuart England* (London: Routledge, 1996); Katy Gibbons, *English Catholic Exiles in Late Sixteenth-Century Paris* (Rochester, NY: Boydell, 2011); Heiko A. Oberman, "Europa afflicta: The Reformation of the Refugees," *Archiv für Reformationsgeschichte* 83 (1992): 91–111; Judith Pollmann, *Catholic Identity and the Revolt of the Netherlands, 1520–1635* (Oxford: Oxford University Press, 2011); Geert H. Janssen, *The Dutch Revolt and Catholic Exile in Reformation Europe* (Cambridge: Cambridge University Press, 2014); Johannes Müller, *Exile Memories and the Dutch Revolt: The Narrated Diaspora, 1550–1750*. Studies in Medieval and Reformation Traditions, 199 (Leiden and Boston: Brill, 2016); Nicholas Terpstra, *Religious Refugees in the Early Modern World: An Alternative History of the Reformation* (Cambridge: Cambridge University Press, 2015). See also Heinz Duchhardt and Horst Lademacher, "Das Heilige Römische Reich und die Republik der Vereinigten Niederlande: Ausgangslage einer Beziehung bis 1648," *Kaufleute und Fürsten: Außenpolitik und politisch-kulturelle Perzeption im Spiegel niederländischdeutscher Beziehungen 1648–1748*, ed. Helmut Gabel and Volker. Niederlande-Studien, 18 (Münster, Munich, et al.: LIT, 1998), 11–38; Christoph Driessen, *Geschichte der Niederlande: von der Seemacht zum Trendland*. 2nd. expanded ed. (2009; Regensburg: Verlag Friedrich Pustet, 2016).

principalities and the Holy See. Those conflicting parties often resorted to the political instrument of sending opponents into exile, if not worse.⁵²

Rüdiger, in the famous Middle High German heroic epic, the *Nibelungenlied* (ca. 1200), stands in as a most remarkable exile figure. He appears at the end of the first part as the emissary of the Hunnish ruler Etzel (Attila), wooing on his lord's behalf for Kriemhilt's hand in marriage. Only once he has promised her that he would avenge any wrong-doing committed against her, which he means in future terms, while she relies on it as a pledge ultimately to help her avenge her first husband Siegfried's murder by Hagen (stanzas 1255–56), does she agree to this proposition.⁵³ When the Burgundians later travel to Hungary to visit their sister – she only intends to lure them into a death trap so that she can get Hagen killed – Rüdiger welcomes them most hospitably and showers them with gifts, but he is not free in his decisions; he must follow his lord's and his queen's orders, and later, when almost everyone at the Hunnish court has already been killed, the exile is bound by his oath to fight against the guest as well, as Etzel and Kriemhilt virtually force him to do. Tragically, he kills scores of his opponents, with whom he is actually closely bonded through their kinship

---

52 David van der Linden, *Experiencing Exile: Huguenot Refugees in the Dutch Republic, 1680–1700* (London: Routledge, 2015). See also the relevant studies: Lauro Martines, "Political Conflict in the Italian City-States," *Government and Opposition* 3.1 (1968): 69–91; Susannah Foster Baxendale, "Exile in Practice: The Alberti Family in and out of Florence, 1401–1428," *Renaissance Quarterly* 44.4 (1991): 720–56; Ann Crabb, *The Strozzi of Florence: Widowhood and Family Solidarity in the Renaissance* (Ann Arbor, MI: University of Michigan Press, 2000); Lorenzo Fabbri, "The Memory of Exiled Families: The Case of the Strozzi," *Art, Memory and Family in Renaissance Florence*, ed. Giovanni Ciappelli and Patricia Lee Rubin (Cambridge: Cambridge University Press, 2000), 253–61; Lorenzo Fabbri, "Da Firenze a Ferrara: Gli Strozzi tra Casa d'Este e antichi legami di sangue," *Alla corte degli Estensi: Filosofa, arte e cultura a Ferrara nei secoli XV e XVI. Atti del Convegno internazionale di studi, 5–7 marzo 1992*, ed. Marco Bertozzi (Ferrara: Università di Ferrara, 1994), 91–108; Margery Ganz, "Paying the Price for Political Failure: Florentine Women in the Aftermath of 1466," *Rinascimento* 34 (1994): 237–57; Heather Gregory, "The Return of the Native: Filippo Strozzi and Medicean Politics," *Renaissance Quarterly* 38.1 (1985): 1–21; Jacques Heers, *L'esilio, la vita politica e la società nel medioevo* (Naples: Liguori, 1997); Fabrizio Ricciardelli, *The Politics of Exclusion in Early Renaissance Florence* (Turnhout: Brepols, 2007); Christine Shaw, *The Politics of Exile in Renaissance Italy* (Cambridge: Cambridge University Press, 2000); Randolph Starn, *Contrary Commonwealth: The Theme of Exile in Medieval and Renaissance Italy* (Berkeley, CA: University of California Press, 1982). I would like to acknowledge here the study by Di Crescenzo and Fisher, "Exile and Imprisonment" (see note 51) who have done already some of the spade work in this field.

53 *Das Nibelungenlied: Mittelhochdeutsch / Neuhochdeutsch*. Nach der Handschrift B herausgegeben von Ursula Schulze. Ins Neuhochdeutsche übersetzt und kommentiert von Siegfried Grosse (Stuttgart: Philipp Reclam jun., [2010]). For an English trans., see *The Nibelungenlied*, trans. A. T. Hatto (1965; London: Penguin, 1969).

and the mutual agreement that his own daughter would marry Giselher, brother of the Burgundian King Gunther. But at the end, in his last duel with Gernot, Gunther's other brother, the two warriors slay each other. This horrible outcome highlights in most dramatic terms how much this life in exile, the cause of which is not explained here, made the individual so dependent on the new lord's goodwill.[54]

Rüdiger operates very impressively, treating the guests most generously, but he is deeply infused with his own sense of being only an exile, not free to carry out his own actions and to realize his personal wishes. When the minstrel-warrior Volker suggests a marriage arrangement with Rüdiger's daughter, the latter responds sorrowfully that the social class difference would certainly prevent that, adding significantly: "wir sîn hi ellende, beide ich und mîn wîp" (stanza 1673/1676, 3; both my wife and myself are strangers here; i.e., exiles). But then Giselher intervenes and offers himself as the young woman's future husband, which the other heroes approve (stanza 1676/1679), and which seems to solve the issue at that moment. Later, however, in the battle, this newly forged family bond does not stand up to the feudal obligations which Rüdiger has toward Etzel and Kriemhilt. Exiles like him do not enjoy full freedom and are subject to the ruler's benevolence and magnificence.

In fact, in that decisive moment when Rüdiger is forced to engage in the fighting against the Burgundians, he tries to return all of King Etzel's previous gifts (stanza 2154/2157), but he is bound by his previous pledges and cannot extricate himself from the feudal commitments, especially as an exile without any outside help, and this is the beginning of his end (stanza 2163/2166). Despite all of his fortunes, his power position as Etzel's margrave, and despite his high esteem, he does not enjoy the freedom to refuse the king's and the queen's request and is forced to obey their order. The person in exile is dependent on the host's hospitality and now has to pay for all that dearly.[55]

---

54 Albrecht Classen, "The Experience of Exile in Medieval German Heroic Poetry," *Medieval German Textrelations: Translations, Editions, and Studies (Kalamazoo Paper 2010–2011)*, ed. Sibylle Jefferis. Göppinger Arbeiten zur Germanistik, 765 (Göppingen: Kümmerle, 2012), 83–110.
55 Previous research has certainly taken the figure of Rüdiger into consideration, especially the anticipation of tragedy as it evolves at his court during the engagement of his daughter with Giselher, but Rüdiger's position as an unfree hero has not attracted much attention; see, for instance, Jan-Dirk Müller, *Spielregeln für den Untergang: Die Welt des Nibelungenliedes* (Tübingen: Max Niemeyer, 1998), 160–63; Irmgard Gephart, *Der Zorn der Nibelungen: Rivalität und Rache im "Nibelungenlied"* (Cologne, Weimar, and Vienna: Böhlau, 2005), 130–33. Both highlight the vassalic relationship with Etzel, but do not address Rüdiger's rather tenuous position as a margrave, who serves there dependent on Etzel's grace in favor of this exile. See now, for a corrective, Albrecht Classen, "Friendship in the Heroic Epics: Rüedegêr in the *Nibelungenlied*," *Friendship in*

5 The Prisoner

While modern-day American history knows especially of the famous prison Alcatraz in San Francisco, California, medieval and early modern English history knows of the Tower of London with such infamous prisoners as Sir Thomas More, King Henry VI, the wives of the of King Henry VIII, and Rudolph Hess, which also resulted in a whole genre of prison literature.[56] And there would hardly be any medieval castle without a dungeon, where the lord could put those individuals he deemed worthy of punishment or from whom he wanted to extort money, privileges, or land.[57]

Some of the most famous avatars following the model more or less provided by Boethius, were, from the sixteenth century onwards to the immediate present, Fray Luis de León (1527–1591), Miguel de Cervantes (1547–1616), Tommaso Campanella (1568–1639), John Bunyan (1628–1688), Marie-Jeanne Rolan (1754–1793), Oscar Wilde (1854–1900), Antonio Gramsci (1926–1937), Dietrich Bonhoeffer (1943–1945), Ann Frank (1942–1944), Jean Cassou (1897–1986), Primo Levi (1919–1987), Irina Ratushinskaya (1982–1986), Ezra Pound (1885–1972), or Nelson Mandela (1918–2013), and Gudrun Ensslin (1940–1977), while here I would not want to dwell on such criminal prisoners as Alphonse Gabriel Capone,

---

the Middle Ages, ed. Albrecht Classen and Marilyn Sandidge. Fundamentals of Medieval and Early Modern Culture, 6 (Berlin and New York: Walter de Gruyter, 2010), 429–43.

56 Ruth Ahnert, *The Rise of Prison Literature in the Sixteenth Century* (Cambridge: Cambridge University Press, 2013); for modern-day prison literature, see now Sandra Berndt, *Haftautobiographik im 20. Jahrhundert: Hafterfahrungen in Tagebuchaufzeichnungen, Briefen, Gedichten, Dokumentationen und Erzähltexten* (Frankfurt a. M., Bern, and Vienna: Peter Lang, 2016). There is a huge amount of relevant primary material concerning this topic; millions of people linger in prison, have suffered in prison, have died in prison, and writing about this experience has been a major outlet for the victims. See, for instance, H. Bruce Franklin, *The Victim as Criminal and Artist: Literature from the American Prison* (New York: Oxford University Press, 1978); Monika Fludernik, *Metaphors of Confinement: The Prison in Fact, Fiction, and Fantasy* (Oxford: Oxford University Press, 2019), traces the history of carceral imagery from antiquity to the modern world.

57 Joachim Zeune, "Verliese, Gefängnisse und Folterkammern," *Burgen in Mitteleuropa. Ein Handbuch*. Vol. 1: *Bauformen und Entwicklung*, ed. Deutsche Burgenvereinigung and Horst Wolfgang Böhme (Stuttgart: Theiss, 1999), 314–15; Daniel Burger, "In den Turm geworfen: Gefängnisse und Folterkammern auf Burgen im Mittelalter und in der frühen Neuzeit," *Burgenbau im späten Mittelalter*, vol. II. Ed. Wartburg-Gesellschaft zur Erforschung von Burgen und Schlössern in Verbindung mit dem Germanischen Nationalmuseum. Forschungen zu Burgen und Schlössern, 12 (Berlin and Munich: Deutscher Kunstverlag, 2009), 221–36. For a large number of photos of medieval and early modern dungeons and similar locations, see https://commons.wikimedia.org/wiki/Category:Dungeons?uselang=de (last accessed on Jan. 15, 2021).

known simply as Al Capone (1899–1947) or Adolf Hitler (1889–1945) before his rise to power.[58] The modern world knows, unfortunately, of many more political and other prisoners, and in some parts of our world, certainly also in the United States, such as in Guantanamo Bay on Cuba, imprisoning people even for the slightest offenses makes money because prisons are increasingly privatized, so prisoners are good business for individual entrepreneurs feeding on other people's lives. But great minds have never been repressed simply by prison walls, as this long list indicates, and the desire for freedom and justice found its way into countless literary, philosophical, and religious works.

This does not mean, however, that the prison mattered less or was of minor significance in the daily lives of pre-modern people, as all the poor victims would be able to confirm quite dramatically, especially since they often actually complained bitterly about it in their various writings. At the same time, to maintain prisons has always been an expensive enterprise, so we only would need to examine the relevant archival documents to find extensive data about prisons also in the Middle Ages as an important instrument in the hands of the authorities, whether the state or the Church.[59] Wherever we look, the prison as an in-

---

[58] Brigitte Sertl, *Carceri e invenzioni: italienische Schriftsteller in Gefangenschaft*. Abhandlungen zur Sprache und Literatur, 79 (Bonn: Romanistischer Verlag, 1995); Rivkah Zim, *The Consolations of Writing: Literary Strategies of Resistance from Boethius to Primo Levi* (Princeton, NJ: Princeton University Press, 2014); *Prison Narratives from Boethius to Zana*, ed. Philip Edward Phillips (New York, NY: Palgrave Macmillan, 2014).

[59] Jean Dunbabin, *Captivity and Imprisonment in Medieval Europe, 1000–1300*. Medieval Culture and Society (Houndmills, Basingstoke, Hampshire; New York: Palgrave Macmillan, 2002). This excellent study traces the development of prisons and their designs, along with the fetters and chains used for prisoners, from late antiquity to the late Middle Ages. As he concludes, "the number of crimes committed almost certainly rose as communities became larger and less intimate. On the other hand, catching the guilty parties was now more difficult, as was preventing their escape once caught. The minds of the prudent therefore turned to thoughts of chains and keys. Whereas, in the earlier part of the period, the interval between the arrest of a criminal, his conviction and his punishment were usually so brief as to obviate the necessity for special arrangements, by 1300 custodial imprisonment before trial had become common across Europe" (171). This means, the rise of prisons and of the number of prisoners in the high and late Middle Ages can be used as a benchmark of the growth of the state as a legal, political, financial, and judicial entity. He continues: "To a certain extent, then, the history of imprisonment does provide a concrete manifestation of the rise of abstract state power. From early claims that important captives should be handed over to princes to the later that only those authorized by princes or podestà should be permitted to keep captives at all, and then normally only after a judgement in a royal, princely or communal court, central control steadily manifested itself. The clearer the concept of sovereignty was in any territory, the greater was the need for prisons. The link between the two, stated cogently in much of Justinian's legislation, was especially persuasive in

stitution mirrored the deep tensions between the individual and the authorities, whether secular or religious, whether we think of the philosopher and theologian Peter Abelard (d. 1142, not in prison yet, but in grave danger of being tried at court for heresy) or the mystic Marguerite de Porète (d. 1310, burned at the stake). We would thus have to write a whole book on prisoners held by the medieval and early modern Inquisition, and on countless war prisoners from early on in order to do justice to this huge and certainly important topic. But I will return to this issue in a variety of contexts further below and examine it more through the lens of literary and cultural history.

6 The Slave

Human beings have always been commodified, either as slaves or as prisoners, and the phenomenon of incarceration and enslavement today does not look good at all, even compared to the late antiquity, the Middle Ages, and the early modern age. However, the true facts concerning modern-day slaves, for instance, are hardly ever brought to light, maybe because the western world likes to think that we live in a post-Enlightenment period where slavery is no longer practiced or really imaginable.[60] The more laws are promulgated, the more individuals are caught by the authorities, the more are brought to 'justice,' the more are thrown into prison, the more the government pays the companies per prisoner bed, etc. Little wonder that those who run those private prisons (such as in the USA, at least in 2020) strongly support arch-conservative politicians who are responsible for many of those very rigid laws. But then there have also been countless political prisoners all over the world, whether we think of the Soviet Archipelago Gulag (as described in the famous text under the same title [1973] by Alexander Solzhenitsyn, 1918–2008), the vast system of prisons and concentration camps in Nazi Germany, or any other incarceration system in North Korea, China, the United States, Chile, South Africa, etc.

---

the Mediterranean areas where the influence of the Bologna law schools spread early and deeply" (172).

60 Give and take, there are currently ca. 136,000 slaves in the UK alone, and 9.2 million black slaves in Africa today; cf. Judith Bergman, "Modern Slavery and Woke Hypocrisy," https://www.gatestoneinstitute.org/16152/modern-slavery (last accessed on Jan. 15, 2021), if we can believe those numbers. Worldwide, there are estimated to exist roughly 40.3 million individuals whom we would call slaves, with 71% of those being female, and 1 in 4 being children (many held for sexual services); for the *Global Slavery Index 2018*, see https://www.globalslaveryindex.org/2018/findings/highlights/ (last accessed on Jan. 15, 2021)

B Freedom

1 Freedom – A Complex Topic Throughout Time

The topic of this study, however, goes beyond the narrow confines – with pardon for this perhaps quite fitting and deliberate pun – of the prison cell, as existential as that experience has always been. The question rather pertains to the issue of what the three terms of freedom, imprisonment, and slavery meant in the pre-modern era, how they were reflected in literature, the arts, philosophy, and religion. In philosophy, the focus normally rests on the issues of free will versus dependency on god, destiny, fate, or some other ineffable power. We might want to consider also the differences between freedom, a personal empowerment allowing the individual to pursue its own path toward happiness, and liberty, a political and social freedom from external restraints, excessive laws, and an authoritarian government, as already outlined by John Stuart Mill (1806–1873). In short, freedom would pertain to subjectivity, the manifestation of the individual in its own determination, whereas liberty characterizes the condition of a society governing itself (e.g., democracy). To what extent the individual who was coerced to do something against his/her own will remains morally responsible constitutes one of the difficult issues in philosophy, morality, and ethics, as outlined perhaps most poignantly by Harry G. Frankfurt.[61]

Freedom has been discussed from many different perspectives, and it represents a highly complex, often shifting notion subject to countless discussions by philosophers, theologians, lawyers, poets, artists, politicians or rulers, and others. It is a topic of great importance both for the ordinary individual and for the philosopher. The term 'freedom' appears in a vast range of semantic fields, per-

---

[61] In a very modern context, both terms are currently even discussed controversially in light of the limited resources of the earth; see *Liberty and the Ecological Crisis: Freedom on a Finite Planet*, ed. Christopher Orr, Kaitlin Kish, and Bruce Jennings. Routledge Explorations in Environmental Studies (London and New York: Routledge, 2020). From a philosophical perspective, see Henry E. Allison, *Kant's Conception of Freedom: A Developmental and Critical Analysis* (Cambridge: Cambridge University Press, 2020). See also *Freedom as a Key Category in Origen and in Modern Philosophy and Theology*, ed. Alfons Fürst. Adamantiana, 14 (Münster i. W.: Aschendorff, 2019); *The Cambridge Companion to the First Amendment and Religious Liberty*, ed. Michael D. Breidenbach and Owen Anderson (Cambridge: Cambridge University Press, 2019). For comparative-religious perspectives, see *The Concept of Freedom in Judaism, Christianity and Islam*, ed. Georges Tamer and Ursula Männle. Key Concepts in Interreligious Discourses, 3 (Berlin and Boston: Walter de Gruyter, 2019). As to Frankfurt's position, see his study "Alternate Possibilities and Moral Responsibility," *Journal of Philosophy* 66.23 (1969): 829–39.

taining to the individual's will, the personal ability to move and act at will, to realize one's wishes without external hindrances, etc. There is 'negative freedom,' meaning the freedom or independence from any obligation or duty, law or regulation, and there is 'positive freedom,' meaning the freedom to do something as one wishes, either individually or as a collective, creating new political, economic, or religious units, though the latter was mostly not possible in the Middle Ages with the Catholic Church, above all, working very hard to prevent any form of heresy.[62] Then we would have to consider the differences between the freedom of an individual and the freedom of a collective, a tribe, a group, a community, or a country.[63] However, apart from the freedom which many imperial cities acquired in the course of time, partially or completely,[64] and this at the latest since the twelfth century,[65] the pre-modern world hardly knew any forms of democracy in the modern sense of the word, perhaps excluding here the world of Icelandic society.[66] But even there the institution of slavery existed, as we will learn below in more detail.

---

62 See, for instance, Malcolm Lambert, *Medieval Heresy: Popular Movements from the Gregorian Reform to the Reformation* (1977; Malden, MA, Oxford, and Carlton, Victoria, Australia: Blackwell Publishing, 2002).
63 For an impressively useful survey article, which covers, however, the entire historical range from antiquity to the present, see online at: https://de.wikipedia.org/wiki/Freiheit (last accessed on Jan. 15, 2021). In this case, Wikipedia proves to be better than its common reputation might imply. The relatively short but highly useful bibliography can be treated as a gateway toward a huge discourse on this very complex issue.
64 Gerd Steinwascher, "Städtische Freiheit und gräfliche Residenz Oldenburg im späten Mittelalter und im Zeitalter der Reformation," *Oldenburg: Stadtgeschichte in Bildern und Texten. Vom Heidenwall zur Wissenschaftsstadt*, ed. Udo Elerd (Oldenburg: Isensee, 2009), 33–44; *Freiheit im Mittelalter am Beispiel der Stadt*, ed. Dagmar Klose and Marco Ladewig. Perspektiven historischen Denkens und Lernens, 4 (Potsdam: Universitäts-Verlag, 2009).
65 Pesch, "Freiheit, Freie" (see note 11), 897; F. B. Fahlbusch, "Freie Städte," *Lexikon des Mittelalters*, Vol. IV (Munich and Zürich: Artemis, 1989), 895–96 (older research literature is listed there). This growing freedom of cities from the local princes (secular or ecclesiastical) found its best expression in the well-known phrase "Stadtluft macht frei" (urban air makes you free). See Paul Schütze, *Die Entstehung des Rechtssatzes: Stadtluft macht frei*. Historische Studien, 36 (Berlin: Ebering, 1903); Ernst Werner, *Stadtluft macht frei: Frühscholastik und bürgerliche Emanzipation in der ersten Hälfte des 12. Jahrhunderts*. Sitzungsberichte der Sächsischen Akademie der Wissenschaften zu Leipzig, Philologisch-Historische Klasse 118.5 (Berlin: Akademie-Verlag, 1976).
66 For a variety of approaches to this topic, see the contributions to *Authorities in the Middle Ages: Influence, Legitimacy, and Power in Medieval Society*, ed. Sini Kangas, Mia Korpiola, and Tuija Aionen. Fundamentals of Medieval and Early Modern Culture, 12 (Berlin and Boston: Walter de Gruyter, 2013); Jesse L. Byock, *Viking Age Iceland* (London: Penguin, 2001); *Social Norms in Medieval Scandinavia*, ed. Jakub Morawiec, Aleksandra Jochymek, and Grzegorz Bartusik. Be-

But it would be erroneous to assume that the discourse on political freedom began only in the eighteenth or nineteenth centuries. On the contrary, all humanistic thinking, whether in antiquity, the Middle Ages, or the early modern age, was deeply dependent on the presence of some degree of freedom, at least in abstract terms.[67] Older scholars still considered the entire discourse on freedom in the Middle Ages as essentially determined by the relationship between the individual and God, between the present time and antiquity as the absolute and final source of all authority, and, above all, the freedom of the human will (Anselm of Canterbury, Peter Abelard, Peter Lombardus, Robert of Melun, Bernard of Clairvaux, et al.).[68]

To what extent has rationality been capable of pursuing a path toward goodness and avoiding evil? How much was it necessary that the individual was free from any constraints in making his/her decisions? Could one identify freedom with one's unfettered will (Thomas Aquinas)? With the human will, hence freedom, the faithful was supposed to aim for the highest good, God, to liberate the soul from its earthly existence. As Aquinas expounded, the drive toward the good, or to absolute freedom, was possible only because the will was, by its nature, determined by the desire for freedom, as Boethius had already argued with respect toward all human quests to gain happiness. Thus, as Pesch formulates it, freedom is the "Seinsgrund des Willens" (1085; the existential foundation of the will).

Freedom would thus be found only in God, clearly a purely theological interpretation favored by those scholastic thinkers like Thomas Aquinas. There would not be any neutral concept of the freedom of will, but this freedom would have to be recognized as the essence of human existence which would find its realization in the merging with God. Duns Scotus later developed this further and identified the freedom of will as the highest entity in human existence, which was not dependent on the drive toward God, but an autonomous entity: "nihil aliud a voluntate est causa totalis volitionis in voluntate" (nothing apart from the will

---

yond Medieval Europe (Leeds: Arc Humanities Press, 2019); *Narrating Law and Laws of Narration in Medieval Scandinavia*, ed. Roland Scheel. Ergänzungsbände zum Reallexikon der Germanischen Altertumskunde, 117 (Berlin and Boston: Walter de Gruyter, 2020).

67 *Freiheit und Gerechtigkeit als Herausforderung der Humanwissenschaften = Freedom and Justice as a Challenge of the Humanities*, ed. Mira Miladinović and Dean Komel (Bern, Berlin, and Vienna: Peter Lang, 2018).

68 O. H. Pesch, "Freiheit. III," *Historisches Wörterbuch der Philosophie*, ed. Joachim Ritter. Vol. 2 (Darmstadt: Wissenschaftliche Buchgesellschaft, 1972), 1083–88.

is the total cause of volition).⁶⁹ If we consider how much all these aspects – the will, freedom, the relationship between the self and God, self-determination, etc. – were hotly debated at the end of the thirteenth century, and keep in mind with what vehemence the Paris Bishop Etienne Tempier tried to condemn many theses in that regard allegedly formulated by the professors at the university in 1277, we understand how much the debate concerning freedom really mattered in theological and also political circles.⁷⁰

These highly esoteric philosophical and theological reflections, in turn regularly implied, considering more the material side of things on a lower, practical level, that there was a clear sense of the danger for the individual of losing that personal freedom, now in political and social terms, either as a punishment (imprisonment) or as the result of unfortunate circumstances, leading to slavery, such as the consequence of a war situation, or when people were waylaid and quickly moved away to an appropriate slave market. The discourse on freedom was normally not, of course, determined by the quest for individual freedom within society, and yet the basic concepts discussed by those scholastics laid the foundation for the practical component as well.⁷¹ The discussion about the nature of freedom of the will and its relationship with God continued throughout the age of Humanism (Erasmus of Rotterdam) and the Protestant Reformation (Martin Luther),⁷² but much of modern philosophy continues to probe this issue.⁷³

As the philosopher Iso Kern now defines this issue: "Die ethische Freiheit des Willens ist die durch das Gewissen ermöglichte Freiheit der Willensentscheidung für ein ethisch mehr oder weniger gutes oder für ein mehr oder weniger schlechtes Handeln" (The ethical freedom of the will is the freedom made pos-

---

69 Pesch, "Freiheit. III" (see note 68), 1086; see also the famous discussion by Hannah Arendt, *The Life of the Mind* (New York: Jovanovich, 1978), 131–33.
70 *Aufklärung im Mittelalter? Die Verurteilung von 1277.* Das Dokument des Bischofs von Paris übersetzt und erläutert von Kurt Flasch. excerpta classica, VI (Mainz: Dieterich'sche Verlagsbuchhandlung, 1989), 202–08, 228–29, 241–42.
71 Mary Elizabeth Ingham, *Ethics and Freedom: An Historical-Critical Investigation of Scotist Ethical Thought* (Lanham, MD: University Press of America, 1989); see also the contributions to *The Routledge Companion to Free Will*, ed. Kevin Timpe, Meghan Griffith, and Neil Levy. Routledge Pilosophy Companions (New York and London: Routledge, 2017).
72 Pesch, "Freiheit. III" (see note 68), 1087. See also Peter Heinrich, *Mensch und freier Wille bei Luther und Erasmus: Ein Brennpunkt reformatorischer Auseinandersetzung – Unter besonderer Berücksichtigung der Anthropologie* (Nordhausen: Traugott Bautz, 2003); Klaus Hammacher, *Die Frage nach der Freiheit* (Baden-Baden: Nomos, 2015).
73 R. Spaemann, "Freiheit, IV," *Historisches Wörterbuch der Philosophie*, ed. Joachim Ritter. Vol. 2 (Darmstadt: Wissenschaftliche Buchgesellschaft, 1972), 1088–98.

sible through the conscience to decide on one's own for an ethical action, more or less good or more or less bad).[74]

This freedom is, however, dependent on the ethical framework determining an individual and the formation of one's consciousness, perhaps first during the time of puberty, which implies that adulthood has to be understood also as the age of one's life in which the individual determines his/her own will and acts accordingly, either ethically or not, but always in pursuit of its freedom. As the global protests against governmental restrictions on people's movements and on the right to gather privately in large groups due to the COVID-19 pandemic indicate, freedom is currently increasingly understood as a form of complete self-enactment without any regard for the neighbors or the collective. But every freedom, a profound privilege hard fought for, comes with obligations and duties as well. No one has the freedom to perform or act as s/he likes it if this hurts innocent others, as the current crisis in 2020/2021 clearly indicates. As Jürgen Habermas now insists, the individual living within a communicative context must demonstrate "Kooperationsbereitschaft" (readiness to cooperate) in order to live peacefully and meaningfully within a historically determined world.[75]

---

[74] Iso Kern, *Der gute Weg des Handelns: Versuch einer Ethik für die heutige Zeit* (Basel: Schwabe Verlag, 2020), 313. The subsequent discussion about the freedom of will then turns considerably toward a rather religious interpretation, warning the individual about the danger of vices that remove the freedom to act according to one's ethical ideals (314).

[75] Kern, *Der gute Weg des Handelns* (see note 74), 314. Jürgen Habermas, *Auch eine Geschichte der Philosophie*. Vol. 1: *Die okzidentale Konstellation von Glauben und Wissen*. Vol. 2: *Vernünftige Freiheit. Spuren des Diskurses über Glauben und Wissen* (Frankfurt a. M.: Suhrkamp, 2019), Vol 1, 14. For an excellent analysis of the right- and left-wing protests against governmental requirements globally imposed in 2020 to wear masks and to observe social distancing in the fight against COVID-19 as the reflection of deeply misunderstood and highly selfish concepts of freedom, see the concise commentary by Jasper von Altenbockum, "Die Aerosole der Freiheitsapostel," *Frankfurter Allgemeine Zeitung* Oct. 24, 2020, https://www.faz.net/aktuell/politik/inland/corona-politik-die-aerosole-der-freiheitsapostel-17017176.html?premium=0x50a3320987f6d5d811c64c7c52ed46e4; in a direct attack against Libertarianism as originally propounded by Ayn Rand leading over to badly misunderstood governmental needs to fight the present pandemic, Paul Krugman warns about the false definition of freedom when the lives of all members of our society are at stake: "When Libertarianism Goes Bad: Liberty Doesn't Mean Freedom to Infect Other People," *The New York Times* Oct. 22, 2020, https://www.nytimes.com/2020/10/22/opinion/coronavirus-masks.html (both last accessed on Jan. 15, 2021). What the protesters against all efforts to contain the virus forget is that their freedom comes with "Eigenverantwortung" (self-responsibility) as the author rightly highlights. See also Mark T. Mitchell, *The Limits of Liberalism: Tradition, Liberalism, and the Crisis of Freedom* (Notre Dame, IN: University of Notre Dame Press, 2018); Stephan Lessenich, *Grenzen der Demokratie: Teilhabe als Verteilungsproblem* (Stuttgart: Philipp Reclam jun., 2019); Larry Alan Busk, *Democracy in Spite of the Demos: Fom Arendt to the Frankfurt School* (London and New York: Rowman & Littlefield In-

While imprisonment is very easy to identify, obviously in negative terms, simply as the absence of freedom, the latter term, freedom, constitutes a profound challenge because there have always been so many different stages of freedom, depending on the context, the hermeneutic categories, the practical use, and the social and political implications. No one is absolutely free, not even today because we are all members of society, bound by rules, obligations, commitments, duties, laws, and precepts. Complete freedom would be an absolute illusion because the individual still needs basic food, shelter, clothing, and protection, which always requires the assistance and support of other members in the community.

Throughout times, people have always been ruled by laws, stipulations, conditions, and regulations, which make up the social, legal, ethical, moral, and religious structure of any society. Total freedom from all social constraints would be the absolute tyranny of the individual over the collective at large, so freedom is a matter of negotiations, bargaining, debates, even bartering because certain freedoms are granted or taken away in return for other values. After all, no human being is completely independent from society, and we all live in some kind of social contract balancing out our individual position in relationship to the needs of the collective – a fundamental idea supporting the existence of laws in the first place, both in the past and in the present.

For instance, what would a medieval farmer have to say about the notion of freedom when his life is mostly contingent on his obligations to his lord, the village authorities, the market, and the weather conditions.[76] As historians have re-

---

ternational, 2020). For somewhat different perspectives, see the contributions to *The State and Its Limits: The Economic and Politics of Freedom for the III Millennium – Essays in Honor of Prince Hans-Adam II of Liechtenstein*, ed. Kurt R. Leube (Triesen: van Eck Verlag, 2020).

[76] This finds its vivid expression in the explanation of the young girl in Hartmann von Aue's "Der arme Heinrich" (ca. 1190) why she wants to sacrifice herself for her lord, suffering from terminal leprosy: "A free Yeoman [God] desires me, and I give myself to Him eagerly. Truly you should give me to Him. Then my life is well taken care of. His plow glides along smoothly; His household is filled with supplies. There neither horse nor cattle die. There crying children are not a bother. There it is never too hot or too cold. There one never grows old in years …. It is there I want to go, fleeing the farm that rain and hail beat down on and floods wash away, though one struggle against them time and again. One can work a whole year long to achieve something and lose it completely in half a day. This is the farm I shall leave behind. I curse this farm" (225–26). *The Complete Works of Hartmann von Aue*, trans. with commentary by Frank Tobin, Kim Vivian, and Richard H. Lawson. Arthurian Romances, Tales, and Lyric Poetry (University Park, PA: The Pennsylvania State University Press, 2001); Karl Brunner and Gerhard Jaritz, *Landherr, Bauer, Ackerknecht: der Bauer im Mittelalter: Klischee und Wirklichkeit* (Vienna: Böhlau, 1985); *Land, Lords and Peasants: Peasants' Right to Control Land in the Middle Ages and the Early Modern Period. Norway, Scandinavia and the Alpine Region*, ed. Tore Iversen. Trond-

peatedly unearthed, the legal, economic, and political situation in the countryside during the pre-modern era was much more complex than we might have assumed, and there were certainly numerous loopholes or privileges for some groups within the rural communities.[77]

Merchants or craftsmen seem to have enjoyed considerably more freedom in social terms than the peasants, but they were equally subject to urban laws and rules, and could arrange their lives only if they observed the regulations and principles of their professions (guilds) and the urban authorities.[78] Peasants in general enjoyed much less freedom, but even within the various rural societies we observe, irrespective of what country we might focus on, a wide range of social ranks and hence different levels of freedom. Especially those peasants who moved to the new territories in central and eastern Europe gained considerable freedoms since the twelfth and thirteenth centuries.[79]

Knights could roam around the world fairly easily, so it seems, but without having a lord whom they could serve they would have been pretty useless, as we observe in the case of Gahmuret in Wolfram von Eschenbach's *Parzival* (ca. 1205) and of the knight mentioned by Chaucer in his *Canterbury Tales* (ca. 1400). The historical evidence certainly confirms this observation as well, which certainly underscores the extent to which our modern world is really anchored in the Middle Ages, both in terms of freedom and the loss thereof.[80] Nevertheless, we would

---

heim Studies in History, 52 (Trondheim: Department of History and Classical Studies, 2005); Claus Kropp and Thomas Meier, "Entwurf einer Archäologie der Grundherrschaft im älteren Mittelalter," *Beiträge zur Mittelalterarchäologie in Österreich* 26 (2010): 97–114; see also the contributions to *Kleine Welten: Ländliche Gesellschaften im Karolingerreich*, ed. Thomas Kohl, Steffen Patzold, and Bernhard Zeller. Vorträge und Forschungen, 87 (Ostfildern: Jan Thorbecke, 2019). There is a vast body of research on peasants and their rights and privileges, if not freedom, in the Middle Ages.

77 Hans Ulrich Rudolf, *Grundherrschaft und Freiheit im Mittelalter* (Düsseldorf: Schwann, 1976).
78 Eberhard Isenmann, *Die deutsche Stadt im Mittelalter: 1150–1550; Stadtgestalt, Recht, Verfassung, Stadtregiment, Kirche, Gesellschaft, Wirtschaft*. 2nd ed. (2012; Cologne, Weimar, and Vienna: Böhlau, 2014).
79 Jutta Goheen, *Mensch und Moral im Mittelalter: Geschichte und Fiktion in Hugo von Trimbergs 'Der Renner'* (Darmstadt: Wissenschaftliche Buchgesellschaft, 1990), 55–59. She rightly emphasizes that gnomic literature such as Hugo's *Der Renner* mirrored much of those social differences between the free and the unfree, 58.
80 See, for instance, Maurice Hugh Keen, *Chivalry* (New Haven, CT: Yale University Press, 1984); Richard W. Kaeuper, *Medieval Chivalry*. Cambridge Medieval Textbooks (Cambridge: Cambridge University Press, 2016); the literature on this topic is legion, of course. For a broader discussion of modernity being enshrined in the Middle Ages, see Fidel Fajardo-Acosta, *Courtly Seductions, Modern Subjections: Troubadour Literature and the Medieval Construction of the Modern World*.

have to differentiate here as well because even among the upper and lower ranks of nobility there were many social and economic distinctions, which do not need to be analyzed here further, and hence many different levels of freedom' as well.

Nevertheless, when we widen our scope of investigation, we can also discover literary documents from the late Middle Ages explicitly advocating the ideal of individual and collective freedom, such as the Swedish song by Bishop Tomas Simonsson in Strängnäs, his "frihetssång" from 1439, consisting of seven stanzas in his "Song of Engelbrekt" in which he expressed his support and admiration for the by then murdered nobleman Engelbrekt who attempted an uprising (1434–1436), supported by the miners and peasants of his region, against Eric of Pomerania, the king of the Kalmar Union, which ultimately, long after Engelbrekt, expelled the Danes from Sweden:

> Frihet är det ädlaste ting
> Som sökas må all verlden kring,
> Den frihet väl kan bära.
> Vill du dig sjelfvan vara huld,
> Du älske frihet mer än guld,
> Ty frihet följer ära.
>
> Frihet må liknas vid ett torn,
> Der väktarn blåser i sitt horn:
> Det klingar så klart och vida!
> Om från det tornet ut du går
> Och en annan det i händer får,
> Då fäller du tårar strida. [81]
>
> [Freedom is the noblest thing
> that is sought all over the world,
> freedom can certainly be accepted.

Medieval and Renaissance Texts and Studies, 376 (Tempe, AZ: Arizona Center for Medieval and Renaissance Studies, 2010), 33–42.

81 I thank my colleague Peter Dinzelbacher (Werfen near Salzburg) for pointing out this important document. Quoted from: https://sv.wikisource.org/wiki/Biskop_Thomas_frihetsvisa. I have slightly adjusted the English translation. For the historical and biographical background, see https://sok.riksarkivet.se/sbl/Presentation.aspx?id=7423; for some background on the uprising and its sad outcome, the murder of Engelbrekt, see http://www.medeltiden.kalmarlansmuseum.se/en/society/the-kalmar-union/the-engelbrekt-rebellion/engelbrekt-engelbrektsson/; https://sok.riksarkivet.se/sbl/Presentation.aspx?id=7423 (all last accessed on Jan. 15, 2021). For solid research on this uprising, see the contributions to *Northern Revolts: Medieval and Early Modern Peasant Unrest in the Nordic Countries*, ed. Kimmo Katajala. Studia Fennica. Historica, 8 (Helsinki: Finnish Literature Society, 2001); see also Lars-Olof Larsson, *Engelbrekt Engelbrektsson och 1430-talets svenska uppror* (Stockholm: Norstedt, 1984); Dick Harrison, *Sveriges historia medeltiden* (Stockholm: Liber, 2002).

If you want to be yourself,
you love freedom more than gold,
for freedom follows glory.

Freedom may be likened to a tower,
where the guard blows his horn:
It sounds so clear and wide!
If from that tower you go out
and another gets his hands on it,
then you shed tears fighting.]

2 Hugo von Trimberg: The Social Discourse in the High and Late Middle Ages

Without a social framework, which automatically limits once's freedom, the individual faces severe difficulties and cannot operate as effectively as s/he could once he is subject to those limits, rules, regulations, etc. Ecclesiastics had to obey strict rules of the Church and/or the monastery and they specifically submitted under God, particularly once they had given their vow of complete obedience (monks/nuns) and had sworn to observe the rules of chastity, observance of the monastic rules, etc. Women fared differently than men, children differently than their parents, and old people were of course dependent on their families, but they all clearly understood the social constraints and limits without which no society can exist. In short, the notion of freedom depends, both in the Middle Ages and today, on a vast number of categories and a wide range of self-concepts. Each society throughout time has determined on its own the relationship between the individual and the collective, and even in the most liberal or free society, rules and laws have existed regulating the extent to which a person could claim a private space for him/herself where no other authority could enter and decide from the outside.

Most people in the pre-modern era did not even know of a specific notion of freedom at least in the way we moderns use it, especially in political terms, and regularly accepted and acknowledged their own role within feudal society, the way how they were born according to God's wishes in a tripartite order of the three estates: those who prayed, those who fought, and those who labored.[82]

---

[82] See the by now 'classic' study by Marc Bloch, *La Société féodale*. Evolution de l'humanité. Synthèse collective, 3, section, 8 (Paris: A. Michel, 1968); cf. also the contributions to *Ständische Gesellschaft und soziale Mobilität*, ed. Winfried Schulze (Munich: R. Oldenbourg, 1988); especially by Otto Gerhard Oexle, "Die funktionale Dreiteilung als Deutungsschema der sozialen Wir-

However, we can be certain that the entire discourse on freedom as we know it today in all of its complexities, emerged already in the Middle Ages in a myriad of critical frameworks, and we could not even imagine any aspect of pre-modern society without taking into consideration the continuous struggle for individual freedom, whether in economic, political, religious, philosophical, material, or physical terms. But we must always be very careful in considering the local conditions, and this in comparison with the broader discourse, especially because pre-modern Europe was a much more complex entity in political, religious, ideological, and economic terms than we might have assumed in the past.[83]

If we can believe the literary-didactic narrative by Hugo von Trimberg, *Der Renner* (ca. 1300), peasants were certainly interested in knowing why they were not free and did not enjoy the same social recognition as the aristocrats. In the chapter "Von gebûr liuten" (vol. 1, 54 ff.),[84] the narrator gets involved with a group of peasants who want to know why they are poor and unfree whereas the nobles are wealthy and free, although all people descend from the same first mother, Eve (1329). Hugo at first refers to the scriptural testimony of Noah and his three sons, with Cham having mocked his father when he was drunk and asleep and in that state of stupor got exposed bodily. While Shem and Japhet covered their father with a cloth in order to protect his honor and were later praised for that, Cham, who had not followed their example, was cursed by

---

klichkeit in der ständischen Gesellschaft des Mittelalters," 19 – 51; *Ordering Medieval Society: Perspectives on Intellectual and Practical Modes of Shaping Social Relations*, ed. Bernhard Jussen. Trans. by Pamela Selwyn. The Middle Ages Series (Philadelphia, PA: University of Pennsylvania Press, 2001); for a useful bibliography and historical illustrations, see https://de.wikipedia.org/wiki/St%C3%A4ndeordnung#Literatur (last accessed on Jan. 15, 2021).

83 Johannes Fried, *Die abendländische Freiheit vom 10. zum 14. Jahrhundert* (see note 21); Fajardo-Acosta, *Courtly Seductions, Modern Subjections: Troubadour Literature and the Medieval Construction of the Modern World* (see note 80), 39–42; cf. also Piotr S. Wandycz, *The Price of Freedom: A History of East Central Europe from the Middle Ages to the Present*. History/Soviet Studies (London and New York: Routledge, 1992); Zdenka Janeković Römer, *The Frame of Freedom: The Nobility of Dubrovnik Between the Middle Ages and Humanism*. Studies in the History of Dubrovnik, 5 (Zagreb and Dubrovnik: Hrvatska akademija znanosti i umjetnosti, 2015); William Chester Jordan, *From Servitude to Freedom: Manumission in the Senonais in the Thirteenth Century*. The Middle Ages Series (Philadelphia, PA: University of Pennsylvania Press, 2016). See also the contributions to *Freedom and Authority: Scotland c.1050 – c.1650; Historical and Historiographical Essays presented to Grant G. Simpson*, ed. Terry Brotherstone (East Linton, Scotland: Tuckwell, 2000).

84 Hugo von Trimberg, *Der Renner*, ed. Gustav Ehrismann. With an epilogue and additions by Günther Schweikle. Deutsche Neudrucke. Reihe: Texte des Mittelalters (1908; Berlin: Walter de Gruyter, 1970), vol. 1, vv. 1309 ff.

Noah when he woke up and realized what had happened to him (Genesis 9:20–23).

Hugo then differentiates further and does not argue that all peasants are subject to this curse, which actually often applies to Jews, Heretics, Pagans, and ignorant Christians who fight against God (1401–04). Instead, there are many peasants who are as free as the aristocrats (1407), even if they do not possess the same wealth as those: "Doch ist er von gebürte frî" (1409; but he is born as a free man). Many nobles would prove to be enemies of God and much worse off than any peasant. True nobility, and hence freedom, would not rest in one's material possessions: "Nieman ist edel denne den der muot / Edel machet und niht daz guot" (1417–18; No one is a noble person unless his/her his mind makes him/her noble; their wealth does not achieve that).[85]

Then Hugo actually turns away from the concrete discussion of freedom and engages, instead, with ethics and the nobility of the mind (1425–29). Those who pride themselves with having many friends and material riches could not claim to be truly noble and virtuous (1428–29). This spiritual nobility would ultimately make possible the entrance into heaven, whereas many a bailiff, more powerful than the peasants would certainly fail in that (1455–56).[86] From here, Hugo enters into further reflections on the various social classes, but no longer examines the notion of freedom itself because he fully accepts the traditional feudal system, divided into the class of peasants, knights, and priests/clerics (2214), each one responsible for their own tasks. The knights are in charge of protecting the others, the priests are in charge of praying, and the peasants are responsible with producing the food, which they share with the others by paying their tithe (2215–20). But, Hugo also warns the aristocrats not to abuse their power against the poor people; otherwise their souls would end up in hell (2221–37), and he has obviously good cause to be deeply worried because he is aware of just too

---

[85] C. Stephen Jaeger, *Ennobling Love: In Search of a Lost Sensibility*. The Middle Ages Series (Philadelphia, PA: University of Pennsylvania Press, 1999), discusses this phenomenon in terms of courtly love. Nevertheless, Hugo's comments deserve to be considered in this context as well.

[86] Catherine Teresa Rapp, *Burgher and Peasant in the Works of Thomasin von Zirclaria, Freidank, and Hugo von Trimberg*. The Catholic University of America Studies in German, 7 Rpt. (1936; New York: AMS Press, 1970); Tobias Bulang, *Enzyklopädische Dichtungen: Fallstudien zu Wissen und Literatur in Spätmittelalter und früher Neuzeit*. Deutsche Literatur, 2 (Berlin: Akademie-Verlag, 2011).

many bad examples and worries about the collapse of the basic social norms and rules due to the fact that too many people have turned to evil (2228–40).[87]

While numerous medieval cities succeeded in the course of time to gain a considerable degree of freedom from the local princes and were soon subject only to the king or the emperor (imperial cities), the situation for the rural class was quite different.[88] Medieval society in its feudal structure was rigidly organized into the three estates, and no one was allowed to rise beyond his/her class without facing severe punishment, as powerfully illustrated by the short verse narrative *Helmbrecht* by Wernher der Gardenære from ca. 1260/1280.

There, the young man, misled by his own arrogance, attractive appearance, luxurious outfit, and his rebellious dreams leaves his family to try to climb the social ladder. He experiences, however, nothing but terrible misery and death at the end after a short and highly criminal existence as a robber knight.[89] As much as he had believed in his personal privilege to assume complete freedom and to disregard the traditional boundaries, as little could he realize his dreams and thus utterly failed in his clumsy and criminal efforts.

Young Helmbrecht assumes that because of his external attributes, especially his fabulous cap, produced by a former nun who had escaped from the convent, but then also an armor, sword (both given to him by his mother), and a horse (given to him by his deeply troubled but nevertheless very weak father), he could simply leave his social class behind and join the aristocracy. His father warns him repeatedly about the dangers of his attempt to rise beyond his peasant class, and urges him repeatedly to abstain from his plans and to keep his afterlife in mind, instead of dreaming of the splendor of aristocracy (e. g., 244–59).

All this is to no avail, of course, and even though young Helmbrecht at first seems to enjoy great success, he commits so many crimes actually against his

---

[87] Research has, of course, dealt with these aspects already for a very long time; see now Scott L. Taylor, "Feudalism in Literature and Society," *Handbook of Medieval Culture*, ed. Albrecht Classen. Vol. 1 (see note 11), 465–76.
[88] Eberhard Isenmann, *Die deutsche Stadt im Mittelalter 1150–1550* (see note 78); Knut Schulz, *"Denn sie lieben die Freiheit so sehr...": Kommunale Aufstände und Enstehung des europäischen Bürgertums im Hochmittelalter* (Darmstadt: Wissenschaftliche Buchgesellschaft, 1992); Flocel Sabaté, *Medieval Urban Identity: Health, Economy and Regulation* (Newcastle upon Tyne: Cambridge Scholars Press, 2015); cf. also the contributions to *Urban Space in the Middle Ages and Early Modern Times*, ed. Albrecht Classen. Fundamentals of Medieval and Early Modern Culture, 4 (Berlin and New York: Walter de Gruyter, 2009).
[89] Wernher der Gärtner, *Helmbrecht. Mittelhochdeutsch / Neuhochdeutsch*, ed., trans., and commentary by Fritz Tschirch (1974; Stuttgart: Philipp Reclam jun.,1991); see also the contributions to *Wernher der Gärtner: 'Helmbrecht': Die Beiträge des Helmbrecht-Symposions in Burghausen 2001*, ed. Theodor Nolte and Tobias Schneider (Stuttgart: S. Hirzel Verlag, 2001).

own social class that he is eventually caught by a judge and his bailiffs. All of his companions are immediately hanged at the gallows; only the protagonist is granted his life, but he loses, as punishment, both of his eyes, a hand, and a foot and thus becomes completely incapacitated; not even his father is willing (or allowed) to grant him asylum, so the young man suffers through a whole year without much help until he is finally apprehended by the peasants whom he had previously injured so badly and quickly lynched, also by hanging, after they have badly roughed him up (1874–1912).

As Wernher der Gardenære thereby signaled, rules and regulations were firmly in place and determined society; and anyone trying to transgress them could face catastrophic consequences. Curiously, however, young Helmbrecht's father and the other peasants enjoyed more freedom within their own social context than the son who tried so hard and so recklessly to leave his family and to partake in the splendors of the knightly existence.[90] Their freedom was guaranteed by the existence of laws, a court, a judge, and the bailiffs. Young Helmbrecht's action amounted to nothing but vicious and reckless criminality, victimizing anyone he could get hold of. The peasants resort to lynching hime it is all over for the already badly punished protagonist, and the narrator comments on this action with approval. Once the young man has been executed, all people can enjoy their safety and freedom as before: "die varent alle nû mit fride, / sît Helmbreht ist an der wide" (1921–22; they all take their course in peace since Helmbrecht is hanging at the willow tree/gallows).

In short, as this verse novella indicates, it would be rather problematic to assume that pre-modern thinkers were in agreement as to the individual's natural rights compared to the social conditions and the traditional feudal structure.[91] We will come back to this entire thorny issue further below when we consider some of the political theory developed in the late Middle Ages.

---

90 Scholarship has paid much attention to this verse narrative; see, for instance, Seraina Plotke, "Polydimensionale Parodie: Verfahren literarischer Verkehrung im 'Helmbrecht' Wernhers des Gärtners," *Parodie und Verkehrung: Formen und Funktionen spielerischer Verfremdung und spöttischer Verzerrung in Texten des Mittelalters und der Frühen Neuzeit*, ed. eadem and Stefan Seeber. Encomia Deutsch, 3 (Göttingen: V&R unipress, 2017), 73–88; Albrecht Classen, "Sarcasm in Medieval German Literature: From the *Hildebrandslied* to *Fortunatus*. The Dark Side of Human Behavior," *Words that Tear the Flesh: Essays on Sarcasm in Medieval and Early Modern Literature and Cultures*, ed. Alan Baragona and Elizabeth L. Rambo. Fundamentals of Medieval and Early Modern Culture, 21 (Berlin and Boston: Walter de Gruyter, 2018), 249–69.
91 Franz Irsigler, "Freiheit und Unfreiheit im Mittelalter: Formen und Wege sozialer Mobilität," *Miscellanea Franz Irsigler: Festgabe zum 65. Geburtstag*, ed. Volker Henn, Rudolf Holbach, Rudolf, Michel Pauly, and Wolfgang Schmid (Trier: Porta Alba Verlag, 2006), 133–52.

3 Eike von Repgow, *Sachsenspiegel*

The Legal Discourse

One of the most influential authors of Low Middle High German law books, Eike von Repgow (ca. 1180–1235), provided a stunningly detailed discussion of the concept of freedom in his famous *Sachsenspiegel* (ca. 1225; The Saxon Mirror), which exerted a tremendous influence on virtually all of Central and Northern Europe by spawning many copies, adaptations, and translations. It can be rightly identified as a major source for information on "medieval communities and the concerns of all their inhabitants, including serfs, free peasants, women, children, and ethnic minorities."[92] Its enormous popularity is documented by the survival of ca. 460 manuscripts, although it was not a law book as such and 'only' recorded in writing the prevailing customary law and thus became a crucial, highly influential model for municipal law books, particularly because Eike made a significant effort to cover almost every aspect of social and communal life as it was to be regulated in legal terms.[93]

Eike at one point also addresses freedom, though he apologizes immediately for not considering the wide range of unfree conditions because that topic would lead him too far afield in his carefully grafted legal outline, focusing on the dominant aspects. Those who are dependent and committed to serve bishops, abbots, and abbesses, above all, live in a highly complex framework of servitude, which would require a separate coverage than he can offer. He does not even address slavery or imprisonment, and instead turns his full attention to the meaning of freedom, which was, since the earliest time, fundamental to all people: "All people were free when our ancestors came here to this land" (Book III, ch. 42, p. 125). It seems inconceivable to him that a human being might lack freedom or belong to another person, and he picks up and destroys all relevant arguments based on the Old Testament.

---

[92] *The Saxon Mirror: A* Sachsenspiegel *of the Fourteenth Century*, trans. Maria Dobozy. The Middle Ages Series (Philadelphia, PA: University of Pennsylvania Press, 1999), 1. See now Madeline H. Caviness and Charles G. Nelson, *Women and Jews in the Sachsenspiegel Picture-Books* (Turnhout: Brepols, 2018), 37–42.
[93] Heiner Lück, *Der Sachsenspiegel: Das berühmteste deutsche Rechtsbuch des Mittelalters* (Darmstadt: Lambert Schneider Verlag/Wissenschaftliche Buchgesellschaft, 2018); Gabriele Olberg-Haverkate, *Die Textsorte Rechtsbücher*. Germanistische Arbeiten zu Sprache und Kulturgeschichte, 55 (Frankfurt a.M.: Peter Lang, 2018); Christa Bertelsmeier-Kierst, "Eike von Repgow: 'Sachsenspiegel'," *Klassiker des Mittelalters*, ed. Regina Toepfer. Spolia Berolinensia, 38 (Hildesheim: Weidmannsche Verlagsbuchhandlung, 2019), 59–81.

Specifically, he insists that "no one may place himself into bondage when his heir clearly opposes it" (ch. 43, p. 125). Granted, he admits that there exists the phenomenon of bondage, but he urges his audience to consider that human beings descended from God and could thus belong only to Him, and not to any worldly master: "At this time each and every person is to be freed whether he desires it or not" (ch. 43, p. 126). In fact, for him, God did not approve of any form of bondage because He created us in His image. However, Eike is realistic enough to acknowledge that lack of freedom was a very common phenomenon at his time, although he specifically opposes it and contrary to divine wishes: "bondage resulted from coercion, imprisonment, and unlawful exercise of force, which has become unjust custom since ancient times, and now people take it to be right and good custom" (ch. 43, p. 126).[94]

Unfortunately, the author does not pursue this topic much further at that point and turns his attention to the historical foundation of the German lands, connecting the founders with Alexander the Great (ch. 45, p. 126). Then we learn about the rules regarding compensation penalties for crimes, the legal status of widows, the court system, and the like. Only when Eike also reflects on the legal system in the German kingdom, does he return, at least to some extent, to the larger issue of freedom, here in political terms. The king is chosen by high-ranking nobles, and after his anointment he is appointed to his task. The emphasis here rests on the 'democratic' process: "The king is elected for the purpose of judging land in free ownership, fiefs, and each man's life" (ch. 53, p. 129). And a little later, we are told: "When the king is elected, he shall pledge allegiance to the realm, swear that he will reinforce justice, thwart injustice, and defend the law of the realm to his best ability and knowledge" (ch. 54, p. 129). No one can be elected as a king who is not "of free and legitimate birth, which means that he retains his legal rights and privileges" (ch. 54, p. 130).

Otherwise, there are many passages in the *Saxon Mirror* where the author addresses the status of a free woman, for instance, who "does not produce servile children" (ch. 73, p. 135), but Eike is generally more interested in the legal relationships, rules for punishments, and power relationships than in the philosophical discourse on freedom. Nevertheless, that principle idea exists for him very clearly, and since he exerted a tremendous influence far and wide, and also for many decades after his death, we can trust Eike as a significant voice that also addressed freedom and insisted that it was a natural law for everyone being free under God.

---

[94] Herbert Kolb, "Über den Ursprung der Unfreiheit: Eine Quaestio im "Sachenspiegel," *Zeitschrift für deutsches Altertum* 103 (1974): 289–311; here 300–05.

Moreover, we can also credit him with having established a universal legal framework that allowed individuals to resort to an authoritative reference and defend their case. Freedom is, of course, not the same as legal justice, but the former cannot fully exist without the latter. Imprisonment or punishment are intimately tied into the notion of freedom, and the *Saxon Mirror* laid the foundation for a fair and equal judicial system already in the early thirteenth century that was copied and practiced far and wide in north-eastern Germany and neighboring countries.[95]

To do full justice to this topic, however, which was certainly not the case here, we would have to include the vast number of other legal law books, such as *The Pipe Roll* of the Bishopric of Winchester, 1208–1209, or the famous Spanish *Siete Partidas* first compiled during the reign of Alfonso X of Castile (1252–1284).[96] The number of relevant sources is simply legion, and the efforts by lawmakers and legal authors to come to terms with the fundamental framework for society's interaction were ongoing, but I am not particularly concerned with the history of law itself, which has already been discussed and examined by scores of experts over the last two hundred years.[97] Eike's statements serve already fully for our purposes, even though we have consulted only snippets, as evidence how much the issues of a well-balanced legal system was of central concern, and this also within the framework of a medieval monarchy.

4 The Quest for Freedom in Medieval Fables

Granted, we would have to wait until the late eighteenth century to witness major revolutions (the American and the French Revolution) which blew away the rule of the aristocracy, at least to some extent and for some time, or to the early twentieth century for the same thing to happen again (the Russian Revolution, 1917), but many efforts were made already in the medieval and early modern period to

---

95 Lück, *Der Sachsenspiegel* (see note 93), 90–94; Stephan Freund, "fride unde reht sint sere wunt: Eike von Repgow, das Reich und Europa in der ersten Hälfte des 13. Jahrhunderts, *Sachsen und Anhalt: Jahrbuch der Landesgeschichtlichen Forschungsstelle für die Provinz Sachsen und für Anhalt-Weimar* 26 (2014): 121–41.
96 Alfonso X el Sabio, *Las siete partidas (El libro del fuero de las leyes)*, intro. and ed. by José Sánchez-Arcilla Bernal (Madrid: Editorial Reus, 2004).
97 For a vast list, see https://sourcebooks.fordham.edu/sbook-law.asp (last accessed on Jan. 15, 2021). For a detailed review of the relevant research, see Scott L. Taylor, "Law in the Middle Ages," *Handbook of Medieval Studies: Terms – Methods – Trends*, ed. Albrecht Classen. Vol. 2 (see note 11), 771–88. See now Arvind Thomas, *Piers Plowman and the Reinvention of Church Law in the Late Middle Ages* (Toronto: University of Toronto Press, 2019).

secure or preserve urban freedom, such as documented by Sebastian Brant's famous *Freiheitstafel* (1517–1519), a collection of fifty-two epigrams composed for frescoes in the Strasbourg city hall created by Hans Baldung Grien.[98]

There were also many attempts to gain freedom for monasteries, bishoprics, pilgrimage sites, or entire territories, such as in the region later to be called *Confoederatio Helvetica* (Switzerland; the term emerged not until 1848).[99] In addition. we have to consider numerous geographically marginal countries such as Iceland where the local population actually succeeded in gaining or maintaining its freedom from external authorities.[100] Iceland was settled by the 'Vikings,' who arrived from Norway and other Scandinavian countries and found an empty island where there was hence no social structure, and everyone who had enough resources was regarded as a free man.[101] Ironically, this promise of independence, unoccupied land, and limitless opportunities, so to speak, which reminds

---

98 See, for example, *Urban Liberties and Citizenship from the Middle Ages Up To Now: actes du colloque 2009 de la Commission Internationale pour l'Histoire des Villes = Städtische Freiheiten und bürgerliche Partizipation vom Mittelalter bis heute*, ed. Michel Pauly and Alexander Lee. Beiträge zur Landes- und Kulturgeschichte, 9 (Trier: Porta-Alba Verlag, 2015); *Freiheit im Mittelalter am Beispiel der Stadt*, ed. Dagmar Klose and Marco Ladewig (see note 64). For comments on Brant's *Freiheitstafel*, see Joachim Knape, *Dichtung, Recht und Freiheit. Studien zu Leben und Werk Sebastian Brants 1457–1521*. Saecvla Spiritalia, 23 (Baden-Baden: Koerner, 1991); id., "Sebastian Brant," *Deutsche Dichter der frühen Neuzeit (1450–1600): Ihr Leben und Werk*, ed. Stephan Füssel (Berlin: Erich Schmidt Verlag, 1993), 156–72; here 168–71; for an edition, see Sebastian Brant, *Das Narrenschiff: nebst dessen Freiheitstafel*, ed. Adam Walther Strobel. Bibliothek der gesammten deutschen National-Literatur von der ältesten bis auf die neuere Zeit: Abteilung 1, 17 (Quedlinburg: Basse, 1839), 301–12. For a digital version, see now https://archive.org/details/dasnarrenschiff00strogoog/page/n330/mode/2up (last accessed on Jan. 15, 2021). See also my article, "Sebastian Brant," *Literary Encyclopedia*, online (https://www.litencyc.com/php/speople.php?rec=true&UID=11830; unfortunately, available only as a paid-service).

99 See, for instance, Wilhelm Baum, *Reichs- und Territorialgewalt (1273–1437): Königtum, Haus Österreich und Schweizer Eidgenossen im späten Mittelalter* (Vienna: Turia & Kant, 1994); Bruno Maier, *Ein Königshaus aus der Schweiz: die Habsburger, der Aargau und die Eidgenossenschaft im Mittelalter* (Baden: Hier + Jetzt, Verlag für Kultur und Geschichte, 2008); Tom Scott, *The Swiss and Their Neighbours, 1460–1560: Between Accommodation and Aggression* (Oxford: Oxford University Press, 2017). The number of historical studies on the medieval history of Switzerland is legion, of course.

100 Okko Leding, *Die Freiheit der Friesen im Mittelalter und ihr Bund mit den Versammlungen beim Upstallsbom* (1878; Walluf bei Wiesbaden: Sändig, 1973).

101 William Ian Miller, *Bloodtaking and Peacemaking: Feud, Law, and Society in Saga Iceland* (Chicago: University of Chicago Press, 1990); R. I. Page, *Chronicles of the Vikings: Records, Memorials and Myths* (Toronto and Buffalo, NY: University of Toronto Press, 1995), 58–76. See now also Carl Phelpstead, *An Introduction to the Sagas of Icelanders* (Gainesville, Tallahassee, et al., FL: University Press of Florida, 2020).

us much of the colonization of North America since the sixteenth century, lured so many people from Norway that King Harald forced everyone ready to leave to pay a fee, as we learn from Arí Thorgilsson's *Íslendingabók* and in the *Landnámabók* (twelfth century).

As barren as Iceland might seem today, for the early settlers, it was a place of enormous hope, as one character, Thorolf, reported: "Thorolf said that butter dripped from every blade of grass in the land they had discovered."[102] However, as the subsequent history clearly relates to us, in the course of time law was introduced to Iceland, a legal system was set up, and social order developed, but all this predicated on the principle that the farmers there were free and agreed to those laws and their own social structure at their meetings held at the *Althingi*. In other words, Iceland represents a 'classical' case of a new country being formed, but not as a kingdom, subject to a royal person, but as the oldest democracy, even in the meaning of the modern term, of the world.[103]

Another interesting case proves to be Old Saxony where Charlemagne had to struggle hard in the late seventh century to gain the upper hand and where there was no tradition of kingship. As the first life of the Anglo-Saxon missionary, St. Lebuinus (eighth century), informs us:

> The ancient Saxons did not have kings, but "satraps" established throughout districts. And it was their custom that once a year they held a general council in the middle of Saxony beside the Weser river at a place called Marklo. All the satraps were accustomed to come together there as one, as well as, from each of the districts, twelve elected nobles and the same number of freemen and of "lidi." There they renewed the laws, adjudicated special cases, and established by common counsel whether during that year they would be at war or in peace.[104]

---

102 Still in the *Landnámabók*, version S; see Page, *Chronicles of the Vikings* (see note 101), 61.
103 Page, *Chronicles of the Vikings* (see note 101), 176–77, with a long quote from Ari Thorgilsson's text; see also Jesse L. Byock, *Viking Age Iceland* (see note 66).
104 Bede, in *Opera Historica*, vol. 2 (Cambridge, MA: Harvard University Press, 1930); 242; I have borrowed this information and the translation from Lisa Wolverton's excellent article, "Why Kings?," *Rethinking Medieval Margins and Marginality*, ed. Anne E. Zimo, Tiffany D. Vann Sprecher, Kathryn Reyerson, and Debra Blumenthal. Studies in Medieval History and Culture (London and New York: Routledge, 2020), 91–106; here 92. See also Eric Goldberg, "Popular Revolt, Dynastic Politics, and Aristocratic Factionalism in the Early Middle Ages: The Saxon Stellinga Reconsidered," *Speculum* 70 (1995): 467–501. For Saxony, see Robert Flierman, *Saxon Identities, AD 150–900* (London: Bloomsbury, 2017); cf. also Matthias Becher, "Non enim habent regem idem Antiqui Saxones ... : Verfassung und Ethnogenese in Sachsen während des 8. Jahrhunderts," *Sachsen und Franken in Westfalen: Zur Komplexität der ethnischen Deutung und Abgrenzung zweier frühmittelalterlicher Stämme. Ergebnisse eines vom 22.–25. April 1997 in Paderborn durchgeführten Kolloquiums zur Vorbereitung der Ausstellung "799 Kunst und Kultur der Karolingerzeit,*

Other Slavic groups, such as the Liutizi, settled east of the middle of the Elbe river, also appear to have enjoyed a considerable degree of independence from royal rule, but in the course of time they were mostly eliminated or subordinated under a royal government. However, as Wolverton observes, the lands of the Czechs and the Moravians, among others, were likewise not completely dominated by a royal ruler, so the notion of medieval kingship as an absolute entity would not hold in those cases either.[105]

As she then concludes, "Such conditions – distinct as they are from, say, England or Bavaria, even Poland – suggest differences as well in the social and economic order in the Czech Lands, whether as cause or consequence of distinct characteristics of the political order. In place of kings and kingdoms, even of 'princes,' I would therefore suggest we focus on 'polities,' recognizing that rulers were as often formed by communities as, by their rule, they were able to mold them."[106] The absence of a central royal power does not necessarily mean the existence of individual freedom, but in all of these cases we recognize considerably large spaces of local freedoms, a phenomenon which rather undermines the general notion of the medieval king as a supreme and absolute head of the state, as in the time of absolutism.[107]

The history of Frisia in the Middle Ages also speaks much about the people's struggle to create a degree of freedom on an individual level.[108] The Frisians successful defense against the Vikings, especially in the battle of Norditi in 841, facilitated an establishment of political freedom rarely ever seen in medieval Europe, characterized by the absence of aristocratic feudal structures, very similar to the situation in Iceland. Allegedly, Emperor Charles the Fat granted them this privilege, the *Fryske frijheid*, which allowed the various representatives of the landed communities (Redjeven) to assemble at the Upstalsboom in Rahe near Aurich (today in the northwest of Germany near the Dutch border, across from Groningen).

Karl der Große und Papst Leo III. in Paderborn", ed. Hans-Jürgen Hässler with Jörg Jarnut and Matthias Wemhoff. Studien zur Sachsenforschung, 12 (Oldenburg: Isensee, 1999), 1–31.
105 Wolverton, "Why Kings" (see note 104), 98.
106 Wolverton, "Why Kings" (see note 104), 100.
107 Susan Reynolds, *Kingdoms and Communities in Western Europe, 900–1300*. 2nd ed. (1984; Oxford: Oxford University Press, 1997); William Ian Miller, *Bloodtaking and Peacemaking* (see note 101).
108 *Eala frya Fresena: die friesische Freiheit im Mittelalter, Ostfriesische Landschaft*, ed. Monika van Lengen. Preparation of the ms. by Uda von der Nahmer and Nicolaus Hippen (Aurich: Ostfriesische Landschaftliche Verlags- und Vertriebsgesellschaft, 2003). For a much older, yet still valuable study, see Karl von Richthofen, *Untersuchungen über friesische Rechtsgeschichte* (Berlin: Hertz, 1880).

The Frisians constantly faced the threat of flooding, so they were acknowledged by the royal powers as a people who deserved by necessity the high privilege of freedom from external influences so they could turn all their attention to building dams against the sea. The situation deteriorated for them by the end of the Middle Ages, although Frisia continued to enjoy a unique political status even during the early modern age.[109] Both the Black Death and a series of major sea storms undermined the social, economic, and political structures, which allowed major figures (*hovedlinge*) to emerge and to assume more of the traditional power for themselves. At the end of the fifteenth and finally in the early sixteenth century Frisia was forcefully integrated into northern dukedoms when various feudal lords, and even the Archbishop of Bremen, took over the control of the various parts of that formerly free land.[110]

Early medieval sources, however, such as the anonymous Anglo-Saxon *Beowulf* (early eighth century), generally depicted the opposite situation, with the people feeling helpless and being victims of strong hostile forces without a good king who could lead them successfully into wars in defense of external attackers. The genre of heroic epics generally followed that trend (see, for instance, the Old French *Chanson de Roland* or the Old Spanish *El Poema de Mío Cid*), although the Icelandic Sagas normally took the oppsite position underscoring the high value of freedom from a royal ruler. The opposite then was expressed a number of times in the fables by Marie de France and Ulrich Bonerius (see below), where the evil ruler is identified as repressive, if not even tyrannical.

Significantly, the idea of individual freedom was also discussed in a variety of texts and made up an important point of various discourses, and this already since antiquity. As Orlando Patterson observes, the term always contains at least three dimensions, some playing a major, others a lesser role. First, there is the freedom from an outside force or power, individual or organization. We are our own agents and can determine our own destiny, independent from an external entity. Second, a truly free person can do whatever s/he pleases, with objects, animals, plants, or other people. Only the nineteenth century witnessed the important proviso that this freedom finds its limit where it threatens to hurt other

---

109 Carsten Roll, "Vom 'asega' zum 'redjeven': Zur Verfassungsgeschichte Frieslands im Mittelalter," *Concilium Medii Aevi* 13 (2010): 187–221 (http://cma.gbv.de/dr,cma,013,2010,a,08.pdf; last accessed on Jan. 15, 2021).
110 Bernd Rieken, *"Nordsee ist Mordsee": Sturmfluten und ihre Bedeutung für die Mentalitätsgeschichte der Friesen*. Veröffentlichungen des Nordfriisk Instituut: Abhandlungen und Vorträge zur Geschichte Ostfrieslands, 186 (Münster and New York: Waxmann, 2005); Paul Kluge, *Friesische Freiheit und die Reformation in Ost-Friesland* (Schortens: Heiber GmbH Druck & Verlag, 2015); Thomas Steensen, *Die Friesen* (Kiel and Hamburg: Wachholtz, 2020).

people (enslavement). Third, there is the freedom to partake in the public power or economic activities on an equal footing with all others, which found its most vivid expression in the classical and especially modern term 'democracy.'

While the institution of slavery continued to hold sway throughout the Middle Ages, often at the same level as in early modern America, and this even in such remote areas as Iceland, an increasing number of medieval individuals identified freedom not so much in contrast to slavery, but in terms of freedom from the dominion of others, as perhaps best expressed in the status of knights who increasingly gained more independence, even when they continued to serve lords.[111]

4.1 Marie de France

The discourse on freedom, almost in the modern sense of the word, comes to the fore most vividly in one narrative contained in Marie de France's *Fables* (ca. 1200), which was in turn based on the old Aesopian tradition. In "De la suriz de vile e de la suriz de bois" (no. 9), a country mouse visits a city mouse and is at first greatly impressed by the luxury of its housing in the cellar, and by the overwhelming amount of food available. But when the butler suddenly appears, the country mouse is deeply scared and barely keeps her life, and once the butler has left again, the country mouse departs as well, preferring her rural existence over the pleasures of the city because there she can live "A seürté e sanz destresce" (51; "In safety and without distress").[112]

About hundred and fifty years later, the Bernese Dominican priest Ulrich Boner/Bonerius picked up the same material in his collection of hundred fables,

---

[111] Olleander Patterson, "The Ancient and Medieval Origin of Freedom," *The Problem of Evil: Slavery, Freedom, and the Ambiguities of American Reform*, ed. Steven Mintz and John Stauffer (Amherst and Boston, MA: University of Massachusetts Press, 2007), 31–66; here 40–41.

[112] Marie de France, *Fables*, ed. and trans. Harriet Spiegel. Medieval Academy Reprints for Teaching (Toronto, Buffalo, and London: University of Toronto Press, 1994), 50–55; cf. R. Howard Bloch, *The Anonymous Marie de France* (Chicago and London: The University of Chicago Press, 2003), chapters four through six and eight, mostly focusing on linguistic and philosophical issues; Charles Brucker, "Marie de France and the Fable Tradition," *A Companion to Marie de France*, ed. Logan E. Whalen. Brill's Companions to the Christian Tradition, 27 (Leiden and Boston, MA: Brill, 2011), 187–208; Sharon Kinoshita and Peggy McCracken, *Marie de France: A Critical Companion*. Gallica, 24 (Cambridge: D. S. Brewer, 2012), 91–104; see now also Baptiste Laïd, *L'élaboration du recueil de fables de Marie de France: " Trover " des fables au XIIe siècle*. Nouvelle bibliothèque du moyen âge, 128 (Paris: Honoré Champion éditeur, 2020), though I could not yet consult it.

Der Edelstein (ca. 1340/50; The Gemstone) and continued with the same issue, criticizing similarly the danger of material seduction in the luxury of urban living, and praising the freedom and happiness of the rural existence: "und wil in armuot vrœlîch leben" (no. 15, v. 55; p. 47; and want [prefer] to live happily in my poverty). The country mouse praises the advantages of the simple life and warns about the constant fears and worries associated with wealth and material possessions.[113]

More important, to return to the fables by Marie de France, in her "Del lu e del chien" (no. 26), she even outlines very specific concepts of the ideal of freedom which would be of higher value than all material possessions. A wolf encounters a dog and is amazed and impressed about its splendid appearance and healthy body, which is the result of the master's good treatment in return for the dog's loyal service watching over his property at night. At first, the wolf is so attracted to the dog's pleasant life, and accompanies it to the city, but then it espies the dog's collar and chain and quickly realizes that the dog has no freedom. The wolf then announces that he much prefers his freedom over the dog's slavery:

> "... I'll never choose to wear a chain!
> I'd rather live as a wolf, free,
> Than on a chain in luxury.
> I still can make a choice, and so
> You fare to town; to woods I'll go" (36–40).

4.2 Ulrich Bonerius

In the parallel version by Ulrich Bonerius (no. 59), the wolf argues the same way, but he emphasizes even more explicitly that his stomach is for him not as important as his freedom (vv. 51–57). For the author, this proves to be the desired nar-

---

113 Ulrich Bonerius, *Der Edelstein*, ed. and trans. Manfred Stange (see note 19); Klaus Grubmüller, "Boner," *Die deutsche Literatur des Mittelalters: Verfasserlexikon*, 2nd, completely revised ed. by Kurt Ruh et al. Vol. I (Berlin and New York: Walter de Gruyter, 1978), cols. 947–52; vgl. auch Johannes Janota, *Orientierung durch volkssprachige Schriftlichkeit (1280/90–1380/90). Geschichte der deutschen Literatur von den Anfängen bis zum Beginn der Neuzeit*, III: *Vom späten Mittelalter zum Beginn der Neuzeit* (Tübingen: Max Niemeyer, 2004), 462–63. For a fundamental study on the medieval fable, and thus also extensively on Bonerius, see Klaus Grubmüller, *Meister Esopus: Untersuchungen zu Geschichte und Funktion der Fabel im Mittelalter*. Münchener Texte und Untersuchungen zur deutschen Literatur des Mittelalters, 56 (Zürich and Munich: Artemis, 1977), esp. 297–374.

rative basis upon which he could develop his lesson. As Bonerius concludes, a poor man, free to pursue his own will, is richer than a rich man who must serve his master and would never be able to shed his worries: "der eigen ist, wâ ist des muot?" (v. 67; he who is a slave, does not have a true inner spirit). And: "es ist nicht sîn, daz selb er hât, / der âne vrîgen willen stât" (vv. 69–70; whatever he might own, it is not truly his property if he does not have a free will).

In several other fables, this Swiss preacher-poet pursed the topic of freedom even further, projecting, for instance, an idyllic country in Asia, Atrîcâ, where people enjoyed complete freedom, not being governed by a king or by any kind of lord (no. 24). One day, however, they appointed a person from the outside as king, who then immediately assumed all royal power and quickly repressed the people, taking away their freedoms and governing as an absolutist ruler, threatening those who might resist his demands with the death penalty: "sî muosten dienen bî der wide" (38: they had to serve him upon the threat of being executed). But Boner has no pity for those people because they had been foolish enough to bring this misery upon themselves.

Similarly, in the famous fable of the free frogs which requested from the god Jupiter that he appoint a king over them (here fable no. 25; in Marie de France's *Fables*, no. 18). Although there would not be any need for such a ruler, they bother Jupiter for such a long time that he eventually throws a log of wood into their pond. The frogs, however soon figure out its true property, so they continue to demand a king to exert power over themselves. Irritated, Jupiter then appoints a stork as their ruler, which immediately begins to devour the frogs as its food, acting as a complete dictator, a term which would not be anachronistic in this context. Terrified, the frogs then request to be freed from this king, but this time Jupiter no longer listens to them and simply allows the stork to keep eating all the frogs.

In his epimythium (the moral conclusion), Boner specifically urges his listeners/readers to pursue their own life with as much freedom as possible: "Wer hêr mag sîn, der sî nicht knecht!" (52; He who can be lord should not be a servant!). Leaving no doubt whatsoever, the poet strongly urges his audience to pursue the ideal of freedom, speaking of the "vrîen muot" (59; free spirit) which one should never allow anyone to repress. More specifically, however, he also implies that people should not be so ignorant and create such a dictatorial system on their own: "der eigen sich enkeinen man" (58: does not make himself subservient to another person).

In her version, Marie de France (no. 18) offers a somewhat different teaching insofar as Destiny blames the frogs for having belittled and maligned their good lord, so that now, being threatened in their lives by an adder, they deserve what they had asked for. For the Anglo-Norman poet, the frogs' demand for a king reflected rather badly on them, especially because they disregarded and shamed the first king – a log thrown into their pond. This is the same what people tend to do, according to the poet, "To a good lord (should they have one): / They always want to stamp their lord; / His honour they don't know to guard" (vv. 47–48).

Despite these fairly small differences in the moral and ethical teachings in these two versions, we can now firmly assert that the high and late Middle Ages also knew of the specific discourse pertaining to individual freedom, a freedom not bound by feudalism or servitude, but a freedom based on individual rights. However, as both Marie and Bonerius also recognized through their telling their fables, most people would not be capable of truly grasping the deeper value of freedom and would anyway easily abandoned it in favor of appointing a king who then would quickly assume dictatorial powers.

Bonerius also projects freedom on a very personal level when he addresses three Roman widows who are all asked by their relatives to remarry (no. 58). The narrator describes them all consistently as highly worthy, noble, independently minded individuals who deeply lament the loss of their beloved first husband and who now refuse to accept the hand of another man in marriage. Their reasons are very rational and virtuous, as the narrator emphasizes himself repeatedly. But it is worth noting that the first woman also clearly spells out that living out her life in widowhood would represent a form of personal freedom: "und wil eine vrîges leben hân" (v. 38; and I want to live the life of freedom).

Although Bonerius has no hesitation to fall back at times to very traditional misogynistic thinking, as reflected in the foregoing fable, no. 57,[114] here he actually supports and advocates for widows who refuse to submit to social pressure to remarry because thus they would be able to enjoy a life determined by loyalty and virtues, and an absence of sorrows and pains (vv. 85–88). He specifically did not argue that marriage was the only acceptable legal status for women and rather promoted widows' personal freedom even within late medieval urban society, particularly because, as he observed it in this case, they would thus be able to maintain their honor, independence, chastity, and virtues.[115]

---

[114] For a long list of relevant texts reflecting this tradition, see *Woman Defamed and Woman Defended: An Anthology of Medieval Texts*, ed. Alcuin Blamires with Karen Pratt and C. W. Marx (Oxford: Clarendon Press, 1992).

[115] *Upon My Husband's Death: Widows in the Literature and Histories of Medieval Europe*, ed. Louise Mirrer. Studies in Medieval and Early Modern Civilization (Ann Arbor, MI: The University of Michigan Press, 1992); *Medieval London Widows, 1300–1500*, ed. Caroline M. Barron and Anne F. Sutton (London and Rio Grande, OH: The Hambledon Press, 1994); Albrecht Classen, "Witwen in der Literatur des deutschen Mittelalters: Neue Perspektiven auf ein vernachlässigtes

Thus, while the notion of freedom proves to be a complex issue that cannot be easily defined and described because so much depends on the specific circumstances and the nuances in meaning of the term,[116] imprisonment and then also slavery were phenomena which always existed and represented straightforward negative values, i.e., the lack of freedom. We might want to go so far as to accept 'imprisonment' as a universal experience because all societies throughout time have depended on some legal structure to protect lives and property, to set limits, to create rules and regulations. Hence, anyone who then broke those laws, was punished, either through the imposition of hefty payments (money or material goods) or exile.

This does not mean, of course, that Bonerius would have regarded marriage as a form of imprisonment, far from it. But we can observe how much the discussion about individual freedom hinged on a vast range of conditions and circumstances. We face, in other words, with these significant terms central metaphors for many different aspects in pre-modern society, which in many ways surprisingly appear quite similar to those we still have to deal with today.

If we pursued the examples provided by both fable authors further, we would encounter many other literary examples where issues of crimes, judgment, and execution are addressed, which sheds important light on the legal conditions in the high and late Middle Ages. In Marie's "Del leün e del vilein" (no. 37; The Lion and the Peasant), for instance, we are told of a baron who is accused of treason, brought to court, and then condemned to death: "And had

---

Thema," *Etudes Germaniques* 57.2 (2002): 197–232; id., "Widows: Their Social and Religious Functions According to Medieval German Literature, with Special Emphasis on Erhart Gross's *Witwenbuch* (1446)," *Fifteenth-Century Studies* 28 (2003): 65–79; Britta-Juliane Kruse, *Witwen: Kulturgeschichte eines Standes in Spätmittelalter und Früher Neuzeit* (Berlin and New York: Walter de Gruyter, 2007); Anne Foerster, *Die Witwe des Königs: zu Vorstellung, Anspruch und Performanz im englischen und deutschen Hochmittelalter*. Mittelalter-Forschungen, 57 (Ostfildern: Jan Thorbecke Verlag, 2018); Katherine Clark Walter, *The Profession of Widowhood: Widows, Pastoral Care, and Medieval Models of Holiness* (Washington, DC: Catholic University of America Press, 2018).

116 See the contributions to *La notion de liberté au Moyen Age: Islam, Byzance, Occident. Penn-Paris-Dumbarton Oaks colloquia IV; session des 12–15 octobre 1982 [Mandelieu-La Napoule]: The Concept of Freedom in the Middle Ages Islam, Byzantium and the West*, ed. George Makdisi (Paris: Les Belles Lettres, 1985). Johannes Fried, in the introduction to *Die abendländische Freiheit* (see note 21), emphasizes the complexity of the term 'freedom,' the meaning of which depends very much on the respective context, definition, and framework. There is, as he outlines it, 1. the notion of the freedom of the will; 2. the freedom of individuals or groups of people; 3. natural, inborn freedom versus acquired freedom; 4. freedom of the spirit or religion; 5. symbolic freedom concerning taxes or interest rates (unclear!); and 6. spatial forms of freedom, such as in a church, a sacred location, etc. (13–14). The individual contributions address those six categories.

him thrown in with his lion – / A lion who'd been long constrained / Within the court where he was chained – This lion killed him straightway" (vv. 28–31).

Bonerius addressed less crimes or legal transgressions; instead, he examined more moral and ethical behavior, both in everyday life and in public, such as in "Von offenunge des rechtes" (no. 62: On the public demonstration of justice). There a young man serving the king as an overseer over the knights feels jealous of another, older administrator at court who is in charge of all provisions. He maligns him to the king by accusing the other servant of embezzling the royal property. In order to prove the validity of his charge, he demands that the king organize an ordeal in which both would fight against each other to confirm the truth of his charge. The older man, completely innocent in this matter (v. 29), is desperate because he knows only too well of the opponent's physical superiority and yet cannnot find any help. Finally, he can convince one of his farmhands to step into the ring and to fight on his behalf, which surprisingly results in the knight's loss, and then his subsequent execution (v. 65).

This account served the poet to warn about the danger of spreading false rumors and of slandering others out of jealousy and envy. Moreover, the older man quickly realized who his friends truly were because no one wanted to come to his rescue, except for the simple farmhand – certainly a direct echo of the teachings by Boethius in his *De consolatione philosophiae* (ca. 524). That simple but honest man wins the ordeal against the younger officer and is subsequently adopted by the older officer as his heir, a quite surprising conclusion considering the huge class difference.

C Imprisonment and Slavery Through Many Different Lenses

The notion of imprisonment was apparently so widely spread that even courtly love poets such as Thibaut de Champagne (1201–1253) could resort to it in order to express their feeling of lacking completely in freedom when they are caught by their amatory emotions for a lady. In his "Ausi com unicorne sui" (no. 57) he describes in highly vivid terms the lover's suffering and helplessness, having lost his heart in the prison of love: "En la douce chartre, en prison" (2, 6; in the sweet dungeon, in prison). Of course, this was all allegorical, but as such the imagery reflects dramatically on common experiences of imprisonment in a frightful prison cell.[117]

Imprisonment is the result of a punishment for some kind of wrongdoing, if not a crime, unless the authority figure or institution simply uses its power to extort money or political gains from the victim. Not every prisoner accepts the reasons for his/her conditions, but society, at least in its majority, or as determined by the authorities, ruled in such a case and meted out punishment. Throughout time, imprisonment was one of the central methods to punish wrong-doings, crimes, violence, uprisings, and riots, and this also applied to the Middle Ages.[118] Slavery, by contrast, constitutes the absolute absence of freedom, but not because of the individual's wrong actions, deeds, or words, but because of material interests by those who captured and sold slaves. Many times, slaves were simply those individuals who were the victims of war, or they were the objects of slave traders who wanted to make money by capturing people and selling them as slaves.

Throughout antiquity, slaves simply constituted an economic good and were treated as a valuable commodity. This phenomenon did not peter out by the eleventh or twelfth centuries, as had been claimed numerous times in the past, but actually grew in intensity by the late Middle Ages, as recent scholarship has con-

---

[117] Brigitte Burrichter, "Thibaut de Chapagne: Lyrik im Gefängnis der Liebe," *Formen der Selbstthematisierung in der vormodernen Lyrik*. Hrsg. von Dorothea Klein in Verbindung mit Thomas Baier, Brigitte Burrichter, Michael Erler und Isabel Karremann. Spolia Berolinensia: Beiträge zur Literatur- und Kulturgeschichte des Mittelalters und der Neuzeit, 39 (Hildesheim: Weidmannsche Verlagsbuchhandlung, 2020), 79–99; here 90–95.

[118] Elizabeth Lawn, *"Gefangenschaft": Aspekt und Symbol sozialer Bindung im Mittelalter, dargestellt an chronikalischen und poetischen Quellen*. Europäische Hochschulschriften, Reihe: 1, 214 (Frankfurt a.M.; Peter Lang, 1977).

vincingly demonstrated, especially in the world of the Mediterranean.[119] The Christianization of medieval Europe especially since the seventh and eighth centuries did not lead over to the abandonment of slavery as an economic principle; instead, here we face one of the common myths about the pre-modern world in contrast to antiquity, the amelioration narrative. However, it would be equally misleading, as most recent research has demonstrated, to assume that the various authors of prescriptive narratives concerning the structure of the early Church all rejected or all supported slavery. Much depended on the individual circumstances.[120]

Modern Marxist scholars have equally misread the Middle Ages in many respects, as Hannah Barker underscores quite dramatically, as a period beyond the classical world with its strong reliance on slavery. Since Marxists relied heavily on the notion of a progressive development from the slave-holding society in the ancient world to feudalism in the Middle Ages, and capitalism in the modern world, ultimately concluding in socialism and then finally in a communist utopia, they could not fashion the idea that slavery existed in the Middle Ages, although the sources are simply filled with references to them.

This phenomenon might well have been more typically of the various Mediterranean societies during the fourteenth and fifteenth centuries, but slavery in general was certainly not extinct north of the Alps either, an issue that rather problematizes the general image of the medieval world determined by Christianity and feudalism.

In the eighth-century heroic epic *Beowulf*, for instance, an unnamed slave suddenly appears at the end shortly before the protagonist's death. He has run away from his master because he wanted to escape from being beating as a punishment for an evil deed. He happens to discover the dragon's lair and steals a jeweled cup, which arises the dragon's infinite ire which it then directs against all the people, so Beowulf has to fight and kill it. The poet did not see any need to explain more about the slave who takes that "cup back to his master

---

119 Hannah Barker, *That Most Precious Merchandise: The Mediterranean Trade in Black Sea Slaves, 1260–1500*. The Middle Ages Series (Philadelphia, PA: University of Pennsylvania Press, 2019); see also my review in *Mediaevistik* 33 (forthcoming). For a detailed study of slaves in Mallorca, see Antoni Mas i Forners, *Esclaus i catalans: Esclavitud i segregació a Mallorca durant els segles XIV i XV*. Trafalempa, 1 (Palma, Mallorca: Lleonard Muntaner, 2005).
120 Hartmut Hoffmann, "Kirche und Sklaverei im frühen Mittelalter," *Deutsches Archiv für Erforschung des Mittelalters* 42 (1986): 1–24. See now Daniel Vaucher, *Sklaverei in Norm und Praxis: Die frühchristlichen Kirchenordnungen*. 2nd ed. Sklaverei – Knechtschaft – Zwangsarbeit, 18 (2017; Hildesheim, Zürich, and New York: Olms / Weidmann, 2020).

as a peace-offering" (ch. 32, p. 81) Undoubtedly, we can affirm, early medieval society knew of slavery and accepted it as a normal social institution.[121]

Jukka Korpela, for instance, has recently demonstrated that Finns and Karelians made up a not so insignificant percentage of those unfortunate individuals who were captured and sold into slavery on the Mediterranean markets, and this already in the early Middle Age well until early modern times.[122] Slaves were of great value for military, agricultural, and general labor purposes, and they were also used for education and sexuality, and this quite similar as in antiquity.[123]

Some of the major slave markets north of the Alps were in Mainz and Verdun in the ninth and tenth centuries, and Rouen in the tenth and the eleventh centuries. S. Lebecq emphasizes, however, that we have to differentiate carefully between slaves used in the household and slaves used in agriculture, especially because the lower rural population often fared hardly better than purchased slaves, or, the other way around, both slaves and the simple peasants enjoyed a certain degree of independence, being granted a small piece of land and a farm house. He also argues that the early Middle Ages witnessed extensive liberation processes, collective transformation of economic relationships and human bondage (*collibertus*), which was often, rather curiously, opposed by the representatives of the Church because the ecclesiastic authors commonly argued that all people should stay in their social class as God had arranged it.

Since many of the Church-owned estates were mostly managed with the help of slaves, it made good sense to hear the theological defense of slavery. Whether

---

[121] Here I draw from *Beowulf:* A Prose Translation with an Intro. by David Wright (London: Penguin, 1957); there are certainly many other excellent editions and translations. As to the history of early medieval slavery, see now Barker, *That Most Precious Merchandise* (see note 119), 5–9; see also Alice Rio, *Slavery after Rome, 500–1100*. Oxford Studies in Medieval European History (Oxford: Oxford University Press, 2017); Jürgen Misch, *Das christliche Sklavenland* (see note 18).

[122] Jukka Korpela, *Slaves from the North: Finns and Karelians in the East European Slave Trade, 900–1600*. Studies in Gobal Slavery, 5 (Leiden and Boston: Brill, 2019). He observes that these two groups of people were highly attractive on the Black Sea slave markets and elsewhere in the eastern Mediterranean because of their blond hair and nordic features. There was obviously a rather flourishing slave trade from Finland through Russia reaching the south, and this over the centuries far into the early modern age.

[123] *Freiheit und Unfreiheit: mittelalterliche und frühneuzeitliche Facetten eines zeitlosen Problems*, ed. Kurt Andermann and Gabriel Zeilinger.Kraichtaler Kolloquium: Kraichtaler Kolloquien, 7 (Epfendorf: Bibliotheca-Academica-Verlag, 2010); *Unfreiheit und Sexualität von der Antike bis zur Gegenwart*, ed. Josef Fischer und Melanie Ulz, together with Marcel Simonis. Sklaverei – Knechtschaft – Zwangsarbeit, 6 (Hildesheim and New York: Olms, 2010); Madeline C. Zilfi, *Women and Slavery in the Late Ottoman Empire: The Design of Difference*. Cambridge Studies in Islamic Civilization (Cambridge: Cambridge University Press, 2010).

hence the institution of slavery slowly but surely disappeared since then, as Lebecq assumes, would have to be examined much more carefully in light of the vast body of archival material than can be done here.[124] We know for sure, however, that the business with slaves increased tremendously since the fourteenth and fifteenth centuries – or maybe simply continued, but by then at an accelerated rate. It might also well be that we have more sources from that time confirming the existence of the slave trade.

Significantly, as recent research has also indicated, slave trade all across Europe was a highly profitable and not at all questioned business in which both Christian and Jewish merchants were equally involved, and this also in the tenth and eleventh centuries under the Frankish and Ottonian rulers. There was hardly any other mercantile commodity more lucrative than slaves, and there are virtually no comments by clerical authors who would have opposed it, except that there were some voices warning that selling slaves to the Arabs in the Iberian Peninsula would strengthen their military might and increase their threatening power because they often elevated their slaves to higher military ranks.[125] However we might have to evaluate the sources, there is no denying any longer that slavery was in full swing throughout the Middle Ages and also the early modern age. What remains to be decided pertains to who were the main organizers in that trade and the main merchants, then to how the slaves

---

124 S. Lebecq, "Sklave," *Lexikon des Mittelalters*, ed. Norbert Angermann. Vol. VII (Munich: Lexma Verlag, 1990), 1977–80; slavery in other parts of Europe is covered by additional entries in the *Lexikon*. See also Susan Mosher Stuard, "Ancillary Evidence for the Decline of Medieval Slavery." *Past & Present* 149 (1995): 3–28, who argues that particularly female slaves continued to be of considerable value in early and high medieval households, whereas the changing agricultural structures made the use of male slaves increasingly unnecessary.

125 Barker, *That Most Precious Merchandise* (see note 119). As to the discussion about early medieval slaves, see Michael Toch, "Wirtschaft und Verfolgung: die Bedeutung der Ökonomie für die Kreuzzugspogrome des 11. und 12. Jahrhunderts. Mit einem Anhang zum Sklavenhandel der Juden," *Juden und Christen zur Zeit der Kreuzzüge*, ed. Alfred Haverkamp. Vorträge und Forschungen. Konstanzer Arbeitskreis für Mittelalterliche Geschichte, 47 (Sigmaringen: Jan Thorbeckek, 1999), 253–85. However, his understanding of the role of Jews as allegedly little invested in slave trade, needs to be questioned extensively; see now Markus J. Wenninger, "*Iudei et ceteri …*: Bemerkungen zur rechtlichen, sozialen und wirtschaftlichen Stellung der Juden in karolingischer und ottonischer Zeit," *Aschkenas* 30.2 (2020): 217–44. As he demonstrates convincingly on the basis of a careful analysis of the available sources, there was fairly little difference between Christian, Jewish, and other merchants in the early Middle Ages, and all of them were keenly interested in buying and selling slaves all over Europe, especially from the Slavic territory all the way down to the Iberian Peninsula. Slave trade was a very common and almost preferred business.

were treated or used for what purpose, and what their relationship was with the larger societies they lived in.

1 Former Slaves as Authors

Freedom, on the other hand, was sought most ardently by those who were forced to live the life of a slave, as we know from the accounts by former victims, especially Johann Schiltberger (1381–ca. 1440) and Georgius of Hungary (ca. 1422/23– 1502), both of whom had been taken as slaves in the wake of Ottoman military victories and managed to escape only after many years of suffering, finally returning to Christian Europe where they then created narratives about their experiences.[126] However, here we might be dealing with rather extreme conditions and not necessarily with a very common situation throughout the early or high Middle Ages, although the final judgment on this issue is still outstanding. Both authors have already been studied to some extent, but it will be useful in our context to re-examine more closely what they had to say about their experiences as slaves in emotional terms.[127] Most of the military details can be left out here, and also the extensive comments about many travels and the cultural observations. Instead, let us pay close attention to how first Schiltberger described in his *Reisebuch* how he was taken prisoner and then made to a slave, examining to what extent he actually ruminated on his own experience. It deserves to be mentioned that there are, as far as I can tell, not many such accounts by former

---

[126] Albrecht Classen, "Global Travel in the Late Middle Ages: The Eyewitness Account of Johann Schiltberger," *Medieval History Journal* 23.1 (2020): 1–28 (online at: https://doi.org/10.1177/0971945819895896); id., "The Topic of Imprisonment in Medieval German Literature: With an Emphasis on Johann Schiltberger's Account About his 30-Year Enslavement in the East," *Studia Neophilologica* (2020): https://www.tandfonline.com/doi/full/10.1080/00393274.2020.1755362 (both last accessed on Jan. 15, 2021).

[127] Schiltberger's account has been edited and translated already several times, so here I will rely primarily on the English text: Johann Schiltberger, *The Bondage and Travels of Johann Schiltberger, a Native of Bavaria, in Europe, Asia, and Africa 1396–1427*, trans. from the Heidelberg ms. ed. in 1859 by Karl Friedrich Neumann by J. Buchan Telfer. With notes by P. Bruun and a preface, introduction and notes by the translator and editor (London: Hakluyt Society, 1897); cf. also the recent edition: Hans Schiltberger, *Als Sklave im Osmanischen Reich und bei den Tataren: 1394– 1427*, ed. Ulrich Schlemmer. Alte abenteuerliche Reiseberichte (Wiesbaden: Ed. Erdmann, 2008); and for a German translation, see *Johann Schiltbergers Irrfahrt durch den Orient: Der aufsehenerregende Bericht einer Reise, die 1394 begann und erst nach über 30 Jahren ein Ende fand*. Aus dem Mittelhochdeutschen übertragen und herausgegeben von Markus Tremmel. Bayerische Abenteuer (Taufkirchen: Via Verbis Bavarica, 2000). I have used some of the material in my previous articles, but updated them in a variety of ways.

slaves, so the statements by these two authors are particularly valuable and can then be placed parallel to similar memoirs or reports from the following centuries, such as by Hans Ulrich Krafft.

1.1 Johann Schiltberger

After the *battle of Nicopolis* was over (Sept. 25, 1396), in which Hungarian, Croatian, Bulgarian, Wallachian, French, Burgundian, German, and assorted troops were defeated by the Ottoman army,[128] the Turkish ruler realized the massive number of his dead troops, so he intended to avenge their deaths by killing all the Christian prisoners. Schiltberger was lucky, however, because of his youth – he was barely sixteenth years of age – they spared him, whereas the others were systematically decapitated (5). While being grouped together with the other youths, none of the older soldiers (above twenty years of age) was spared, and the killing went from morning to vespers. Only upon the intervention of the king's counselors did this blood-bath come to an end, and those who survived were assigned as slaves to whoever had earned such rewards for military accomplishments. Considering the large number of slaves, none of whom managed to escape, we gain a good idea of the high level of administrative capabilities on the side of the Turks. But Schiltberger himself does not comment on his own situation; instead, he reports of their collective experience, being stuck in a prison for a long time, then being shipped east, and so forth (6–7).

Smaller groups of young slaves were then sent to the various rulers in that region as gifts of respect, so these young Christians had completely lost their freedom and were treated as chattel to be bartered, passed on, used for work, and employed in military service. Schiltberger himself was primarily tasked for six year with being a runner in front of the king, wherever he went. Following, for another six years, he was promoted and from then on rode on horseback, but also only in the procession with the king. We are not given any details as to Schiltberger's life itself, how he was treated, whether he learned the foreign language, what kind of accommodations he and the other slaves had, how they were fed, or what uniforms were given to them. Instead, the focus rests only on the military operations carried out by the Turkish king, as if Schiltberger

---

128 David Nicolle, *Nicopolis 1396: The Last Crusade*. Campaign Series (London: Osprey Publishing, 1999); Attila Bárány, "Nicopolis, Battle of," *The Oxford Encyclopedia of Medieval Warfare and Military Technology*, ed. Clifford J. Rogers. Vol. 3 (Oxford: Oxford University Press, 2010), 57–59. The most detailed and yet succinct account, however, proves to be the anonymous article online at: https://en.wikipedia.org/wiki/Battle_of_Nicopolis (last accessed on Jan. 15, 2021).

considered himself primarily as a chronicler, as he obviously avoided to place himself particularly in the foreground. At one point, however, in chapter six, he relates how sixty of the slaves escaped together as a group, but were caught again by a whole battalion of Turkish soldiers.

After some negotiations, the commander convinced them to give themselves up to him on his pledge that he would ensure that they would not be killed. Without that oath, they all would have been finished, as the Turkish king (Weyasit) at first ordered upon their return. Instead, they are all thrown into a prison for nine months, during which twelve of them died. But thereafter, they were released again, after having promised never to escape again. Surprisingly, this then resulted in them all receiving back their horses and even an increase in their pay for the service (12), as if nothing significant had happened. While we hear in subsequent chapters about religious issues causing serious conflicts or aristocratic prisoners, the slaves, Schiltberger being one of them, seem to have been ignored in that regard.

He himself reports, however, about a duke and his son who were both captured and put into prison, where the father died. His son, however, accepted the Islamic faith to save his own life (14). The author, writing, of course, from the retrospect more than thirty years later after having managed to escape after all, explicitly uses the term "Infidels" for the Muslims (14) so as to mark clearly the difference between the Christian slaves and their owners. Schiltberger relates his account from the bottom up, so to speak, reflecting the major military and political events, but he mostly leaves out to comment about his own situation as a slave. We learn of horrible casualties of war, of the decimation of the entire population of cities, and of thousands of prisoners taken to slavery (20, ch. 12), but the author does not emote about these terrific events, obviously because he himself was not in a much better situation at that time and composed his entire account out of a retrospective anyway, making sure to be as dramatic as possible to appeal to his audience. The ten surviving manuscripts and scores of incunabula and early modern prints underscore the extent to which he was actually very successful in that attempt – the last printing dates from as late as 1678![129]

---

[129] The only accurate and latest update about these manuscripts can be found at http://www.handschriftencensus.de/werke/3859 (last accessed on Jan. 15, 2021). See also the useful summary and overview by Nicolaus Ruge, "Schiltberger, Hans," *Deutsches Literaturlexikon: Das Mittelalter*, ed. Wolfgang Achnitz. Vol. 3: *Reiseberichte und Geschichtsdichtung* (Berlin and Boston: Walter de Gruyter, 2012), 594–96. For the record of sixteenth- and seventeenth-century prints, see the catalogs VD 16 and VD 17, both online.

During his thirty or so years as a slave, Schiltberger passed on to various different rulers, such as to the infamous Tamerlane (1336–1405),[130] but it did not seem to have matter to him particularly, as he leaves no personal comments about such transitions. Instead, we are entertained with gruesome details about slaughter, executions, military operations, political structures, and cultural aspects, and hear very little about the slave himself. Schiltberger prided himself with having seen many different countries, always serving one ruler or the other, but we cannot tell whether he enjoyed these experiences or not. For most of his account, Schiltberger presents himself as an eyewitness of the major events he was involved with, and this basically as a chronicler, leaving out his own situation as a slave. After having mentioned a number of cities in the Black Sea region, he emphasizes, for instance, "I have been in them all" (41). Or he remarks: "I have been in all the above-named countries, and have learned their peculiarities" (43), as if he were another Marco Polo or Odorico da Pordenone. The author also considers the religious practices and teachings by the Greek-Orthodox and the Muslims, and endeavors greatly to outline the details so as to make his report as informative as possible.

Only at the near end of his account we are finally informed how he and four other slaves managed to escape, and this after thirty years of enslavement. Having arrived with their lord near the Black Sea, they use the opportunity and get away, though it proves difficult for them to find a ship master willing to take them on and to help them cross over to the Christian territory. Only after they have proven that they still know the *Pater noster* and other prayers identifying them as members of his own faith, does he believe them and allows them to enter his ship. The journey back home, however, proved to be arduous, complicated, difficult, and often rather dangerous, but eventually Schiltberger completed his journey through the Balkans, Poland, Bohemia, and Bavaria, finally to reach his home city near Freising, and this after thirty-two years having suffered through slavery.

The account concludes with rather scant comments, but some of them deserve to be quoted because the author emphasizes here his great relief about having returned to Christianity still healthy in body and mind:

> And when I had almost despaired of coming [away] from the Infidel people and their wicked religion, amongst whom I was obliged to be for xxxii years, and of any longer hav-

---

[130] Ron Sela, *The Legendary Biographies of Tamerlane: Islam and Heroic Apocrypha in Central Asia*. Trans. Clements R. Markham. Cambridge Studies in Islamic Civilization (Cambridge: Cambridge University Press, 2011); Ahmad Ibn Arabshah, *Tamerlane: The Life of the Great Amir*, trans. J. H. Sanders (1936; London and New York: I. B. Tauris, 2018).

ing fellowship with holy Christianity, God Almighty saw my great longing and anxiety after the Christian faith and its heavenly joys, and graciously preserved me from the risk of perdition of body and soul. (102)

However, apart from his early imprisonment, which was due to his escape attempt, Schiltberger remains almost completely quiet about his private life as a slave and focuses instead on the military events, conquests, the different religions, and cultural idiosyncracies. We do not even learn anything about how he communicated with his various masters, fellow prisoners and slaves, and his military superiors. How were they treated in prison after they had been captured again following their first escape? In what way did Schiltberger's various masters ensure that he would not repeat his effort to gain his freedom from slavery? It also would be helpful to learn how he might have felt serving in his military role and yet being a slave? Finally, there are no comments as to his own religious orientation and possible attempts by his owners to make him convert to Islam. We can be certain, however, that he must have been treated fairly well since he did not starve, did not die from malnutrition, beatings, unhealthy conditions, or as 'cannon fodder.' He managed to preserve his knowledge of the German language but must have learned enough other languages to cope in that foreign world as a military man.

Consequently, although many answers are missing, we can be certain that Schiltberger fared fairly well, survived more than thirty years in slavery, and was still strong and healthy enough at the end to get away and to journey for many months until he finally reached his home again back in Bavaria. He also must have saved enough money during those many years to pay for all the services rendered that were necessary on his escape and then the journey all the way from the Black Sea to southeast Germany. All this might force us to reconsider the meaning of slavery under the Ottomans and others during the late Middle Ages, but we would have to consult many other sources to gain a clearer picture.

1.2 The Slave Georgius of Hungary

Georgius was born around 1422/1423 in Siebenbürgen (Transylvania, today Romania), probably in Rumes/Romos, and grew up speaking either Hungarian or German, or more probably both. In 1437 he moved to Mühlbach (today: Sebeş, northwest of Sibiu) to join a Dominican school there, but soon enough that city was besieged by the Turks, and the young man was one of the last defenders of a tower irrationally and fanatically hoping to set up a successful resistance against the overwhelming hostile army. When the enemy finally set fire to the tower, the small band of Christian soldiers still alive fell into their hands, and they were all put into chains and soon sold as slaves on the slave market of Edirne (today: south of the border to Bulgaria). Shortly thereafter, still driven by his youthful desire for freedom, Georgius twice attempted to escape, yet he was caught each time, then condemned to being heavily chained, as he reports in vivid terms, calling his account an "infelicitatis historiam" (148). A series of further attempts followed, but obviously all to no avail. Then there is a gap in his account, and we find him again in the house of a lord who treated him very well and where Georgius stayed for the next fifteen years. Finally, however, despite the relatively comfortable life that he had enjoyed with his last master, he escaped again, then for the eighth and final time, finally being able to leave the Ottoman Empire without being captured and taken back. His slavery had ended. The years between 1439 and 1443 remain a blank page in his account, perhaps because he later felt so ashamed of his succumbing to the 'temptation' of the Muslim faith and wanted to draw a veil of silence over them.[131]

His last lord seems to have been a kind man, older in age, married, and with a child. He had offered Georgius a *pactum libertatis*, which promised him the liberation after a certain time in return for a specific amount of money. Georgius was apparently accepted into the family, took his meals with them, enjoyed free time during which he eventually turned much attention to the study of the Muslim faith. The author also had a pleasant relationship with his lord's wife, and it seems rather surprising that Georgius at the end abandoned all that and fled for good, returning to Europe.

His master had allowed him to travel only because Georgius had claimed to seek further religious instructions from some dervish. Georgius first aimed for Pera, north of Constantinople, and then he traveled to the island of Chios, where he joined the Dominican order. Subsequently he turned to Rome where he lived for the rest of his life and where he also composed the tract about his life as a slave, about his trials and tribulations during his imprisonment, his punishments, his temptations by the other religion, about his rediscovery of

---

131 Georgius de Hungaria, *Tractatus de Moribus, Condictionibus et Nequicia Turcorum. Traktat über die Sitten, die Lebensverhältnisse und die Arglist der Türken*. Nach der Erstausgabe von 1481 herausgegeben, übersetzt und eingeleitet von Reinhard Klockow. Schriften zur Landeskunde Siebenbürgens, 15 (Cologne, Weimar, and Vienna: Böhlau, 1994); cf. Anton Schwob, "'Toleranz' im Türkentraktat des Georg von Ungarn: Eine Infragestellung," *"swer sînen vriunt behaltet, daz ist lobelîch": Festschrift für András Vizkelety zum 70. Geburtstag*, ed. Márta Nagy and László Jónácsik, together with Edit Madas and Gábor Sarbak (Piliscsaba and Budapest: Katholische Péter-Pázmány-Universität, Philosophische Fakultät, 2001), 253–59.

the Christian faith, and his long-term endurance in surviving his time of enslavement.[132]

Similar to Schiltberger, Georgius's account attracted considerable interest, and even appealed to Martin Luther, among many others, not only because the comments about slavery as such, but because of the great fear throughout Christian Europe of the imminent danger of the Ottoman constant conquests and attacks on the Balkans, then Hungary, and even Austria.[133] His *Tractatus de Moribus, Condictionibus et Nequicia Turcorum* first appeared in print in 1481 (perhaps as late as 1482), and for the last time in 1559 (twelve incunabula and early modern prints; there are also seven manuscripts, copied by hand from some of the printed Latin editions), deeply stirring people's minds, apparently because of its vivid eye-witness account and the more or less novel perspective about the Ottomans from a slave who actually embraced a rather positive attitude about his masters and the Turkish-Muslim culture, and who nevertheless withstood all religious temptations and remained a committed Christian.[134]

Despite his apocalyptic perspective in light of the victorious and every growing Ottomans, as outlined in the prologue, Georgius offers many rather surprisingly positive comments about the highly developed Muslim culture and reveals indirectly that he would have almost converted to Islam as well, but then remembered his own Christian faith. The treatise thus served apologetic purposes, and also as a warning for other Christians who might fall into the Turks' hands, because they and their culture appear as relatively appealing also for Europeans.

---

132 Albrecht Classen, "The World of the Turks Described by an Eye-Witness: Georgius de Hungaria's Dialectical Discourse about the Foreign World of the Ottoman Empire," *Journal of Early Modern History* 7.3–4 (2003): 257–79; id., "Life Writing as a Slave in Turkish Hands: Georgius of Hungary's Reflections About His Existence in the Turkish World," *Neohelicon* 39.1 (2012): 55–72.
133 *Chronica unnd Beschreibung der Türckey. Mit eyner Vorrhed D. Martini Lutheri. Unveränderter Nachdruck der Ausgabe Nürnberg 1530 sowie fünf weiterer "Türkendrucke" des 15. und 16. Jahrhunderts*. Mit einer Einführung von Carl Göllner. Schriften zur Landeskunde Siebenbürgens, 6 (Cologne and Vienna: Böhlau, 1983); see also Aslı Çrakman, *From the "Terror of the World" to the "Sick Man of Europe": European Images of Ottoman Empire and Society from the Sixteenth Century to the Nineteenth*. Studies in Modern European History, 43. (2002; New York, Washington, DC, Baltimore, et al.: Peter Lang, 2005).
134 For a detailed list of all available print copies, see http://www.mirabileweb.it/title/demoribus-conditionibus-et-nequitia-turcorum-geor-title/19202; cf. also the excellent bibliographical overview at http://www.geschichtsquellen.de/werk/4950; Albrecht Classen, "*Tractatus de moribus, condictionibus et nequicia Turcorum*," *Christian-Muslim Relations: A Bibiographical History*. Vol. VII: *Central and Eastern Europe, Asia, Africa and South America (1500–1600)*, ed. David Thomas and John Chesworth (Leiden and Boston: Brill, 2015), 36–40, online at: http://dx.doi.org/10.1163/2451-9537_cmrii_COM_24643 (all last accessed on Jan. 15, 2021).

As his prologue underscores, this text served to illustrate the allegedly horrendous, inhumane, almost devilish kind of persecutions which the unfortunate and badly victimized author had to undergo, and to warn people of the impending doomsday, as prophesied in the Old and the New Testament. Books and other printed texts containing ancient texts are no longer necessary for warnings about the imminent catastrophe, as the author states, because the danger from the East, the emergence of the Turkish empire, is clearly visible, tangible, and almost unavoidable. He regarded himself as a martyr in the cause of God and insisted that he did not tell any fables or fictions, having actually gone through a long period of suffering in the Ottoman empire. But he also admits frankly that his destiny would have taken a very different turn if he had simply accepted the peace treaty between the city and the Turks. Duke Vlad II, the Voivode of Wallachia from 1436 to 1442, and again from 1443 to 1447, who had fought on the side of the Ottoman army, had negotiated a peace agreement with the citizens which allowed the nobles, once they had turned over the city to the enemy, to depart safely and to turn to the duke's land, while the others were supposed to move to the Turkish territory and to settle there. Everyone was later granted the opportunity, once the conquest had been completed, to return home. Georgius openly admits: "Que ominia, ut promiserat, impleta uidimus" (152; All those promises were later fulfilled, as we witnessed). If our author had accepted this accord, he would not have suffered more than two decades of slavery, but one noble lord and a group of young men proved to be too hot-headed and set up the strong resistance, which unfortunately led to all of their demise, including Georgius's, for whom the situation appeared like an opportunity to embrace his own martyrdom (152).

This *Tractatus* subsequently served particularly as a narrative mirror about the author's personal experiences as a slave, very similar to the account by Schiltberger. Considering the large number of slaves from all over eastern Europe, the Middle East, and North Africa sold on Ottoman markets (called "Esir" or "Yesir") well into the eighteenth century and beyond, many of whom subsequently enjoyed considerable respect and rose in military, administrative, or educational rank, we can be certain that the archives contain many more slave narratives in a variety of languages.[135]

---

135 Brian L. Davies, *Warfare, State and Society on the Black Sea Steppe*. Warfare and History (London and New York: Routledge, 2007). For relevant sources from the eighteenth and nineteenth centuries, see Eve M. Troutt Powell, *Tell This in My Memory: Stories of Enslavement from Egypt, Sudan, and the Ottoman Empire*. History, Middle East Studies (Stanford, CA: Stanford University Press, 2012); Nur Sobers-Khan, *Slaves Without Shackles: Forced Labour and Manumission in the Galata Court Registers, 1560 – 1572*. Studien zur Sprache, Kultur und Geschichte der

The Turks, however, were not the only ones who bought and used slaves, and this for many different purposes, but for the European public, as hypocritical as it may have been, the Ottoman empire represented the greatest danger in those terms because they were so successful in military terms and experienced a tremendous ascendancy also in economic and political terms during the fifteenth and sixteenth centuries. Examining the way how Georgius viewed and evaluated his own experiences as a slave, can later be used as a valuable springboard for modern studies on slave narratives, especially in North America, though this is beyond the chronological framework of this book.[136]

The author almost lost his Christian faith and began to follow the Muslim practice and embraced its religious foundation: "de fide Christi non modicum dubitaui" (146; I doubted the Christian faith not a little). Only God's own grace rescued him, as he adds immediately, to avoid that danger, although he had already sunk in deeply and had been close to lose himself. Although the author primarily aims at introducing the culture, customs, living conditions of, and, as he hastens to add, the evil attitudes of the Turks, all that really serves as a foil for his own self-reflections. In this regard Georgius's *Tractatus* emerges, after all, as another valuable piece of life-writing, somewhere located between an autobiography and a learned treatise, a religious tract and a travelogue.

More important, behind the factual account we recognize the author's deep concerns about the shaky teachings of the Christian faith because its dogma by itself does not seem to be solidly anchored in people's minds. Consequently, they become easy victims of an intellectually superior enemy who knows exceedingly well how to propagate his own faith to the detriment of the Christian one. Georgius's life writing thus serves as the foil for a sophisticated counter strategy for future victims of Ottoman attacks who certainly would experience the same deliberate temptations by their new lords and masters to accept the Islamic religion. Indirectly, the author thus also attacks the Christian Church for having neglected its duties to teach the faithful how to understand, defend, and bolster

---

Türkvölker, 20 (Berlin: Schwarz, 2014). As to the complex relationships between slaves and their masters, cf. the contributions to *Slaves and Slave Agency in the Ottoman Empire*, ed. Stephan Conermann and Gül Şen. Ottoman Studies / Osmanistische Studien, 7 (Göttingen: V&R Unipress, 2020).

136 *The Slave Narrative*, ed. Kimberly Drake. Critical Insights (Ipswich, MA: Grey House Publ./ Salem Press, 2014). The contributors focus especially on the voices by Frederick Douglass, Harriet Jacobs, and Solomon Northup, but also on Ottoman slaves and modern slave novels. See also *The Cambridge Companion to the African American Slave Narrative*, ed. Audrey A. Fisch (Cambridge: Cambridge University Press, 2007); *The Oxford Handbook of the African American Slave Narrative*, ed. John Ernest (Oxford: Oxford University Press, 2014). The research on modern slave narratives, especially in the American context, is legion.

their own faith in a world where strong competing forces could dominate. Georgius reveals a sense of abandonment throughout his treatise, and tries to outline for his readers how to armor themselves in dogmatic terms if they might ever face the same situation as the one our author had to suffer through.

There is much criticism of the Christian Church and the Christian monarchies in Europe, but the author describes his enslavement in most somber terms as a true danger for the well-being of his own soul. He never complains about physical hardship in any particular way, but emphasizes regularly how much the attractiveness of the Turkish culture could appeal to a European, in fact could penetrate him even down to his heart: "ut ad intima cordis penitret nec etiam ipsius anime precordia <non> infecta derelinquat" (176; that it could reach down to the bottom of the heart and does not even preserve the center of the soul from infection).

Whereas most other commentators about the Ottoman Empire replicated generic information, borrowed from second-hand informants, or from published studies and tracts, Georgius's account proves to be so fascinating and valuable for our investigation because of his personal eye-witness account and religious reflections in face of in-depth familiarity with the other side. At the same time, he is most interested in using his autobiographical report as a basis to criticize the Western world over and over again, so when he charges the Church with being entirely given over to the sin of simony, a practice which seems to have become the norm, as the author observes most clearly after his return from his slavery (184). Similar tendencies can be observed in parallel tracts dealing with life in Turkey, the so-called "Türkendrucke."[137]

By contrast, and that proves to be the most exciting component of the *Tractatus*, almost every aspect of daily life, of the politics, and of the military operations carried out by the Ottomans, the Janissaries, or their handling of prisoners emerges as ideal and most impressive, especially for a European reader who had never seen the like back in his home country. For instance, Georgius underscores that the Turks take great efforts to avoid the killing of any of their opponents and always prefer to keep them alive as "tributarios" or as slaves (192). But he does not perceive this as a humanitarian gesture; instead he accuses the Muslims of thus hurting their victims in reality twice, first by gaining money through selling

---

[137] Carl Göllner, *Tvrcica: Die europäischen Türkendrucke des XVI. Jahrhunderts*. 2 vols. (Bucharest: Editura Academiei; Berlin: Akademie-Verlag, 1961); *Europa und die Türken in der Renaissance*, ed. Bodo Guthmüller and Wilhelm Kühlmann. Frühe Neuzeit, 54 (Tübingen: Niemeyer, 2000); see also Gregory J. Miller, *The Turks and Islam in Reformation Germany*. Routledge Research in Early Modern History (New York and London: Routledge, 2017).

them into slavery, and second by exposing them to the temptations by the devil (194).

Considering the traumatic experience of his enslavement and his many years subsequently fighting against his utter subordination, we realize how important it proved to be for him to reject Islam outright and to cast it as a most deceptive, devastating, and illusionary religion. Little wonder that his European audience quickly chimed in, supported his arguments, and internalized them, such as Martin Luther, though often for many different reasons and not so secret agendas.

The early phase of his enslavement must have been hard, even if Georgius certainly exaggerated the dramatic events to some extent. By emphasizing his long period of suffering and enduring great fears ("anime periculo sustinui, 156), he appealed to his audience to feel deep empathy with his personal history. In later phases of his enslavement, the situation appears to have been quite different, and he survived well, after all, without having sustained lasting physical injuries. Nevertheless, his own account was to serve as a warning for all Christians to keep their death in mind and hence the well-being of their soul. The *Tractatus* thus turned into a platform to preach about the Seven Deadly Sins and to warn people about their own moral and ethical shortcomings and failures (170).

In a rather apocalyptic and self-pitying fashion Georgius characterized his entire time which he had to spend as a Turkish slave as determined by constant dread of death: "tot mortibus interii, quot inter Turcos dies vixi" (176; I suffered as many deaths as I lived days among the Turks). But when we examine his own report, we find fairly little information as to his actual experiences as a slave, apart from general comments concerning the entire group of slaves as chattel. Thus, he provides details as to the actual sale of the slaves, who are taken to the markets, tied up with chains. On the market, they have to take off all clothing and are thus examined by men and women at all body parts as to their physical health (194–96).

The author describes this, of course, as a deeply shameful procedure, and those who demonstrate some resistance out of embarrassment, are hit even harder and then have to follow orders after all. They are all treated as nothing but chattel, and neither social status nor age, neither gender nor family relationships matter, they are all sold to individual buyers, and not even mothers are allowed to stay with their babies (198). Movingly, Georgius emphasizes that the slaves lose all hope and feel completely abandoned to their destiny, never to see freedom again. Full of lament, the author concludes his jeremiad with remarks about the utter desperation of the slaves, many of whom either commit suicide or try to flee, but then die from hunger and thirst (200). The poor souls of the slaves find themselves separated from the Christian community and exposed to the physical attacks by worldly forces, or rather, to intensifies this image, handed over to the power of the devil (200). At the same time, the author also admits that for every self-respecting Turk, head of a household, it was a matter of honor and social esteem to own at least one male or female slave (202).

He also describes how virtually all slaves think about how to escape, though hardly anyone ever succeeded in that, and then had to face severe consequences. Some slave owners, however, pursued the different path and offered their slaves contracts through which she could gain their freedom after they would have paid a certain amount of money (204). Georgius also complains bitterly about those dishonest people who pretend to offer an opportunity for gaining one's freedom through a payment, but who do nothing else but to resell the poor victim several times (206). Most interestingly, however, proves to be his comment that most of those who manage to regain their freedom through a money transaction do not return home to Christian lands because they have already established personal connections (marriage: "familiaritatem contraverunt," 208) or face too many difficulties in their endeavor. Finally, a huge number of young men are accepted in the Sultan's military service and form the famous units of the janissaries who had no reason to turn their back to the Muslim ruler.[138]

Georgius's main impetus remains, however, the deeply conflicting phenomenon that he had to realize the Turks' extraordinarily highly developed public culture and refinement, far superior to most European societies, including the public administration and government, and yet their adherence to a religion the Christian author rejected with all of his might. He himself felt for quite some time strongly attracted to Islam, but eventually, he could resist and then actually escape, allowing him to return to the Christian world.[139]

Altogether, however, Georgius pays the most attention to anthropological descriptions of the Turkish culture and society and especially of Islam, which seems to attract such huge numbers of people from all over the territories which the Ottomans had conquered, whereas Georgius's own experience as slave receives only secondary attention. After lengthy reflections on the differences between Islam and Christianity, and many attempts to explain why the latter was entirely superior, or rather, the only true religion, Gregorius concludes with a

---

[138] Godfrey Goodwin, *The Janissaries* (London: Saqi Books, 1994); David Nicolle *The Janissaries*. 11th ed. Elite Series, 58 (1995; London: Osprey Publishing, 2008); see also online at: https://en.wikipedia.org/wiki/Janissary (last accessed on Jan. 15, 2021) for a surprisingly solid bibliography, a well-structured historical overview, and images.

[139] Nancy Bisaha, *Creating East and West: Renaissance Humasists and the Ottoman Turks* (Philadelphia, PA: University of Philadelphia Press, 2004), 135–73.

few comments about the way how he managed to leave Turkey and to return home. His master, and the rest of the entire family tried with all their might to convince him not to depart for further scholarly studies, obviously afraid that he might use that explanation only as a pretext. The author openly admits that he was greatly loved by his master, but he had to make his way out of the world of slavery toward his long-aspired freedom.

He expressed with great relief that he was finally save from all further temptations to convert to Islam, a temptation which was obviously significant and could have achieved the break-through, otherwise he would not have resorted to the strong formulation: "diabolica infectione absolutus" (410; absolved from this devilish infection). He might have been a bit disingenuous in this regard, since he had truly felt inspired to take that path, and he also overplayed the 'slavery card' to some extent, commenting at the end one more time how horrible his 'imprisonment' had been (410). Indeed, he had lost his freedom, and he had been sold into slavery, but the author also seems to have experienced a fairly comfortable life with a certain degree of personal freedom to pursue his interests in studying Islam.

This does not mean, of course, that we could or should minimize his actual suffering, which comes through in various comments throughout the text, though it is not systematically put together. In the sixteenth chapter, for instance, Georgius outlines in general terms how he was treated by his first owner, a cruel peasant ("crudelitas," 298). Curiously, however, after he had been apprehended again following his first attempt to escape, this owner repressed his anger and did not mistreat the slave. Yet, he warned him about dire consequences if he ever dared to attempt another escape. Just this threat encouraged Georgius to do just that because he wanted rather to die than to live ("magis mori quam uiuere optabam," 298). His desire to experience a martyrdom thus was still strongly in him at that point.

The second escape followed soon, and this one also failed. The author then must have experienced horrible tortures, though he did not die from them. The less he goes into details here, the worse the punishment must have been: "hoc solum dico, quod non solum ea, que minatus fuerat, perfecit, sed omnia, que citra morten possunt fieri, sine aliqua misericordia crudeliter peregit" (298; I am telling you only so much that he did not only did that to me what he had threatened me with, but everything else what can be done except causing death, and this cruelly). Surprisingly, the owner's sisters then began to plead for the slave, so he was finally released from his shackles because they pledged for me that I would not flee again.

Georgius endeavored six more times to free himself, and always failed, which left him behind as a spiritually broken man: "fatigatus atque fractus"

(300). That final condition also triggered in him a curiosity about Islam as a possible alternative for his desperation and loss of faith in the Christian God (300–02). Nevertheless, he ultimately managed to preserve his original faith, and emerged unscathed as a good Christian, but not without many temptations, as this autobiographical account illustrates impressively. Georgius's *Tractatus* thus served specifically as a model narrative for many other possible victims who might end up in the same situation and then abandon their faith, as was actually the case in large numbers following the highly successful military operations by the Ottomans.[140]

We could here also refer to the famous Spanish poet Miguel de Cervantes (1547–1616), who was, together with his brother Rodrigo, while traveling by ship from Naples to Barcelona taken captive by Ottoman corsairs on September 26, 1575. Everyone on board was transported to Algiers to be sold as slaves, but the two brothers were held in prison to be released upon the payment of a ransom. In 1577, the lower middle-class family managed to secure the ransom money for Rodrigo, but not for Miguel. He remained in prison, but seems also have been taken to Istanbul for some time to work there in the construction of the Kılıç Ali Pasha Complex. Only in 1580, Miguel was freed after the Trinitarians, specializing in this Christian relief effort, had intervened and come up with the required sum of money. He returned to Madrid, but it is not clear what his occupation was there.[141]

Imprisonment and slavery were almost ubiquitous experiences throughout time, and the more we probe the lives and works of writers and poets in the pre-modern world, the more we encounter tragic cases of people who lost their freedom when they were attacked by pirates and became victims of the misfortunes of war. We might never find out the true numbers of all those prisoners, but they all certainly yearned to gain their freedom.

---

140 Tobias Graf, *The Sultan's Renegades: Christian-European Converts to Islam and the Making of the Ottoman Elite, 1575–1610* (Oxford: Oxford University Press, 2017). As outlined online about this book: "Examines why the figure of the renegade-a European Christian or Jew who had converted to Islam and was now serving the Ottoman sultan-is omnipresent in writings on the fifteenth to seventeenth century Ottoman Empire, when the Ottoman sultans posed a major political, military, and ideological challenge to Christian princes in Europe."
141 James Fitzmaurice-Kelly, *The Life of Miguel de Cervantes Saavedra*. Rpt. (1892; Norderstedt: Hansebooks GmbH, 2017); Maria Antonia Garcés, *Cervantes in Algiers: A Captive's Tale* (Nashville, TN: Vanderbilt University Press, 2002); Donald P. McCrory, *No Ordinary Man: The Life and Times of Miguel de Cervantes* (London: Peter Owen, 2005).

1.3 The Slave Harck Olufs

Considering the case of Harck Olufs (1708–1754), who was, along with the crew, taken a captive by Algerian pirates on their voyage from Nantes (south of the Normandy) to Hamburg – hence in the Atlantic waters, and not at all near Algeria – and then was sold on the slave market of Algier in 1724, we have clear evidence that the business of slavery continued well into the early modern age. His family, just like the Cervantes, could not afford to pay the ransom sum for their young son – he was only sixteen years of age at that time – and did not receive any help from the Slavery Fund of the Danish kingdom. Harck Olufs had been born in Northern Frisia, on the island of Amrum, which at that time belonged to the Danish crown. However, since his ship had traveled under the Hamburg flag, the appeal for financial help was rejected. The existence of such a fund indicates all by itself that the problem of high-sea piracy with resulting enslavement was commonly known and regarded as a great hardship for those affected. However, Denmark did not consider itself responsible for those who worked on German ships. Olufs's father, the sea captain Oluf Jensen, eventually succeeded in getting together the ransom sum, but it was then used to purchase back another man with the same name.

It would also be important to find out how the Algerian pirates communicated with Olufs's family back home, but we can be certain that capturing a ship and its crew served their desired goal only if the goods and the people could be commodified, so Olufs' destiny appears to have been a rather common one, whether on the Atlantic or in the Mediterranean. Basically, no one daring to go on a voyage or to work on a mercantile ship was safe from experiencing this destiny, as Hannah Barker has recently confirmed in her highly detailed, well-researched monograph, *That Most Precious Merchandise*.[142]

The young Olufs was thus stuck and could not regain his freedom, but he did not have to suffer as much as Georgius of Hungary or Johann Schiltberger, so it seems. From 1724 to 1728 he was a slave servant of the Bey of Constantine and advanced in responsibility to become the Bey's *gasnadal* (treasurer). Between 1728 and 1732 he was made Commander of the Life Guards. In 1732 he became Agha ed-Deira, Commander-in-Chief of the local cavalry. At some point, Olufs accompanied his lord, the Bey, on a pilgrimage to Mecca, which indicates that he must have converted to Islam and thus enjoyed his master's great respect. In 1735, he took part in the conquest of Tunis by the Algerian army during the disposal of Al-Husayn I ibn Ali. As a reward, Olufs was released on October 31 and

---

142 Barker, *That Most Precious Merchandise* (see note 119).

was allowed to return to Amrum in 1736, now a wealthy man who could afford to establish a family, although he seems to have had difficulties to reintegrate into his old, Christian, society.

Olufs wrote a lengthy autobiographical account about his destiny as a slave in Danish under the title *Avantures* published in Copenhagen in 1747, which was translated into German in 1751: *Harck Olufs aus der Insul Amron im Stifte Ripen in Jütland, gebürtig, sonderbare Avanturen, so sich mit ihm insonderheit zu Constantine und an andern Orten in Africa zugetragen.* He died in 1754 and was buried in Amrum, with his gravestone providing an abbreviated account of his adventurous life.[143] Although he was a slave, he experienced a rather pleasant life at court, where he first learned Turkish and Arabic, and served in ever more responsible functions, earning a good wage, which eventually allowed him to return home as a rich man.[144]

But every military conflict led to scores of people either being killed or taken prisoner, as we often hear in passing, whether in chronicles or in fictional texts (heroic epics). What the situation might have been like for those prisoners of war would be hard to imagine; considering modern cases as a result of the First or the Second World War, we can certainly assume that most of those miserable victims faced extremely hard times and were lucky if they even got out of that situation alive without too many damages to their health and physical being.[145]

---

143 Martin Rheinheimer, *Der fremde Sohn: Hark Olufs' Wiederkehr aus der Sklaverei.* Nordfriesische Quellen und Studien, 3 (Wachholtz: Neumünster 2001). For an edition of his autobiography, and similar reports of other victims, see *Verschleppt, Verkauft, Versklavt: deutschsprachige Sklavenberichte aus Nordafrika (1550–1800). Edition und Kommentar*, ed. Mario Klarer (Vienna: Böhlau, 2019). For images of his house, the gravestone, and the cover of his autobiography, see https://commons.wikimedia.org/wiki/Category:Hark_Olufs?uselang=de (last accessed on Jan. 15, 2021). See also *Muslimische Sklaverei: ein "vergessenes" Verbrechen. Die muslimische Sklaverei*, ed. Manfred Pittioni. Muslimische Sklaverei, 1 (Berlin and Münster: LIT, 2018).
144 For the German translation, see online at: https://web.archive.org/web/20120216001038/http://www.web.sdu.dk/mrh/autgerm.htm (last accessed on Jan. 15, 2021).
145 There are many bookshelves with studies addressing modern situations of prisoners of war all over the world; for the pre-modern era, see Rémy Ambühl, *Prisoners of War in the Hundred Years War: Ransom Culture in the Late Middle Ages* (Cambridge: Cambridge University Press, 2013); see now also the contributions to *Medieval Hostageship c.700-c.1500: Hostage, Captive, Prisoner of War, Guarantee, Peacemaker*, ed. Matthew Bennett and Katherine Weikert. Routledge Research in Medieval Studies (New York: Routledge, 2017).

2 Dante Alighieri and Boethius, Again

Imprisonment and Freedom in Theological Terms

And yet, there was a clear sense of freedom observed already in philosophy and in chronicles. Even medieval poets included numerous examples of individuals suffering in prisons, which I will reflect upon below in greater detail. Almost ironically, the worst, absolute, and final imprisonment was the one described by Dante Alighieri in his *Inferno*, the first part of his *Divina Commedia* (completed in ca. 1320).[146] Those 'sinners,' even including ancient philosophers and poets, such as Homer and Virgil, and also unbaptized children, are lost in this prison set up by God from which there is no escape.[147] Dante, however, only tours this underworld and experiences a kind of *catabasis*, being allowed to depart again while guided by the Roman poet through this divine prison. Yet, there is truly no way out of hell, as the inscription on top of the gate spells it out most ominously: "Abandon every hope, all you who enter" (Canto III, 9). As Virgil soon explains about the shrieks and laments they hear as soon as they have entered the first circle, those originate from those souls who "have no hope of truly dying, / and this blind life they lead is so abject / it makes them envy every other fate" (Canto III, 46–48). Similarly, the infernal ferryman Charon confirms this observation, shouting at these two wanderers through hell: "Give up all hope of ever seeing Heaven: / I come to lead you to the other shore, / into eternal darkness, ice, and fire" (Canto III, 85–87). Of course, the two pilgrims finally are able to leave hell, the eternal prison, but all the other evil souls have to stay behind and suffer badly. The psychological terror which this first part of Dante's *Divina*

---

146 Dante Alighieri, *The Divine Comedy*. Vol. I: *Inferno*, trans. with an intro., notes, and commentary by Mark Musa (see note 41); for a recent review of relevant Dante research, see Zygmunt G. Barański, "On Dante's Trail," Italian Studies 72.1 (2017): 1–15; *Dante Worlds: Echoes, Places, Questions*, ed. Peter Caravetta. Circolarità mediterranee, 2 (Rome and Bristol, CT: "L'Erma" di Bretschneider, 2019); *Ethics, Politics and Justice in Dante*, ed. Giulia Gaimari (London: UCL Press, 2019); *The Cambridge Companion to Dante's Commedia*, ed. Zygmunt G. Barański and Simon A. Gilson (Cambridge: Cambridge University Press, 2019); Alessandro Vettori, *Dante's Prayerful Pilgrimage: Typologies of Prayer in the Comedy*. Medieval and Renaissance Authors and Texts, 22 (Leiden and Boston: Brill, 2019).

147 Alan E. Bernstein, *The Formation of Hell: Death and Retribution in the Ancient and Early Christian Worlds* (London: UCL Press, 1993); *Himmel, Hölle, Fegefeuer: das Jenseits im Mittelalter*, ed. Peter Jezler (Zürich: Verlag Neue Zürcher Zeitung, 1994); Petra Korte, *Die antike Unterwelt im christlichen Mittelalter: Kommentierung – Dichtung – philosophischer Diskurs / Autoren*. Tradition – Reform – Innovation, 16 (Frankfurt a.M.: Peter Lang, 2012); Eileen Gardiner, "Hell, Purgatory, and Heaven," *Handbook of Medieval Culture* (see note 11), 653–73. See also the contributions to *Imagining the Medieval Afterlife*, ed. Richard Matthew Pollard (Cambridge: Cambridge University Press, 2020). The book was not yet out when I finished this study, so I could not yet consult it.

Commedia exerted is completely palpable and frightening, but it was not at all the only literary or artistic expression of hell as the ultimate and divine prison. Apart from countless narratives engaging with this pit, the lowest point of all existence, what Romanesque or Gothic church would not display at least some scenes of hell, of the day of Judgment, and the terrifying sensation of losing all of one's freedom for eternity?[148] And where would we fail to observe the very opposite, the glory of heaven, the realm of utmost, ultimate freedom?[149]

At the same time, we can also find direct parodies of this infernal universe, the absolute and final prison for the countless sinners here in this world. In his *Decameron* (ca. 1350), Boccaccio, in the eighth story told by Lauretta, presents the case of a crude farmer who is secretly locked away in a dark cell on behalf of the abbot who wants to have free access to his wife and sleep with her for ten months. This Ferondo firmly believes that he has ended up in Purgatory, receiving a beating twice a day by an 'angel,' one of the abbot's loyal monks helping him to carry out this charade. But once Ferondo's wife has become pregnant, the abbot arranges the 'prisoner's return to life, placing his newly intoxicated body into a tomb from which he then can rise as if indeed returning from purgatory. Anyone familiar with Dante's *Divina Commedia* would have immediately recognized the element of parody here.[150] I will return to this story below, placing it then into a different context.

Dante's major allegorical poem, the keystone of all of medieval literature, as we might say, addressing both the notion of the absolute and finite prison and the concept of ultimate freedom through the grace of God, thus takes us back in a major arc to Boethius, whose *Consolatio de philosophiae* was, after all, the foundational rock of the same noetic building. Philosophically and spiritually, the metaphor of the eternal prison was of greatest significance and exerted deep influence on all people in the pre-modern age, and this although the New Testament had more or less explicitly promised a liberation of all people

---

148 For a rather religious interpretation, focusing on the notion of personal guilt, both in biblical and modern psychological terms, see now Hermann Wohlgschaft, *Schuld und Versöhnung: das Letzte Gericht und die größere Hoffnung* (Würzburg: Echter, 2019). See also the contributions to *A Companion to the Premodern Apocalypse*, ed. Michael A. Ryan. Brill's Companions to the Christian Tradition (Leiden and Boston: Brill, 2016).

149 Peter Dinzelbacher, *Himmel, Hölle, Heilige: Visionen und Kunst im Mittelalter* (Darmstadt: Primus Verlag, 2002), offers a wide selection of primary material in medieval literature and art. See also the excellent catalog accompanying an exhibition, *Himmel, Hölle, Fegefeuer: Das Jenseits im Mittelalter*, ed. Peter Jezler (see note 147).

150 Angelo M. Mangini, "Il purgatorio di Ferondo, e quello di Forese: L'intertestualità dantesca in Decameron III.8 e la questione dei suffragi," *Lettere Italiane* 69.1 (2017): 59–82.

through Christ's harrowing of hell (1 Peter 4:6; Ephesians 4:9; Acts of Pilate, also known as the *Gospel of Nicodemus*).[151]

Before we proceed too quickly, we hence need to examine first how this late antique philosopher and politician reflected on his experience in prison and how he translated it into a universal lesson that has carried over until today and can be regarded as the most seminal critical reflection upon the basic human condition here on earth.[152] While Thomas More, with whom I began, quickly transformed the lesson provided by Boethius into a Christian teaching, the sixth-century philosopher did not pursue a religious perspective; instead, he argued in abstract, logical terms and outlined not a spiritual reading, but a critical approach to the question what might constitute true happiness. Boethius has the allegorical figure of Philosophy appear in his prison cell and engage in a deep conversation about the actual nature of Fortune, which proves to be nothing but fickle, though it is constant in its very fickleness and can be trusted in that regard because change is its very nature.

Fortune entrusts individuals with power, wealth, fame, personal physical happiness, and the like, but it also takes all of those away again, deconstructing the trust which human beings place in those mundane forms of happiness. In this regard, Fortune provides a sense of truth because when misfortune strikes, only then one fully learns who is one's friend. And those who suffer from misfortune also realize the truth that they had lived a life of contingency which can never be trusted. Moreover, Philosophy also points out the disconnect between Boethius's long life filled with happiness and the present miserable

---

[151] There are many solid entries in various theological lexica; see, for instance, A. Grillmeier, "Höllenabstieg Christi, Höllenfahrt Christi," *Lexikon für Theologie und Kirche*. 2nd completely rev. ed. by Josef Höfer and Karl Rahner. Vol. 5 (Freiburg i. Br.: Herder, 1960), cols. 450–55; but see also the excellent material on the web, especially visual representations, https://en.wikipedia.org/wiki/Harrowing_of_Hell#Scripture (last accessed on Jan. 15, 2021).

[152] There are many good editions and translations of this text; here I rely on Boethius, *Consolation of Philosophy*, trans., with intro. and notes, by Joel C. Relihan (Indianapolis, IN, and Cambridge: Hackett Publishing, 2001). For critical studies, see, for instance, *Boethius: His Life, Thought and Influence*, ed. Margaret Gibson (Oxford: Basil Blackwell, 1981); Ralph McInerny, "Boethius," *Medieval Philosophers*, ed. Jermiah Hackett. Dictionary of Literary Biography, 115 (Detroit and London: Gale Research, 1992), 110–17; Joachim Gruber, *Kommentar zu Boethius De Consolatione Philosophiae*. Texte und Kommentare – eine altertumswissenschaftliche Reihe, 9 (Berlin and New York: Walter de Gruyter, 1978); John Marenbon, *Boethius* (Oxford: Oxford University Press, 2004); cf. also the contributions to *The Cambridge Companion to Boethius*, ed. John Marenbon (Cambridge: Cambridge University Press, 2009); *Boethius Christianus? Transformationen der "Consolatio Philosophiae" in Mittelalter und Früher Neuzeit*, ed. Reinhold Glei (Berlin and New York: Walter de Gruyter, 2010); Joachim Gruber, *Boethius: eine Einführung*. Standorte in Antike und Christentum, 2 (Stuttgart: Anton Hiersemann, 2011).

state that is guaranteed to lead to his execution. So, she alerts him to the fact that he has plenty of reasons to be happy about his good fortune in the past.

Most important, though, we do not find real happiness in this material existence because everything is contingent and hence fleeting. By contrast, true happiness is defined logically by self-sufficiency, oneness, or wholeness, or unity, which are different words for the supreme good. Of course, this makes Boethius to a Neo-Platonist, but he can thus explain in a logical manner how the individual can make his way through the endless waves of life that all pretend to offer happiness, but only serve an illusion of the real form of it. All beings desire to be reunited with the original self, so they only need to allow that inner instinct to come to full fruition in order to experience the rapproachment of self and the inner good by way of self-sufficiency, i.e., not needing any influx from the outside. This then leads over to more philosophical and ethical question regarding the existence of evil, which Philosophy essentially denies because the worldly manifestation of evil constitutes only a form of self-deception. In our daily lives, there are evils, of course, and Boethius himself is suffering from evil individuals who brought false charges against him, but Philosophy argues that those are evil individuals who are the weakest of all because they cannot even follow their own instinct toward the good and so turn actually against their own inner self.[153]

There are many more issues addressed in *De consolatione philosophiae*, but suffice it here for us to be content with the realization that Boethius successfully transformed his prison experience into a staging ground for his most influential development of these philosophical ideas. Where do we actually find him at the beginning of Book One? In prison, and thus we are granted a universal forum of prison writing, but here with the unique twist that the physical loss of freedom translates into a spiritual form of freedom for Boethius, and subsequently all of his successors throughout the following centuries.

However, the treatise begins with quite different terms, that is, with poetry in which Boethius pours out the sorrows of his heart over his personal misery, having lost all of his previous power and being handed over to grief and weeping. Appealing to the muses, he endeavors to find the right words for his deep sorrow so he can give vent to the truly miserable experience he finds himself in: "lachrymose elegy's truth" (4). He contrasts his own present stage, being an old miserable man, with the delights of his youth: "Pain gave the order; its years now must be added to mine" (10). Death should come not to those who enjoy the

---

[153] Albrecht Classen, "Boethius' 'De consolatione philosophiae'. Eine 'explication du texte'," *Jahrbuch für internationale Germanistik* XXXII.2 (2000): 44–61.

pleasures of youth, but to those who are "stricken with grief" (14), i.e., are old and ailing. At the same time, Boethius laments the changing face of Fortune: "she's darkly transformed her appearances, ever deceitful" (19), but there is no answer, until suddenly Philosophy arrives and greets him as her old student who should know better and only has forgotten her previous lessons. Imprisonment thus turns into a metaphor for the notion of lack of freedom in intellectual, spiritual, and mental terms.

The first task for Philosophy is to chase away the muses who are sitting at the victim's bedside and inspire him to compose his verses of doom and gloom (p. 3). She calls them: "these the women who choke out the rich fields of reason's fruits; theirs are the barren brambles of the passions; they acclimatize the mortal mind to disease, and do not liberate it" (p. 3). What this teacher then does is to remedy the "confusion of my mind" (p. 3) and to provide Boethius with the very lesson outlined above. His real problem proves not to be his imprisonment, but the fact that he "has forgotten himself for a time" (p. 5). Nevertheless, she is confident that "he'll remember easily enough, since he knew us once before" (p. 5).

For Boethius, it seems strange at first to observe Philosophy here in the prison cell together with him, maybe because she suffers from equally "trumped-up charges" (p. 6). This is, of course, not the case, though she quickly alerts him to previous cases of major philosophers who had to suffer their untimely death because they had been charged with treason, such as Socrates who "won the victory of an unjust death while I stood at his side" (p. 7).

Imprisonment as the result of the actions by the mob, as Philosophy herself calls it, has regularly affected the righteous and the wise, the intelligent and the leaders of their people. Mob mentality determines the masses of the envious, jealous, ignoramuses, cowards, and power-hungry, whereas Philosophy stands high above them all, aloof and unaffected by the raging of the foolish masses: their army "is not led by any general but is only yanked this way and that, at random, by a berserk aimlessness" (p. 7). She assures Boethius that "we laugh at them from on high as they snatch at each and every worthless thing—we are safe from all their maddened riot, protected by a wall that marauding stupidity is forbidden to assault" (p. 8–9). The mob was, in other words, already at work in antiquity, and then also in the Middle Ages, threatening the well-being of the intellectual, ethical, and spiritual elite, throwing them into prison, robbing them of their freedom and then also of their lives.[154] Boethius at least

---

[154] Albrecht Classen, "Die Gefahren des Massenwahns aus literarhistorischer Sicht: Von Walther von der Vogelweide und Heinrich Wittenwiler zu Thomas Mann und Gustave Le Bon," *Im*

bitterly complains about the malfiesance committed against him when someone fabricated a letter in which he allegedly desired to bring about Roman liberty and thus committed treason against the Ostrogoth King Theoderic I. As Boethius then bitterly bursts forth: "sacrilegious men have undertaken lawless efforts against virtue" (p. 11), whereupon he goes one step further and voices not only astonishment, but bitterness and a feeling of incredulity: "that the lawless … are powerful against innocence while God is watching over it – this is like some monstrosity" (p. 12).

In other words, the prisoner Boethius is completely aghast that God would even tolerate such uncalled-for injustice against people like him who have worked hard their entire life to protect and serve the state. As he then formulates full of protest and anger: "For what sort of a crime did even a full and open confession ever produce judges so unanimous in their mercilessness that neither the fallibility of human intelligence nor the universal unpredictability of human fortune and circumstance could make som of them bend" (p. 12).[155] The abomination of the false court and false witnesses, the failure to accept Boethius's complete innocence, makes him scream out at Philosophy, asking desperately for an explanation of this horrible situation with no justice left (p. 13). As he also formulates: "It disgusts me to bring to mind what the gossip is now, how discordant and how diverse are the popular beliefs" (p. 13). The workings of Fortune disgust him, and that is, of course, the core of his inner sickness, as Philosophy then

---

Clash der Identitäten: Nationalismen im literatur- und kulturgeschichtlichen Diskurs, ed. Wolfgang Brylla and Cezary Lipiński. Andersheit – Fremdheit – Ungleichheit: Erfahrungen von Disparatheit in der deutschsprachigen Literatur, 1 (Göttingen: V&R unipress, 2020), 185–99; for modern approaches to the phenomenon of the masses, see Petra Kuhnau, *Masse und Macht in der Geschichte: zur Konzeption anthropologischer Konstanten in Elias Canettis Werk "Masse und Macht"*. Epistemata. Reihe Literaturwissenschaft, 195 (Würzburg: Königshausen & Neumann, 1996); Uwe Israel, "Masse und Stadt: die Bewältigung großer Menschenmengen im Mittelalter am Beispiel von Nürnberg," *Concilium medii aevi: Zeitschrift für Geschichte, Kunst und Kultur des Mittelalters und der Frühen Neuzeit* 15 (2012): 151–83.

155 See the contributions to *Treason: Medieval and Early Modern Adultery, Betrayal, and Shame*, ed. Larissa Tracy. Explorations in Medieval Culture, 10 (Leiden and Boston: Brill, 2019); cf. also Albrecht Classen, "Treason: Legal, Ethical, and Political Issues in the Middle Ages: With an Emphasis on Medieval Heroic Poetry," *Journal of Philosophy and Ethics* 1.4 (2019): 13–29; https://www.sryahwapublications.com/journal-of-philosophy-and-ethics/pdf/v1-i4/2.pdf (last accessed on Jan. 15, 2021). For valuable reflections on treason from antiquity to the present, see now the contributions to *Verräter: Geschichte eines Deutungsmusters*, ed. André Kritscher (Vienna, Cologne, and Weimar, 2019). The editor emphasizes correctly that recent nationalist trends globally have suddenly profiled the notion of treason or of the traitor intensively. Traitors such as Judas, Brutus, King Tasso III of Bavaria, and traitors in the *Nibelungenlied* or in Dante's *Divina Commedia* are the focus of those studies dealing with the issue in antiquity and the Middle Ages.

quickly realizes, whereupon she has to embark on her teaching to heal her student from his profound misunderstanding and self-deception.

We do not need to pursue the treatise much further here, since our interest is only focused on the tension between freedom and imprisonment, and hence, at least in this case, between justice and injustice. It might seem surprising, but Boethius's vehement protests could actually have been formulated even today:

> the wicked workshops of lawless men overflowing in joy and jubilation; every last degenerate making threats with brand-new deceptions and denunciations; good men fallen, laid low by their fear of this crisis of mine; every last criminal encouraged to dare a crime because he will go unpunished, and to commit it because he will be rewarded; and the guiltless deprived not only of their safety but even of their defense (p. 14).

Significantly, once the treatise has progressed further, the actual prison situation is mostly lost out of sight, and at the end we do not even hear anything anymore about it. Instead, Philosophy concludes with the generic advice: "Avoid vice, cherish virtues; raise up your minds to blameless hopes; extend your humble prayers into the lofty heights" (150). Certainly, Boethius raises the issue several times throughout the narrative why evil exist, why evil people have so much power over good ones, especially at the beginning of Book IV, but he is quickly instructed by Philosophy about the true nature of evil, which is really a no-entity and the complete opposite of goodness toward which all beings actually strive. Even though the prisoner is suffering badly from his miserable situation, facing certain death despite his repeatedly claimed innocence, Philosophy ultimately enlightens him that the actions of evil people are nothing but self-deception because they struggle against their own self and deny the natural instinct toward goodness, meaning that they ultimately eliminate themselves.

Materially, Boethius has to accept his condition in prison, his complete lack of freedom, but in philosophical terms, as this treatise illustrates, what matters is not freedom or the lack thereof, but the individual awareness about the nature of Fortune and the true idea of all being, that is, the movement toward the Good. Both the false charges against Boethius and his condemnation to death are nothing but weak expressions of those evil people's attempt to fight against their own instinct, namely to aim for the Good, and the more Boethius and others have to suffer at the hands of the evil individuals, the more the latter deconstruct themselves, at least in idealistic terms. Freedom and imprisonment thus prove to be negotiable terms that cannot be easily be defined, as this philosopher indicated already through his treatise.

At the end, Philosophy, in her arguments with the prisoner, goes so far as to suggest that freedom and slavery are actually the results of one's own intellectual capacity and need to be understood in metaphysical terms above all, irrespective of the actual suffering by the individual:

> Now it is necessarily the case that human souls are indeed at their freest when they preserve themselves intact within the contemplation of the divine mind; but they are less free when they fall away toward bodies, and still less free when they are tied to limbs of earthly matter. At the possession of the reason that belongs to them because they have sturrended themselves to vices. For once they have cast their eyes down from the light of the highest truth to the lower and shadowy realms, they are soon darkened over by the cloud of unknowing, they are caught in the whirlwind of destructive passions. By yielding to these passions and agreeing with them they help along the slavery that they have brought down upon themselves and, in a certain sense, they are the captives of their own liberty. (p. 129, Book V, Prose Two)

3 Freedom and Imprisonment since Antiquity

Kurt Raaflaub, among many others, has already succinctly summarized the historical idea of freedom in the ancient world which was clearly characterized by many different discourses on the role of the individual vis-à-vis society, hence freedom versus lack thereof. Many of the wars during that earlier period were predicated on the desire to gain freedom from a hegemon, but it did not mean completely individual freedom, as we might conceive of it. Much more important proved to be the notion of ideal freedom:

> The use of freedom in philosophy was more complex. Fifth-century sophists emphasized the strong individual's right to erupt from enslavement by the conventions of nomos and rule over the weaker in accordance with nature (Antiphon, Callicles in Plato's Gorgias). Others contested the validity of traditional social distinctions; Alcidamas declared slavery as contrary to nature. Despite Aristotle's elaborate refutation (Politics 1), this view was echoed by the Stoics (see Stoicism) and discussed thoroughly by Roman jurists. Yet other sophists propagated cosmopolitanism, individualism, and 'freedom from the state' (Aristippus).[156]

While philosophers such as Plato scoffed at the notion of personal freedom as something irrelevant, the Epicureans and Stoics fully embraced this ideal as the ultimate goal in life. The situation in ancient Rome underwent a complex process, with political freedom increasingly abandoned as an ideal publicly de-

---

[156] Kurt Raaflaub, "freedom in the ancient world," *The Oxford Companion to Classical Civilization*, ed. Simon Hornblower and Antony Spawforth (Oxford: Oxford University Press, 1998; published online, 2003), https://www.oxfordreference.com/view/10.1093/acref/9780198601654.001.0001/acref/9780198601654-e-276 (last accessed on Jan. 15, 2021).

fended, especially in the wake of the rise of the Roman empire. At the same time, Christianity taught a spiritual form of freedom, though not here in this world, but in the afterworld under God. "Christians did not oppose slavery as an institution, but in accepting slaves into their community they anticipated the universal brotherhood of the free expected in another world."[157] But late Roman society was aflush with slaves, many of whom performed critical tasks in the household, and also in the military. Whether slavery then declined during the early and high Middle Ages proves to be a complex issue, as I have indicated already above. The difficulty of this topic consists of its high level of fluidity because each society, each social group, and each political entity defined itself in different terms and thus had different concepts about the meaning of freedom and slavery. However, we can be certain, unfortunately, that the struggle for freedom continues until today, and this in constant negotiations with governmental forces, legal stipulations, fundamental laws, and, probably the most important, countless different power structures.

In fact, slave trade continues until today, though no longer in the open. Kidnapping happens all the time in many parts of our world, and the prison population is growing rapidly, especially in the United States. To what extent would we be willing to abandon our freedoms in order to have the government protect us from the COVID-19 virus, or to allow the police to exert its power and authority over us in order persecute criminals? These are modern questions, but Boethius felt very much in the same situation when he was stuck in his prison cell. We grasp, in other words, that these two extremely opposed aspects constitute truly fundamental issues for all societies throughout history. At issue is not only individual freedom, but social freedom, meaning, the form of government in place during the various phases from antiquity to today.[158] This does not even address the huge question of gender-specific forms of freedom because in most societies until today men's freedom differed from that of women.

Much of philosophy and religion are determined by the question regarding the relationship between individual and the authorities/God, so our reflections would immediately fling wide open any limitations we might want to pursue to get a good handle of the central ideas determining this volume. But the very breadth of concepts regarding freedom already underscores the universal

---

157 Raaflaub, "freedom in the ancient world" (see note 156). See now also Alexander Demandt, *Magistra Vitae: Essays zum Lehrgehalt der Geschichte*. Historica Minora, 4 (Vienna, Cologne, and Weimar: Böhlau, 2020), 93–216.
158 See the studies on "Herrschaft" in antiquity (Hans Kloft), the Middle Ages (Hans-Werner Goetz), and the early modern time (Johann Baptist Müller) in *Europäische Mentalitätsgeschichte: Hauptthemen in Einzeldarstellungen*, ed. Peter Dinzelbacher (see note 8), 519–61.

value and importance of this topic. Tom Denter, for instance, alerts us to the following sequence of names in the long tradition of engaging with freedom: Plato already indicated in his allegory of the cave the extent to which all people are dependent on their perception of reality. Socrates (d. 399 B.C.E.) was forced to drink poison as a punishment for his demands that thinking should enjoy all freedom. Emperor Marcus Aurelius (121–180 C.E.) realized in his *Meditations* (170–180) the limitations of human freedom, always subject to our desires, and sought to find a place for the self within the universe. Thomas Aquinas identified the human dependency from God in his *Quaestio disputata de malo* (ca. 127), and Martin Luther fought for the freedom of every Christian from the authorities (*Freiheit eines Christenmenschen*, 1520). René Descartes highlighted again that all people are dependent on the divine *creatio continua* (*Meditationes de prima philosophia*, 1614).

The list goes on, and we could thus determine the philosophical discourse as being predicated on comprehending the correlation between the individual and the divine, between freedom and lack thereof, as is also beautifully and movingly expressed in Marguerite de Navarre's allegorical poem *Les Prisons*, left unfinished at her death in 1549, in which she reflects on the soul's need to liberate itself from the prison of love and from the prison of material existence.[159] Freedom can pertain to our inner thoughts, our faith, or ideology, and it can pertain to our political empowerment or lack thereof. Does the individual possess a free

---

159 Tom Denter, "Freiheit," *Lexikon der Geisteswissenschaften: Sachbegriffe – Disziplinen – Personen* (Vienna, Cologne, and Weimar: Böhlau, 2011), 207–19. As to Marguerite's work, see her *Les Prisons*, ed. and commentary by Simone Glasson. Textes littéraires français, 260 (Geneva: Droz, 1978); Marguerite de Navarre, *The Prisons of Marguerite de Navarre: An English Verse Translation*, trans. Hilda Dale (Reading, United Kingdom: Whiteknights Press, 1989); Marguerite de Navarre, *Les prisons: A French and English Edition*, ed. Claire Lynch Wade. American University Studies. Ser. 2: Romance Languages and Literature, 99 (New York, Bern, et al.: Peter Lang, 1989). Very movingly, she begins: "Beloved Friend, I will confess to you / That I for many a year almost despised / Sweet liberty with all its happiness, / Content to be in prison, where I lay / Through love of you; for torments suffered there / Were pastimes dear, and welcome were its chains. / Then did the darkness seem to bring me light / And sunlight was as darkness and deep gloom; / I cried and wept but thought I laughed and sang, / While iron doors enclosing me, with bolts / And bars, grilles, chains and walls of stoutest stone, / More grateful were to me than open fields" (1–12). Although aiming at an allegorical reading of the prison as a symbol of her love and life, the poet still succeeded in outlining some of the concrete realities of a prison cell, more than most other poets before her. At the same time, she explicitly formulated the wonders of liberty, here in spiritual terms, beginning in book two when she gets out of her prison and gazes at the miraculous beauty of nature. Most recently, see Cynthia Skenazi, "Les Prisons' Poetics of Conversion," *A Companion to Marguerite de Navarre*, ed. Gary Ferguson, Gary and Mary B. McKinley. Brill's Companions to the Christian Tradition, 42 (Leiden: Brill, 2013), 211–35.

will, or is it dependent on destiny or providence? Certainly, this was an issue that extensively occupied Boethius, and after him countless generations of other philosophers. To do justice to this topic, we would have to illuminate the theoretical concepts as developed by Immanuel Kant and other Enlightenment philosophers, but it is obvious enough for our purposes that the issue has always been of critical importance for each society, its ideology, and theoretical and religious frame of mind, as reflected, above all, in Johann Gottlieb Fichte's *Wissenschaftslehre* (1793–1813), who aimed at creating a platform in intellectual terms where all individuals could aspire for their philosophical freedom, finding themselves and their ideas being without limitations. Kantian idealism, empiricism, pragmatism, existentialism, determinism and indeterminism, but then also questions pertaining to democracy, dictatorship, tyranny, and other forms of political systems have deeply determined the debate regarding freedom.

Following many of the standard lexica and encyclopedia dedicated to the Middle Ages, however, the notion of freedom does not seem to have been of significance; often, there are no lemmata included to address this issue.[160] By contrast, recent years have seen an upswell or growth in relevant studies focused on the issue of tyranny.[161] The reasons for this renewed interests are quite obvious because the critical examination of the form of royal government allows us profoundly to comprehend the power structures prevalent in the various medieval and early modern kingdoms. Hans Joachim Schmidt now looks at the individual models of government as outlined already in the Old Testament, in ancient sources, in early medieval encyclopedias (Isidor of Seville), in theological writings (St. Augustine), and papal treatises (Gregory the Great), and then moves to the dominant concepts as practiced by Charlemagne, Louis the Pious, and their suc-

---

160 See, for instance, *The Oxford Dictionary of the Middle Ages*, ed. Robert E. Bjork, 4 vols. (Oxford: Oxford University Press, 2010). Vol. 2, for instance, contains only entries for "free cities," "free royal cities," "free spirit, doctrine of," and "free will" (668–69). Aryeh Grabois, *The Illustrated Encyclopedia of Medieval Civilization* (London: Octopus Books; Jerusalem: The Jerusalem Publishing House, 1980), does not even include any lemma concerning freedom. I must admit that I did not think about this topic either when I put together the *Handbook of Medieval Culture: Fundamental Aspects and Conditions of the European Middle Ages*, ed. Albrecht Classen (see note 11).
161 Mario Turchetti, *Tyrannie et tyrannicide de l'Antiquité à nos jours*. Bibliothèque de la Renaissance, 11 (Paris: Classiques Garnier, 2013); see now the contributions to *Criticising the Ruler in Pre-Modern Societies – Possibilities, Chances, and Methods*, ed. Karina Kellermann, Alheydis Plassmann, and Christian Schwermann. Macht und Herrschaft, 6 (Göttingen: Bonn University Press/V&R unipress, 2019); see my review in *Mediaevistik* 33 (forthcoming in 2021); Hans-Joachim Schmidt, *Herrschaft durch Schrecken und Liebe: Vorstellungen und Begründungen im Mittelalter*. Orbis mediaevalis, 17 (Göttingen: V&R unipress, 2019).

cessors, the negative image of Attila the Hun, kingship in the twelfth and thirteenth centuries (especially Emperor Frederick II), political instructions of rulers (mirrors for princes), and finally, which almost comprises the bulk of his study, the political discourse in urban settings during the late Middle Ages (Aegidius Romanus, Engelbert of Admont, John Duns Scotus, Remigio dei Girolami, Henry of Ghent, Geoffrey of Fontaines, Brunetto Latini, Marsilio of Padua, William of Occam, and others. One of the highlights often proves to be the question how the ruler can learn to love his people and serve as their ruler in the name of God, serving the entire community, and abstaining from dictatorial positions: "Liebe als Klebstoff des Staates" (Love as the glue that holds the state together).[162] In light of these extensive investigations, it appears quite surprising that the notion of individual freedom does not emerge as we might have expected, but we would always have to keep in mind that pre-modern society was deeply determined by a hegemonic thinking, subjecting each individual into a social order which was ultimately governed by God in His omnipotence.[163]

In the world of the laws, however, the notion of freedom, of free people and the opposite individuals mattered critically, if we think, for instance, of the famous *Sachsenspiegel* (Saxon Mirror) from ca. 1225/30 where we read, for instance:

> Freemen and imperial ministerials can certainly be witnesses before the realm and determine a judgment. By these means, each performs his service to the realm according to his legal status. However, ministerials of the realm may not reach a judgment concerning a person of the *Schöffen* class or be witness for him when it may damage life, reputation, or health. (Book III, 19)[164]

Charters and legal records quickly reveal the extent to which the notion of 'freedom,' certainly in its medieval context, mattered critically since cities, monasteries, abbeys, territories, and other entities were keenly concerned with their own liberty and guarded themselves carefully against any attempts by the superior lord, or king, to swallow them up and rob them of their freedom. In charters, we commonly hear of liberty, meaning the privilege granted to a landowner. The *Formulary of Marculf* (compiled after 700 C.E.) contains the note that a bish-

---

162 Schmidt, *Herrschaft durch Schrecken und Liebe* (see note 161), 663.
163 For an anthology of relevant texts regarding tyrannicide in the Middle Ages, see *Tyrannentötung: eine Textsammlung*, ed. Wilhelm Baum (Munich: Herbert Utz Verlag, 2017). However, there does not seem any good chronological or thematic order, as Baum compiles texts from antiquity to the present in a rather disorganized manner.
164 *The Saxon Mirror: A Sachsenspiegel of the Fourteenth Century* (see note 92), 120; see also 93, 107, 127, 129, 130, 197, 198 (cf. also the lemmata for 'freehold' and 'freedmen').

op granted *libertatis privilegium* to an abbey. Similarly, bishops, churches, and monasteries requested privileges from the rulers to guarantee their independence from local authorities, freeing them from paying taxes or providing service. Grants of territorial liberty consequently required the assent of many power players, such as bishops, counts, and the king.[165] Of course, the relationship between a king and his subjects differed from country to country, and we would have to review a vast tapestry of individual political entities across medieval Europe and beyond in order to understand the complex power structures as they evolved over the centuries.

The signing of the *Magna Carta* in 1215 and the rise of the Swiss Confederation at about the same time are only two of the major political events during the thirteenth century in which the political will toward freedom gained momentum and was increasingly carved out of the central power structure.[166] In general, we would have to be very careful in our assessment of medieval power structures since the king was certainly dependent on many different forces and had to negotiate virtually all of his moves and decisions, which allowed a considerable degree of freedom to enter the political stage, at least for the high-ranking barons and princes.[167] Even though we might have to accept a rather broad definition of freedom in this context, we still can recognize the extent to which all power structures are contingent and hardly ever absolute, especially in the Middle Ages. It would be entirely erroneous, for instance, to talk about 'sovereignty' of a medieval ruler because neither kings nor emperors, and also not the popes, could ever hope to achieve absolute dominion, such as in the case of the famous and glorious French ruler, Louis XIV. Sovereignty was only the hallmark of early modern rulers, especially during the time of absolutism. Medieval kings, by con-

---

165 Alan Harding, "Political Liberty in the Middle Ages," *Speculum* 55.3 (1980): 423–43.

166 Dēmētrios L. Kyriazēs-Gubelēs, *Magna Carta: Palladium der Freiheiten oder Feudales Stabilimentum*. Schriften zur Verfassungsgeschichte, 36 (Berlin: Duncker & Humblot, 1984); James C. Holt, *Magna Carta*. 2nd ed. (Cambridge and New York: Cambridge University Press, 1992); John Hamilton Baker, *The Reinvention of Magna Carta 1216–1616* (Cambridge: Cambridge University Press, 2017); Jennifer Jahner, *Literature and Law in the Era of Magna Carta*. Oxford Studies in Medieval Literature and Culture (Oxford: Oxford University Press, 2019); Mario Caravale, *Magna carta libertatum* (Bologna: Il mulino, 2020).

167 Lucy K. Pick, *Her Father's Daughter: Gender, Power, and Religion in the Early Spanish Kingdoms* (Ithaca, NY, and London: Cornell University Press, 2017). Though she focuses on the role of Iberian queens, she also uncovers the significant element of royal dependency at large: "Power in the early Spanish kingdoms, and indeed throughout the medieval world, worked through networks of relationships. The king may have been the apex or focal point of the network, but for his power to be exercised, it had to be shared" (19). See now also the contributions to *Criticising the Ruler in Pre-Modern* (see note 161).

trast, were deeply dependent on countless different forces, and had to grant their barons and other nobles a considerable degree of independence, if not freedom.[168] Hence, both in legal and in political terms, there are many loopholes and opportunities to be found which individuals utilized throughout the Middle Ages to pursue their own lives, to stay clear of the rule and dominance of a territorial ruler, a bishop, a king, or even an emperor.

Already Boethius had pointed out this fundamental weakness of all rulers and the infinite strength of the spiritually free individual:

> Once a tyrant thought that he would by torture compel a free man to betray his partners in a conspiracy formed against him; but that man bit his own tongue and cut it off and spat it out in the face of that infuriated tyrant. And that was how a wise man made his tortures an opportunity for virtue, when the tyrant had thought that they were an opportunity for bloodletting" (Book II, Prose 6, 40).

And in a slightly different context:

> What is this power that cannot banish the gnawing of their anxieties [of the tyrants], that cannot avoid the stings and barbs of their fears? To be sure, they would themselves wish to live without such anxieties, but they cannot; and thereupon they boast about their power .... Do you think a man is powerful when he travels in the company of bodyguards, when he is more faraid of those whom he intimidates than they are of him, when the appearance of his power is placed in the hands of those who serve him. (Book III, Prose 5, 60)

It would go much too far to claim that the modern discourse on freedom, democracy, and, its very opposite, dictatorship originated directly from the Middle Ages, but by the same token freedom and imprisonment have always been regarded as fundamental contrasts people are deeply concerned with, and this also in the pre-modern era. To be clear, however, we are not discussing here philosophical issues such as freedom and will within the cosmic order correlating

---

168 Strangely, Brett Edward Whalen, *The Two Powers: The Papacy, the Empire, and the Struggle for Sovereignty in the Thirteenth Century* (Philadelphia, PA: University of Pennsylvania Press, 2019), argues just the opposite, at least in the introduction and the epilogue, but stays mostly clear from this notion throughout his entire study. See now the review by Cary J. Nederman, forthcoming in *Mediaevistik* 33 (2021). For a classic study on the problematic issue of sovereignty, see Quentin Skinner, *Foundations of Modern Political Thought*. 2 vols. (Cambridge and New York: Cambridge University Press, 1978); Dieter Grimm, *Sovereignty: The Origin and Future of a Political and Legal Concept*. Columbia Studies in Political Thought / Political History (New York: Columbia University Press, 2015); Martin Philipp Sommerfeld, *Staatensouveränität und ius cogens; eine Untersuchung zu Ursprung und Zukunftsfähigkeit der beiden Konzepte im Völkerrecht. State Sovereignty and ius cogens*. Beiträge zum ausländischen öffentlichen Recht und Völkerrecht, 287 (Berlin: Springer, 2019).

the individual with God, as St. Augustine, as one of the first major thinkers in the post-Roman era, elaborated those categories in *De civitate dei* 14.7, *De libero arbitrio* 3.74; *Ad Simplicianum* 1.2.21; *De civitate dei* 1.16 – 28; *De duabus animabus* 15; and *Contra Iulianum* 6.70.[169] Boethius also reflected deeply on the relationship between providence and free will, but these are very abstract notions that do not concern us here.

Instead, our focus rests on the concrete physical experience of having lost one's freedom of movement, being stuck in a prison cell for whatever reason, whether justified or not, as Boethius clamored loudly and clearly. Every society, whether the Carolingian Empire or late medieval Portugal, pursued its own laws and set up rules regarding what was considered legal and what not. In this regard, the Icelandic epic poem, *Njáls' Saga* (twelfth century?) proves to be most eye-opening because there we encounter a society in the making, with Njál constantly trying to formulate new laws and setting up more advanced legal structures in order to fend off blood-feuds and open violence. Tragically, of course, at the end he succumbs to the very chaotic conditions in his society that he tried to regulate, but there is hope that subsequently social, legal, ethical, moral, and religious values can be relied on and trusted, at least more than in the past.[170]

4 The Magna Carta

Legal and Political Efforts to Establish Early Forms of Freedom

Even if the notion of 'freedom' as expressed in the *Magna Carta* cannot be easily identified with that which we today hold up so highly as the foundation of our modern, western system, there is general agreement that all discussions about 'freedom' ought to use this famous document as a bedrock of the entire political discourse, at least in England since the early thirteenth century. It was signed by King John of England at Runnymede, near Windsor, on June 15, 1215 and reissued it the next year, and then once again in 1225 in order to gain the privilege to raise new taxes. As we can see in the case of King Edward I, who followed the same pattern, reconfirming the validity of the *Magna Carta* in May of 1270 and 1297, the issue of freedom, at least for the political grandes, became a bargaining chip for money and influence.

---

[169] Christian Tornau, "Saint Augustine," *The Stanford Encyclopedia of Philosophy* (Summer 2020 edition), ed. Edward N. Zalta, https://plato.stanford.edu/archives/sum2020/entries/augustine/ (last accessed on Jan. 15, 2021).
[170] *Njal's Saga*, trans. with intro. and notes by Robert Cook (London: Penguin, 1997).

The document had been first drafted by Archbishop of Canterbury Stephen Langton who intended with it to achieve establishing peace between the unpopular king and a group of rebel barons. In particular, the *Magna Carta* promised the protection of Church privileges, protection for the barons from illegal imprisonment, access to swift justice, and limitations on feudal payments to the Crown. In order to maintain the validity of these mutually agreed regulations, a council of twenty-five barons was set up to observe the practical implementations. Even though neither side upheld its commitments, and even though the charter was annulled by Pope Innocent III, which then led to the First Barons' War. The barons were led by Robert Fitzwalter, who attacked King John with the help of a French army, which in turn was led by the future Louis VIII of France. John died in September of 1216, which convinced many of the barons to switch sides. Subsequently, the French suffered heavy losses at Lincolnshire and Sandwich in 1217, so Louis was forced to sign the Treaty of Lambeth in September of that year. The *Magna Carta* received its official title only then and from then on was regarded as part of the Statue Law of England, despite modifications throughout the subsequent decades and even centuries.[171]

First and foremost, the Church and all of its members received the privilege of freedom: "the English Church is to be free and to have all its rights fully and its liberties entirely" (1). Most importantly, inheritance patterns became regulated, which prevented the king from taking over the property of families when the male ruler died and left only underage children. This also entailed the freedom that "[h]eirs are to be married without disparagement" (6), meaning that the king could not meddle in dynastic politics. Widows could keep their dowry, which significantly cut into the king's power to take over the land after a nobleman's

---

171 Faith Thompson, *Magna Carta – Its Role in The Making of The English Constitution 1300– 1629* (Minneapolis, MN: University of Minnesota Press, 1948); Austin Lane Poole, *From Domesday Book to Magna Carta 1087–1216*. 2nd ed. (1951; Oxford: Oxford University Press, 1993); Howard, A. E. Dick, *Magna Carta: Text and Commentary*. Revised Edition (1964; Charlottesville, VA: University Press of Virginia, 1998); Peter Linebaugh, *The Magna Carta Manifesto: Liberties and Commons for All* (Berkeley, CA: University of California Press, 2009); *Magna Carta: Law, Liberty, Legacy*, ed. Claire Breay and Julian Harrison (London: The British Library, 2015); Ralph Turner, *Magna* Carta (London: Taylor and Francis, 2016); *Challenges to Authority and the Recognition of Rights: From Magna Carta to Modernity*, ed. Catharine MacMillan and Charlotte Smith (Cambridge: Cambridge University Press, 2018). The critical literature on this famous document is legion, of course. For an edition of the Latin and Anglo-Norman French text, see *Magna carta libertatum*, ed. Mario Caravale. Introduzioni. Diritto (Bologna: Il mulino, 2018). For an online version in English translation of the charter as edited by King Edward, prepared by Nicholas Vincent, National Archives and Records Administration, see https://www.archives.gov/files/press/press-kits/magna-carta/magna-carta-translation.pdf (last accessed on Jan. 15, 2021).

death. And, by implication, this also meant: "No widow shall be distrained to marry for so long as she wishes to live without a husband, provided that she gives surety that she will not marry without our assent if she holds of us, or without the assent of her lord, if she holds of another" (7).

London, but then also all other cities, boroughs, and vills were allowed to keep their traditional freedom, though details are not listed at length (9). However, we also read the significant stipulation regarding building projects necessary for the royal logistical system: "No town or free man is to be distrained to make bridges or bank works save for those that ought to do so of old and by right" (15). The king also committed himself not to take over any property if a delay in debt payments had occurred, granting the owner a chance to come up with the money without losing their land in a dictatorial fashion: "Neither we nor our bailiffs will seize any land or rent for any debt, as long as the existing chattels of the debtor suffice for the payment of the debt and as long as the debtor is ready to pay the debt, nor will the debtor's guarantors be distrained for so long as the principal debtor is able to pay the debt" (8).

There is a particular focus on the appropriate measurement of penalties for smaller offences:

> A freeman is not to be amerced for a small offence save in accordance with the manner of the offence, and for a major offence according to its magnitude, saving his sufficiency (*salvo contenemento suo*), and a merchant likewise, saving his merchandise, and any villain other than one of our own is to be amerced in the same way, saving his necessity (*salvo waynagio*) should he fall into our mercy, and none of the aforesaid amercements is to be imposed save by the oath of honest and law-worthy men of the neighbourhood (14).

Even if the *Magna Carta* was more of a tentative attempt to establish some balance of power and to remove the royal influence from the courts, it was reissued numerous times and constituted a basis for much of the future discourse on political and legal freedom, leading over to the development of the early modern democracy in the United States of America, in France, and in other countries.[172]

---

[172] For the public performance of late medieval kingship, see Katherine J. Lewis, *Kingship and Maculinity in Late Medieval England* (London and New York: Routledge, 2013).

5 *Waltharius:* An Early Medieval Heroic Poem in Latin

Conquest, Warfare, Enslavement, Liberation

Indeed, the topic of freedom and imprisonment finds countless manifestations in many different texts, literary narratives, poems, or chronicles, from throughout the entire Middle Ages and far beyond.[173] Intriguingly, however, in many cases we observe that poets addressed slightly different notions more typical of the pre-modern age because the political and military conditions were not quite the same, of course. This finds a most vivid expression in the Latin heroic epic of *Waltharius*, which a monk wrote down while drawing from an older Germanic oral source, quite parallel to the Old English *Waldere* (eighth or ninth centuries; hence possibly a source, after all). Our text was composed sometime in the ninth or tenth century and exerted a deep influence on the various famous medieval heroic epics, including the Latin *Ruodlieb*, the anonymous *Chanson de Roland*/Priest Conrad's *Rolandslied* (ca. 1150/1170), the *Nibelungenlied* (ca. 1200), and the *Þiðrekssaga* (thirteenth century). The debates about the authorship – perhaps the monk Ekkehard I of St. Gall (d. 973), perhaps an otherwise unknown Geraldus, perhaps an anonymous Carolingian writer – have not yielded any satisfactory answer, and we do not need to solve this puzzle here.[174]

We encounter here a wonderful opportunity to reflect upon the notion of freedom and slavery in a wider heroic and political context, proffering us evidence from the early Middle Ages, but still deeply connected with classical antiquity, written in elegant Latin dactylic hexameters (1456 in total), reflecting both traditional heroic history and also early concepts of courtly love. In essence, the poem tells the story of Walter, prince of Aquitaine, held as a hostage at the court of the ruler of the Huns, Attila. After having achieved yet another victory for his lord, Walter decides to escape from his captivity, taking his be-

---

[173] Elizabeth Lawn, *"Gefangenschaft": Aspekt und Symbol sozialer Bindung im Mittelalter* (see note 118).
[174] *Waltharius*, ed., trans., and intro. by Abram Ring. Dallas Medieval Texts and Translations, 22 (Leuven, Paris, and Bristol, CT: Peeters, 2016). For the thirteen manuscripts containing this poem, see Ring, ed., 20–24; cf. also, though strangely incomplete, http://www.handschriftencensus.de/werke/2319. For a good online edition of the Latin text, see https://www.thelatinlibrary.com/waltarius1.html (both last accessed on Jan. 15, 2021). See now Jan M. Ziolkowski, "Waltharius," *The Virgil Encyclopedia*, ed. id. and Richard F. Thomas. Vol. 3 (New York: Wiley, 2014). Following previous scholarship, he also strongly emphasizes that the poet drew intensively from Virgil, but always made sure to render his source into his own words and concepts, thus proving to be a creative, learned, and flexible poet (https://doi.org/10.1002/9781118351352.wbve2221; last accessed on Jan. 15, 2021); see also Otto Zwierlein, "Das Waltharius-Epos und seine lateinischen Vorbilder," *Antike und Abendland* 16 (1970): 153–84.

loved, the Burgundian princess Hildegund with him. They succeed in their plans, having made the entire Hunnish court company so heavily drunk that everyone has fallen asleep, which gives them a long time to flee without being noticed at all. However, and this would be the center piece of *Waltarius*, after the hero has crossed the river Rhine on a ferry boat, King Gunther traces him and wants to force him to turn over his treasures that he had brought with him from the Huns.

Unfortunately for Gunther and his men, Walter is not only well placed at the entrance of a cave, he is also the most skillful warrior and can thus kill one man after the other who had tried to carry out the king's order to demand the treasure and the woman to be turned over to the king. At the end, Gunther can force Hagen, Walter's old comrade, to fight together with him against the stranger, yet the king loses one of his legs, while Hagen loses his right eye, whereas Walter's left hand is cut off. This then ends the fighting, and the three men agree to establish piece, which allows the protagonist to continue on his journey, together with his bride, reaching his homeland of Aquitaine, where he marries her and assumes the kingship ruling happily for thirty years.[175]

What is relevant in *Waltharius* for our purpose consists of the early dramatic experiences. Attila, the ruler of the Huns, marches westward and threatens every people before him with war and annihilation. No ruler is able or willing to resist his mighty force, so first the king of the Franks, Gibicho, then the king of the Burgundians, Hereric, and finally the king of Aquitaine, Alphere quickly give up all resistance, offer a peace treaty in return for massive treasures, and, above all, hostages. Gibicho's son Gunther is still too young to serve in that function, so they send the noble child Hagen. Hereric has only a single daughter, Hildegund, who has to accept her destiny as a hostage and move to the Hunnish kingdom. Finally, Alphere designates his son Walter as the pawn for peace, although he clearly loves him: "dilectum ... natum" (v. 90). None of these rulers is said ever to have considered an alliance, and since they were all mediocre kings in comparison with Attila, they have to succumb to the threat and oblige the opponent with treasures and most precious hostages.

---

175 Gustav Adolf Beckmann, *Gualter del Hum –Gaiferos – Waltharius*. Beihefte zur Zeitschrift für romanische Philologie, 359 (Berlin and New York: Walter de Gruyter, 2010); Claudia Händl, "Il 'Waltharius' – un poema eroico germanico in lengua latina?," *Il ruolo delle lingue e delle letterature germaniche nella formazione dell'Europa medievale*, ed. Dagmar Gottschall (Lecce: Milella, 2018), 119–31; Andrea Ghidoni, "Narrazioni eroopoietiche mediolatine: 'punteggiature' nell'evoluzione delle letterature profano-volgari," *Mittellateinisches Jahrbuch* 53.3 (2018): 399–422; cf. also Tyler Flatt, "The Book of Friends: Hagen and Heroic Traditions in the 'Waltharius'," *Journal of English and Germanic Philology* 1154 (2016): 463–85.

Surprisingly, perhaps, but probably not unheard of in the early Middle Ages, Attila treats the two exiled children like a father: he "bid that they be raised as his own" (49), though he never leaves them out of his sight. In other words, despite his kindness toward them, they are still prisoners and not free to go wherever they want to. We also never hear of their actual fathers ever making any efforts to ransom their sons or their daughter, so these three young people are entirely raised at the Hunnish court. The two young men quickly rise to being the most outstanding warriors who enjoy greatest respect everywhere, while Hildegund can equally earn high esteem by Attila's queen Ospirin, who, at last, appoints her as "the steward to watch over all the king's treasure" (49). In fact, Walter rises to the level of general, leading Attila's army, winning every battle for his lord. Nevertheless, all three remain exiles, captives, and they suffer, though the poet is not very explicit about it, from the loss of their freedom.

Things change rapidly when the news arrive that the king of the Franks, Gibicho, has died, succeeded by his son Gunther, who immediately dissolves the treaty with the Huns on his own, although this does not have any military consequences for either side because the Huns no longer seem to be bent on their traditionally vast expeditions to conquer many parts of the world. However, Hagen uses this change of conditions as the long-awaited opportunity and escapes: "at night he undertook flight and hastened to his lord" (49). This is, to some extent, in parallel with Hagen's situation in the thirteenth-century *Kudrun*, except that there he had been caught as a young child by a griffin and taken to a remote island as food for the young ones, but can escape their clutches. Together with three princesses (from Portugal, India, and Iceland [?] they leave their cave, wander through a forest for twenty-four days to reach the coast, where the discover a ship with pilgrims who, after some hesitation due to their fear, finally accept them on board and thus help them to get home again.[176] However, trying to establish closer connections between both narratives would stretch the meaning of the term 'imprisonment' excessively because in the Latin epic poem the young man is forced out of military and political conditions to go into exile, i.e., into imprisonment at the Hunnish court.

In *Waltharius*, Hagen serves as a proxy for the child Gunther, and he is later completely committed to him as his lord, which forces him at the end to fight together with him against Walter, but this does not concern us here further. However, at the point when Hagen realizes that the right moment has arrived due to the death of the Frankish king, he immediately takes action and disappears over

---

[176] *Kudrun*. Nach der Ausgabe von Karl Bartsch herausgegeben von Karl Stackmann. Altdeutsche Textbibliothek, 115 (Tübingen: Max Niemeyer, 2000).

night. Walter, by contrast, does not accompany his friend Hagen; instead, he is at that point in time leading the Hunnish army into a war which he wins decidedly for his lord. Yet, Attila's wife clearly senses the grave danger that Walter could also escape since no particular loyalty would hold him back. Losing both men would constitute a grave danger for the Hunnish kingdom because both those captives, serving basically as mercenaries, had become the major pillars upon which the power of the royal house rested.

Ospirin urges her husband to offer Walter a bride from among his highest nobles, but the young man rejects this offer since it would distract him too much from his military goals, discipline, and make him lose some of his drive and energy. He also emphasizes: "Nothing is so sweet to me as to be faithfully obedient to my lord" (53). But, when we follow the subsequent events, Walter proves to be rather disingenuous, being a clever strategist just as on the battlefield. Hardly has he returned from his triumphant victory, does he engage in a private conversation with Hildegund and secretly plots both their escape from the Hunnish kingdom, which appears to be a very risky enterprise.

While she prepares all the treasures they plan on taking with them on their flight, he organizes a major feast for Attila and his entire court at which everyone gets so badly drunk that they fall deeply asleep and do not wake up until late the next day, by when the couple has already managed to flee. The narrator leaves no doubt about the extent to which these two hostages had waited for this moment, remarking about Walter: "he anxiously starts to leave the hated land" (67; "invisa trepidus decedere terra," v. 340). We are clearly told how much they long to return home and to leave the land of their exile behind (69), and the narrator outlines in unmistakable terms how much this attempt at escape represented a great risk for both: "they turn their nervous steps this way and that through the pathless wild" (69). Considering the rage which subsequently fills Attila once he has learned the news, and the ominous words by Ospirin about the danger to their country with the hostages having left secretly – "Today the pillar of our empire has clearly fallen. Behold! Your strength and famous courage have gone far from here" (71) – it is obvious how much value these two people constituted for the Hunnish ruler.

The subsequent events then focus on the conflict between Walter and Gunther, the latter proving to be an arrogant, duplicitous, and untrustworthy king who attacks the traveler with a band of his best men, most of whom are killed by Walter in hand-to-hand combat until Gunter and Hagen take up the weapons against the hero. In this final melee, each one is severely wounded, when Walter cuts off Gunther's leg, loses his right hand, and then cuts out one of Hagen's eyes and six of his teeth. Only then do the hostilities end, all three men taunt each other, realizing that there is nothing else to do in face of their serious wounds, and Walter and his fiancée are finally free to go, but all this represents a different topic and does not need to be investigated further at this point.[177]

For us, of central importance proves to be only the highly dramatized operation to escape from Hunnish enslavement. Although Walter and Hildegund enjoy Attila's and Ospirin's greatest respect, and have complete freedom to operate at the court as it pleases them, they are deeply frustrated about them being forced to stay in the land of the Huns. Their masters are aware about the precarious situation and endeavor with all their skill and means to keep them firmly within their sphere of power, but they fail because the desire for personal freedom supersedes all material and political temptations by the foreign ruler.

Hagen already had shown them the way, and Ospirin becomes rather wary about the danger that Walter might follow him soon. We are not told how Hagen managed seemingly so easily to slip away, but the poet makes it abundantly clear that Walter must take greatest precautions to prepare his own move. If anyone had learned of his plans, and would have betrayed him to Attila, the young man would not have survived it, despite all the military glory and triumphs that he has gained on behalf of his ruler. The refugee travel only under the cover of the dark and proceed most carefully, being fully aware that they as slaves would be mercilessly killed if captured, and yet they face all dangers, crossing through hostile lands, and Walter does not take a real rest the whole time until they have found that cave west of the Rhine. He sleeps in Hildegund's lap, but alerts her: "'Keep a careful watch'" (83). And as soon as she recognizes the band of men arriving tracking down Walter's and her path, she wakes up the hero, who is immediately ready to fight.

Freedom, that is the highest ideal for Walter, and he even refers to the potentiality that one of Gunther's men could take him captive, but this only mockingly: "He has not thrust me into a prison cell or twisted my hands behind my back and bound them in chains, has he?" (91). Walter is even willing to pay for his free transit, and doubles his offer (95), but since Gunther is greedy, rash, unconsidered, and even contemptuous toward Hagen who does not want to be involved in this fighting (93),[178] the tragedy evolves without delay, with

---

[177] Jan Ziolkowski, "Fighting Words: Wordplay and Swordplay in the 'Waltharius'," *Germanic Texts and Latin Models: Medieval Reconstructions*, ed. K. E. Olsen, A. Harbus, and T. Hofstra. Mediaevalia Groningana, 2 (Leuven, Paris, and Stirling, VA: Peeters, 2001), 9–51.

[178] This could be considered a noteworthy parallel with the figure of Rüedegêr in the *Nibelungenlied* who refuses for a long time to get involved in the fight against the Burgundians because they are his own kin, or at least tribesmen, until Kriemhilt at the end forces him to live up to his feudal oath toward her and to take up arms against the horrendous guests. There is a high level of likelihood that the poet/scribe of the *Nibelungenlied*, a cleric in the service of Bishop Wolfger

one man after the other being slaughtered by Walter. We thus recognize several major points of criticism: 1. against the weak kings in the Frankish territory; 2. against the ridiculous Hunnish ruler Attila whom Walter can dupe so easily; 3. against the rash and almost insane (sic) Frankish King Gunther ("male sana mente gravatus," 530); and 4. all those authority figures who believe that they can keep a slave for good or that they can despoil anyone crossing through their territory.[179]

However, all this does not mean that early medieval literature was uniformly determined by a hatred of a 'slave-holding' Hunnish ruler. *Waltharius* proves to be rather complex in that regard because Attila is not projected as an evil character, though he tries everything in his power to hold on to this pillar of his power, Walter. If we consider, by comparison, the more or less contemporary Old High German "Hildebrandslied" (ca. 820, Fulda, two scribes),[180] we confront a rather different situation because the old Hildebrand had to leave with his lord Theoderic ("Theotrihhe") fleeing from Odoacer's vengeance, and then served in the Hunnish army, as documented by the heavy rings out of gold which he tries to give to his son as gifts and as symbols that he is actually his long-lost father. Hildebrand is, however, rudely rejected by his opponent, Hadubrand, because the young man, also a leader of his own army (Germanic), had been told by sailors already a long time ago that his father had died in battle. Subsequently, since their communication breaks down, the two begin to fight against each other, and we can only surmise – the poem has survived only as a fragment – that tragedy will be the outcome, with the either the father killing his son, the son killing his father, or both killing each other. There is considerable bitterness on both sides, with Hadubrand voicing deep anger about his father having abandoned the family already before his own birth, irrespective of his great respect for the father's fame and honor he himself is actually proud of, and with Hildebrand feeling rejected, and disregarded by the young man, whom he has to fight to protect his own life and honor. But the anonymous poet/s did not reflect on

---

von Erla in Passau, was aware of the *Waltharius*, also written by a cleric, though in Latin. See Victor Millet, *Germanische Heldendichtung im Mittelalter: Eine Einführung*. de Gruyter Studienbuch (Berlin and New York: Walter de Gruyter, 2008), 105–21; here esp. 109.
179 Simon MacLean, "'Waltharius': Treasure, Revenge and Kingship in the Ottonian Wild West," *Emotion, Violence, Vengeance and Law in the Middle Ages: Essays in Honour of William Ian Miller*, ed. Kate Gilbert and Stephen D. White. Medieval Law and Its Practice, 24 (Leiden and Boston: Brill, 2018), 225–51.
180 *Althochdeutsche Literatur* (see note 50), 68–71; Albrecht Classen, *Verzweiflung und Hoffnung. Die Suche nach der kommunikativen Gemeinschaft in der deutschen Literatur des Mittelalters*. Beihefte zur Mediaevistik, 1 (Frankfurt a. M., Berlin, et al.: Peter Lang, 2002), 1–52; Millet, *Germanische Heldendichtung im Mittelalter* (see note 178), 24–47.

the exile any further and only indicates that Hildebrand had to undergo thirty years of hardship, determined by his vassalic loyalty toward his lord. In short, the poem reflects on exile itself, but not on imprisonment, freedom, or slavery.[181]

Both men are completely determined by their warrior mentality, so for Hildebrand there had never been any option, as far as we can tell, whether he should have departed together with his lord or not. His family obligations were only second. This exile, hence, is determined purely by military necessities, whereas in *Waltharius* all three young people were forced to leave home and submit under captivity because their fathers were too weak and fearsome to fight against or to resist the Huns. Consequently, the fact that Hildebrand happens to encounter his son Hadubrand at the head of an army, which quickly leads to a mortal confrontation, seems to be nothing but circumstance. The old man still leads a Hunnish army, and he is highly decorated with Hunnish gold, so there is no noticeable sense of imprisonment or his loss of freedom anywhere in the poem. The only time when Hildebrand voices some bitterness is when he laments that he himself had to go into exile ("recceo," v. 49; 'rekko' or 'rekkeo'= the one who is exiled, banned, ostracized),[182] whereas his young opponent has never had to experience this destiny, and thereupon Hildebrand only appeals to the gods, or destiny, and gives in to the fighting mode which knows of no family bonds or emotions. The contrast with *Waltharius* brings out quite remarkably how much the protagonist in the latter poem indeed feels like he is choking in the Hunnish land and must risk everything, his fame, his fortune, his power, and Attila's love for him just to get back into freedom. The "Hildebrandslied" knows nothing of that sort.

In fact, when we review other parallel heroic poems, there is no indication that within the framework of heroism poets might have paid particular attention to any of those political and legal issues. Granted, in the Old Spanish *El Poema de mío Cid* (ca. 1000) the protagonist suffers specifically from the destiny of being exiled from the royal court, but he is completely free to fight for his own destiny, to establish his own new power base, and to appeal to the king to accept his gifts and ultimately himself again as his loyal vassal. In the *Chanson de Roland* (second half of the eleventh century) or in Priest Konrad's *Rolandslied* (ca. 1170) the central issues focus on betrayal, heroic battles, defeat, revenge, the punishment of the traitor.

---

181 Albrecht Classen, "The Experience of Exile in Medieval German Heroic Poetry" (see note 54), 83–110.
182 Gerhard Koebler, *Althochdeutsches Wörterbuch*, 6th ed. (2014), online at: http://www.koeblergerhard.de/ahd/ahd_r.html (last accessed on Jan. 15, 2021).

In the *Nibelungenlied*, we hear about many heroic deeds, conflicts, murder, and Kriemhild's enormous desire to avenge her husband's death, but no one suffers from the loss of freedom. By contrast, the monkish poet of *Waltharius*, perhaps because he was so deeply steeped in the classical tradition (Ovid, Vergil), predicated the entire work on the issue of captivity, if not slavery, from which the three main figures can eventually extract themselves.

Imprisonment and freedom are also important topics in some of the precourtly *Spielmannsepen*, such as *König Rother* (ca. 1150/1160), where the king's messengers to the emperor of Constantinople, who are supposed to woo for the princess's hand on behalf of their lord, are immediately imprisoned and suffer for a long time until Rother himself arrives to liberate them and to gain his bride. The narrator outlines their misery in the dungeon in great detail, emphasizing the darkness of their cell, the cold, and moisture. The prisoners suffer from hunger, and the only water they can drink they find on the ground. Remembering their glorious life at court back home, they shed tears over their terrible condition in this prison and lament that they have to endure this punishment without any fault of their own.[183] However, they will be freed, and they are not forced or sold into slavery as is the case with Waltharius. We will hear about that theme once again only in the later Middle Ages, especially when historically confirmed individuals could eventually escape their slavery and return home to Europe where they then reflected upon their destiny through their memoirs.

6 Marie de France: Marriage as Prison?

Switching gears and moving into a different genre and a different period, we discover a perhaps unexpected type of literary treatment of imprisonment, though there the concern with the lack of freedom proves to be surprisingly similar after all. The Anglo-Norman poet Marie de France (fl. ca. 1160–1200) injects a sense of terrible subjugation and repression in the first of her twelve *lais*, in "Guige-

---

[183] *König Rother: Mittelhochdeutscher Text und neuhochdeutsche Übersetzung* von Peter K. Stein. Ed. Ingrid Bennewitz together with Beatrix Koll and Ruth Weichselbaumer (Stuttgart: Philipp Reclam jun., 2000), 342–85. See now Sarah Bowden, *Bridal Quest Epics in Medieval Germany. A Revisionary Approach*. Bithell Series of Dissertations, 85 (London: Modern Humanities Research Ass., 2012); Jens Weißweiler, *Gewaltentwürfe in der epischen Literatur des 12. Jahrhunderts: zur narrativen Verortung von Gewalt im "König Rother" und im "Straßburger Alexander"*. Germanistische Literaturwissenschaft, 12 (Baden-Baden: Ergon Verlag, 2019).

mar."[184] Although most of her *lais* aim at the achievement of personal happiness, the poet also recognized many times how character flaws, feelings of hatred, jealousy, envy, and the desire to exert control and power over the partner, or simply fear of the other, prevented the achievement of this goal.[185]

Nothing in "Guigemar" at first seems to indicate that an individual might suffer from the loss of freedom in legal or prosecutorial terms. The protagonist enjoys the comfortable lifestyle of a nobleman, but he does not know anything about love. Through a magical adventure he is mysteriously transported across a

---

184 *Les lais de Marie de France*, ed. Jean Rychner. Les classiques français du Moyen Âge (Paris: Champion, 1978); cf. also Marie de France, *Lais: texte original en ancien français; manuscrit Harley 978 du British Museum*, ed. Nathalie Desgrugillers-Billard (Clermont-Ferrand: Éd. Paleo, 2007); Marie de France, *Lais: Guigemar, Bisclavret, Lanval, Yonec, Laüstic, Chievrefoil*. Altfranzösisch/Deutsch, ed. Philipp Jeserich (Stuttgart: Philipp Reclam jun., 2015); Marie de France, *Die Lais*. Übersetzt, mit einer Einleitung, einer Bibliographie sowie Anmerkungen versehen von Dietmar Rieger. Klassische Texte des romanischen Mittelalters, 19 (Munich: Wilhelm Fink, 1980). Currently the best bilingual edition is *The Lais of Marie de France: Text and Translation*, ed. and trans. by Claire M. Waters (Peterborough, Ont.: Broadview, 2018), from which I will quote. Research on Marie de France is legion; see, for instance, Judith R. Rothschild, *Narrative Technique in the Lais of Marie de France: Themes and Variations*. North Carolina Studies in the Romance Languages and Literatures, 1 (Chapel Hill, NC: U.N.C. Dept. of Romance Languages, 1974); cf. also the contributions to *In Quest of Marie de France: A Twelfth-Century Poet*, ed. Chantal A. Maréchal (Lewiston, NY, Lampeter, Wales, and Queenston, Ont.: Edwin Mellon Press, 1992); Howard Bloch, *The Anonymous Marie de France* (see note 112); Sharon Kinoshita and Peggy McCracken, *Marie de France: A Critical Companion* (see note 112); Albrecht Classen, *Reading Medieval European Women Writers: Strong Literary Witnesses from the Past* (Frankfurt a. M.: Peter Lang, 2016), 83–118.

185 Albrecht Classen, "Happiness in the Middle Ages? Hartmann von Aue and Marie de France," *Neohelicon* XXV.2 (1998): 247–74; id., "The Erotic and the Quest for Happiness in the Middle Ages. What Everybody Aspires to and Hardly Anyone Truly Achieves," *Eroticism in the Middle Ages and the Renaissance: Magic, Marriage, and Midwifery*, ed. Ian Moulton. Arizona Studies in the Middle Ages and the Renaissance, 39 (Tempe, AZ, and Turnhout, Belgium: Brepols, 2016), 1–33; somewhat related to this topic, *Tears, Sighs and Laughter: Expressions of Emotions in the Middle Ages*, ed. Per Förnegård, Erika Kihlman, Mia Åkestam, and Gunnel Engwall. KVHAA konferenser, 92 (Stockholm: Kungl. Vitterhets Historie och Antikvitets Akademien, 2017). There is a vast amount of research on the history of emotions, but here I only try to emphasize the experience of happiness in a love relationship. For happiness in philosophical terms, see James M. Powell, *Albertanus of Brescia: The Pursuit of Happiness in the Early Thirteenth Century*. The Middle Ages Series (Philadelphia, PA: University of Pennsylvania Press, 1992); Katarzyna Dybel, *Etre heureux au Moyen Age: d'apres le roman arthurien en prose du XIIIe siècle*. Synthema, 2 (Louvain, Paris, and Dudley, MA: Peeters, 2004), but there is no reference to Marie. There are many global studies on happiness; see, for instance, *Glück: The New World Book of Happiness, mit den neuesten Erkenntnissen aus der Glücksforschung*, ed. Leo Bormans and Sofia Blind (Cologne: DuMont, 2017).

body of water and reaches a harbor where an unhappily married young woman welcomes him, heals his wound, but causes a much bigger wound of love in him. The two spend about one year and a half together until they are discovered, and he is forced to leave with the same ship again. The jealous husband would have killed him, but the fact that the magical ship has docked at the harbor just in time and is ready to pick him up again saves his life. However, he has to leave his lady behind, and she suffers badly in her loneliness, longing for Guigemar, while being locked in a 'prison cell' by her old husband for two years. She is so despondent at the end that she is prepared to commit suicide by throwing herself off the cliff and drowning in the sea. Surprisingly, at that very moment there is no more a lock or a key in the door, and almost as if through magic she can leave her room and get to the harbor without being stopped or disturbed by anyone. Fitting for the fairy tale character of this *lai*, the black ship is already waiting for her, and hardly has she stepped onto it, when she is automatically transported over the sea where she eventually encounters her beloved again who can finally liberate her from lord Meriaduc who had discovered here on that ship through a military operation, which concludes the narrative with a happy end.

Marie de France obviously lamented the destiny of young women who are forced by their parents to marry old and rich husbands so that the dynastic connections could be of profit for both sides. But let us consider more carefully how the poet describes the situation of the lady because her condition can only be identified as a prison. She lives in a little chamber situated within an orchard, which in turn is surrounded by an insurmountable wall out of green marble (220–22). Only one door provides access to the garden, and hence to the housing for this lady. But the side to the sea is open because no one is expected to come up there, though this is the very point from which Guigemar can enter the harbor and thus meet the lady.

In order to safeguard his wife, the old lord has created the little house for her: "Pour mettre i sa femme a seür" (230), to which is attached a little chapel. Inside, however, the walls are richly decorated with a mural painting depicting the goddess of love, Venus, and the ways how men should behave in love, a direct allusion to Ovid, of course, with his *Ars amatoria* (2 C.E.). But there is more to this because the paintings also show how Venus tosses a follow-up book, Ovid's *Remedia Amoris*, which instructs the readers how to avoid getting hurt by love or how to free oneself from the feelings of love, into the flames.[186] All

---

[186] Logan E. Whalen, "A Medieval Book-Burning: Objet d'art as Narrative Device in the Lai of Guigemar," *Neophilologus* 80.2 (1996): 205–11.

this strongly suggests that the old husband is trying to manipulate and to force his wife to develop love for him, after all, although the strategy to influence the young woman's feelings in a mechanistic fashion obviously fails. We observe a significant parallel to the contemporary treatise by the Parisian cleric Andreas Capellanus, *De Amore* (ca. 1180/1190), where the third part attempts to ridicule love, to reject love outside of the bonds of marriage, and to characterize women at large as contemptible and vile.[187] Both here and there, male strategies to determine a woman's emotions prove to be useless and absurd, if not paradoxical.

While the images on the wall are supposed to achieve the desired effect through visual influence, a young girl, the lord's niece, serves as a guardian staying in the lady's company all the time. In short, this unhappy wife is virtually kept in a prison cell: "La fu la dame enclose e mise" (245). The door to the gate in the wall surrounding the orchard is closely kept by an old priest who is identified as a eunuch, otherwise he would not have been entrusted with that task. In short, the husband is extremely afraid that his wife might ask for any contact with the outside world, which would probably, so he must fear, make her immediately fall in love with another man. Ironically, while the priest is allowed to serve in his function because "Les plus bas membres out perduz" (257), we might assume that the husband himself is probably impotent; there is never a word about the lady getting pregnant.

However, even the most secure prison is breachable, especially when love is involved, as is the case here as well. As if predetermined by an outside force, the black (ebony) ship, highly symbolic by itself,[188] transports the badly wounded Guigemar to the harbor where the imprisoned lady and her maid discover him. In their exchange she divulges to him explicitly that her husband treats her like a prisoner: "he has shut me up in this enclosure" (345). She curses the old man, but also admits that she is completely at his mercy. Nevertheless, in this situation she dares to transfer the knight secretly to her chamber and to

---

[187] John W. Baldwin, *The Language of Sex: Five Voices from Northern France Around 1200*. The Chicago Series on Sexuality, History, and Society (Chicago and London: The University of Chicago Press, 1994); Peter L. Allen, *The Art of Love: Amatory Fiction from Ovid to the* Romance of the Rose. The Middle Ages Series (Philadelphia, PA: University of Pennsylvania Press, 1999); Albrecht Classen, "Epistemology at the Courts: The Discussion of Love by Andreas Capellanus and Juan Ruiz," *Neuphilologische Mitteilungen* CIII.3 (2002): 341–62; id., "Dialectics and Courtly Love: Abelard and Heloise, Andreas Capellanus, and the *Carmina Burana*," *Journal of Medieval Latin* 23 (2013): 161–83; Don A. Monson, *Andreas Capellanus, Scholasticism, & the Courtly Tradition* (Washington, DC: The Catholic University of America Press, 2005); Paolo Cherchi, *Andreas and the Ambiguity of Courtly Love* (Toronto: University of Toronto Press, 2016).
[188] Emanuel J. Mickel, Jr., "Guigemar's Ebony Boat," *Cultura Neolatina* 37 (1977): 9–15.

take care of him. While she cures him, indeed, she also hurts him badly at the same time because love is kindled in his chest, just as in her case. The love story then develops, although both are stuck in her prison cell, as we could say. Nevertheless, this secret room almost transforms into a *locus amoenus* behind the chamber walls. Ironically, the mural paintings only now make perfect sense because the *Remedia amoris* are completely disregarded, whereas the two practice the *Ars amatoria*, while the old husband, the guardian of the prison, proves to be the one who is shut out. Everything he had tried to achieve with the beautifully decorated chamber, the complete seclusion of his wife, the protection by the old priest, the wall around the orchard, all that has failed to work the way he had envisioned because the competitor for the lady's heart has arrived from the sea where there is no protection which the old husband could have erected but failed to do. Love and water thus prove to be intimately interconnected, especially because the automatic ship, functioning like an automaton, had specifically transported Guigemar to the harbor and thus directly to the young lady.[189]

Once the two lovers have been discovered, Guigemar is threatened with death, but since he stands ready to defend himself with all his might, the old lord inquires about his background and how he had reached this place. The mysterious story of the doe and then the black ship convince the husband that this is an extraordinary situation, so he challenges the stranger to present evidence, the ship itself, which in fact proves to be moored in the harbor and is ready to transport the protagonist promptly back to his home country. Guigemar has no choice but to board the ship, and the poor woman stays behind alone, now shut up more securely than ever before in a real prison cell located in a tower – the analogy to the situation with Tristan leaving his beloved Isolde at the end of Gottfried's eponymous romance (ca. 1210) proves to be striking, though there are also differences in detail. Her husband is not willing to grant her any freedom, any enjoyment, or any pleasure, which removes her emotionally even further away from that old man. The terrible solitary confinement – that is the only reasonable characterization of her destiny – leads her to deep depression, even to thoughts of suicide.

---

189 For this large topic, see E. R. Truitt, *Medieval Robots: Mechanism, Magic, Nature, and Art*. The Middle Ages Series (Philadelphia, PA: University of Pennsylvania Press, 2015). She does not know, unfortunately, of the case of the ship in Marie's *lai*, and she is also unaware of other literary examples of robots, such as in The Stricker's *Daniel von dem Blühenden Tal* (ca. 1220). As to the role of water regarding the development of this love affair, see Albrecht Classen, *Water in Medieval Literature: An Ecocritical Reading*. Ecocritical Theory and Practice (Lanham, MD, Boulder, CO, et al.: Lexington Books, 2018), 89–104.

Then, one day, virtually by magic, the cell is open and she can leave, walks down to the harbor, finds the same ship, as if it had been waiting for her, and is thus transported to the country where here lover resides. Ironically, however, at first, she is basically taken a prisoner once again, this time by another mighty lord who is named, i.e., Meriaduc, who feels deeply attracted to her, yet cannot sway her heart. He treats her most respectfully, and yet denies her the freedom to move wherever she might want to go, and in particular he refuses Guigemar the right to take the lady as his beloved: "Jeo la trovai, si la tendrai" (851; "I found her, I will keep her"). Although the narrator claims that Meriaduc loves her with his full heart, he really treats her as chattel, just like her old husband did, so she is not free, and has only exchanged one prison with another.

As comfortably as the lady is treated in material terms, she lacks all freedom; not even Guigemar has any entitlement on her, cannot help her out of this new prison, and at the end he must leave the castle. But, he takes all the other knights with him, abandoning the tournament. And they all join Meriaduc's enemy, return to the castle, besiege und conquer it, with Guigemar being at the lead: "He destroyed and captured the castle / and killed the lord within" (679–80). Only then does the lady gain her long-sought freedom and can live with her true love, Guigemar, though the narrator does not say anything about her at the end in specific terms and emphasizes only that thereby the protagonist's suffering had come to an end (882).

Marie operated here with a quite common literary motif dealing with the wife as an involuntary *inclusa*, such as in *Le Roman des Sept Sages de Rome* from ca. 1200 (4223–4240), which in turn was based on the *Historia septem sapientum* (a Latin translation of an ancient Persian text, which was first translated into Arabic, later into Latin since the twelfth century), where the wooing knight operates, however, much more strategically to win his beloved for himself by deceiving the husband in an ingenious manner, which involves serving him under pretense, building a house next to the tower where the lady is 'imprisoned,' and a secret doorway between both structures. Another significant example would be the *Roman de Cassidorus* (thirteenth century) or the first story told on the fourth day in Boccaccio's *Decameron* (ca. 1350), at least in the structural elements, and then the various pan-European adaptations of the *Roman des Sept Sages de Rome*, such as *Die Historia von den Sieben weisen Meistern und dem Kaiser Diocletianus* (middle to the end of the fifteenth century).[190]

---

190 There are many critical studies of "Guigemar," but rarely have scholars focused on the poor woman's prison experience; see, however, Jean-Marie Kauth, "Barred Windows and Uncaged Birds: The Enclosure of Woman in Chrétien de Troyes and Marie de France," *Medieval Feminist*

We encounter, to return to Marie's *lais*, a parallel case of a beautiful young woman who was forced to marry a very old man who treats her like a prisoner. This *inclusa* appears in "Yonec." Although she is well fed and provided with everything she needs, she is closely guarded by her husband's sister: "Pur li tenir meuz en justise" (32). Even though there are other women in neighboring rooms, the lady is not allowed to speak to them; she does not receive visitors, and is basically kept, once again, in solitary confinement, which leads to her feeling depressed, abandoned, and forlorn. It is worth noting that she also is not getting pregnant, although her husband has controlled her in this fashion already for seven years. The lady comments explicitly on her own status as prisoner: "Que en si grant prison me tient" (72), and laments that she is not even allowed to hear mass in church, not to mention any opportunity to meet other people: "Si jo puisse od gent parler" (78). Marriage of that kind thus proves to be tantamount to terrible imprisonment without the prisoner having committed any

---

Forum 46.2 (2010): 34–67. For the critical edition of *Le Roman des sept sage*, see *Le Roman des Sept Sages de Rome. A Critical Edition of the Two Verse Redactions of a Twelfth-Century Romance*, ed. Mary B. Speer. The Edward C. Armstrong Monographs on Medieval Literature, 4 (Lexington, KY: French Forum Publisher, 1989); see also Yasmina Foehr-Janssens, *Le temps des fables: Le Roman des sept sages ou l'autre voie du roman*. Nouvelle bibliothèque du moyen âge, 27 (Paris: Champion, 1994); for a critical examination, see the concise article by Udo Gerdes, "'Sieben weise Meister' (Zyklische Rahmenerzählung orientalischer Herkunft)," *Die deutsche Literatur des Mittelalters: Verfasserlexikon*, ed Burghart Wachinger et al. 2nd completely rev. ed. Vol. 8 (Berlin and New York: Walter de Gruyter, 1992), col. 1174–89; N(orbert) H. Ott, "Sieben weise Meister," *Lexikon des Mittelalters*, Vol. VII (Munich: Lexma Verlag, 1995), col. 1836–39. For the editions of the other works, see *Le Roman de Cassidorus*, ed. Joseph Palermo. Société des Anciens Textes Français, 1 and 2 (Paris: Picard 1963–1964); see also *Le Roman de Helcanus*. Édition d'un texte en prose du XIIIe siècle par Henri Niedzielski. Textes Littéraires Françaises, 418 (Geneva: Droz 1966), and Meradith Tilbury McMunn, "*Roman de Kanor*: Édition critiqued'un texte en prose du XIIIe siècle," Ph.D. diss., Storrs, University of Connecticut, 1978; *Die Historia von den Sieben weisen Meistern und dem Kaiser Diocletianus*, ed. Ralf-Henning Steinmetz. Altdeutsche Textbibliothek, 116 (Tübingen: Max Niemeyer, 2002), no. XIII. The topic of the 'inclusa' is also discussed by Detlev Fehling, "Die Eingesperrte (Inclusa) und der verkleidete Jüngling (Iuvenis femina). Neues zur Traditionsgeschichte zweier antiker Komödienmotive nebst einem Beitrag zur Geschichte des ›Sindbad‹-Zyklus, " *Mittellateinisches Jahrbuch* 21 (1986): 186–207; see now Abdoulaye Samaké, *Liebesträume in der deutsch-, französisch- und italienischsprachigen Erzählliteratur des 12. bis 15. Jahrhunderts*. Traum – Wissen – Erzählen, 6 (Paderborn: Wilhelm Fink Verlag, 2020), 54–87, for comparative perspectives. His central interest, however, rests on the function of dreams, and not on the suffering of the 'imprisoned' wife and her desperate attempts to gain her freedom.

crime. The only reason for her lingering away in this prison is that her family married her off to this old jealous man (81–85).[191]

Only once she has formulated in her mind the ardent desire that she could be rescued from her prison, does suddenly a goshawk appear flying through a window into her room. He quickly transforms into a young knight who declares his love for her and asks that she returns his feelings in kind. Only because she had explicitly asked for help had he been able to fly to her, although he had loved her already for a long time. The lady happily accepts him, though she is rather worried about the magical bird, a kind of male fairy.[192] From then on, the hawk-man visits her regularly, and this changes the woman's life completely, making her cheerful and giving her a positive outlook, taking much more care about her own self in body and dress. In other words, the prison has suddenly become, just as in the case of "Guigemar," a *locus amoenus*, but the dream of the erotic utopia is always shattered, whether here or in Gottfried von Straßburg's *Tristan* (ca. 1210). The lovers are discovered, and the husband has then spikes placed into the window, one of which mortally wounds the hawk-knight, who then departs, but not without telling her that she is pregnant with their child.

Again, this *lai* operates with a heavy dose of fictional material, like in a fairy tale, as the sorrowful lady then follows her lover, climbing through a window and jumping down twenty feet without hurting herself. She traces the track of her lover's blood and finds him, indeed, lying on his bed in the private chamber of his own castle, about to die. However, he comforts her, gives her a ring which would help her husband forget everything about those events, and a sword which she is later to pass on to her son when he will have learned who his true father was.

---

191 The original clearly says: 'parent' (81), so there is no reason to translate this phrase in such general terms as "relatives."
192 We face here the reverse concept of the "Martenehe," the marital relationship between a human being and a fairy, such as in any of the many *Melusine* versions, but then also in Walter Map, *Thomas off Ersseldoune*, and *Huon de Bordeaux*. For the wide range of related fairy tales all over the world, see Christoph Schmitt, "Mann auf der Suche nach der verlorenen Frau (AaTh 400)," *Enzyklopädie des Märchens*, ed. Rolf Wilhelm Brednich. Vol. 9 (Berlin and New York: Walter de Gruyter, 1999), cols. 195–210; Lydia Zeldenrust, *The Mélusine Romance in Medieval Europe: Translation, Circulation, and Material Contexts*. Studies in Medieval Romance (Cambridge: Cambridge University Press, 2020). See also Armin Schulz, "Spaltungsphantasmen – Erzählen von der "gestörten Mahrtenehe"," *Wolfram-Studien* 18 (2004): 233–62; Janin Pisarek, "Mehr als nur die Liebe zum Wassergeist: Das Motiv der 'gestörten Mahrtenehe' in europäischen Volkserzählungen," *Märchenspiegel. Zeitschrift für internationale Märchenforschung und Märchenpflege* 27.1 (2016): 3–8.

Indeed, she returns without being bothered by anyone, although loud bell-ringing and lamentations soon set in when the corpse of the knight is discovered. The ring protects the lady, and from that time on she spends an ordinary life with her husband, without being reproached and, especially, without being guarded, or imprisoned: "Ne ne messdist ne ne garda" (454). But the prophecy formulated by her dying lover comes true, and once her son, Yonec, has understood his mother's long suffering under the mean and cruel old man, and once she has fallen on the tomb holding her true love and has died, he takes hold of the sword and decapitates the man who was really only his stepfather: "he thus avenged the sorrow of his mother" (542).

Again, there are many possible approaches when trying to analyze the content and meaning of this lai.[193] What matters for us is that Marie here presents another case of a truly imprisoned lady who is completely contained in her private chambers and is not allowed to see anyone, except when she calls for a priest to give her the last rites, or the *Viaticum*, which her lover, in her shape, takes in order to prove to her that he is a good Christian. Most importantly, the old husband does not only try to catch the hawk-man with those spikes in the window; he thus bars his wife even further away from the outside, demonstrating thus his absolute control over her, a complete prisoner, subject to his whims and fears.

However, she is able, after all, to escape through a window – une fenestre" (337) – in order to follow her badly wounded lover, and later to re-enter through it somehow, without details being given. Love thus represents such a force that even the best prison cannot hold the lady back who is desperately trying to re-unify with her lover, not being worried about death herself. This does not mean at all that for Marie de France marriage was tantamount to solitary confinement, only bad and enforced marriage, arranged by the parents purely for dynastic or financial interests.

---

193 Elizabeth Liendo, "The Wound that Bleeds: Violence and Feminization in the Lais of Marie de France," *Neophilologus* 104 (2020): 19–32, approaches both *lais* with the typically feminist or Lacanian perspectives in mind, recognizing in the shared narrative motif of the male protagonist being impaled and shedding much blood a strategy to reverse, or feminize, their gender. The imagery might indeed lend itself for such a post-modern reading, but it proves to be the result of the author having been trapped by Freudian theories anachronistically imposed on medieval narratives. Otherwise, every medieval knight stabbed or killed by a sword or a spear would have to be read in those terms, and all medieval warfare would thus have to be explained in terms of sexual penetration. For a more solid analysis, see Joanne Findon, "Supernatural Lovers, Liminal Women, and the Female Journey," *Florilegium* 30 (2013): 27–52; cf. also Matthieu Boyd, "The Ring, the Sword, the Fancy Dress, and the Posthumous Child: Background to the Element of Heroic Biography in Marie de France's Yonec," *Romance Quarterly* 55.3 (2008): 205–30.

After all, "Guigemar" concludes with a happy end, presumably in marriage; in "Milun" we witness the two lovers finally being able to come together and marry after her first husband has passed away; and in "Eliduc," the wife withdraws from their actually happy marriage so that he can marry a young princess and live out his complete joy with her. In "Laüstic" the situation might sound similar to "Guigemar" or "Yonec," but the problem there only consists of the wife being in love with her neighboring knight, not being able to be with him, though both can talk to each other from their windows until her husband intervenes and has all the nightingales killed that allegedly keep her awake at night.

In extreme cases, however, as we have seen above, the ill-matched marriage results in her being terribly caught in a veritable prison where she is held in a solitary cell and suffers badly despite the luxury that surrounds her. In "Guigemar," the lady finally manages to flee unhampered and unharmed, and, with the help of the ship, to find her true lover again. In "Yonec," the lover who had managed to come to visit her, is mortally wounded by the traps set up by the husband, but both she and her wooer ultimately can join in death, whereas her husband is killed by the stepson, who avenges his mother's long-term imprisonment in this bad marriage. In each case, the old husband, apparently important, keeps the young wife as his personal prisoner, which the poet severely condemns, alerting us to the high principle that marriage be between two people joined by one will, and not a form of forced cohabitation, with him being the master and she being the slave.[194] These women suffer from extreme forms of imprisonment, not because they have to suffer from material deprivation, but because they are stuck in a marital deadlock and have to exist in complete social isolation.

---

[194] Marriage in the Middle Ages has been discussed already from many different perspectives; see, for instance, Neil Cartlidge, *Medieval Marriage: Literary Approaches, 1100–1300* (Cambridge: D. S. Brewer, 1997). Curiously, however, although he draws from numerous literary sources as well as historical documents, Marie de France is mentioned only briefly and in passing. The same applies to David d'Avray, *Medieval Marriage: Symbolism and Society*. D. L. d'Avray (Oxford: Oxford University Press, 2005). For the opposite approach, see Albrecht Classen, *Der Liebes- und Ehediskurs vom hohen Mittelalter bis zum frühen 17. Jahrhundert*. Volksliedstudien, 5 (Münster, New York, Munich, and Berlin: Waxmann, 2005), 32–72.

D Literary Treatment of Imprisonment and Slavery

1 Boccaccio's *Decameron*

The Monastic Prison as Purgatory

Sometimes we also hear of husbands being imprisoned because they are extremely jealous and overly protect their wives, treating almost like prisoners. This is the case in the eighth story told on the third day in Boccaccio's *Decameron* (ca. 1350), where the wife of the yeoman Ferondo who is a very wealthy but crude man, complains to an abbot about being mistreated by her overly jealous husband, and this on a daily basis, while he is also failing in bed with her (255–56), that is, lacking in potency. The abbot, certainly an excessive womanizer, immediately plans on using this situation to his own advantage, concocts a plan to which she soon agrees, both because she is sick and tired of her foolish and mean husband, and because the abbot offers her a valuable ring, paying for her sexual favors.

Ferondo is put into a coma by means of a drug, and then placed in a secret and windowless vault. Once he has woken up, he learns to his surprise and consternation that he has died and now has landed in the Purgatory. A monk arrives regularly in his cell, gives him a beating twice a day, and food and drink which his wife had allegedly donated to the abbey on behalf of her deceased husband's soul. In the meantime, the abbot, in the disguise of Ferondo's clothing, visits the lady every night, and for ten months they both enjoy a heated affair, until she is getting pregnant, which forces the abbot to bring the 'prisoner' back to life, who from then on promises never to demonstrate any sign of jealousy of his wife, having learned his lesson in 'Purgatory.'[195] The outcome is to the great satisfaction of everyone: Ferondo is happy to be back to life and living with his wife; she is happy to have a husband who displays no more any sign of jealousy and gives her enough freedom, whenever the occasion arises, to sleep with the abbot; and the latter, of course, because his reputation as a saint has grown tremendously, and yet he can continue having an affair with the lady. For Ferondo, however, the experience in the prison was a life-long lesson; not connected too much with suffering, except for the two daily beating, the loneliness, the darkness, he has understood that he must not control his wife excessively because she needs her own freedom. Of course, whether this resolves his problem of lack-

---

195 Boccaccio, *The Decameron*, trans. with an intro. and notes by G. H. McWilliam (see note 47).

ing in sexual potency, we do not learn, but since his wife enjoys enough diversion in that regard with the abbot, she is completely content as well.[196]

As wrong, of course, as the abbot's action proves to be, breaking his vow of chastity, faking being a saintly figure when he is really acting in a criminal fashion, abusing his own monastery as a private prison to serve his person purposes to have a sexual affair with a married woman, not fearing at all of being detected, as startling is the account of a prison operated by a rich urban citizen, an innkeeper, for the purpose of satisfying his wife's inexhaustible sexual desires.

2 Heinrich Kaufringer: Further Examples in Late Medieval *mæren*

In the Middle High German verse narrative, "The Search for the Happily Married Couple" by the South-German poet Heinrich Kaufringer (fl. 1400), a husband is deeply dissatisfied with his wife because of her perceived miserliness, while she is angry with him over his excessive generosity and hospitality. Finally, he leaves her for several years searching for a happily married couple, pledging that he would not return home until he would have been successful. He has, however, a very hard time in achieving that goal, always stumbling on marital conflicts and strife amongst all the couples he encounters. Twice, however, he seems to have discovered a truly happily married couple, but each time he learns quickly that even in those cases he was deceived. Luckily, at the end he realizes that his own wife's shortcomings, as he views it, amount to a really negligible aspect, while she enjoys great respect and honor in their community.[197]

---

196 Martin Eisner, "The Tale of Ferondo's Purgatory (III.8)," *The Decameron Third Day in Perspective*, ed. Francesco Ciabattoni and Pier Massimo Forni (Toronto: University of Toronto Press, 2014), 150–69.
197 Heinrich Kaufringer, *Werke*, ed. Paul Sappler. Vol. 1: *Text* (Tübingen: Max Niemeyer, 1972); for an English translation, see Albrecht Classen, *Love, Life, and Lust in Heinrich Kaufringer's Verse Narratives*. Medieval and Renaissance Texts and Studies, 467. MRTS Texts for Teaching, 9 (Tempe: Arizona Center for Medieval and Renaissance Studies, 2014; rev. and expanded 2nd ed., 2019). The most comprehensive critical study on Kaufringer was written by Marga Stede, *Schreiben in der Krise: die Texte des Heinrich Kaufringers*. Literatur, Imagination, Realität, 5 (Trier: Wissenschaftlicher Verlag Trier, 1993); but much new research has come out since then; see, for instance, Albrecht Classen, "Mord, Totschlag, Vergewaltigung, Unterdrückung und Sexualität. Liebe und Gewalt in der Welt von Heinrich Kaufringer," *Daphnis* 29.1–2 (2000): 3–36; id., "Love, Marriage, and Sexual Transgressions in Heinrich Kaufringer's Verse Narratives (ca. 1400)," *Discourses on Love, Marriage, and Transgression in Medieval and Early Modern Literature*, ed. Albrecht Classen. Medieval and Renaissance Texts and Studies, 278

The second time, when he is about to return home, in the conviction that he has finally discovered two ideal people, the husband confides in him, takes him down deep into his cellar and leads him to a secret corner where he keeps a prisoner, a man from the countryside, whom he had kidnapped years ago to have a sex slave for his wife, whom he himself could not satisfy. Maybe, this innkeeper is impotent, because his wife needs to visit this prisoner on a regular basis: "He makes love to her until she is satisfied and has no further demands" (49, v. 415–16). The husband treats him with greatest care, providing him with the best food and wines so as to keep him strong and willing:

> I take better care of him, by my honor, than of myself in order that he may sleep with my wife so that she will be sexually satisfied and does not look for the pleasure of sex elsewhere, as she used to do. That brought shame and disgrace upon me in the past. I tell you truly, this torture I have endured for ten years. During that time my wife has not had sex with any other man. Dear guest, look at the children whom I have under my care. Everyone assumes they are my own. This is a cause of great pain for me because they are the peasant's offspring, all six of my children. (49)

But this sex slave also leaves a horrifying impression: he "was terrible to look at, strong, and evil. H e was locked with a strong and solid chain so that he could not leave. He stood there as if a stormy breeze had disheveled his hair, and he appeared to be very threatening" (48).

Even though this figure evokes the image of the famous 'wild man' in Hartmann von Aue's *Iwein* (ca. 1190), the difference could not be bigger, although there are some fundamental issues shared both here and there. That sylvan character in Hartmann's Arthurian romance actually represents complete individual freedom, self-control, and dominance over all the ferocious animals in the forest, but he is also someone who knows nothing about the courtly world, knighthood, and civilization. Nevertheless, he does not have to obey any lord and rules all by himself over all the animals, so he represents the very opposite to Kaufringer's

---

(Tempe, AZ: Arizona Center for Medieval and Renaissance Studies, 2004 [appeared in 2005]), 289–312; id., "The Agency of Wives in High Medieval German Courtly Romances and Late Medieval Verse Narratives: From Hartmann von Aue to Heinrich Kaufringer," *Quidditas* 39 (2018): 25–53, online at: https://humanities.byu.edu/rmmra/pdfs/39.pdf (last accessed on Jan. 15, 2021; the search tends to lead nowhere at first, hence, look under vol. 39); id., "Das Paradox der widersprüchlichen Urteilsprechung und Weltwahrnehmung: göttliches vs. menschliches Recht in Heinrich Kaufringers 'Die unschuldige Mörderin' – mit paneuropäischen Ausblicken und einer neuen Quellenspur ('La femme du roi de Portugal')," *Neuphilologische Mitteilungen* CXX.II (2019): 7–28. I have not yet been able to consult Martin Schneider, *Kampf, Streit und Konkurrenz: Wettkämpfe als Erzählformen der Pluralisierung in Mären*. Aventiuren, 15 (Göttingen: V&R unipress, 2020), but his topic does not seem to be related to the present investigation.

figure of the enslaved peasant who is kept in the prison cell to serve as a sex slave for the innkeeper's wife.[198]

Edgar Allan Poe's horror story "The Cask of Amontillado" from 1847 might be a distant avatar, with the grizzly imprisonment of the miserable victim (Fortunato) in the crypt deeply underneath a river in an Italian town at the hand of a man called Montresor as a punishment for unspecified injuries and insults – he is chained, walled in, and thus has to die a horrible death.[199] However, here, in Kaufringer's case, the prisoner has an important task to fulfill and must be fed well in order to maintain his sexual potency for the host's wife. Without the prisoner, the husband would not enjoy honor in his community, and would be the butt of public jokes because of his lack of manliness, being cuckolded by his wife all the time. The prison thus assumes an essential counter-role for the house above – private versus public, sex versus impotence – just as in the case of Boccaccio's story, though there the abbot simply moves the farmer out of the way for ten months so that he can have free access to the wife's body, and then allows him to return to the living in order to make the pregnancy look legitimate.

We face, in other words, an odd mirror perspective, with Kaufringer's husband capturing an innocent man from the countryside for his wife's sexual needs, while with Boccaccio the abbot takes the husband out of 'business,' so to speak, and substitutes for him for ten months in secret. It would be worthwhile to explore the relationship between both narratives further because of the intriguing correlations between the individual figures, but suffices it here to state that imprisonment serves both authors in an intricate fashion to work out a surprising love relationship keeping out the public and preserving the secrecy of the extramarital sexual affair.

---

198 Hartmann von Aue, *Iwein*. 4., überarbeitete Auflage. Text der siebenten Ausgabe von G. F. Benecke, K. Lachmann und L. Wolff. Übersetzt und Nachwort von Thomas Cramer (Berlin and New York: Walter de Gruyter, 2001), 418–599. For a discussion of the famous frescoes showing also this Wild Man in Castle Rodenegg, Southern Tyrol, see Volker Schupp and Hans Szklenar, *Ywain auf Schloß Rodenegg: Eine Bildgeschichte nach dem 'Iwein' Hartmanns von Aue* (Sigmaringen: Jan Thorbecke, 1996), esp. 58–59, figs. II and III. Cf. now Udo Friedrich, *Menschentier und Tiermensch: Diskurse der Grenzziehung und Grenzüberschreitung im Mittelalter* (Göttingen: Vandenhoeck & Ruprecht, 2009); for a copy of the image online, see https://de.wikipedia.org/wiki/Iwein#/media/Datei:Iweinwaldmensch.jpg (last accessed on Jan. 15, 2021).
199 Edgar Allan Poe, *The Selected Writings of Edgar Allan Poe: Authoritative Texts, Backgrounds and Contexts, Criticism*, selected and ed. by Gary R. Thompson (New York: Norton, 2004). For an online version of the text, see http://www.poedecoder.com/Qrisse/works/amontillado.php (last accessed on Jan. 15, 2021).

Boccaccio's *Decameron* could easily serve us to probe further the experience of imprisonment as reflected on in late medieval literature, such as in the sixth story told on the second day or in the second and sixtth story told on the fourth day. In fact, we often hear of secular and of clerical prisons, such as in monasteries where ill-behaved monks have to spend time as punishment for their evil deeds. Even though these are 'only' literary examples, they clearly underscore how fundamental it was for all pre-modern societies to set up rules, promulgate laws, have a police force, and to send off to prison those who had acted criminally or who were supposed to be removed for political reasons.[200]

3 Interim – Slavery in Historical Terms: A Few Examples in Support of the Literary Evidence

This represents a welcome segue to widen our perspective and to include also the phenomenon of slavery as the worst case of losing one's freedom. Granted, we do not often hear of slaves within European medieval courtly literature, and this despite the fact that the practice of trading in and using slaves in many different roles and functions was quite extensive even in the late Middle Ages,[201] at least around the Mediterranean. Virtually all major port cities had larger slave markets, both east and west, both Muslim and Christian, simply because bartering with unfree people was good business.[202] And slaves were of high value, being used in countless functions, from low to high, many being half free, half enslaved, or were eventually set free for their good services, all depending on the circumstances.[203] The role of female slaves for sexual services, or as wet nurses, also would have to be considered.[204]

One of the main reasons for the growth in slave trade since the mid fourteenth century seems to have been the massive loss of laborers due to the pandemic of the Black Death, which resulted in a extensive growth of salaries. To

---

200 Wolfram Hoyer OP, "Volumus ut carceres fiant: Medieval Dominican Legislation on Detention and Imprisonment," *Making and Breaking the Rules: Discussion, Implementation, and Consequences of Dominican Legislation*, Cornelia Linde. Studies of the German Historical Institute London (Oxford: Oxford University Press, 2018), 323–48.
201 Barker, *That Most Precious Merchandise* (see note 119).
202 Kevin Mummey, "Women, Slavery, and the Notarial Process in Late Fourteenth-Century Mallorca," *Rethinking Medieval Margins and Marginality* (see note 104), 110–28.
203 Jeffrey Fynn-Paul, "Empire, Monotheism and Slavery in the Greater Mediterranean Region from Antiquity to the Modern Era," *Past and Present* 205 (November 2009): 3–40.
204 Kevin Mummey, "Women and Chains: Women, Slavery, and Community in Late Fourteenth-Century Mallorca," Ph.D. diss., University of Minnesota, 2013.

have slaves substitute for free laborer was apparently an economic advantage.[205] As the Mallorcan documents reveal, there were surprisingly many women, especially widows, involved in buying and selling slaves, some at almost shockingly high prices. Sometimes a network of women joined forces to acquire slaves because they needed help in running their businesses or estates, especially when the husbands had deceased. And many times, the slave could sign a contract with his/her master to purchase his/her freedom after a certain number of years.[206] It also deserves to be pointed out that within a marriage, husband and wife could each have their own slaves, which sometimes led to strife among them over individual slaves both seem to have claimed for themselves. At times, the records even seem to indicate that the relationship between slave owner (female or male) and the slave was almost cordial or friendly, though this did not change anything in the legal and financial conditions of the slaves.[207] Contrary to many modern assumptions, the slaves were not at all exclusively of African origin. In Valencia, for example, the group of local slaves were Tartars, Circassians, and Russians, as well as Moros from Africa and the Canary Islands, and the picture becomes even more colorful when we turn to other port cities and urban centers with a larger slave population.[208]

4 Slavery in Icelandic Sagas – Fleeting but Revealing References

But we also learn of slaves in the perhaps most unexpected context, in the Old Norse Sagas, such as in the *Njál's Saga* (late thirteenth century), where a slave operates in a rather critical context, triggering a whole sequence of violent acts

---

205 A. R. Bridbury, "The Black Death," *Economic History Review*, 2nd Ser. 26 (1973): 557–92; Roser Salicrú i Lluch, "L'esclau com a inversió? Aprofitament, assalariament i rendibilitat del treball esclau en l'entorn català tardomedieval," *Recerques: història, economia, cultura* 52–53 (2006): 49–85.
206 Onofre Vaquer Bennàssar, *L'Esclavitud a Mallorca, 1448–1500* (Palma, Mallorca: IEB, 1997); Mummey, "Women, Slavery, and the Notarial Process in Late Fourteenth-Century Mallorca" (see note 202), 116.
207 Debra Blumenthal, *Enemies and Familiars: Slavery and Mastery in Fifteenth Century Valencia* (Ithaca, NY: Cornell University Press, 2009).
208 Charles Verlinden, *L'esclavage dans l'Europe medieval*. 2 vols. Rijksuniversiteit te Gent; Werken uitgegeven door de Faculteit van de Letteren en Wijsbegeerte, 119e aflevering, 162 (Bruges: "De Tempel", 1955).

which ultimately endanger society at large.[209] While Icelandic society was primarily determined by new settlers, they brought with them all of their families, or founded their own, and this seems to have entailed a variety of subordinated figures as well, such as the thralls, or slaves, who are mentioned more often than we would have expected (see, for instance, *Grettir's Saga*) and who certainly occupied a noteworthy low corner of that nordic world.

A closer examination of the relevant archival evidence, also in the region north of the Alps, reveals that slavery was not at all unknown there.[210] Thus it does not come as a surprise that those who settled so far northwest of continental Europe, and even further away from the Mediterranean, also brought their own slaves with them.

Normally, the main figures in this saga a free men, rich landholders, lawmakers, traders, and wise men, and their wives, but in one case we also hear of a slave. In *Njál's Saga*, Hallbjorn, brother of Otkel and Hallkel, has brought with him a slave named Melkolf, who originated from Ireland and who is identified immediately as "unlikeable" (79). Although only a slave, he seems to enjoy considerable freedom to voice opinions, such as when he requests the privilege to stay with Otkel who "was kind to him and gave him a knife and a belt a full set of clothes" (79). Hallbrjorn is willing to sell the slave to him, but he has a negative opinion of Melkolf and considers the value of this man as too highly

---

209 *Njal's Saga*, trans. with intro. and notes by Robert Cook (see note 170). As to slaves in that nordic country, see Marlis Wilde-Stockmeyer, *Sklaverei auf Island: Untersuchungen zur rechtlich-sozialen Situation und literarischen Darstellung der Sklaven im skandinavischen Mittelalter*. Skandinavistische Arbeiten, 5 (Heidelberg: Universitätsverlag Winter, 1978); Jukka Korpela, *Slaves from the North: Finns and Karelians in the East European Slave Trade, 900–1600*. Studies in Global Slavery, 5 (Leiden and Boston: Brill, 2018). For an insightful comparative study placing this text within the European context, see Alois Wolf, *Die Saga von der Njálsbrenna und die Frage nach dem Epos im europäischen Mittelalter*. Beiträge zur Nordischen Philologie, 53 (Tübingen: A. Francke Verlag, 2014). For the texts of the Icelandic Sagas, such as *Grettis's Saga* (also written down in the thirteenth or fourteenth century), see now the excellent online collection, https://sagadb.org/index_az (last accessed on Jan. 15, 2021). For the history of the 'thralls' in Iceland and elsewhere, see now Ben Raffield, "The Slave Markets of the Viking World: Comparative Perspectives on an 'Invisible Archaeology'," *Slavery & Abolition* 40.4 (2019): 682–705; Thomas K. Heebøll-Holm, ""Piratical Slave-Raiding – The Demise of a Viking Practice in High Medieval Denmark," *Scandinavian Journal of History* June 4 (2020), online at: https://www.tandfonline.com/doi/full/10.1080/03468755.2020.1748106 (last accessed on Jan. 15, 2021).

210 Charles Verlinden, *Slavenhandel en economische ontwikkeling in Midden-, Oost- en Noord-Europa gedurende de hoge middeleeuwen*. Mededelingen van de Koninklijke Academie voor Wetenschappen, Letteren en Schone Kunsten van België, Klasse der Letteren, 41.2 (Brussel: Paleis der Academiën, 1979).

placed, as the subsequent narrative then also confirms: "Once Otkel owned the slave his work got worse and worse" (79).

Subsequently, Otkel sells Melkolf to Gunnar, who had actually asked whether he could buy hay and food from him during a famine and was denied all. Gunnar is advised by one of his companions to resort to violence and to rob those items, but he refuses to do that as well, though he accepts the slave as a commodity. The narrative then quickly switches to Njál who learns about the bad exchange between those two men, and, prodded by his wife Bergthora, he takes plenty of those items and brings them as gifts to his friend Gunnar. However, Gunnar is married to an unevenly tempered woman, Hallgerd, who always pursues her own agenda, which eventually will mean her husband's death.

One of her evil strategies consist of creating a major damage to the people of Kirkjubaer, led by Otkel, stealing butter and cheese and to set fire to their storage shed. She orders the slave to carry out this deed on her behalf. Even though he hesitates at first, he does not enjoy the freedom to resist her. He admits: "I've been bad, but I 've never been a thief" (81), but she retorts that he had already committed murder in the past and would be killed now if he dared to refuse. At any rate, as the narrator makes abundantly clear, this is a man with a very poor character and with no morals, which finds its expression, for instance, in the way how he treats one of the dogs keeping guard at Kirkjubaer. Since it recognizes Melkolf and welcomes him as its friend, not turning to barking, highly unusual for dogs both then and today.[211] However, after Melkolf has broken into the shed and taken the horses and food, he "then set fire to the shed and killed the dog" (81). He is a callous, criminal, and mean-spirited character, though this has no bearing on the fact that he is a slave.

In fact, Hallgerd is to be blamed as the instigator of this theft and arson, and when Gunnar learns that the cheese and butter on their dining table had been stolen, he slaps her on the face, for which she will later take revenge by refusing to help her husband in his final battle, which makes her partly responsible for his death in the fight (82; for Gunnar's defeat ultimately brought about because Hallgerd refuses to give him some locks of her hair from which

---

[211] In Gottfried von Straßburg's *Tristan*, the protagonist takes a hunting dog, Hiudan, with him when the two lovers are expelled from the court and withdraw to their secret love cave. In order to keep their hiding place secure, he trains the dog to go hunting without barking (vv. 17254–60), which is another sign of Tristan's ability to transform nature into art; Albrecht Classen, "Hunde als Freunde und Begleiter in der deutschen Literatur vom Mittelalter bis zur Gegenwart: Reaktion auf den 'Animal Turn' aus motivgeschichtlicher Sicht," *Etudes Germaniques* 73.4 (2018): 441–66.

he could make a substitute bow string, see 128). The subsequent events blow out of proportion because other evil people get involved and offer malicious advice, which then makes the case of the theft balloon into a public scandal of enormous proportions, but Gunnar succeeds, with the help of Njál's advice, to extricate himself from this conflict, establishing a settlement that proportions acceptably the various damages done. For Gunnar, however, it is also important to get rid of the slave, whom he characterizes publicly as an evil man:

> "My terms are," he said, "that I should pa the value of the storage shed and the food that was in it. For the slave Melkolf's doings I will pay nothing becauseyou hid his faults me me, and I return him to you, since ears belong best in the place where they grew. I also find that you summoned me with intent to disgrace, and for that I award myself nothing less than the value of the shed and the contents that were burned. (89)

If we take into consideration the *Landnámabók* and the *Islendingasôgur*, we hear many times of slaves being taken in Ireland and Scotland through Viking raids. They were quite common 'commodity,' and were sold frequently on international markets, such as in Russia, where Swedes sold slaves to Arab merchants.

However, it was also possible that native Scandinavians could be taken as slaves in the wake of raids, or as punishments for crimes and unpaid debts. When slaves were hurt or killed, the party responsible for those acts had to pay compensation, but not to the victims; instead the owner received that money or payment. The Law of Uppland (1296, most of central Sweden) was deliberately aimed at ameliorating the conditions of slaves and regulated the fines and amounts of compensation, but this did not remove the institution of slavery in the Scandinavian countries far in the late Middle Ages. In parts of Denmark and Sweden, slaves were even allowed to marry, and their children kept their mother's social status, which thus prolonged slavery over generations. If one of the parents was a Christian, however, the child was free, at least according to the Law of Uppland and other law codes. Slaves were integrated into the larger families and did more or less the same labor as the other farm hands.

The poet's disrespect for the slave Melkolf in the *Njál's Saga* is reverberated and even emphasized in *Rígsþula*, where the slaves face open contempt and are ridiculed and belittled in many different ways.[212] To quote from a quick summary,

> Rígr was walking along the shore and came to a farm-hut owned by Ái (great-grandfather) and Edda (great-grandmother). They offered him shelter and poor, rough food for a meal. That night Rígr slept between the pair in their bed and then departed. Nine months later, Edda gave birth to a son who was svartan (dark). They named him Þræll (thrall, serf, or slave). Þræll grew up strong but ugly. He married a woman named Thír (slave girl or bondswoman), and they had twelve sons and nine daughters with names mostly suggesting ugliness and squatness. They became the race of serfs.[213]

In the course of time, Christian owners of slaves tended to grant them freedom, but this did not simply end the institution of slavery.[214] In 1335 the Swedish Skara Ordinance prohibited that Christians were taken as slaves, but this did not prevent others to purchase non-Christians as slaves. Yet, altogether, as Ruth Mazo Karras concludes, "By the later Middle Ages, the free population of Scandinavia was much more stratified socially than before, and not all free people had full political rights, but there was no longer a need for a formal category of slave."[215]

---

[212] The outcome of Rig's creation of human races is that there are various social classes, including the serfs and slaves. See stanza 13:
    Daughters had they, | Drumba and Kumba,
    Ökkvinkalfa, | Arinnefla,
    Ysja and Ambott, | Eikintjasna,
    Totrughypja | and Tronubeina;
    And thence has risen | the race of thralls.
http://www.voluspa.org/rigsthulaintro.htm (last accessed on Jan. 15, 2021). See also the commentary by Géza von Neményi, *Kommentar zu den Götterliedern der Edda*. Vol. 3: *Die Vanenlieder Skirnisfor, Grógaldr, Fjolsvinnsmál, Rígspula, Hyndluljóð: Textausgabe nach der korrigierten Übersetzung von Karl Simrock mit ausführlicher Einleitung (im Teil 1) und Kommentierung zu den Liedstrophen aus heidnischer Sicht*. Reihe altheidnische Schriften (Holdenstedt: Kersken-Canbaz-Verlag, 2014).

[213] *The Elder Edda: A Book of Viking Lore*, trans. with intro. and notes by Andy Orchard (London: Penguin, 2011), 241–47, stanza 13; see also https://religion.wikia.org/wiki/R%C3%ADgs%C3%BEula (last accessed on Jan. 15, 2021).

[214] *Eurasian Slavery, Ransom and Abolition in World History, 1200–1860*, ed. Christoph Witzenrath (Farnham, Surrey, and Burlington, VT: Ashgate, 2015).

[215] Ruth Mazo Karras, "Slavery," *Medieval Scandinavia: An Encyclopedia*, ed. Phillip Pulsiano (New York and London: Garland, 1993), 598–99; here 599. She briefly mentions the Saga literature, but does not go into any details, such as to the slave in the *Njál's Saga*. See also her *Slavery and Society in Medieval Scandinavia*. Yale Historical Publications, 135 (New Haven, CT: Yale University Press, 1988).

By contrast, the *Njál's Saga* emphasizes the high value of freedom as enjoyed by the individual landholders, such as Gunnar and Njál. The various protagonist are described in their free lives, interacting with each as the great masters of their estates, often getting into conflict with some neighbors, but trying to handling the situation as good as possible. The narrative gaze rarely wanders down the social ladder, but when it happens, then we hear of some slaves as well, especially when they prove to be outstanding individuals, or when they are evil characters.

In the *Saga of the People of Laxardal*, or *Laxdæla Saga*, the unusual figure of Asgaut appears on the stage, also a slave. He had arrived in Iceland together with his master, Thord Goddi, a mighty, powerful, and wealthy man who had immigrated from somewhere (Norway?) to Iceland and had brought with him this Asgaut. The narrator praises him considerably as a noteworthy and highly loyal individual: "He was a large and capable man, and, though he was called a slave, there were few among those called free men who could regard themselves as his equal... . Thord had other slaves, but only Asgaut is mentioned by name."[216] He can actually travel by himself and serves his master so well that one day, when he returns home, Thord's wife Vigdis praises him and gives him, as his reward for his labor, his freedom. He uses that freedom to leave on a ship, traveling first to Norway and then to Denmark, where is settles enjoying high respect.

Another man, Hoskuld, is said to purchase a slave woman from Gilli the Russian, who owns eleven others all sitting in his tent, waiting to be bought. Gilli demands more money for the one woman Hoskuld has chosen because of her beauty, but Gilli also admits that she has a fault because she does not seem to be able to speak. Hoskuld then agrees to the price, and already the same night he sleeps with her, and the next morning he gives her much more splendid clothing than those she was dressed in as Gilli's property (17). At that point, the narrator does not go into any further details, especially not about the other slave women, but he pursues the odd situation that the new owner does not even know her name in more detail. Hoskuld is already married to Jorunn, who only inquires about this curious fact but does not demonstrate any other concern for her husband having bought a concubine.

Once being home, Hoskuld sleeps only with his wife and ignores the slave-woman, who displays a unique character and quality, though she does not speak, not even when she delivers a boy whom the father calls Olaf, a most beautiful and strong child that grows up rapidly. Jorunn soon demands that the slave-

---

[216] *The Saga of the People of Laxardal and Bolli Bollason's Tale*, trans. Keneva Kunz, ed. with an intro. by Bergljót S. Kristjánsdóttir (London: Penguin, 1997), 15.

woman make herself useful on the farm, and her husband makes her serve on him and his wife. After a while, he discovers the mother and her child at an isolated spot, both talking with each other, and only then does she finally reveal her secret. Her father is Myrkjartant, a king in Ireland, while she was taken a captive when she was only fifteen years of age. She also reveals her name, Melkorka, but she remains a slave, and there is no indication that anyone might try to ransom her; instead, she continues serving her master and mistress, though Jorunn develops jealousy of her, and it then comes to blows between them, which Hoskuld can stop from escalating when he enters the room.

We can sense what psychological tensions flared up there between those two women, but the narrator refrains from telling us the specific motivations. But Hoskuld then takes the slave-woman to another farm where she is well taken care of and lives mostly independently. Even though she is a slave, she soon operates quite independently and takes on a rather harsh and demanding role regarding her son Olaf's destiny, which Hoskuld determines through a variety of arrangements. Later, however, he grows tired of this responsibility and refers to Olaf as the one who should be in charge (35–36).

In fact, Melkorka, though still fully aware of her relatively low social status as a slave woman, freedly decides to accept Thorbjorn's hand in marriage, especially because this facilitates her son's effort to prepare a ship to journey to Ireland to visit his family (36). She also turns over to him a valuable gold ring which she herself had received from her father as a child which would help Olaf to be recognized as the Irish king's grandson (37). Again, there is no explanation of the slavery, or what this status means for Melkorka, who only cares for her son gaining full recognition as the heir to the Irish throne. After all, she even had taught him Irish "so that you'll be able to speak to people anywhere you make land in Ireland" (37). The narrative then follows Olaf's experiences in Ireland, but ignores the background, his mother's enslavement a long time ago, a woman of high Irish origin, but who does not seem to care about the return home. She would have liked her wet-nurse to have accompanied Olaf back to Iceland, but that did not happen.

Later, Hoskuld tries to marry his son to Egil's daughter Thorgerd, but she carries strong prejudice against Olaf, who is, to her, nothing but "some slave-girl's son" (47), although her father points out Melkorka's royal origin. Ultimately, the two young people talk it all over themselves and agree to get married, and there is no more talk about the slave-woman's low social status. Only Jorunn later brings this up again (50), but only in a rather encouraging manner, and the specific account of Olaf's life is concluded at that point with a story about a ghost appearance against whom Olaf has to fight (52). Future events happen, but they are not relevant for our discussion.

In *Grettis saga Ásmandarsonar*,²¹⁷ composed sometime in the early fourteenth century, maybe ca. 1310–1320, the protagonist at one point, accompanied by his brother Illugi, hides on the island of Drangery, but they are certainly not alone and have actually also slaves with them. Because the slave Þorbjorn glaumr is neglectful and allows the fire to go out, Grettir is forced to swim ashore to get a new fire from a farm on the mainland, where he is met with mockery by the farmer's daughter and maidservant about his small penis.²¹⁸ The passage about the slave tells us specifically:

> The thrall began to get very slack at his work; he grumbled much and was less careful than before. It was his duty to mind the fire every night, and Grettir bade him be very careful of it as they had no boat with them. One night it came to pass that the fire went out. Grettir was very angry and said it would only be right that Glaum should have a hiding. The thrall said he had a very poor life of it to have to lie there in exile and be ill-treated and beaten if anything went wrong (ch. 74).

There is later another side-remark about his slave, but the poet was obviously not interested in elaborating on this figure any further. Those slaves do not have a free will, but it might be worth investigating further what actual conditions determined their lives in legal and social terms.²¹⁹ However, the poets of the Icelandic sagas do not go much into detail about those slaves, but there is no doubt that they existed, even if they did not live under the same circumstances as in other parts of the Continent and the Middle East.²²⁰ Grettir, for instance, does not respond in any negative terms to the slave's negligence and simply attempts to compensate for the latter's failure. In many other contexts, we hear of slaves as simple farmhands working under the command of the various protagonists, the mighty rulers of rural estates. This then makes it rather difficult for us to assess the legal and economic conditions of those unfree individuals.

---

217 *Grettir's Saga*, trans. Denton Fox and Hermann Palsson (1977; Toronto, Buffalo, and London: University of Toronto Press, 2002); here I am quoting from *Grettir's Saga*, trans. G. A. Hight (s.l: s.p., 1914); online at: https://www.sagadb.org/grettis_saga.en2 (last accessed on Jan. 15, 2021).
218 Phelpstead, *An Introduction to the Sagas of Icelanders* (see note 101), 130.
219 Phelpstead, *An Introduction to the Sagas of Icelanders* (see note 101), refers to slaves at times, but does not examine this institution.
220 P. H. Sawyer, *Kings and Vikings: Scandinavia and Europe AD 700–1100* (New York and London: Routledge, 2002), 39; Niels Skyum-Nielsen, "Nordic Slavery in an International Context," *Medieval Scandinavia* 11 (1978–1979): 126–48. See also Marlis Wilde-Stockmeyer, *Sklaverei auf Island* (see note 209). Cf. now Neil Price, *Children of Ash and Elm: A History of the Vikings* (New York: Basic Books, 2020), 141–46, 150–54; for further references, see 531–32; for an excellent review, see William Sayers, in *Mediaevistik* 33 (forthcoming, 2021).

These "thralls" originated from many different locations, often having been captured during any of the many Viking expeditions of looting and pillaging. But it often remains unclear what the differences might have been between those slaves and ordinary farmhands and maids.[221] In the case of *Grettir's Saga*, at least, the slave works closely with his masters, but this also means that he brings great misfortune upon Grettir who receives a severe wound in his leg from trying to cut a log with his ax. Grettir had rejected that log already twice, out of justified fear that there might be a spell placed on it by Thorbjorn's foster-mother, and so had tossed it out to the water, but the slave, in his ignorance, later brought it back in, without Grettir then knowing what kind of wood it was: "'He who meant me evil has prevailed; it will not end with this. This is the very log which I twice rejected. Two disasters have you now brought about, Glaum; first you let our fire go out, and now you have brought in this tree of ill-fortune. A third mistake will be the death of you and of us all'" (ch. 79).

To what extent we could call Glaum a thrall, or slave, however, appears rather ambivalent: "He was a vagrant, had no mind to work and swaggered much. It was the habit of some to make game of him or fool him. He became very familiar and told them much gossip about the district and the people therein" (ch. 69). But ultimately, Glaum fails in his duties, sleeps all day, does not pull up the ladder that makes possible the access to the island, which then allows the enemies to come up, who then eventually kill Grettir and take Illugi with them, only to kill him later. The slave is also slaughterhed by them: they "slew him there where he was, crying as loud as he could until he was killed" (ch. 82). The leader of the enemy band, Thorbjorn Angle, had only words of mockery for this thrall when he scoffed at him: "'True is the ancient saying that Old friends are the last to break away, and also this, that It is ill to have a thrall for your friend – such a one as you, Glaum! You have shamefully betrayed your liege lord, though there was little good in him'" (ch. 82).[222]

5 *Aucassin and Nicolette:* The Female Slave as the Beloved

From here, we can move to another literary text of a very different genre where we also hear of a slave woman, Nicolette, who is loved by the young protagonist, Aucassin, but hated by his father, Count Garin of Beaucaire, because of her low

---

[221] Ruth Mazo Karras, *Slavery and Society in Medieval Scandinavia* (see note 215).
[222] Phelpstead, *An Introduction to the Sagas of Icelanders* (see note 101), 124–34.

social status, which would bring down the reputation of his family.[223] This Old French *chantefable* from ca. 1220–1240; if not somewhat earlier, which consists of a mixture of poetry and prose, known as prosimetrum, has enjoyed a high level of popularity particularly in nineteenth- and twentieth-century art and music.[224] The verse narrative proves to be rather deceptive at first because the focus rests so deeply on emotional aspects, the conflict between father and son, the intensive love between the prince Aucassin and the former slave girl Nicolette, the conflicts they experience within society, their escape from prison, the experience of a kind of utopia in the kingdom of Torelore, the kidnapping by pirates, similar to the situation in *Apollonius of Tyre*, and other adventurous elements. But for our purpose, we must not ignore one of the critical issues, her origin and destiny, intimately tied in with slavery and imprisonment, and hence also about freedom, which confirms how much these topics concerned people in the pre-modern age since those themes could also easily enter such playful poetic texts such as *Aucassin et Nicolette*.

Very parallel to the situation in the *Laxdæla Saga*, here we encounter, once again, the tragic situation of a young princess, though this time she is the daughter of the ruler of Carthage, hence a Muslim king, and now in the possession of Christian aristocrats, the Viscount of the town where Garin of Beaucaire rules. The entire text is certainly strongly determined by fanciful feature, playful elements, satirical comments, and emotional expressions, projecting a near-imaginary world. Nevertheless, there is enough cultural-historical background to gain a good sense of how the poet drew from common experiences at his time and

---

223 *Aucassin and Nicolette: A Facing-Page Edition and Translation* by Robert S. Sturges (East Lansing, MI: Michigan State University Press 2015); see also *Aucassin et Nicolette*, ed. critique. 2nd rev. and corrected ed. by Jean Dufournet (Paris: GF-Flammarion, 1984). See also *Aucassin et Nicolette*, trans. and photo-ill. by Katharine Margot Toohey (2017), online at: https://quemarpress.weebly.com/uploads/8/6/1/4/86149566/aucassin_and_nicolette_-_translation_by_k.m._toohey.pdf; for further online links to older editions, see https://en.wikipedia.org/wiki/Aucassin_and_Nicolette (both last accessed on Jan. 15, 2021); for some critical comments, see Roger Pensom, *Aucassin et Nicolete: The Poetry of Gender and Growing Up in the French Middle Ages* (Bern, Berlin, et al.: Peter Lang, 1999); Albrecht Classen, "Aucassin et Nicolette," *Encyclopedia of Medieval Literature*, ed. Jay Ruud (New York: Facts on File, 2005), 44–46; Philippe De Wolf, "La critique de l'amour courtois dans la littérature médiévale: Le 'De amore' d'André le Chapelain et 'Aucassin et Nicolette' (fin du XIIe-début du XIIIe siècle)," Ph.D. Université libre de Bruxelles, 2010; Robert Stuart Sturges, "Race, Sex, Slavery: Reading Fanon with Aucassin et Nicolette," *Postmedieval* 6 (2015/16): 12–22.
224 https://commons.wikimedia.org/wiki/Category:Aucassin_et_Nicolette?uselang=de (last accessed on Jan. 15, 2021).

injected those into his fictional account. As Francis William Bourdillon had already formulated:

> And here before us is of all pretty love-stories perhaps the prettiest. Idyllic as Daphnis and Chloe, romantic as Romeo and Juliet, tender as Undine, remote as Cupid and Psyche, yet with perpetual touches of actual life, and words that raise pictures; and lightened all through with a dainty playfulness, as if Ariel himself had hovered near all the time of its writing, and Puck now and again shot a whisper of suggestion.[225]

He also assumed that the original story had been composed in Spain, and was transposed only later, maybe during the early part of the thirteenth century, to northern France, as the many geographical and personal names indicate, though there is no guarantee for this thesis. The text has survived only in two manuscripts, but it certainly mirrors common entertainment literature during the high Middle Ages.[226] Here we learn about feuds between two local lords, conflicts between father and son, criticism of war as such, budding love between the prince Aucassin and the former slave Nicolette, their elopement, travel, music, and so forth.

What does the text reveal about Nicolette's origin and status? She was bought by the Viscount of the town of Valence (Valencia?) on a Muslim slave market, but not only as a worker in his household and estate. He took her on virtually as his own daughter, had her baptized and raised by teachers, preparing her for a good marriage with a wealthy man from the urban community, at least fitting for her social class. None of that is respectable enough for Aucassin's father who has aspiring plans for his own son whom he would like to see married to a royal princess or at least a count's daughter. His son, however, disregards all those social criteria and only wants to pursue his love for Nicolette, whom he praises in the highest possible terms. The poet remarks that she originated from Carthage (maybe, however, from Cartagena, south of Murcia?) and represents a severe threat to Count Bourgars's marriage and dynastic plans for his son. So, he urges the owner to eliminate the young woman (kill her?) because her influence represents a major danger to the future development of this noble family. The Viscount quickly agrees, although he had obviously bonded with the

---

225 *Aucassin and Nicolette*, trans. from the Old French by Francis William Bourdillon (London: Kegan Paul, Trench, and Trübner, 1908), 8.
226 Paris, Bibliothèque nationale de France, français, 2168, f. 70rb-80va (with musical notations), and Paris, Bibliothèque nationale de France, Arsenal, 2770, a copy of 2168. For a detailed description of both manuscripts, along with an impressive bibliography of modern editions, translations, and critical studies, see https://www.arlima.net/ad/aucassin_et_nicolette.html (last accessed on Jan. 15, 2021).

girl, having made her to his god-daughter, especially because he believes to have 'rescued' her from the Islamic faith.

In order to comply with the Count's request, he basically puts Nicolette in the same kind of garden setting as Marie de France had used in the case of "Guigemar," once again a kind of *locus amoenus*, a garden surrounded by a tall wall, but a pleasant location, with plenty of provisions for the young woman and a female companion for fellowship. Even the door to the garden is firmly sealed, and he keeps open only a window, which altogether constitutes, once again, a prison for the poor lady, the true heroine, but abused and imprisoned by the old male characters: "puis si fist l'uis seeler c'on n'i peust de nule part entrer ne iscir, fors tant qu'il i avoit une fenestre par devers le gardin assés petite dont il lor venoit un peu d'essor" (Then he had the door sealed up, so that there was no way to go in there, nor to go out, except that there was a window overlooking the garden, small enough, through which there came to them a little fresh air).[227] Just as in the case of Marie's verse narrative, the female prisoner is also stuck in a cell with delightful wall paintings, though here we are not told about their didactic purposes.

Nicolette's disappearance creates an uproar in the country, obviously because she was much liked and highly esteemed, and Aucassin severely challenges the Viscount, inquiring about his beloved's whereabout, but he is given the same comments about the foolishness to love a woman of such a low social status.

Subsequently, the war situation worsens for Aucassin's father who then begs his son to help him fight the enemy, but his son only agrees on the condition that he lets him see his beloved and to allow him to kiss her once. Even though the count agrees, and even though his son then achieves the military goal, his father reneges on his promise and actually throws his own son into the dungeon hoping to make his mind change regarding this Saracen girl.

As in a good modern detective or crime story, Nicolette soon manages to escape from her prison by tying bedcloths and towels together to climb out of the window. She can even talk with her imprisoned lover, but eventually she has to run away and disappear in the woods. In the meantime, the Count Garin let's his son out of the prison and actually sends him out to the countryside to cheer him up because he assumes that Nicolette has disappeared. In reality, however, she is hiding in the middle of the forest, so the two lovers then can find each other, and the highly entertaining story continues from there.

---

227 http://www.umilta.net/aucassin.html (last accessed on Jan. 15, 2021), ch. IV.

5 Aucassin and Nicolette: The Female Slave as the Beloved — 137

This *chantefable* represents, of course, a literary dreamworld with many fanciful, entertaining, imaginary components, including the world of Torelore where the king lies in bed assuming that he is about to deliver a child, while his wife is out on the field waging a war agains their enemies, but using only food items as weapons. But for our purposes, what really matters is that both protagonists are thrown into prison as a means to separate them and to bring them to 'reason,' at least according to dynastic interests pursued by the father.

However, in terms of freedom and imprisonment/enslavement, life proves to be unstable and completely contingent, since they both are captured and taken as slaves when pirates besiege and conquer the castle of Torelore.[228] Aucassin is bound tightly and taken to one ship, whereas Nicolette is brought to another, so both have now completely lost their freedom, all hope, and they face near death. Curiously, however, ship with Aucassin is driven by the storm to the Castle of Beaucaire and is wrecked there, conveniently with him being the only survivor, which is quite parallel to the situation of the Muslim princess Alatiel in Boccaccio's *Decameron* (ca. 1350, seventh story, second day), though the outcome differs considerably, with the poor Arabic woman there used by many different men as a concubine until she is finally saved, returned to her father, and then sent off again to her future husband.[229]

Nicolette, by contrast, returns to Carthage from where she had been kidnapped from as a small child. Though her memories are dim, she remembers enough to realize that she has actually come home, and her father and brothers all rejoice and acknowledge her, soon trying to marry her off to a Muslim king, again in their typically male attitudes concerning their control over the female members of their family. But Nicolette quickly evades those attempts, transforms into a minstrel, changes her appearance, and soon disappears with a merchant

---

228 The history of piracy already in the Middle Ages (and actually antiquity), has recently attracted more attention; see, above all Emily Sohmer Tai, "Restitution and the Definition of a Pirate: The Case of Sologrus De Nigro," *Mediterranean Historical Review* 19 (2004): 34–70; eadem, "The Legal Status of Piracy in Medieval Europe," *History Compass* 10.11 (2012): 838–51; Peter Lehr, *Pirates: A New History, from Vikings to Somali Raiders* (New Haven, CT, and London: Yale University Press, 2019); for a collection of sources, see *Piracy in the Early Modern Era: An Anthology of Sources*, ed. and trans., with an intro. by Kris Lane and Arne Bialuschewski (Indianapolis, IN, and Cambridge: Hackett, 2019); *Piracy and Captivity in the Mediterranean, 1550–1810*, ed. Mario Klarer. Routledge Research in Early Modern History (Abingdon, Oxon: Routledge, 2019). Most recently, see Kathryn Reyerson, "Pirates as Marginals in the Medieval Mediterranean World," *Rethinking Medieval Margins and Marginality* (see note 104), 186–203.
229 Giovanni Boccaccio, *The Decameron* (see note 47); see also Sharon Kinoshita and Jason Jacobs, "Ports of Call: Boccaccio's Alatiel in the Medieval Mediterranean," *Journal of Medieval and Early Modern Studies* 37.1 (2007): 163–95.

ship aiming for the Provence where she indeed finds her beloved again, and soon reveals herself to him, which then concludes the narrative with a joyful ending.

Just as much as the tale itself consists of prose and verse, as much does it contain also dramatic ups and downs for the protagonists, once being high-ranking individuals enjoying great public esteem, next them being thrown into the dungeon and suffering in their loneliness and misery. Once they experience complete freedom, having escaped successfully from Beaucaire, they soon enough are captured by Muslim pirates, virtually an archetypal experience often mirrored in medieval literature (*Apollonius of Tyre*). But miraculous events turn everything to the better, so tragedy is replaced by comedy. As playful as the entire tale proves to be, as much do we realize here the extent to which people could easily lose their freedom, become enslaved, lose their lives, or recover from shipwreck. Behind the facetious literary facade obviously looms the dark reality of prisons and slavery. Even though the poet, like most of his contemporaries, does not address freedom as such, its absence through imprisonment clearly indicates the difficulties for individuals to lead their lives according to their own free will, especially with regard to marriage or the marriage partner.

This overly sentimental, almost motley fictional account also serves exceedingly well as a literary source for the further examination of slavery in the late Middle Ages. Not even the children of royal couples were safe, as the case of Nicolette illustrates, from being kidnapped. But instead of trying to retrieve their daughter, the young girl simply seems to have disappeared from her parents' view and concern, though fifteen years later when she happens to reappear by accident, they are greatly delighted and fully acknowledge her as part of the family. Of course, at that point, Nicolette has been raised as a Christian, she loves the Christian lord Aucassin, so there is nothing that can hold her back and keep her in Carthage, but this does not concern us here further.

6 *Floire et Blanchefleur*

Remarkably, we hear of raiding, killing, kidnapping, and enslavement being done by both sides of the political and religious divide. While in *Aucassin et Nicolette* the little girl had been taken violently from her parents to be sold on a slave market, where the Viscount acquired her as his possession, in the pan-European narrative of *Floire and Blanchefleur* (originally in Old French, ca. 1180), a Muslim force from southern Spain attacks Galicia in the north and does not only rob, destroy, burn, and kill, it also ambushes Christian pilgrims on the way to Santiago de Compostella. Tragically, a knight and his pregnant but widowed daughter become the warriors' victims, him being killed, while she is dragged off and turned over to the Muslim King, Fenix.[230] As it turns out, Fenix's wife had requested a female slave of noble descent to serve in her household (111–12), so the army had deliberately been on the lookout for such a person to capture in order to satisfy the queen's demands.

Surprisingly, the young captured woman is royally treated, receives a separate room by herself, and is allowed to keep her Christian faith (136–137). Both women, however, are pregnant, having conceived on the very same day, so they partake in their suffering and share the difficult time together almost like close friends irrespective of their religious difference and the fact that one is aqueen, the other a slave. After the two babies have been born, the Christian woman is charged with taking care of both, who, as the narrator is not tired of emphasizing repeatedly, loves both children dearly and takes the best care of them. Once Floire has reached the age of five, he is to be sent to a teacher, but he refuses to go without Blanchefleur, which his father eventually grants, as if the girl were not the daughter of a slave woman.

Events turn sour, however, once both have reached the proper age of marriage, and the sultan realizes that Floire truly and deeply loves Blanchefleur, who would not at all be an appropriate wife for him. The sultan thus wants the young woman to be decapitated immediately, as he suggests to his wife, otherwise "Our lineage will be debased" (296). She advises against such a radical measure and suggests instead to resort to a ruse. Her mother must pretend to be sick and in need of the girl's care, whereas the boy should go to see his teacher, to be followed by Blanchefleur within two-weeks time.

Insofar as this is a deeply emotional love story, it does not come as a surprise that young Floire is so insistent and hangs on to Aucassin with all his might, and this very parallel to Aucassin and Nicolette. Once being forced to leave for his schooling, he suffers extremely from love-sickness and quickly fades away, the news of which cause his parents great concern, and again the sultan wants Blan-

---

230 Robert d'Orbigny, *Le conte de Floire et Blanchefleur: nouvelle édition critique du texte du manuscrit A (Paris, BNF, fr.375)*. Publié, traduit, présenté et annoté par Jean-Luc Leclanche. Champion Classiques. Série "Moyen Age", 2 (Paris: Champion Classiques, 2003); for an English trans., see *The Romance of Floire and Blanchefleur: A French Idyllic Poem of the Twelfth Century*, trans. Merton Jerome Hubert. University of North Carolina Studies in the Romance Languages and Literatures, 63 (Chapel Hill, NC: The University of North Carolina Press, 1966). For the Middle High German version, see Christine Putzo, *Konrad Fleck: 'Flore und Blanscheflur': Text und Untersuchungen*. Münchener Texte und Untersuchungen zur deutschen Literatur des Mittelalters, 143 (Berlin and Boston: Walter de Gruyter, 2015). For a global study, interdisciplinary study on this narrative, see Patricia E. Grieve, *Floire and Blancheflor and the European Romance*. Cambridge Studies in Medieval Literature, 32 (Cambridge: Cambridge University Press, 1997).

chefleur to be killed. Again, his wife intervenes, and suggests to sell the girl on the slave market because there are many rich merchants from Babylon who would be eager to buy such a valuable 'commodity' (413–19). Indeed, two merchants pay a huge price for the girl, but they make double the profit for her when they present her to the emir of Babylon, who is greatly delighted about her beauty and orders his men "to guard her well" (513), especially because her physical appearance reveals her noble origin (509).

Once Floire has returned home, he immediately wants to see his beloved, but his parents pretend that she has died, as documented by a fake tomb. But the young man is so dejected and is in danger of committing suicide out of despair that his mother has to reveal the truth to him, whereupon the actual story sets in, with Floire following Blanchefleur's tracks and eventually finding her and winning her back as his wife, in the course of which he can change the emir's heart, who becomes their protector and takes care of all of their needs, making sure that he can knight Floire and thus to give Blanchefleur a worthy husband (2876–91).

The emir had actually been a cruel ruler who held a whole harem of young women, among them Blanchefleur, and married one of them for one year. Thereafter, she was then decapitated, and the same routine began anew. But when the two lovers are discovered, they display such intense care and love for each other that the emir's heart melts and he suddenly changes his mind completely, which we do not need to pursue further here. But we need to keep in mind how much the narrator emphasized the flourishing market of slaves, in this case especially of young women, and if Floire had not arrived in time and rescued his beloved, and if both had then not been so dedicated to each other that each one wanted to die in order to spare the other person's life, the horrible carousel of killing those slave women would have continued.

Obviously, the poet (and all others who developed this story in their own language) was fully aware of an intensive and complex system of slave trade, especially in the port cities of the Mediterranean.[231] Raids are carried out in other countries not only to conquer, to rob, to steal, or to plunder, but specifically to capture people as 'commodity' and to use them either for new owner's purposes, or to sell them further. Slave merchants can be found everywhere, whether in Muslim or Christian communities, and for a good price they are always willing to accept the offer to buy a valuable person and to resell that slave to the highest

---

231 Olivia Remie Constable, "Muslim Spain and Mediterranean Slavery: The Medieval Slave Trade as an Aspect of Muslim-Christian Relations," *Christendom and Its Discontents: Exclusion, Persecution, and Rebellion, 1000–1500*, ed. Scott L. Waugh, and Peter D. Diehl (Cambridge: Cambridge University Press, 1996), 264–84.

bidder. The literary evidence confirms what the historical sources inform us about, since the entire Mediterranean operated with slaves as a "precious merchandise."[232] But slave trade was not at all limited to the lands south of the Alps; otherwise, the various literary texts popular throughout the rest of Europe and which addressed slavery in one way or the other would not have achieved their success; the individual authors obviously addressed topics that were well known and represented tragic cases of human beings, rich or poor, Christians or Muslims, who could easily lose their freedom and become a merchandise.

7 Konrad Fleck: The Middle High German Version

Ironically, however, and this can certainly be attributed to the fictional freedom which the individual poets enjoyed, Blanchefleur, or Blanscheflur, as she is called in Konrad Fleck's Middle High German version, is assigned a palatial room in a tower with twenty maids serving her because the Admiral (not the emir, as in the French version) recognizes her noble character and acknowledges her extraordinary physical attractiveness. He clearly realizes that she is filled with sorrow and longing for her lover, but he urges her to take a year of reprieve, to overcome and abandon those feelings, to change her mind, and turn all her feelings toward him because he would then marry her and make her the queen ruler over all his lands.[233]

This sentimental romance focuses, however, mostly on the feelings of both lovers, at that point vastly separated, her being completely caught in this new prison, while he knows very little of her whereabout. Blanscheflur also worries deeply about the social difference between her and Flore, him being a king's son, whereas she herself knows nothing about her original family and feels socially subordinated and perhaps not even worthy of his love (1794–800). She herself worries about their difference in religion, but she dismisses that thought quickly because love bonds them so strongly (1808–11).

It might also be pure fiction, but Fleck provides many details about how much the merchants have to pay for Blanscheflur, which amounts to a veritable fortune (1540–56). In particular, they hand over a most valuable chalice, which is of ancient origin and engraved with the entire story of Troy, a 'classical' case of ekphrasis of great interest for the poet in his effort to display his rhetorical

---

232 Barker, *That Most Precious Merchandise* (see note 119). See now also Lori De Lucia "The Space between Borno and Palermo: Slavery and Its Boundaries in the Late Medieval Saharan-Mediterranean Region," *Rethinking Medieval Margins and Marginality* (see note 104), 11–25.
233 Putzo, *Konrad Fleck* (see note 230), vv. 1687–1730.

skills.[234] Once having arrived in Babylon, they can then sell their slave to an even higher price because the Admiral recognizes her value as his own future wife (1682–86). The entire set-up with the tower and its enormously luxurious interior, holding seventy rooms for all the ladies in there, as detailed by the old innkeeper Daries, amounts to pure fantasy, and represents a form of Orientalism *avant la lettre*, especially considering that the Admiral has purchased a slave, nothing more, and yet wants to make her to his wife (4151–4402).

Altogether, the theme of slavery matters centrally in the various versions of *Flore and Blanchefleur*, but it is quickly superseded by an intensive love story determined by sacrifice, complete dedication and loyalty, suffering, and enormous struggle by the young man to regain his beloved from the Babylonian ruler. After all, Blanscheflur is no ordinary slave, but rather the highest priced commodity in the Admiral's empire. Of course, within this fictional space, the poet can dream of a major change of the ruler's heart once he has witnessed the two lovers' absolute dedication to each other, their willingness to die so that the other can be spared. In reality, nothing of that sort was probable, but the literary discourse itself outlines the common practice of slaves being bartered all over the world, some for a very small, others for a huge price, all depending on the circumstances, the slave's 'qualities,' and the use which the owners wanted to make of their 'commodity.' We also need to keep in mind that the poet quickly transforms his figure of the Admiral from being a cruel and brutal tyrant or dictator into a surprisingly benevolent ruler who even listens to the advice of a Christian bishop at his court to forgive everyone who had helped Floris to achieve his goal (7337–67).

What matters for us consists of the open, concerned, and intensive discussion of slavery both within the Mediterranean as well as in the Eastern world of Babylon. Moreover, which opens an additional perspective which we need to keep in mind as well, the Admiral lets all the female slaves go, granting them freedom, and he himself then marries Blancheflur's friend and companion, Claris (7545), which seems to indicate the end of slavery by itself, as also confirmed by the subsequent courtly festival and tournament, all determined by courtly joy, as we often hear in Arthurian romances that are normally free of any references to slavery (7564).[235]

---

234 Haiko Wandhoff, *Ekphrasis: Kunstbeschreibungen und virtuelle Räume in der Literatur des Mittelalters*. Trends in Medieval Philology, 3 (Berlin and New York: Walter de Gruyter, 2003), 191–93, 301–20. See also Monika Fludernik, *Metaphors of Confinement* (see note 56).
235 Siegfried Christoph, "The Language and Culture of Joy," *Words of Love and Love of Words in the Middle Ages and the Renaissance*, ed. Albrecht Classen. Medieval and Renaissance Texts and Studies, 347 (Tempe: Arizona Center for Medieval and Renaissance Studies, 2008), 319–33.

8 Wolfram von Eschenbach, *Willehalm*

Rennewart, the Saracen Slave

In cases such as Wolfram von Eschenbach's *Willehalm* (ca. 1218), we might not come across an opportunity to reflect on the notions of freedom and imprisonment because it is an epic narrative (perhaps heroic romance?) in which a deadly war is pitting Christians against Muslims, and there are no prisoners taken because death awaits those who are defeated. Nevertheless, at closer analysis we discover a remarkable connection between *Willehalm* and the previous narratives, though there many sentiments and emotions dominate the events. In the background, or in the margin, Wolfram also reflects on these issues that concern us here, by introducing a most remarkable character, Rennewart, a slave first in the French king's service, then in Willehalm's, but he is a most mighty warrior, stronger and much more courageous and resolute than the entire French army. I would not go so far as to draw closer parallels with the protagonist in *Waltharius*, but there are significant similarities in the way how both poets project slaves as major military leaders for rulers who own them actually as property.[236]

Willehalm had been, which we find out only in the Old French source, *Aliscans* (ca. 1180–1190; ca. 8000 verses), a prisoner in Muslim hands, but the wife of his captor, Arabel, fell in love with him, so both eventually escaped back to Europe where she converted to Christianity and assumed the new name, Gyburc.[237] The epic narrative basically sets in with a huge heathen army under the leadership of her former husband, her father, and her son attacking Willehalm's castle. The protagonist barely survives in the first battle, but his entire

---

[236] Wolfram von Eschenbach, *Willehalm: nach der Handschrift 857 der Stiftsbibliothek St. Gallen*, mittelhochdeutscher Text, Übersetzung, Kommentar; mit den Miniaturen aus der Wolfenbütteler Handschrift, ed. Joachim Heinzle. Mit einem Aufsatz von Peter und Dorothea Diemer. Bibliothek des Mittelalters, 9 (Frankfurt a. M.: Deutscher Klassiker Verlag, 1991); for an English translation, see Wolfram von Eschenbach, *Willehalm*, trans. Marion E. Gibbs and Sidney M. Johnson (London: Penguin, 1984).

[237] See the contributions to *Guillaume et Willehalm: les épopées françaises et l'oeuvre de Wolfram von Eschenbach: actes du colloque de 12 et 13 janvier 1985*, ed. Danielle Buschinger. Göppinger Arbeiten zur Germanistik, 421 (Göppingen: Kümmerle, 1985); Thordis Hennings, *Französische Heldenepik im deutschen Sprachraum: Die Rezeption der Chansons de geste im 12. und 13. Jahrhundert – Überblick und Fallstudien – *. Beiträge zur älteren Literaturgeschichte (Heidelberg: Universitätsverlag Winter, 2009). However, he does not examine the relationship to the Old French *chanson de geste* in particular detail. For the Old French version, see *Aliscans*, texte établi par Claude Régner. Champion classiques, 21 (Paris: Champion, 2007); and *Aliscans: das altfranzösische Heldenepos nach der venezianischen Fassung M*, eingeleitet und übersetzt von Fritz Peter Knapp. De Gruyter Texte (Berlin and Boston: Walter de Gruyter, 2013).

army is decimated. With difficulties, Willehalm can make his way to the court of the French king and to appeal to him to protect Christianity. After various conflicts, they all agree that the attack by the Muslims against the Provence represents a *cause celèbre*, meaning that the protagonist is finally granted the help of the royal army.

The second part of the epic covers the renewed battle, and this time the Christians gain a devastating victory, after which the few Muslim survivors retreat and return to their homelands. For several decades, Wolfram's narrative has gained increasingly in respect and is now regarded as one of the masterpieces of medieval literature at large, being extent in the amazing number of seventy-nine manuscripts.[238]

While recent research has blossomed considerably, examining a plethora of important themes, figures, events, and motifs,[239] here the interest rests only on the figure of Rennewart, a slave owned by Willehalm. We encounter him first as serving as a kitchen boy who is badly abused by the cooks and squires, and eventually he avenges their merciless mocking and teething. In reality, he is the son of the heathen King Terramer, who is besieging now Willehalm's castle. As a child, he had been captured and was then sold by slave traders to the French king who knew about his royal status and therefore granted that he be raised together with his little daughter Alyze. Just as in the case of *Flore and Blancheflur*, the two young people fall in love with each other, and there is a clear sense that both are supposed to get married later in life.

Rennewart refused to accept conversion to Christianity, and for that reason he was punished to serve in the kitchen, until Willehalm recognizes him as an Arab child. Both can speak in Arabic, which Willehalm had learned during his own imprisonment, which is barely addressed by Wolfram, but commented on extensively in later versions of the Rennewart account. Rennewart appears like a giant, and he fights, revealingly, not with a sword, but with a huge club, the typical insignia of giants. Only once this club has broken, is he forced to resort

---

238 http://www.handschriftencensus.de/werke/440 (last accessed on Jan. 15, 2021).
239 See, for instance, Christopher Young, *Narrativische Perspektiven in Wolframs "Willehalm": Figuren, Erzähler, Sinngebungsprozeß*. Untersuchungen zur deutschen Literaturgeschichte, 104 (Tübingen: Max Niemeyer, 2000); *Wolframs "Willehalm": Fifteen Essays*, ed. Martin H. Jones and Timothy McFarland. Studies in German Literature, Linguistics, and Culture (Rochester, NY: Camden House, 2002); Florian Nieser, *Die Lesbarkeit von Helden: uneindeutige Zeichen in der "Bataille d'Aliscans" und im "Willehalm" Wolframs von Eschenbach* (Stuttgart: J. B. Metzler, 2018); Angila Vetter, *Textgeschichte(n): Retextualisierungsstrategien und Sinnproduktion in Sammlungsverbünden: der "Willehalm" in kontextueller Lektüre*. Philologische Studien und Quellen, 269 (Berlin: Erich Schmidt Verlag, 2018).

to a sword, and he proves to be a supreme champion for the Christian cause, basically deciding the war almost all by himself. Curiously, however, at the end he disappears from the narrator's view, and we do not learn, at least not in Wolfram's poem, about his future actions. Willehalm himself is rather perplexed and wonders aloud whether his favorite warrior might have been killed (453, 7). He also calls him the key figure in his entire army:

> you have won this land for me, and you have served my own life here and Giburc ... Were it not for your exceptional bravery, my old father would be lost... You were the rudder for my ship, the favouring wind for my sails that has allowed Heimrich's sons to drop anchor on Roman soil. No man's renown has come soaring in such high nobility among all people living today. You freed my kinsmen, fighting on sea and on land. (219)

There are significant differences in the way how the anonymous French poet and Wolfram describe Rennewart in his character and manner, with the latter casting the young man in a much better courtly light. In *Aliscans* he (Renoart) is already converted to Christianity, but the king had withheld the baptism, which finally happens at the end of the second battle (7894 ff.). In Wolfram's poem, it is Rennewart who refuses to accept the Christian faith because he mistrusts the religious-political power structures which are not to his own advantages.[240]

The French King Lôîs relates, "Merchants brought him across the sea after buying him in Persia. No one saw a face or a body more handsome. The woman who brought him into the world would be honoured if only he did not reject baptism" (102; Book IV, chapter 191, 11–18). It is unclear why Lôîs cares so much for this heathen pagan, but he first rejects Willehalm's request to let him have the foreign squire, but then, upon his daughter's pleading, he finally gives in. The encounter between Willehalm and Rennewart proves to be astonishing because the latter at first pretends not understand his French, but when the former turns to Arabic ("kaldeis und kôatî," 192, 8), which he had learned during his imprisonment, their conversation begins to flow. As the young man reveals, he was born in Mekka, was raised as a Muslim, but has turned his back to Islam because he has never been helped by Mahmete (Mohammed) despite his many prayers. In secret, hence, he has turned to Christ, but still refuses to get baptized because "it just does not suit my nature, and so night and day I have lived as if I had never had a powerful man for a father" (103).

---

[240] Elke Brüggen and Joachim Bumke, "Figuren-Lexikon," *Wolfram von Eschenbach: Ein Handbuch*, ed. Joachim Heinzle. Vol. II: *Figuren-Lexikon, Beschreibendes Verzeichnis der Handschriften, Bibliographien, Register und Abbildungen* (Berlin and Boston: Walter de Gruyter, 2011), 919–20.

Although Rennewart is never leaving the status of being a slave, he finds himself now in Willehalm's service, who treats him with respect, even calls him his friend at a later moment (105), and provides him with everything he might need for the war against the Muslims. In return, the squire promises him that he will avenge the margrave's massive losses in the first battle: "Sire, if you are the Marquis who has lost that magnificent army in battle against those who came across the sea, then I have been given over to you to help you in the nick of time. I shall avenge those men if I love to do so. I pledge myself to follow your advice" 103). There is no further word about his destiny as a slave; on the contrary, Willehalm treats him like the worthiest vassal, grants him full freedom to chose his own armor and weapons (only a mighty club). In fact, Willehalm often approaches him as 'his friend' and worthy warrior, and Giburc recognizes his royal origin, especially because she and the young man look so much alike (140–41).

Only later does the narrator return to telling us more about Rennewart's background, emphasizing that the slave merchants had sought him out particularly because of his royal status, which would make him especially precious as a slave commodity (144). They taught him French and also warned him to keep quiet about his original family if he wanted to stay alive. Once having sold him to the French king, he was allowed to be raised with the princess Alize, but due to his refusal to accept baptism, he was sent to the kitchen to do the dirty work down there. Most significantly, as the narrator informs us,

> The boy bore a grudge against his father and his other relative because they had not secured his release. He thought that they were violating their own loyalty, yet his anger was not justified, for they did not know anything about him. If a messenger of his had come to them, or if anyone had demanded ransom money, such sums would have been offered for him that the French would be weighing the gold to this day. (145; Book VI, ch. 285, 1–10)

At the same time, there is a strong and budding love between Rennewart and Alize, which clearly foreshadows the same sentimental relationship as described in *Aucassin et Nicolette* and in any of the versions of *Floire and Blanchefleur*. This young man is, as we then learn, the son of mighty Terramer (147), hence Giburc's brother, which is, however, never fully revealed, despite the clear external and internal indications: "all the time she did not take her eyes off him, for she discerned something in him which startled her deep in her heart" (148). And: "her heart could see that he was certainly born of her race, however he might have been lost" (148). In their conversation, they reach a point where just one more word would have been enough to reveal the fact of both of them being brother and sister (149), but Rennewart breaks off the exchange before this can happen and assures Giburc that he would fight on Willehalm's side with all of his might: "In doing so I shall have my revenge for the shameful suffering from which the heathens should have released me a long time ago" (149).

Subsequently, he is splendidly armored, and the court maids provide him with polite entertainment and diversion, as ordered to do so by Giburc. There is no more word about Rennewart being a slave; on the contrary, in the battle which then arises he emerges as the most valiant fighter who actually decides the victorious outcome.[241]

9 The Literary and the Historical Dimension Intertwined

Intermediate Reflections

All these literary examples shed a curious light on the entire phenomenon or institution of slavery. While it was most commonly a mercantile business to capture people wherever possible to sell them for the highest possible price, here we observe a very different kind of slave, namely the attempt by the traders to capture members of royal families because those fetched then truly astronomical prices on the markets. We have also observed that the various poets projected those royal slaves in a variety of functions, assuming highest responsibilities at court, on estates, and in war. These unique slaves were rather sought after by the various rulers because, so it seems, they enhanced the owner's reputation and esteem. It was even conceivable that a princess bought as a slave could rise so much in her status that the Admiral or Sultan decides to marry her and thus to make her to the ruling queen. Religious differences appear regularly, but they do not concern anyone much because the emotional connections between the prince and the slave girl, or the other way around, supersedes those potential conflicts.[242] In another context, the male slave could prove to be the

---

241 Fritz Peter Knapp, *Rennewart: Studien zu Gehalt und Gestalt des "Willehalm" Wolframs von Eschenbach*. Dissertationen der Universität Wien, 45 (Vienna: Verlag Notring, 1970); Carl Lofmark, *Rennewart in Wolfram's Willehalm: A Study of Wolfram von Eschenbach and His Sources*. Anglica Germanica, 2 (Cambridge: Cambridge University Press, 1972); Ines Hensler, *Ritter und Sarrazin; zur Beziehung von Fremd und Eigen in der hochmittelalterlichen Tradition der "Chansons de geste": Struktur und Funktion des Sarrrazin-Bildes*. Beihefte zum Archiv für Kulturgeschichte, 62 (Cologne, Weimar, and Vienna: Böhlau, 2006); Florian Schmitz, *Der Orient in Diskursen des Mittelalters und im "Willehalm" Wolframs von Eschenbach*. Kultur, Wissenschaft, Literatur: Beiträge zur Mittelalterforschung, 32 (Berlin: Peter Lang, 2018), 292–98.
242 Albrecht Classen, *Toleration and Tolerance in Medieval and Early Modern European Literature*. Routledge Studies in Medieval Literature and Culture, 8 (New York and London: Routledge,

best military asset, as was the case already in the early medieval *Waltharius*. Wolfram von Eschenbach drew on the same motif and has Rennewart basically beat the entire Muslim army single-handedly, especially because he is filled with so much rage over this family having forgotten or abandoned him. The narrator, however, just as in *Aucassin et Nicolette*, assures us that the family simply did not know the whereabout of their lost son or daughter; otherwise they would have certainly made every possible effort to ransom their child.

10 *Apollonius of Tyre*

Slavery in a Pan-European Literary Perspective

Slave markets must have existed at many locations, especially harbor cities. When we turn to the pan-European *Apollonius of Tyre*, originally composed in Greek or Latin in the second or third century C.E., which later became a true 'bestseller' throughout the Middle Ages and far beyond (William Shakespeare, *Pericles Prince of Tyre*, 1609), we have a great opportunity to study the practicalities and common practices of how people were captured and sold into slavery.[243]

Apollonius travels across the sea together with his pregnant wife in order to take over the country of King Antiochus. She delivers a healthy baby girl during the voyage, but seemingly dies in the process and is placed in a coffin which the sailors set out to the sea in order to get rid of the corpse. She is, however, not really dead and will recover from her coma once the coffin has been washed up at the coast of Ephesus and once a young doctor has skillfully treated her stiff body, but this is of no concern for us here. Apollonius, in his despondency,

---

2018); id., *Religious Toleration in the Middle Ages and Early Modern Age: An Anthology of Literary, Theological, and Philosophical Texts* (Berlin: Peter Lang, 2020).
243 Elizabeth Archibald, *Apollonius of Tyre: Medieval and Renaissance Themes and Variations. Including the text of the* Historia Apollonii Regis Tyri *with an English translation* (Cambridge: D. S. Brewer, 1991); see now *Historia Apollonii regis Tyri: A Fourteenth-Century Version of a Late Antique Romance*. Ed. from Vatican City, Biblioteca Apostolica Vaticana, MS Vaticanus latinus 1961, by William Robins. Toronto Medieval Latin Texts (Toronto: Pontifical Institute of Mediaeval Studies, 2019); *The Middle English "Kynge Appolyn of Thyre", Historia Apollonii regis Tyri with a parallel text of the Medieval French "La cronicque et hystoire de Appollin, roy de Thir": La cronicque et hystoire de Appollin, roy de Thir*, trans. Robert Copland, edited from the text published by Wynkyn de Worde (1510) by Stephen Morrison with Jean-Jacques Vincensini (Heidelberg: Universitätsverlag Winter, 2020). I have reviewed the last two editions in *Mediaevistik* 33 (forthcoming, 2021). For a commentary of the foundational text, see Stelios Panayotakis, *'The Story of Apollonius, King of Tyre': A Commentary*. Texte und Kommentare, 38 (Berlin and Boston: Walter de Gruyter, 2012).

continues the journey, lands in Tarsus, and entrusts his daughter Tarsia to foster parents, Stranguillio and Dionysias. He himself then departs and disappears from the scene for many years to come.

When Tarsia has grown up, her foster mother Dionysias becomes deeply jealous of her because she is so much more beautiful than her own daughter. Very similar to traditional fairy tales (avatars, hence, of *Apollonius of Tyre*), Dionysia then plots Tarsia's murder, ordering an overseer, Theophilus, carries out the ghastly deed. She promises him his freedom in return (146/147), and both this highly desirable reward and strong pressure on him since he might feel severe consequences in the case of disobedience convince him quickly to follow the order.

Tarsia, however, is spared her life because Theophilus allows her first to pray to God before he would be forced to murder her: "I do not commit this crime willingly" (147). At that moment, however, pirates arrive, threaten the overseer, who runs away and hides, while they capture the girl and sail away. As they explain themselves, they are not determined by pity for the young woman, or because they might be attracted to her physically, but they simply pursue mercantile interests in her: "This girl is booty for us, not your victim" (147).

Theophilus is more than happy that he did not have to commit the crime, but he still pretends to have done it. However, when he requests the reward for his deed, Dionysias reneges on her promise and sends him back to the farm, threatening him with bad consequences for him if he were to object to her command. At the same time she arranges a fake tomb for Tarsia who, as she lets people learn, has died from a stomach flu, and she and her husband put on funeral clothes and pretend to mourn the loss of Tarsia.

The narrative focus then shifts to the slave market in Mytilene, where a pimp is most eager to purchase her, realizing her great value for his business, a brothel (151). The local prince of the city, Athenagoras, also becomes aware that Tarsia is of noble origin and shines through her intelligence and beauty, so he bids a huge amount of money for her. The pimp immediately ups his amount, and once he has offered hundred thousand sesterces, and pledged that he would always outbid any competitor with ten thousand more, Athenagoras gives up his attempt because the cost for the girl would force him to sell several slaves, and since the pimp would make her available as a prostitute, he plans on deflowering her as the first customer (151).

The poet situates us squarely in the world of late antique and also medieval prostitution, though the situation for those women is worse than for regular prostitutes since they are nothing but slaves and have no freedom whatsoever.[244] Tarsia is of particular value for the pimp because she is still a virgin, and her first customer would hence have to pay a high price for the 'pleasure' of deflowering her. As the pimp informs his overseer: "after that she will be open to the public for one gold piece" (151).

Surprisingly, Tarsia can move all of her customers to tears with her story of suffering, and all the men, beginning with Prince Athenagoras, pay her huge amounts of money without touching her, allowing her to keep her virginity. Even the overseer, whom the pimp had ordered to deflower her, follows this pattern, and soon Tarsia is allowed, under Athenagoras's protection, so to speak, to entertain the public with her music and eloquent talk, which brings much more money from men and women than any sexual service would.

The narrative then switches back to Apollonius, who is made to believe by Dionysias that his daughter has died, indeed, so he leaves and roams the eastern Mediterranean until he reaches Mytilene as well. While hiding in the hold of the ship, the prince arrives, realizes Apollonius's deep depression, and orders Tarsia to come and to console the suicidal man below the deck. In the course of their conversation, critically determined by riddles, Apollonius realizes that he is facing his own daughter, and the narrative thus quickly nears its happy end. He agrees to let the prince marry Tarsia, but first he wants to avenge his daughter's suffering at the hand of the pimp, for which he orders the destruction of the city. Athenagoras appeals to the citizens to protect themselves, and they rush to capture the pimp and burn him at the stake, which solves all the problem, giving Tarsia back her freedom, dissolving the brothel, and making the marriage between the two young people possible.

Most significantly for our context, we learn that Tarsia decides to give much money to the overseer and to liberate all the other prostitutes: "because you were slaves with me, you shall be free with me from now on" (171). While there are no doubts about the existence of slavery in late antiquity, that is, at the time when

---

244 Dagmar M. H. Hemmie, *Ungeordnete Unzucht: Prostitution im Hanseraum (12.–16. Jahrhundert): Lübeck – Bergen – Helsingør* (Cologne, Weimar, and Vienna, 2007); Albrecht Classen, *Prostitution in Medieval and Early Modern Literature: The Dark Side of Sex and Love in the Premodern Era*. Studies in Medieval Literature (Lanham, MA, Boulder, CO, et al.: Lexington Books, 2019). See now also Michael M. Hammer, *Gemeine Dirnen und gute Fräulein: Frauenhäuser im spätmittelalterlichen Österreich*. Beihefte zur Mediaevistik, 25 (Berlin: Peter Lang, 2019). See also Jamie Page, "Masculinity and Prostitution in Late Medieval German Literature," *Speculum* 94.3 (2019): 739–73.

this 'novel' was originally composed,[245] its astounding popularity far into the early modern age confirms that the destiny of those who fell into slavery was not unknown, might have been actually quite common, and was, nevertheless, viewed with compassion and pity. Economic conditions, however, made slavery appear in very different light.

Late medieval translations, such as Heinrich Steinhöwel's *Apollonius* (1471) closely follow the course of events, including the entire section with the pimp, the brothel, and the prostitutes. Here as well, Tarsia demonstrates great generosity, announcing that the overseer had acted kindly toward her, which makes him deserving a large amount of money, and that the other prostitutes also should gain their freedom.[246]

As much as *Apollonius of Tyre* demonstrates its origin in late antique culture and literature, especially the world of the eastern Mediterranean, as much did it appeal to many different audiences throughout the entire Middle Ages and well beyond. This allows us to conclude that all those specific topics of slavery, piracy, prostitution, freedom, and liberation from slavery were fully understandable to the listeners/readers, probably because they were most likely fully familiar with them, despite the somewhat exotic context of this account. Prostitution was very common in western Europe particularly in the fourteenth and fifteenth centuries, but it is here specifically connected with slavery. The pimp buys Tarsia and he offers her to the highest paying customers for sexual pleasures. Interestingly, and this connects *Apollonius* with many other medieval narratives, both the pirates and the pimp pursue specific interests, capturing high-ranking female slaves who appealed to the customers most, hence the high price for those slaves.

Curiously, though, while the literary authors regularly voice their severe concern about this phenomenon, condemning slavery because it affects their female protagonists despite their high-ranking social status, the reality looked very differently, with slave markets operating openly and legally all over the Mediterranean and elsewhere. As Hannah Barker observes: "Slavery was legal and socially acceptable throughout the Mediterranean, in Venice and Genoa as well as in

---

245 Kyle Harper, *Slavery in the Late Roman Wworld, AD 275–425* (Cambridge: Cambridge University Press, 2011).
246 Tina Terrahe, *Heinrich Steinhöwels* Apollonius: *Edition und Studien*. Frühe Neuzeit, 179 (Berlin and Boston: Walter de Gruyter, 2013), 239. Terrahe also includes the parallel text in Latin by Geoffrey of Viterbo, *Pantheon* (ca. 1185) and from the *Gesta Romanorum* (late thirteenth or early fourteenth century).

Alexandria and Cairo. It was a universal threat, a misfortune that could befall anyone; masters one day might find themselves enslaved the next."[247]

11 *Kudrun:* A Thirteenth-Century Heroic Epic

A Female Prisoner Turned Peace-Weaver

Sometimes, however, literary characters lose their freedom because they become victims of political and dynastic manipulations and because their own people cannot protect them sufficiently. In the anonymous heroic epic poem, *Kudrun*, composed in ca. 1250, the female protagonist is about to marry the high-ranking prince Herwic of of Sealand when she is abducted by Hartmut of Normandy. Bridal quests and subsequent abductions are not uncommon themes in the various pre-courtly romances such as *König Rother* or *Oswald* (both ca. 1170 or 1180), and this also happened to Kudrun, who had been abducted by Herwic. But in the subsequent battle, he and her father Hetel had reached a point where neither side could defeat the other, so they finally put down their weapons and reach a marriage agreement. However, Kudrun's mother, Hilde, insists on a waiting period of one year during which she wants to prepare her daughter properly for marriage and her future role as queen. Hartmut, however, is not content with accepting this changed situation and kidnaps Kudrun in order to impose his will upon her and her family. Tragically, when her father pursues the criminal suitor, he and many of his men die in the battle, and only few survivors return, with empty hands.

This does not mean, however, that Hartmut would then have an easy game with this woman; instead, Kudrun flatly refuses to submit under his will, and she insists that she will uphold her pledge to marry Herwic. This recalcitrance irritates Hartmut's mother to such an extent that she treats the young woman under her command like a slave and forces her to do hard labor, washing the royal clothing in the cold sea, and this for fourteen years. By that time, Kudrun's brother Ortwin has grown up, and with a vast army of allied forces he can travel to Normandy, attack the castle, overpower the enemy, and liberate his sister. Both his parents die in this military melee, whereas Kudrun then intervenes, orders the end of all fighting, grants Hartmut his life, and eventually changes the policies back home, which makes it possible that all previous conflicts are overcome by means of marriages. Kudrun becomes a 'peace-weaver,' and despite the

---

247 Barker, *The Most Precious Merchandise* (see note 119), 209.

ten years of imprisonment, if not enslavement, she does not hold a grudge against Hartmut and can thus establish long-term peace.[248]

Whether the king's daughter is abducted or convinced to elope, the narratives with those bridal-quest motifs always insinuate that the women lose their freedom and become victims of male manipulations on the highest level. But in *Kudrun*, the poet added the additional feature with Hartmut's mother Gerlind who badly abuses the prisoner and turns into a kind of slave-driver:

> Wicket Gerlind had Kudrun serve her and never let er sit down to rest. Kudrun, whom one would always have expected by her right to find among the children of noblemen, was not to be found among the servants. The old she-wolf said to her in a hateful way: "I want Hilde's daughter to ser me; since she is so resolute in her animosity towards us, she will perform service for me unlike anything she has done before." (112)

Even the cold temperatures during winter do not sway Gerlind to let off her harsh treatment of this foreign woman whom she obviously hates to an enormous degree. Speaking to the maid Hildeburg, she comments:

> "You will have much suffering to bear. However hard a winter we may have, you will have to go out in the snow and wash the clothes in the cold winds, so that you will often wish you could be back in the warm chamber." (113)

Kudrun's and Hildeburg's suffering is described in most moving terms, which underscore that she is not only a prisoner, but treated as a hated person, perhaps even worse than a slave:

> And in truth, this situation prevailed for a long time, so that they had to go on washing clothes for five-and-a-half years and prepare white garments for Hartmut's knights. No women had ever been in a worse state, given the suffering they had to put up with outside the Norman castle. (113)

---

248 *Kudrun*. Nach der Ausgabe von Karl Bartsch, ed. Karl Stackmann (see note 176); for a solid English translation, see *Kudrun*, trans. by Winder McConnell. Medieval Texts and Translations (Columbia, SC: Camden House, 1992); cf. Barbara Siebert, *Rezeption und Produktion: Bezugssysteme in der "Kudrun"*. Göppinger Arbeiten zur Germanistik, 491 (Göppingen: Kümmerle, 1988); Winder McConnell, *The Epic of Kudrun: A Critical Commentary*. Göppinger Arbeiten zur Germanistik, 463 (Göppingen: Kümmerle, 1988); Gisela Vollmann-Profe, "Kudrun – eine kühle Heldin: Überlegungen zu einer problematischen Gestalt," *Blütezeit: Festschrift für L. Peter Johnson zum 70. Geburtstag*, ed. Mark Chinca, Joachim Heinzle, and Christopher Young (Tübingen: Max Niemeyer Verlag, 2000), 231–44; Albrecht Classen, "Eine einsame Stimme für den Frieden im Mittelalter: Der erstaunliche Fall von *Kudrun*," *Thalloris* 1 (2016): 69–90.

Although many researchers have closely engaged with *Kudrun*, the specific theme of imprisonment and slavery has not yet been addressed clearly enough. There is no doubt that Hartmut, and then especially his mother Gerlind, hold Kudrun as a prisoner and badly abuse her in order to break her strong will and mind. Yet, they fail, and the young woman arises triumphantly from her imprisonment, gaining great respect and power, especially because she does not fall back, after her liberation, into the cycle of blood feuds, revenge, and mutual slaughter.[249] We face both here and in a variety of other literary cases the odd situation of a princess being held as a prisoner or even a slave because she represents significant political power and proves to be of significant value in a political context. Hence, Hartmut and Gerlind cannot go so far as to kill Kudrun or to abuse her so badly that she might succumb to her suffering and die; she is an important pawn in their strategies to gain influence, esteem, and might on the international stage. Interestingly, she is fully aware of this unique situation and possesses enough acumen, personal strength, and self-respect to resist all their efforts to break her will and make her obey their commands.

Neither Tarsia in *Apollonius of Tyre* nor Kudrun reveal any weakness in their mind or character and can thus sustain their long period of physical and mental suffering out of which they manage to emerge rather triumphantly and royally. For Kudrun's brother Ortwin, there are some doubts as to her endurance under those circumstances, and when he finds her at the beach, he even goes so far as to inquire about the children whom she might have born to Hartmut. Her response deserves to be quoted at length because it reveals the true degree of her resolve not to let this imprisonment undermine her social rank and character:

> "How could I have ever borne children? All of Hartmut's kin know that he could never persuade me to accept him as my husband. It is for this reason that I am forced to work in this way." (132)

As much as this calms Herwic's concerns regarding his fiancée's loyalty to him, as little does he understand at that moment how to handle the situation in an honorable fashion. He would like to abduct Kudrun on the spot, take her

---

[249] For more recent research, though even there these critical aspects are hardly addressed, see, for instance, Susanne Knaeble, "Im Zustand der Liminalität – Die Braut als Zentrum narrativer Verhandlungen von Gewalt, Sippenbindung und Herrschaft in der Kudrun," *Genus und generatio. Rollenerwartungen und Rollenerfüllungen im Spannungsfeld der Geschlechter und Generationen in Antike und Mittelalter*, ed. Hartwin Brandt, Anika M. Auer, and Johannes Brehm. Bamberger historische Studien, 6 (Bamberg: University of Bamberg Press, 2011), 295–314; Vanessa Betti, *Das Zusammenspiel von Raum, Zeit und Figuren in der "Kudrun"* (Baden-Baden: Tectum Verlag, 2019).

home, marry her, and thus get done with it all. Ortwin does not allow that; instead he insists on the most honorable fashion to liberate the prisoners, pointing out that otherwise they would operate in the same evil manner as Hartmut and his men had done: "Even if I had a hundred sisters, I would prefer to let them die before I would stoop to such measures as hiding in a strange land and rescuing by stealth from my archenemy the people who have been taken from me by force" (132). He demands that they pursue an honorable path of action (133) and also rescue all the maidens who had also been captured by the Normans, which would require a massive military action. Hence, the two men have to leave again in order to organize the full onslaught on the castle with their army, as much as this distresses Kudrun, who feels, for the time being, completely abandoned: "Once I was considered among the highest and now I have been degraded to one of the lowest. In whose hands have yo left me and who will offer me solace, wretched orphan that I am?" (133).

However, Kudrun has also suddenly regained her hope and her pride, and instead of washing the dirty laundry, she throws it all into the sea where it floats away (134). Back in the castle, she confronts Gerlind who is about to have her flocked and flayed as punishment for her sudden recalcitrance, but her prisoner suddenly promises to marry Hartmut, which seems to change everything. It is, of course, only a secret strategy to put her opponents into a happy mood and to relax in their attentiveness, making the attack by Kudrun's family and friends easier, especially because Hartmut, urged on by his future 'wife,' then sends out lots of messengers to announce the wedding festivities and to invite the nobles all over the country to join them as guests. As the narrator laconically comments: "This was a sly trick" (137), and the outcome proves that Kudrun understood very well how to operate in this precarious situation, which contributes critically to the successful attack and hence to her liberation at the end.

Kudrun thus proves to be an extraordinary literary example reflecting on the fundamental experience of freedom and imprisonment, presenting the conditions of all those women suffering in slavery and the subsequent changes in their situation. Moreover, once victory has been achieved, the few survivors, Hartmut and his men, end up in imprisonment themselves, "all of whom were hostages that had been taken prisoner there. They were to spend many long, endless days with their captors" (160). The suffering and sorrow of imprisonment, the rapid changes of fortune, and the consequences of criminal or military actions that easily can fall back onto the perpetrators find most vivid expression in this 'heroic' epic poem.

But Kudrun at the end manages to convince her mother Hilde not to "repay evil with evil" (164) and to demonstrate true nobility and dignity in treating the defeated enemies, which even entails that they are released from their irons, are given a bath and fine clothing, and then accepted at court on their promise "not [to] try to escape and [to] swear an oath that they will not ride off from here without my permission" (164). As the narrator finally concludes: "A full reconciliation was achieved and the hatred that they had felt towards each other vanished" (164). Although we know nothing about the poet, this outcome, with new marriage bonds, constitutes a humanistic approach that brings an end to the entire tradition of heroic epics and to the notion of blood feuds, revenge, and mutual destruction as the fundamental *modus vivendi*. The same kind of criticism was already voiced in the famous follow-up poem *Diu Klage* (*The Lament*), which follows the *Nibelungenlied* in almost all the relevant manuscripts,[250] but only the poet of *Kudrun*, composed ca. fifty years later, combined the two major themes of heroism and subsequent bridal quest, on the one hand, with the critical examination of imprisonment and slavery involving the princess and all of her maids.

12 *Das Lied vom Hürnen Seyfrid*

The Imprisoned Princess in Heroic Poetry

The late Middle Ages also witnessed the rise of the heroic ballad where oftentimes a princess is kidnapped by a dragon or griffin and kept as a prisoner, if not slave. In *Kudrun*, we heard already of three princesses abducted by a griffon, who are then joined by Hagen, another victim, but since Hagen, once having grown up, manages to kill the monster, they all can leave the island and return to human society. Audiences in the late Middle Ages apparently enjoyed this theme as presented in woodcuts and balladic poems. The best example for this case proves to the *Das Lied vom Hürnen Seyfrid* (The Song of the Horn-Skinned Seyfrid), which exists primarily in printed versions from the sixteenth century, but might have been created originally already in the fifteenth century, if not much earlier, considering its connections with the Middle High German *Nibelungenlied* and the Old Norse Prose Edda, including the *Völsunga Saga* (middle of the thirteenth century), and the heroic epic songs from the Faroe Islands, such

---

[250] *Diu Klage, mittelhochdeutsch – neuhochdeutsch. Einleitung, Übersetzung, Kommentar und Anmerkungen,* von Albrecht Classen. Göppinger Arbeiten zur Germanistik, 647 (Göppingen: Kümmerle, 1997); *The Lament of the* Nibelungen *(Div Chlage),* trans. and with an intro. by Winder McConnell. Studies in German Literature, Linguistics, and Culture (Columbia, SC: Camden House, 1994).

as *Regin Smiður* and *Brinhild*.²⁵¹ Without any difficulties we can recognize here clear echoes of the much older myth of St. George (d. 303 C.E.) and the dragon, a favorite Christian account, best formulated in the thirteenth century by Jacobus de Voragine in his *Golden Legend* (ca. 1259–1266). For our purposes, however, I want to focus only on the suffering of the imprisoned princess, who is eventually liberated by the hero Seyfrid who kills the mythical dragon, another archetypal theme, the ultimate symbol of oppression, enslavement, control, and imprisonment.²⁵²

Beginning with stanza 16, we are informed about the four children of King Gybich and his wife, three sons and one daughter. The young woman is standing at a window one day when a dragon suddenly arrives and kidnaps her, flying high up to the clouds and disappearing, leaving behind completely distraught parents (stanza 18, 8). The dragon, a huge monster casting a show of a quarter of a mile, takes the virgin with it to the mountains where he puts her down, taking good care of her because it is highly attracted to her beauty. She is certainly supplied with all the food and drink she might need, and this for four years, but she is a captive and does not see any human being (stanza 20). The poet emphasizes her emotional suffering, expressed through her constant crying: "ir ellendt thet ir wee" (stanza 20, 8; her exile/imprisonment was painful for her).

The situation with the dragon might seem ridiculous or unbelievable, as the poet realizes him/herself because we are assured that even though the dragon placed its head into the virgin's lap (stanza 21, 2), it's enormous power and weight are said to be so great that when it breathed in or out, the entire mountain trembled (stanza 21, 7).

One day at Easter, the dragon turns into human shape, and informs her that in five year's time – the poet confuses this to some extent, having stated before (stanza 20) that Krimhilt had stayed a prisoner already for four years – it would permanently regain its original appearance of a man and would then sleep with her. She would never see any of her family again, or any other human being be-

---

[251] *Das Lied vom Hürnen Seyfrid*, ed. Maike Claußnitzer and Kassandra Sperl. Relectiones (Stuttgart: S. Hirzel Verlag, 2019). See also *Die faröischen Lieder der Nibelungensage*. Vol. 1: *Regin Smiður/Regin der Schmied*, ed. Klaus Fuss. Göppinger Arbeiten zur Germanistik, 427 (Göppingen: Kümmerle, 1985).

[252] Timo Rebschloe, *Der Drache in der mittelalterlichen Literatur Europas*. Beiträge zur älteren Literaturgeschichte (Heidelberg: Universitätsverlag Winter, 2014); Martin Arnold, *The Dragon: Fear and Power* (London: Reaktion Books, 2018); *Drachenblut & Heldenmut*, ed. Stefanie Knöll (Regensburg: Steiner + Schnell, 2019). See also Rüdiger Vossen, "Drachen und mythische Schlangen im Kulturvergleich: Drachen von Ostasien bis Westeuropa seit dem 4. Jahrtausend v.Chr.," *Auf Drachenspuren: Ein Buch zum Drachenprojekt des Hamburgischen Museums für Völkerkunde*, ed. Bernd Schmelz and Rüdiger Vossen (Bonn: Holos-Verlag, 1995), 10–24.

cause thereafter both would travel down to hell and stay there in eternity (stanzas 25–28), which carries deeply biblical symbolism, which does not need to be explored further here. The young woman is entirely distraught about this horrible prospect, and she appeals to the Virgin Mary, at first to no avail.

Then, however, Seywfride/Seyfrid appears and is described as more powerful than any other mortal person, able to catch lions and to hang them into trees as a form of entertainment (stanza 33). He discovers the dragon and pursues it through a dark forest, where he encounters the king of the dwarfs, Eugleine (stanza 45), who reveals to him his own family history Seyfrid had been unaware about. The dwarf also informs him about the female princess, whose name, Krimhilt, is mentioned here the first time (stanza 51, 3). Seyfrid admits that they both had had a love affair in the past, and then forces Eugleine/Eugel to help him in the battle against the dragon.

First, Seyfrid has to fight against the giant Kuperan, who holds the key for the door leading up to the mountain where the princess is kept a prisoner (stanza 59). The ferocious battle would have almost cost Seyfrid's life, but he is stronger than the giant, causes him many wounds, and can thus force him to submit under his command. But Kuperan breaks his oath and soon attacks Seyfrid from behind, striking him down to the ground. In this situation, the dwarfs comes to Seyfrid's rescue and hides him with an invisibility cloak (stanza 89). Again, a fierce fights erupts, and the protagonist would have almost killed the giant when the latter warns him that without his key the opponent would never get through the mountain to the female prisoner (stanza 96).

Krimhilt is overjoyed and soon pledges her hand in marriage to Seyfrid, if they might get away alive (stanza 106). Surprisingly, at that point the disloyal giant Kuperan provides crucial help with a sword which would be the only weapon in the world good enough to kill the dragon (stanza 107). Yet, immediately afterwards, he commits yet another act of disloyalty, hitting Seyfrid and causes him a bad wound. The two then wrestle with each other, with the protagonist winning once again. Kuperan then begs for forgiveness, admitting that he had betrayed him three times (stanza 113) – certainly a highly symbolic number with deep religious connotations, though the outcome here takes a different term. Seyfrid no longer believes Kuperan and throws him down the rocks so that he dies, breaking up into hundred pieces (stanza 114).

Seyfrid can finally relax, eat and drink, royally served by the dwarf and his companions (stanza 119), when the dragon arrives, which requires the hero's renewed effort, but he vanquishes also this enemy, particularly with the unique sword provided to him by Kuperan, and is thus finally able to take Krimhilt with him, thus liberating her for good after years of imprisonment and suffering. The dragon had been cursed by a woman whom he had wooed (stanza 125), and thus he had turned into this devilish creature (stanza 124), although he would have been delivered from this curse after having kidnapped that beautiful virgin and having kept her as a prisoner for five years (stanza 126) – a rather confusing narrative sequence which leaves many questions unanswered. Another irony proves to be the fact that the dragon's own flames which heat up everything around it also soften its own horny skin, which then finally makes it possible for Seyfrid to cut deeply into the dragon and thus to kill it (stanzas 147–48).

Not only has the protagonist killed the dragon and thus freed Krimilt, he has also liberated the dwarfs who had suffered under the dragon's mistreatment for a long time (stanza 154) and who would have all died at the hand of the giant Kuperan if Seyfrid had not overcome him at the end (stanza 157). With the death of both monsters, however, both the world of people and the world of dwarfs have become freed and can enjoy their liberty from evil. However, only eight years later, as Eugel prophecies him based on his astrological prediction, he would be murdered, which then actually happens, reconnecting the *Lied vom Hürnen Seyfrid* with the events as they are reported in the *Nibelungenlied*,[253] with the hero at first enjoying great respect, but then encounters so much hatred by King Günther – the name is suddenly changed from Gybich to Günther (stanza 173) – and his brothers that they altogether plot Seyfrid's murder. which then completes this epic poem.

Whereas all other literary examples of imprisonment and enslavement discussed above and to be considered below conceive of this loss of freedom as the result of human machinations and strategies, here in the *Lied vom Hürnen Seyfried* a mythical being operates as the crucial kidnapper and prison guard which needs the virgin prisoner for its own liberation from the curse. But Krimhilt is clearly an innocent victim, ultimately of another woman's cursing of her wooer, who then had turned into the dragon controlled by the devil.[254] Undoubtedly, despite the considerable popularity of this epic poem, there are numerous inconsistencies in the plot development and the explanations of the dragon's origin and its plans with Krimhilt. We only know for sure that the dragon has no

---

253 In contrast to the *Nibelungenlied*, however, Seyfrid is the one who retrieves the hoard from the mountain, where the dwarfs have placed it, takes it with him to Worms, and dumps it himself into the Rhine river (stanza 167). The narrator points out, however, that the true owners of the hoard had been the dwarfs (stanza 168).
254 Claußnitzer and Sperl, ed., *Das Lied vom Hürnen Seyfrid* (see note 251), 73, discuss the inverted mythological dimension of this dragon. While in most other literary cases the cursed individual represents a positive figure, here the dragon-man constitutes a most evil monster. See also Uwe Steffen, *Drachenkampf: Der Mythos vom Bösen*. Buchreihe Symbole. 2nd ed. (1984; Stuttgart: Kreuz-Verlag, 1989).

plans whatsoever to release the virgin, since he informs her explicitly that she would never see her parents again and would have to go down to hell together with it (stanza 25).

13 Rudolf von Ems: *Der guote Gêrhart*

Trade in Captives and Goods

Imprisonment and slavery can also be the result of unfortunate circumstances, and yet require intensive efforts by friends or outsiders to rescue the misfortunate individuals. One of the most dramatic examples for such a case can be found in the Middle High German *Der guote Gêrhart* by Rudolf von Ems (ca. 1220) which tells the highly unusual story of a most successful merchant from Cologne who makes his business globally, who speaks fluently German (native), French, and English, and excels so much in his character that people have given him the epithet of 'the good one.' While traveling home across the Mediterranean, Gerhart arrives at a Moroccan harbor where he has an astounding experience involving pirates, imprisonment, hostages, ransom, and trade of innocent prisoners with merchandise. The poet was obviously somewhat aware of the central location of that country as the major gateway for the growing slave trade, mostly from Africa to Europe, even though in his romance he does not speak explicitly of slavery; only of prisoners held for ransom.[255] Whatever the circumstances might be, here and elsewhere, the shared denominator proves to be that human beings are used as commodity for a huge profit.

---

[255] Steven A. Epstein, *Speaking of Slavery: Color, Ethnicity and Human Bondage in Italy*. Conjunctions of Religion & Power in the Medieval Past (Ithaca, NY, and London: Cornell University Press, 2001); Chouki El Hamel, *Black Morocco: A History of Slavery, Race, and Islam*.African Studies (Cambridge: Cambridge University Press, 2013); Michael A. Gomez, *African Dominion: A New History of Empire in Early and Medieval West Africa* (Princeton, NJ, and London: Princeton University Press, 2018), 43–57. Gomez, however, is mostly concerned with the notion of race in that part of the world. For the slave trade and piracy in the early modern age, see Daniel Hershenzon, *The Captive Sea: Slavery, Communication, and Commerce in Early Modern Spain and the Mediterranean* (Philadelphia, PA: University of Pennsylvania Press, 2018). The abstract available online confirms entirely what Rudolf projects for the early thirteenth century: The author "explores the entangled histories of Muslim and Christian captives – and, by extension, of the Spanish Empire, Ottoman Algiers, and Morocco – in the seventeenth century to argue that piracy, captivity, and redemption formed the Mediterranean as an integrated region at the social, political, and economic levels. Despite their confessional differences, the lives of captives and captors alike were connected in a political economy of ransom and communication networks shaped by Spanish, Ottoman, and Moroccan rulers; ecclesiastic institutions; Jewish, Muslim, and Christian intermediaries; and the captives themselves, as well as their kin."

The poet hailed from the area of Bregenz southeast of the Lake of Constance in modern-day Austria who made his career at the court of the Bishop of Constance.[256] Rudolf also composed a religious conversion story indirectly borrowed from an ancient Indian source, *Barlaam und Josaphat* (ca. 1225–1230), a courtly romance, *Willehalm von Orlens* (ca. 1245), a world chronicle, the *Weltchronik* (ca. 1254), and perhaps the hagiographical narraive *Eustachius* (today lost). The large number of manuscripts containing his narratives demonstrates that Rudolf was a very successful poet of his time.[257] However, by contrast, his *Der guote Gêrhart* has survived in only two manuscripts (Vienna, Österreichische Nationalbibliothek, Cod. 2699; first half of the fourteenth century; and Vienna, Österreichische Nationalbibliothek, Cod. 2793; ca. 1473).[258] It might well be that Rudolf's choice of topic, focusing on a Cologne merchant, and also his willingness to introduce a rather tolerant Muslim ruler enjoying a close friendship with the protagonist did not appeal to his audience. We could also speculate that the treatment of imprisonment of so many Norwegian and English nobles was too horrifying for the readers and listeners. However, the situation described in this romance provides important literary reflections on a situation which was obviously rather common in the western (and eastern) Mediterranean, that is, a flourishing business practice.[259]

---

256 Rudolf von Ems, *Der guote Gêrhart*, ed. John A. Asher. Altdeutsche Textbibliothek, 56. 3rd ed. (1971; Tübingen: Max Niemeyer, 2013; online: Berlin and Boston: Walter de Gruyter, 2017); Albrecht Classen, *An English Translation of Rudolf von Ems's* Der guote Gêrhart (Newcastle upon Tyne: Cambridge Scholars Press, 2016). Interestingly, there is also a Japanese translation, *Zennin gēruharuto: Ōkō kishitachi shimintachi*, trans. Hirao Kōzō (Tōkyō: Keiō Gijuku Daigaku Shuppankai, 2005). For three excellent studies, see Wolfgang Walliczek, *Rudolf von Ems, 'Der guote Gêrhart'*. Münchener Texte und Untersuchungen zur deutschen Literatur des Mittelalters, 46 (Munich: C. H. Beck, 1973); Werner Wunderlich, *Der "ritterliche" Kaufmann: literatursoziologische Studien zu Rudolf von Ems' "Der guote Gêrhart"*. Scriptor-Hochschulschriften / Literaturwissenschaft, 7 (Kronberg/Ts.: Scriptor-Verlag, 1975); cf. also Sonja Zöller, *Kaiser, Kaufmann und die Macht des Geldes* (see note 14); Meinolf Schumacher, "Toleranz, Kaufmannsgeist und Heiligkeit im Kulturkontakt mit den 'Heiden'. Die mittelhochdeutsche Erzählung "Der guote Gêrhart" von Rudolf von Ems," *Zeitschrift für interkulturelle Germanistik* 1.1 (2010): 49–58.
257 Xenja von Ertzdorff, *Rudolf von Ems: Untersuchungen zum höfischen Roman im 13. Jahrhundert* (Munich: Fink, 1967); Helmut Brackert, *Rudolf von Ems: Dichtung und Geschichte*. Germanische Bibliothek: Reihe 3. Untersuchungen und Einzeldarstellungen (Heidelberg: C. Winter, 1968); Wolfgang Walliczek, "Rudolf von Ems," *Die deutsche Literatur des Mittelalters: Verfasserlexikon*. 2nd, completely rev. and expanded ed. by Kurt Ruh et al. Vol. 8 (Berlin and New York: Walter de Gruyter, 1992), col. 322–345.
258 http://www.handschriftencensus.de/werke/1599 (last accessed on Jan. 15, 2021).
259 Still valuable for us today for the historical background and parallel cases: Jarbel Rodriguez, *Captives and Their Saviors in the Medieval Crown of Aragon* (Washington, DC: Catholic Uni-

It would go too far here and side-track us extensively to engage with the poet's theoretical reflections on goodness in the prologue to his romance, with his criticism of the German Emperor Otto (I or IV), and with his treatment of the contemporary political conditions in the Holy Roman Empire. Suffices it, instead, to emphasize what the protagonist experiences during one of his extensive trips through the eastern world, when his ship is driven by a strong storm to the coast of Morocco. He finds a friendly welcome by the local Muslim castellan, Stranmûr, and both soon invite the respective other to view their merchandise and treasures. Gerhart's ship is filled to the brim with valuable goods from the various markets in the eastern world. The castellan, by contrast, presents a most curious treasury, prison cells filled with chained people whom he wants to ransom for a considerable amount of money, especially because of their high social status.

The visitor is horrified, of course, recognizing them as being a large group of English noblemen, who have been stuck in this miserable condition for more than a year without having received any help. Worse even, he then learns of the destiny of the Norwegian princess in another cell, who is free of shackles, but still a prisoner, together with her fourteen maids.[260]

They all have lingered in these terrible circumstances because bad winds had driven their ship right into one of the castellan's harbor, which allowed him to take hold of them and put them into his prison, waiting for the time that someone would pay the ransom. Geographically speaking, this would not make too much sense, considering how far away Norway is located from Morocco, but the distance also explains why none of the relatives in that Scandinavian country and in England have made any effort to pay the ransom and thus to liberate the prisoners.

The princess is the daughter of the Norwegian King Reinmunt who had been supposed to get married to the English Prince Willehalm. But winds had driven them all off their path, with the prince seemingly lost on the high sea and being

---

versity of America Press, 1900); see now the contributions to *Seeraub im Mittelmeerraum: Piraterie, Korsarentum und maritime Gewalt von der Antike bis zur Neuzeit*, ed. Nikolas Jaspert and Sebastian Kolditz. Mittelmeerstudien, 3 (Munich and Paderborn: Wilhelm Fink and Ferdinand Schöningh, 2013), and the contributions to *Merchants, Pirates, and Smugglers: Criminalization, Economics, and the Transformation of the Maritime World (1200–1600)*, ed. Thomas Heebøll-Holm, Philipp Höhn, and Gregor Rohmann. Discourses of Weakness and Resource Regimes, 6 (Frankfurt a.M. and New York: Campus, 2019).

260 Wolfgang Walliczek,"Rudolf von Ems" (see note 257); Mike Malm, "Rudolf von Ems," *Deutsches Literatur-Lexikon: Das Mittelalter*, ed. Wolfgang Achnitz. Vol. 5: *Epik (Vers – Strophe – Prosa) und Kleinformen* (Berlin and Boston: Walter de Gruyter, 2013), 393–408.

presumed to be dead (1735–60). Stranmûr is certain that he would make a huge profit with these prisoners, but neither the Norwegian nor the English king have apparently tried to learn about the destiny of their children. This proves to be the same situation in Wolfram von Eschenbach's *Willehalm* (ca. 1220) where young Rennewart, a Saracen slave, appears to have been abandoned by his family after he had been kidnapped and sold on the market. Similarly, in the anonymous *Aucassin and Nicolette* (ca. 1220–1240), Nicolette's Muslim family does not seem to have bothered much to track down their lost daughter.

In Rudolf's narrative, at least, there are no contacts, and the castellan therefore offers his prisoners to the German merchant Gêrhart in return for all of his wares. He is sure that his new friend would be able to gain more in ransom money than from all of his merchandise, but he himself would not have a good opportunity to deliver them to the 'customers,' himself being a Muslim, hence he would need Gêrhart as an intermediary on the Christian 'market': "I will give them to you and assure you / that they will pay double the amount of money as ransom / which you will give me for them" (1762–64).

Stranmûr assures Gêrhart that the princess's father would not rest until he would have freed his daughter from this terrible predicament, and would willingly pay any amount which the merchant would request for her – this is never to happen, in fact. But the merchant is deeply troubled by the entire proposition and needs a bit of time to think about the implications and what it all would mean to him. He is, after all, not a slave trader, and finds the entire idea of slavery highly objectionable, as revealed by his great pity for the prisoners. In a dream at night an angel urges him strongly to do what God expects him to do, that is, to be good and to help those poor people, so he demonstrates his willingness to the castellan one he has inquired with him the next day about his decision.

Gêrhart at first displays some hesitation because he does not know whether the prisoners would agree with the deal offered to them, but the princes and the maids are in such a miserable shape that they beg and plead with him to accept the proposition so that they finally could regain their freedom after more than a year in their prison cell. However, the merchant approaches them rather cautiously at first, inquiring about their mind-set and how they would view him as a lower-ranked merchant after he would have 'purchased' them from the castellan. In fact, as he explains to them, he is worried that they might abuse him subsequently, causing him thereby a huge monetary loss. Of course, as expected, the English lords, desperate as they are, urgently appeal to him to help them out of this imprisonment, and promise to double the ransom money if only he would make it possible for them to regain their freedom. The princess similarly pleads with him, refers to the Virgin Mary, begs him with all of her inner strength to rescue her from heathendom, and to arrange everything with her as it would please him: "I will travel with you to your country, / and whatever you want I also want. / My father will happily ransom me, / for which I will vouch" (2268–70).

Of course, Gêrhart is both a good Christian and a deeply sympathetic man, and it does not take much coaxing to convince him that the swap of his merchandise for the prisoners is the only reasonable thing to do, which provides the princess and the English lord with profound relief and new-found happiness because it means the end of a long period of suffering with no hope in sight. Surprisingly, when they finally leave, there is no hard feeling on the side of the Muslim lord and the local population; on the contrary, they also express considerable sympathy for the former prisoners' suffering (2478–85). At the point of departure, the emotions that bond the castellan and Gêrhart reach new heights, and there is no hostility, no enmity at all. In fact, all of them share a festive meal together, and Strânmur even prays both to the Christian God and to his own gods that their voyage will turn out well with a safe return home. Both men shed tears when the time has come for the ship to leave, and the castellan goes so far as to promise that he would honor Christianity in the future out of his great respect and love for Gêrhart.

However, the poet does not simply let all this happen as if both men acted out of pure altruism. Instead, the narrator clearly emphasizes that both were very pleased with the exchange and felt content with the outcome, neither one having been cheated by the other: "He believed to have made a profit, / and I also thought the same / believing that my profit would not be lost" (2591–93). But those economic interests quickly fade away, even when the point during their journey has reached to separate, with one ship sailing in the direction of England, the other in the direction of Austria – certainly landlocked, but this is an irrelevant point in the narrative. Even though the English lords do not want to separate from Gêrhart, insisting that they themselves would be the safest guarantee that he would be paid for their release from imprisonment, the protagonist does not accept it and sends them their way. He himself travels home to Cologne with the Norwegian princess, hoping that her fiancé would one day reappear or that her father would pay for the ransom.

The narrative continues from here for still ca. four thousand verses, but the themes of imprisonment and slavery, as important as they certainly were for the protagonist and the captives, are quickly left behind. Strangely, we never hear from the Norwegian king, but the English prince eventually appears, almost too late, when Gêrhart is already about to marry the young woman to his own son. This problem is then solved, to the great disadvantage of Gêrhart's son (who has the same name as his father), and when they all travel to England, the merchant can also overcome a bitter internecine strife there, and thus help Willehalm to ascend to his father's orphaned throne.²⁶¹

For Stranmûr, however, taking Christians as captives and treating them as his property that can be ransomed represents a common practice, and he never demonstrates any compunctions regarding the miserable condition his prisoners have to live under. After all, as historical records also confirm, here we identify an obviously not unusual type of business involving pirates, established merchants, but also the various royal houses, especially in the entire Mediterranean.²⁶² As historians have demonstrated, this type of business with people (prisoners and/or slaves) was wide-spread during the Middle Ages and continued well into the early modern age.²⁶³ Neither religious nor political concerns had any particular impact, and all participants in the wider Mediterranean world were fully involved, as many historians have already confirmed. But Rudolf's romance provides an intriguing perspective because he views this situation through the lens of a German merchant who has obviously extensive experiences all over the known world, speaks fluently English and French, and has open access to the most far-flung harbors and markets. Granted, *Der Guote Gêrhart* is not specifically concerned with slavery as such, but the narrative framework and the conditions under which those prisoners have to suffer strongly suggest that the poet had a very similar scenario in mind.

The protagonist, being confronted with those prisoners, all of them completely innocent and simply victims of weather hazards, is deeply shocked, and their suffering evokes profound empathy in him. This makes him ready to venture his entire merchandise to gain their freedom. Although he pretends

---

261 Scholarship has practically ignored this critical aspect in Rudolf's romance, despite many valuable studies addressing the clash between the social classes, the superiority of the merchant even over the Emperor Otto in spiritual and moral terms, and the significant component of toleration. See, for instance, Meinolf Schumacher, "Toleranz, Kaufmannsgeist und Heiligkeit" (see note 256); Albrecht Classen, "Medieval Transculturality in the Mediterranean from a Literary-Historical Perspective: The Case of Rudolf von Ems's *Der guote Gêrhart* (ca. 1220–ca. 1250)," *Journal of Transcultural Medieval Studies* 5.1 (2018): 133–60; id., *Religious Toleration in the Middle Ages and Early Modern Age* (see note 242), 69–115.
262 Jarbel Rodriguez, *Captives and Their Saviors in the Medieval Crown of Aragon* (Washington, DC: The Catholic University of America Press, 2007); see also James W. Brodman, *Ransoming Captives in Crusader Spain* (see note 14).
263 Robert C. Davis, *Christian Slaves, Muslim Masters: White Slavery in the Mediterranean, the Barbary Coast, and Italy, 1500–1800* (New York: Palgrave Macmillan, 2003); *Slavery and the Slave Trade in the Eastern Mediterranean (c. 1000–1500 CE)*, ed. Reuven Amitai and Christoph Cluse. Mediterranean Nexus 1100–1700, 5 (Turnhout: Brepols, 2017); Daniel Hershenzon, *The Captive Sea* (see note 255).

for a long time to operate purely as a merchant, ultimately he completely forgoes all pretenses to secure ransom money and let's them all go, which demonstrates once again why he carries the epithet of 'the good one.'

His initial reaction when he is led to the prison cell where the English noblemen are kept, speaks volumes about his own character and also about his unfamiliarity with the entire institution of enslavement for mercantile interests: "My heart began to lament their suffering / and to share through the lament their burden, / which they suffered in such misery / and with such great heartfelt pain" (1561–64). Despite some initial hesitation, obviously because he is not sure how to react to this situation and to the castellan's unusual offer, Gêrhart soon comes up with the right decision to act as a good Christian is supposed to do, and he frees them from their imprisonment without ever receiving any payment or remuneration for his selfless actions. An angel informs him in a dream what God expects him to do, so he accepts the castellan's offer and barters all of his goods for the prisoners. However, he first carefully inquires whether this would also be their wish, and whether they would live up to their part of the bargain regarding the ransom. Gêrhart is, after all, still a merchant at heart, and he does not accept the deal simply out of pure goodness.

14 Geoffrey de Villehardouin's *Conquête de Constantinople*

Enslavement of the Civil Population as Collateral Damage

The literary examples discussed so far normally focus on just one person in prison or only on a small group of people. In historical chronicles, however, especially when they discuss war situations and the destruction of a whole region, with all settlements or cities being destroyed, we hear more commonly of vast numbers of prisoners, though the details then escape us, especially regarding their individual suffering. In Geoffrey de Villehardouin's (1160–ca. 1212) *De la Conquête de Constantinople* (Conquest of Constantinople; ca. 1207, in Old French), for instance, we hear of King Johanitza (Kaloyan, also known as Kalojan, Johannitsa or Ioannitsa, the King of Bulgaria, 1196–1207; cf. p. 79) who attacked Demotika (today: Didymoteicho, in Macedonia, Greece), conquered and destroyed it, burning down the towns and villages. Then, the chronicler remarks: "After that he overran the whole region, taking men, women, and children from their homes and cattle from the fields, and, in short, indulging in wholesale destruction wherever he went."[264] It remains unclear to us whether they were then

---

[264] Joinville and Villehardouin, *Chronicles of the Crusades*, trans with an intro. by M. R. B.

simply slaughtered, taken as pawns, as slaves, or whether they were moved completely to clear the land and make it useless for the approaching enemy.

According to the chronicler, Emperor Henri followed him with the specific intention "to rescue the men and women he had captured and was taking away" (144). Later we hear that those prisoners along with their carts holding their possessions and their cattle had been taken to a valley, and after a fierce encounter, Johanita's troops were defeated, which meant that the captives were freed and could return. The movement of all those people was tremendous, being free and independent one day, prisoners and refugees the other:

> The captives numbered a good twenty thousand, men, women, and children together; there were, besides, about three thousand carts, loaded with clothes and other belongings, to say nothing of a vast number of cattle. As they passed along from the valley to the camp the line of people, carts, and cattle covered about a couple of leagues. It was night by the time they arrived in camp. (145)

The emperor was delighted about the people's rescue, and has them camp separately from the troops, with strong guards set up to prevent any conflicts, thefts, rape, or other crimes. Later he allowed them to leave and to return to wherever they wanted to go. More details are not provided, as to be expected because the focus rests, of course, on the military and political events. We gain, however, a remarkable insight into the suffering of the ordinary people who were regularly innocent and helpless victims of the many different war campaigns the Middle Ages and the early modern age were filled with. There is the distinct possibility that the Bulgarian ruler might have sold them all into slavery, but the chronicler does not go into further details. But when would medieval chroniclers have ever cared much about the suffering of the ordinary people. The few comments here are already quite remarkable and shed important light on the true consequences of a war campaign with the siege and conquest of cities.

Shaw (London: Penguin, 1963), 144 (for an online version, see the translation by Frank T. Marzials from 1908: https://sourcebooks.fordham.edu/basis/villehardouin.asp; last accessed on Jan. 15, 2021). For critical perspectives on the chronicler, see Colin Morris, "Geoffroy de Villehardouin and the Conquest of Constantinople," *History. The Journal of the Historical Society* 53.177 (1968): 24–34; Jeanette Beer, *Villehardouin: epic historian*. Études de philologie et d'histoire, 7 (Geneva: Droz, 1968); Cristian Bratu, "Je, aucteur de ce livre: Authorial Persona and Authority in French Medieval Histories and Chronicles," *Authorities in the Middle Ages: Influence, Legitimacy and Power in Medieval Society*, ed. Sini Kangas, Mia Korpiola, and Tuija Ainonen. Fundamentals of Medieval and Early Modern Culture, 12 (Berlin and Boston: Walter de Gruyter, 2013), 183–204.

Earlier on, Villehardouin also includes comments about political events on the highest level, which often involved taking prisoners of the opponents or their sons, such as in the case of Emperor Alexius whom Murzuphlus and others kidnapped and threw into a prison. The latter tried to poison him secretly, but since that did not work he later strangled him personally, but he pretended that "his death was due to natural causes" (84) – a direct parallel to the events as developed in *Apollonius of Tyre* involving Tarsia. But the large number of civilians often being taken as prisoners during the war campaigns hardly evokes any emotions, and there are virtually no comments on what subsequently happened to those poor people. Emperor Henri, for instance, makes a surprise attack on the town of Philia in Thrace where he and his men "gained much booty in the way of cattle and clothing, as well as taking a good number of prisoners. These they put into boats and sent down the straits to the camp" (85). We can only ask what their destiny might have been, but no answer is given. Were they all sold into slavery?

At least in one case, we learn more about the bitter outcome for the prisoners of war. Once the town of Serrès (northern Macedonia) was taken by Johanitza, the defenders were first treated quite friendly, but three days later, their fortune changed tragically:

> He had them seized, stripped of all their possessions, and led away to Wallachia, naked, unshod, and on foot. Those who were poor, or of meaner birth, and therefore of little importance, he sent away to Hungary; as for the rest, he had their heads cut off. Such was the infamous treachery King Johanitza could commit. (130)

15 Boccaccio's *Decameron* in a New Context

Saladin and His Noble Prisoner

This allows us to move to the late medieval (or early modern) Italian poet Boccaccio who also includes the themes of imprisonment and loss of freedom in a variety of contexts. Most directly connected with the comments in the Old French chronicle proves to be the case in the ninth story told on the tenth day in his *Decameron* (ca. 1350).[265] At first sight, the issues of freedom or slavery do not seem

---

[265] *Decameron*, ed. Vittore Branca. Sixth rev. and corrected ed. (1980; Turin: Giulio Einaudi, 1987). There are many other good editions as well, but here I quote from Branca's which proves to be the most reliable and critically trustworthy. For an excellent online platform with a text edition, translation (by J. M. Rigg, 1903, which is still one of the best despite its antiquated language), commentary, etc., see http://www.brown.edu/Departments/Italian_Studies/dweb/ (last

to be of any relevance, whereas the display of courtliness, nobility, generosity, and other social values assumes central importance. But, as we have already observed numerous times, even the highest ranked members of feudal society are not exempt from experiencing the loss of their freedom and could easily face the danger of being imprisoned once the circumstances change.

The narrator Dioneo takes his audience back to the time of Emperor Frederick I Barbarossa (1152–1190) who launched the Third Crusade to regain the Holy Land for Christianity. His opponent was the famous Kurdish ruler Saladin, here identified as the Sultan of Babylon, but ruling in Egypt.[266] Intelligently, Saladin wanted to prepare himself for the upcoming war, put on the clothing of a wealthy merchant-pilgrim and toured the western world in order to spy on the military preparedness of his opponents. One day, he encounters, while crossing northern Italy, the noble-minded Messer Torello, who quickly realizes the nobility of the foreigners and immediately offers them the greatest possible hospitality which seems not to know any limits. Very similar to the situation in *Der guote Gêrhart*, these two men obviously strike a close friendship, both being deeply impressed by the respectively other's character strength, education, and gentility. Saladin, as the narrator emphasizes above all, hardly can believe that an ordinary merchant like Torello could display such degree of nobility in words and deeds: "He talked a great deal to his companions about Messer Torello and his lady,

---

accessed on Jan. 15, 2021). Giovanni Boccaccio, *The Decameron*, trans. with an intro. and notes by G. H. McWilliam (see note 47). There is much modern research on Boccaccio; see, for instance, Giuseppe Mazzotta, *The World at Play in Boccaccio's Decameron* (Princeton, NJ: Princeton University Press, 1986); Pier Massimo, *Adventures in Speech: Rhetoric and Narration in Boccaccio' Decameron*. Middle Ages Series (Philadelphia, PA: University of Pennsylvania Press, 1996); Alessandro Archangeli, *Recreation in the Renaissance: Attitudes Towards Leisure and Pastimes in European Culture, c. 1425–1675* (Houndmills, Basingstoke, Hampshire: Palgrave Macmillan, 2003); Valerio Ferme, *Women, Enjoyment, and the Defense of Virtue in Boccaccio's* Decameron. The New Middle Ages (New York: Palgrave Macmillan, 2015); see also the contributions to *"Umana cosa è aver compassione degli afflitti": raccontare, consolare, curare nella narrative europea da Boccaccio al Seicento*. Special issue of *Levia Gravia: quaderno annuale di letteratura italiana* (Alessandria: Ed. dell' Orso, 2015).

266 Both figures are too famous and too well known that it would be necessary to engage with their biographies here in detail; see, for a solid introduction, Christie Niall, *Muslims and Crusaders: Christianity's Wars in the Middle East, 1095–1382, From the Islamic Sources*. Sec. ed. (Abingdon, Oxon, and New York: Routledge, 2020); Jonathan Phillips, *The Life and Legend of the Sultan Saladin* (London: The Bodley Head, 2019); John B. Freed, *Frederick Barbarossa: The Prince and The Myth* (New Haven, CT, and London: Yale University Press, 2016); *The Crusade of Frederick Barbarossa: The History of the Expedition of the Emperor Frederick and Related Texts*. Crusade Texts in Translation, 19 (London: Taylor and Francis, 2016). The number of relevant studies on both figures, in German, English, French, Arabic, etc., is simply legion.

and about all the things he had done for them, waxing more eloquent in his praises on each occasion he returned to the subject" (771–72).[267]

The subsequent events can be summarized quickly: Torello participates in the crusade, but the Christians are defeated, and the protagonist, with many others is taken captive. They are all marched to various cities where they have to serve as slaves. Torello is taken to Alexandria where he is assigned to train the hawks for hunting, an art which he commands to perfection. However, he keeps his true identity a secret for a long time, although he soon attracts great attention for his outstanding skill. Saladin, without knowing anything about him, then frees him and appoints him as his falconer (773), but he calls him only 'Christian,' not being aware of who he truly is. In the meantime, a group of Genoese emissaries arrives to negotiate the freedom of some of their fellow citizens, something which never happens in Rudolf's romance, for which reason the captives have to suffer for such a long time without any relief.

Torello writes a letter to his uncle, the Abbot of San Pietro in Ciel d'Oro in Pavia, to ask for his help, and hands that letter over to one of the Genoese in the hope that this would contribute to his release from enslavement. Tragically, this letter never reaches its destination because, what Torello finds out only much later, the ship sank on their way home. In the meantime, the Sultan suddenly recognizes the man behind his slave and immediately treats him in the most friendly manner and raising him to the highest position of respect at his court.

The situation for Torello back him is worse than he can imagine because he is presumed to be dead because another man with the same name had died on the very day when the Christian army had been defeated by Saladin, so most people simply believe that the protagonist has lost his life. Consequently, the entire family wants Torello's wife to remarry, but she is so deeply grief-stricken that she refuses for a long time until she finally agrees to accept this proposition once the time would have passed which her husband had set for her to wait until his return at a specific date in the future. This date is now approaching, and Torello learns to his horror that his letter had never been delivered because of the shipwreck (776). He believes that he has hence lost his wife to another man, despairs, and is prepared to die. Saladin, however, who loves him dearly, cheers him up and offers him the help of one of his magicians, who indeed manages to transport Torello at night directly back to Pavia, where then the story ends happily,

---

[267] Cristelle L. Baskins, "Scenes from a Marriage: Hospitality and Commerce in Boccaccio's Tale of Saladin and Torello," *The Medieval Marriage Scene: Prudence, Passion, Policy*, ed. Sherry Roush, Cristelle L. Baskins, and Timothy D. Arner (Ithaca, NY, and London: Cornell University Press; 2005), 81–99.

with the couple happily being reunited, and Torello maintaining his close friendship with the Sultan.²⁶⁸ As the narrator relates: "Messer Torello informed Saladin, through more than a single messenger, of his felicitous return to Pavia, declaring himself to be his friend and servant" (783).

The outcome thus proves to be basically the same as in the case of Rudolf von Ems's *Der guote Gêrhart*; the imprisonment or enslavement lasts only a certain period of time; the protagonist is eventually liberated, and the former captive and master entertain strong bonds of friendship that last many years. In Rudolf's romance, the Muslim castellan disappears from our view once the Christian company has left the Moroccan harbor, but the emotional reactions upon their departure are equally strong on both sides. But what matters for us here centrally is that both writers projected a situation involving highest ranking members of society being in the prison of a Muslim lord. It is never easy to regain the freedom, especially because the ransom money is extremely high and because those who could afford that money are either not aware of the situation or not able/willing to pay that huge amount. In Boccaccio's case, we also observe that the Sultan treats his prisoners/slaves rather civilly and respectfully. Torello is assigned a rather noble task, training hawks, and because of his extraordinary skills in that matter, he easily regains his freedom.

16 Don Juan Manuel, *El Conde Lucanor* – Medieval Spanish Reflections

We find also excellent illustrations of the basic plot elements in Boccaccio's tale when we turn to the near contemporary collection of narratives (fables and otherwise), *El Conde Lucanor* (ca. 1335) by the Spanish poet Don Juan Manuel (1282–1348), nephew of Alfonso X of Castile, son of Manuel of Castile and Beatrice of Savoy. In the twenty-fifth story we hear of the count of Provence who travels to the Holy Land, obviously on a crusade, and is taken prisoner by Sultan Saladin. Very similar to the situation in Boccaccio's tale, the Spanish narrator projects Saladin as a noble and worthy individual who "recognized [the count's] great vir-

---

268 Valerio C. Ferme, "Torello and the Saladin (X, 9): Notes on Panfilo, Day X, and the Ending Tale of the Decameron," *Medievalia et Humanistica: Studies in Medieval and Renaissance Culture* 35 (2009), 33–55. Albrecht Classen, "Magic in the Middle Ages and the Early Modern Age – Literature, Science, Religion, Philosophy, Music, and Art: An Introduction," *Magic and Magicians in the Middle Ages and the Early Modern Time: The Occult in Pre-Modern Sciences, Medicine, Literature, Religion, and Astrology*, ed. Albrecht Classen. Fundamentals of Medieval and Early Modern Culture, 20 (Berlin and New York: Walter de Gruyter, 2017), 1–108; here 31–33.

tues" and treated his captive full of respect. "And so wise was his counsel and so great the Sultan's trust in him that although he was a prsioner, he was as powerful, as highly esteemed and as well treated throughout Saladin's lands as he would have bee in his own."[269] Despite his lack of freedom, the count is allowed to operate as one of the Sultan's highest-ranked advisors, and when the time has come for his by then nubile daughter, he consults with his lord whom he should choose as his son-in-law. The level of mutual trust and friendship proves to be very solid, but this does not mean that the count could leave and manage his own affairs back home.

Saladin does not know anything about the various contenders for the hand of the count's daughter, but he recommends that only that person should be chosen who has the character and status of an "omne" 158; man). He means thereby an individual of great inner character and strength of ethics, and not a person of any particular social standing. The count accepts this advice, and indeed one man is then chosen who is free of all blemishes and moral shortcomings, despite (or perhaps because of) his low social status. All this is communicated via letters because the count is not allowed to leave, still being the Sultan's prisoner.

That young man, once he has received the offer, and once the wedding has taken place, decides immediately to do what seems to be his moral obligation, so he journeys to the kingdom of Armenia (162) where, at least according to this story, Saladin resides. The visitor spends a long time at the Sultan's court and virtually become's the latter's confident, without ever accepting any gifts from him. At one point, when they both entertain themselves with hunting using falcons, the count's son-in-law manages to surprise the Sultan and to take him prisoner on one of his ships. Saladin would regain his freedom only if he were to release the count, which Saladin happily agrees to, particularly because he learns that this man is just the one whom he himself had recommended as the future husband of the count's daughter. At the same time, he is deeply grate-

---

[269] Juan Manuel, *El Conde Lucanor: A Collection of Mediaeval Spanish Stories*. Ed. with an Intro., trans. and notes by John England (Warminster: Aris & Phillips, 1987), no. 25, 157. Cf. Reinaldo Ayerbe-Chaux, *El conde Lucanor: materia tradicional y originalidad creadora*. Ensayos (Madrid: Ediciones J. Porrúa Turanzas, 1975); Aníbal A. Biglieri, *Hacia una poética del relato didáctico: ocho estudios sobre* El conde Lucanor. North Carolina Studies in the Romance Languages and Literatures, 233 (1988; Chapel Hill, NC: North Carolina Studies in the Romance Languages and Literatures, 1989); Jonathan Burgoyne, *Reading the Exemplum Right: Fixing the Meaning of* El Conde Lucanor. North Carolina Studies in the Romance Languages and Literatures, 289 (Chapel Hill, NC: North Carolina Studies in the Romance Languages and Literatures, 2007); see also the contributions to *Lectures de "El Conde Lucanor" de Don Juan Manuel*, ed. César García de Lucas and Alexandra Oddo-Bonnet. Didact Espagnol (Rennes: Presses universitaires de Rennes, 2014).

ful that he had given his advice to the count because this son-in-law certainly has proven to him what kind of a man he truly is. Subsequently, the count is finally given back his freedom, and everyone at court is deeply impressed both by the young man's intelligence, courage, and integrity (164). Simultaneously, we are also told how much everyone admired the Sultan and the count, each man regarded as an ideal character, which finds its final confirmation when Saladin grants the count "double the income which he would have received from his lands during the time he was imprisoned, and sent him back home rich and prosperous" (165).

The primary purpose of this tale is to illustrate the best method how to choose the right man for one's daughter, selecting an honorable, upright, intelligent, and courageous individual. For our purposes, however, we also recognize her the extent to which Juan Manuel also mirrored, similar to Boccaccio, the situation of prisoners taken by the Muslims during the crusading war campaigns. Significantly, however, just as in the case of Torello, Saladin treats his captives most honorably and with greatest respect, though he does not easily grant them freedom. In Boccaccio's story, Saladin acknowledges Torello's great need to return home in time to save his marriage, whereas in Juan Manuel's story the son-in-law must resort to a military ruse to force the Sultan to do so. Despite Saladin's friendly relationship with the count, there does not seem to be any opportunity for the latter to regain his freedom; he cannot even pay a specific ransom, as was the case in Rudolf von Ems's *Der guote Gêrhart*.

E Famous Historical Prisoners

1 Richard I: The English King as Prisoner

We have already heard of major late medieval poets such as Sir Thomas Malory whose literary creativity was, so it seems, particularly stimulated through their life in prison. The situation for royal prisoners, captives as the result of war, was, without any doubt, rather difficult and required intensive negotiations, as we know already from the case of Henry of Castile the Senator (1225–1304, known as Infante Enrique), who spent, for a variety of military and political reasons, twenty-three years in captivity – in the castle of Canossa from 1268 to 1277, and in Castel del Monte from 1277 to 1291.[270]

Similarly, but much better known today, the English King Richard I the Lionheart (1157–1199; King of England since 1189) had to endure a highly humiliating captivity from which he was released only after a huge ransom had been paid on his behalf. He was one of the three rulers leading the Third Crusade to the Holy Land, after the Ayyubid Sultan Saladin had defeated the Christians in the Battle of Hattim in 1187, which allowed him to retake Jerusalem. Richard had made peace with the King of France, Philip II, in January of 1188 in order to coordinate his crusading plans, which also involved the German Emperor Frederick I – in this regard the chronicle accounts and Boccaccio's later tale intriguingly interlace. The crusaders managed to regain the coastal city of Acre, but then decided to break off their efforts, especially because Frederick had drowned in a river on his way across the Balkans in 1190. His successor in the crusading enterprise was Leopold V, Duke of Austria, also known as The Virtuous, who likewise returned home, while Richard and Saladin concluded the Treaty of Jaffa in 1192, which granted the control over Jerusalem to the Muslims, but allowed Christian pilgrims and merchants to visit that holy city.[271]

---

270 Norbert Kamp, "Enrico di Castiglia," *Dizionario Biografico degli Italiani* 42 (1993); online at: https://www.treccani.it/enciclopedia/enrico-di-castiglia_%28Dizionario-Biografico%29/ (last accessed on Jan. 15, 2021); Margarita Torres, *Enrique de Castilla* (Barcelona: Plaza & Janés, 2003); Luca Demontis, *Enrico di Castiglia senatore di Roma (1267–1268): diplomazia, guerra e propaganda tra il comune di "popolo" e la corte papale*. Medioevo, 28 (Rome: Antonianum, 2017); see now also Richard P. Kinkade, *Dawn of a Dynasty: The Life and Times of Infante Manuel of Castile*. Toronto Iberic, 46 (Toronto: University of Toronto Press, 2020). Although the focus here is not directly on Enrique, Kinkade incorporates many references to him; unfortunately, he tells us almost nothing specific about his capture and long-term imprisonment (128).
271 Gerhard Volfing, *Von Akkon nach Dürnstein: Herzog Leopold V. und König Richard Löwenherz* (Salzburg: Österreichischer Milizverlag Salzburg, 2016); Klaus Lohrmann, *Die Babenberger*

These three Christian leaders did not go along well and bitterly quarreled over the spoils of the city of Acre after it had fallen. They also disagreed strongly regarding the appointment of the new king of Jerusalem, and especially Leopold left the Holy Land with a strong sense of frustration. Richard continued his military campaign against Saladin, and at one point he had 2,700 of the Muslim prisoners in his control decapitated, and this in full view of the opponents who could not do anything to help them. In return, Saladin had all the Christian prisoners in his control killed. We do not have names, only numbers, and yet those speak a gruesome language about the true meaning of being a prisoner of war, especially during the Crusading period. Richard then succeeded in conquering Jaffa in September of 1191, which meant that he controlled almost the entire coastal stretch, a critical precondition for the conquest of Jerusalem. The fortunes of war went back and forth, neither side making any decisive victory, and on September 2, 1192, Richard and Saladin signed a peace treaty, which was, however, dissatisfactory for both sides. A month later, Richard departed from the Holy Land and took the land route through Austria, where Leopold, deeply irritated about the English king's behavior and decisions during their shared crusading efforts, managed to take Richard as prisoner in December of that year; however, this imprisonment had already been planned the year before by Emperor Henry and King Philipp.[272]

Allegedly, the English king was kept in the prison of the castle Dürnstein on the Danube, between Krems and Melk; and later he was transferred to the control of the German Emperor Henry VI. The latter demanded the huge ransom of one hundred and fifty thousand marks, which was difficult to secure even for Richard's family or the kingdom at large, but it was finally paid in 1194, whereupon he could return home and resume his throne – after two humiliating years in

---

und ihre Nachbarn (Vienna, Cologne, and Weimar: Böhlau, 2020); see now also Ingrid Bennewitz, "'Karl und König Artus hat er übertroffen . . .': Der Mythos von Richard Löwenherz in der Literatur des Mittelalters und seine Rezeption in der Neuzeit," *Richard Löwenherz, ein europäischer Herrscher im Zeitalter der Konfrontation von Christentum und Islam: Mittelalterliche Wahrnehmung und moderne Rezeption*, ed. eadem and Klaus van Eickels, together with Christine van Eickels. Bamberger interdisziplinäre Mittelalterstudien. Vorträge und Vorlesungen, 8 (Bamberg: Bamberg University Press, 2018), 149–70.

272 Walter Pohl, *Die Welt der Babenberger: Schleier, Kreuz und Schwert*, ed. Brigitte Vacha (Graz: Verlag Styria, 1995); Heinz Dopsch, *Die Länder und das Reich: der Ostalpenraum im Hochmittelalter*. Österreichs Geschichte 1122–1278 (Vienna: Ueberreuter, 1999). For a good summary of the smaller historical details, and more research literature, see https://de.wikipedia.org/wiki/Leopold_V._(%C3%96sterreich) (last accessed on Jan. 15, 2021).

captivity. However, at some point he received a crossbow bolt wound and died already in 1199.[273]

Everything about this imprisonment was rather embarrassing, considering the high rank enjoyed by the king and his triumphs he had celebrated during the Crusade in the Holy Land. But he had various bitter enemies, such as Duke Leopold. Richard had to put on a disguise for his journey through the Alpine territories, and yet he was recognized by Duke Meinhard von Görz in December of 1192. At first, the king could escape, but once he reached the territory of Leopold, he was caught by surprise and taken prisoner, as Otto of St. Blasius related in vivid details.[274] The famous chronicler Otto von Freising mockingly described the humiliating situation for Richard, dressed as a simple pilgrim, being surprised while he was frying some chicken on a stick, as if he were nothing but a kitchen boy. For medieval audiences, a king had to live up to specific expectations, and the way how Richard was caught by surprise and then taken prisoner was deeply humiliating and shameful.[275] The German sources, such as the chronicle by Otto von Freising (ca. 1112–1158), his *Gesta Friderici Imperatoris*, continued by his disciple Rahewin, closely followed the negative model in their evaluation of this situation,[276] whereas the English chroniclers, such as Roger of Howden, Radulph of Coggeshall, William von Newburgh, and Richard

---

273 *Chronicle of the Third Crusade, a Translation of Itinerarium Peregrinorum et Gesta Regis Ricardi*, trans. Helen J. Nicholson. Crusade Texts in Translation, 3 (Aldershot: Ashgate, 1997); James Reston, *Warriors of God: Richard the Lionheart and Saladin in the Third Crusade* (New York: Doubleday, 2001); David Nicolle, *The Third Crusade 1191: Richard the Lionheart and the Battle for Jerusalem*. Osprey Campaign, 161 (Oxford: Ospre, 2005); Thomas F. Madden, *The Concise History of the Crusades*. 3rd ed. (1999; Lanham, MD: Rowman & Littlefield Publishers, 2013); Robert-Tarek Fischer, *Richard I. Löwenherz: Ikone des Mittelalters*. 2nd rev. ed. (2006; Vienna: Böhlau, 2019), ch. VI, 187–212. He emphasizes that Richard commanded, despite his imprisonment, full authority to rule as the English king, receiving, in his prison cell, high-ranking visitors from all parts of the Angevin empire, and issuing relevant executive orders (202). This was not an ordinary prisoner, to be sure.

274 *Ottonis de Sancto Blasio chronica: Ad librum septem chronici Ottonis Frisingensis continuatae historiae appendix Chronica*, ed. Adolf Hofmeister. Monumenta Germaniae Historica, 1.7. Scriptores, rer. Germ., 47 (Hanover and Leipzig: Hahn, 1912), 57–58. See also the translation by Franz-Josef Schmale, *Die Chronik Ottos von St. Blasien und die Marbacher Annalen*. Ausgewählte Quellen zur deutschen Geschichte des Mittelalters, 18,a (Darmstadt: Wissenschaftliche Buchgesellschaft, 1998), 15–157, here 111.

275 Knut Görich, "Verletzte Ehre: König Richard Löwenherz als Gefangener Kaiser Heinrichs VI.," *Historisches Jahrbuch* 123 (2003): 65–91.

276 Bischof Otto von Freising und Rahewin, *Die Taten Friedrichs oder richtiger Cronica*, ed. Franz-Josef Schmale, trans. Adolf Schmidt (Darmstadt: Wissenschaftliche Buchgesellschaft, 2000).

of Devizes, projected a quite different situation, claiming that the king tried his best to maintain his honorable position even under the worst circumstances, defending himself, but being overwhelmed, could not help and was unable to resist the arrest.[277]

Despite all of his military successes in the Holy Land, despite his royal rank, and despite the lack of true charges against him, the least of which would have been 'treason,' Leopold V cared little for the English king and his honor because he blamed him bitterly for having insulted him and his dynasty during the siege of Acre; so he did not only gain a huge profit when he finally turned him over to the emperor gaining thereby a massive ransom, he also could redeem his own hurt honor in the view of the public. In other words, not even Christian kings were necessarily spared this terrible destiny, and princesses had often to endure such suffering as well as a conquest of bridal quests or for other reasons. For many contemporaries, imprisoning a crusader king was a severe blow to Christianity and an act of sinfulness, although many chroniclers such as Magnus von Reichersberg argued poignantly that Richard had deeply insulted Leopold and had belittled his political and military rank and so deserved to be humbled himself as a prisoner.[278]

After his capture, Richard was handed over to the Austrian nobleman Hadmar II von Kuenring, one of the ministerials of the dukes of Babenberg, and imprisoned in the castle Dürnstein on the Danube, west of Vienna and near Krems. On December 28, 1192, Emperor Henry VI informed the French King Philipp II about this imprisonment, identifying the English king as: "inimicus imperii nostri, et turbator regni tui" (enemy of our empire and threat to your kingdom). Pope Coelestin III, however, was incensed and protested against this vehemently, and in 1194 he actually went so far as to excommunicate Duke Leopold.

The entire situation turned into a highly political controversy, with the emperor trying to instrumentalize Richard's captivity for his own purposes in the Holy Roman Empire, so he had the king delivered to Regensburg on January

---

[277] Knut Görich, "Verletzte Ehre" (see note 275), 67–68. For an exceptionally good summary of the various viewpoints and the relevant research, see, online at: https://de.wikipedia.org/wiki/Richard_L%C3%B6wenherz#Gefangenschaft_bei_Kaiser_Heinrich_VI (last accessed on Jan. 15, 2021). For more recent research, see, above all, Dieter Berg, *Richard Löwenherz. Gestalten des Mittelalters und der Renaissance* (Darmstadt: Wissenschaftliche Buchgesellschaft, 2007); John Gillingham, *Die Gefangenschaft des englischen Königs Richard I. als Wendepunkt in der mittelalterlichen deutschen Geschichte*, trans. from the English by Helmut Schlieger. Schriftenreihe zur Geschichte und Baukunst des Trifels, 4 (Annweiler: Freundeskreis für mittelalterliche Geschichte und höfische Kultur auf Burg Trifels e.V., 2018).
[278] Magnus von Reichersberg, *Chronicon*, ed. Wilhelm Wattenbach. Monumenta Germaniae Historica, Scriptores, 17 (Hanover: Hahn, 1861), 519.

6, 1193, though he did not stay there for long and was taken back when the negotiations between Henry and Leopold did not achieve the desired results. Richard was imprisoned again, but he could obviously communicate well with his nobles back home and continue with the political business over the long distance.

On February 14, 1193, Henry and Leopold finally signed a contract that stipulated the payment of 100,000 marks of silver, to be split among them in equal halves. It took until March 25 of that year when Richard finally agreed to the peace treaty, but he stayed in imprisonment on castle Trifels in the Palatinate until the middle of April, and later he spent time at the court of Henry, operating very freely. The final 'release' contract was signed on June 29, which by that time increased the amount of money to be paid to 150,000 marks of silver, a payment which was very difficult to make for the English crown, requiring a hefty increase in the tax rate to 25% and the sale of many royal lands. It took, however, until February 4, 1194 when Richard was officially released from his captivity, which took place at the Mainz imperial diet.

Many literary legends developed quickly around this most scandalous history, especially dramatic accounts about an imaginary poet (*ménestrel*) Blondel who allegedly succeeded in discovering Richard in his Dürenstein prison by singing a special tune they both had composed during his youth, to which the king responded. Blondel was thus able to report back home where Richard was imprisoned, and the nobles then sent representatives to negotiate his release against a huge ranson.[279] The Middle High German poet Ulrich von Zatzikhoven's *Lanzelet* (ca. 1194) was surely influenced by some of those accounts, since a certain Hugh de Morville, who served as one of the hostages for Richard Lionheart to guarantee the payment for his release, apparently provided Ulrich with a copy of a Anglo-Norman version of this poem.[280] In his epilogue, Ulrich specifies the circumstances, giving us remarkable insights into the larger political framework of this infamous imprisonment:

> The captive king gave him, as hostages, noble lords of very high birth from foreign lands far away: counts, barons, and their peers. But Emperor Henry ordered they be sent to him in his German territories, according to his will. Hugh de Morville was the name of one of these very hostages, and in his possession first appeared among us the French book of Lanzelet. (133)

---

[279] Jean Flori, *Richard Coeur de Lion: le roi-chevalier*. Biographie Payot (Paris: Payot & Rivages, 1999), 191–92.
[280] Ulrich von Zatzikhoven, *Lanzelet*, trans. Thomas Kerth (see note 30), 7.

As far as we can tell, various troubadour poets such as Peire Vidal, Arnaut Daniel, Guiraut de Borneil, and Bertram de Born (the Elder) spent time in Richard's vicinity, or were patronized by him, while he himself was highly active in coordinating many political activities and promoted his public appeal. We are hence not forced to assume that this high-ranking man idled away in a dark hole, somewhere in the castle's dungeon or in an urban prison. Imprisonment also knows of all the social distinctions, and there are wealthy and powerful prisoners, and poor and miserable ones. The records, however, mostly tell us only of the former group. Little wonder that such events inspired many poets to use the accounts about Richard and to develop their own versions since the idea of a king being thrown in a prison moved and agitated the minds of the audiences throughout time.[281]

How could a sovereign, a crusader knight who had done so much for Christianity, be so badly treated for some perceived insults against Duke Leopold of Austria? Little wonder that English propaganda regarded all this as a grave insult and damage to the honor of their own kingdom, and the many legendary accounts about Richard Lionheart that circulated a long time after his death underscored the great respect, if not even mythical status, of this famous ruler and prisoner. Ranulf Higden, for instance, in his *Polychronicon*, compared him with such luminaries as Alexander the Great, Charlemagne, and King Arthur. Roger of Hoveden assumed that Richard was in the possession of the famous source Excalibur, the unique attribute of Arthur.

The legend about the minstrel Blondel, created around 1260, though completely fictional, dramatized intensively the alleged suffering of this famous prisoner and intensified his mythical status as an innocent victim who was, however, in clear contrast to the famous late antique philosopher Boethius, eventually liberated against the huge ransom.[282] In fact, we can thus preliminarily conclude at least in this case that this presumably innocent suffering in a ducal and then royal prison strongly contributed to the growth of the myth of Richard Lionheart as a glorious hero.[283] Not only was he greatly admired as a crusader and as the

---

281 Broughton B. Bradford, *The Legends of King Richard I, Coeur de Lion: A Study of Sources and Variations to the Year 1600*. Studies in English Literature, 25 (The Hague: Mouton, 1966).
282 Rüdiger Krohn, "'Richardes lob gemêret wart mit hôher werdekeit': Der Löwenherz-Mythos in Mittelalter und Neuzeit," *Herrscher, Helden, Heilige*, ed. Ulrich Müller und Werner Wunderlich. Mittelalter Mythen, 1 (St. Gall: UVK-Fachverlag für Wissenschaft und Studium, 1996), 133–53.
283 *Richard Coeur de Lion in History and Myth*, ed. Janet L. Nelson. King's College London Medieval Studies, 7 (London: King's College, Centre for Late Antique and Medieval Studies, 1992); David Miller, *Richard the Lionheart: The Mighty Crusader* (London: Weidenfeld & Nicolson, 2003); Ralph V. Turner and Richard R. Heiser, *The Reign of Richard Lionheart: Ruler of the Ange-

English king, but his victimization by these continental rulers, which put him into dire straits as a result of a string of misfortunate circumstances, was virtually the stuff of much public debate and literary creativity.

2 The French King Louis IX as Prisoner of the Mamluks of Egypt

The Mis/Fortunes of War
Very briefly, let us also consider the destiny of the probably most famous medieval prisoner, King Louis IX of France, whose crusading army was badly defeated in the Battle of Al Mansurah which was fought from February 8 to February 11, 1250. He faced tremendous opposition and had to fend off mighty Ayyubid forces led by Emir Fakhr-ad-Din Yusuf, Faris ad-Din Aktai, and Baibars al-Bunduqdari.

The crusaders had realized that the power center in the Islamic world had shifted to Egypt and tried to win a major victory there, but utterly failed for many different reasons. The decisive battle took place near the harbor of Damietta, and despite the Europeans' best efforts, they were not familiar enough with the terrain and failed to see through their opponents' guerilla tactics and sophisticated war strategy, trapping the Christian army in Al Mansurah, presumed to have been vacated. Only few of the Knights Templars survived, and scores of other soldiers were killed. The army retreated in disorder to its camp, set up defense structures, but the Mamluks could cut them off their supply lines, destroyed their ships, and in the last battle of the Seventh Crusade, the Battle of Fariskur, the Muslims won an overwhelming victory.

Even King Louis was captured on April 6, along with his brothers, Charles d'Anjou and Alphonse de Poitiers, chained in the house of Ibrahim Ibn Lokman, the royal chancellor, and placed under the guard of a eunuch named Sobih al-Moazami. Details of the conditions of their captivity elude us, but they were apparently well treated, representing most valuable war 'booty.' Louis had to pay 400,000 dinars as ransom, and he had to pledge never to return to Egypt. 12,000 other prisoners were also released, and all returned to Europe, having been badly, if not catastrophically defeated and deeply humiliated. Louis regained his freedom on May 6, 1250 and immediately journeyed to Acre where he stayed until all his soldiers were let go as well. This was basically the end

---

vin Empire, 1189–1199. The Medieval World (Harlow, Munich, et al.: Longman, 2000); W. B. Barlett, *Richard the Lionheart: The Crusader King of England* (Stroud, Gloucestershire: Amberley Publishing, 2018). Research on this major English king is really legion.

of all further crusading efforts, especially after the king had left the Holy Land for good on April 24, 1254. The Arabs' victory ensured the rise to complete power by the Mamluks, but the wider political and military context does not need to be considered here and has been discussed already by much more competent scholars.[284]

As this military catastrophe indicates, not even kings were exempt from being taken prisoners, but Louis IX was still rather fortunate because the rising Mamluk dynasty in Egypt apparently was just glad to get rid of him and his remaining army, all imprisoned, once the huge payment was done.[285] Other rulers, actually, suffered a similar, if not even a worse destiny. But Louis IX and his men dealt with rather noble-minded opponents who quickly accepted the terms of negotiations, as the chronicler Joinville reported: "When the Saracens had seen that they could not prevail over our good king with threats, they had come back to him and asked him how much money he was prepared to pay the sultan, and whether he would also surrender Damietta."[286] Once Louis had agreed, the sultan exclaimed in amazement: "'By Allah! this Frank is a very generous-minded man not to have haggled over paying so great a sum! So go and tell him I'll let him off a hundred thousand livres of the ransom money'" (250). We learn much about the destiny of the king and his high-ranking officers, but not much, of course, of the destiny of the masses of prisoners, the ordinary soldiers, most of whom were simply executed after they had been captured by the victors. Only those who promised, because of their social rank, to be worth a considerable ransom, were spared. The horror of war affected particularly the Christian army, but King Louis got away after having paid a huge amount of money,

---

284 The Seventh Crusade has been discussed already by many historians; see, for instance, William Chester Jordan, *Louis IX and the Challenge of the Crusade: A Study in Rulership* (Princeton, NJ: Princeton University Press, 1979); Dirk Reitz, *Die Kreuzzüge Ludwigs IX. von Frankreich 1248/ 1270*. Neue Aspekte der europäischen Mittelalterforschung, 3 (Münster: LIT, 2005); Wayne B. Bartlett, *The Last Crusade: The Seventh Crusade & the Final Battle for the Holy Land* (Stroud, Gloucestershire: Tempus, 2007); Xavier Hélary, *La dernière croisade: Saint Louis à Tunis (1270)* (Paris: Perrin, 2016); for sources, see *The Seventh Crusade, 1244–1254: Sources and Documents*, ed. Peter Jackson. Crusade Texts in Translation, 16 (Aldershot: Ashgate, 2007). See also *al-Sulūk li-Ma'rifat Duwal al-Mulūk*, ed. 'Ata, Muhammad 'Abd al-Qadir (Beirut, Lebanon: Manshurat Muhammad 'Ali Baydun, Dar al-Kutub al-'Ilmiyah, 1997). Although written more for the lay audience, see Roger Crowley, *Der Fall von Akkon: Der letzte Kampf um das Heilige Land*, trans. from the English by Norbert Juraschitz (2019; Darmstadt: Theiss, 2019), 36–55.
285 For one of the best sources from the French perspective, see the old translation, *The Memoirs of the Lord of Joinville: A New English Version (Vie de Saint Louis)*, by von Ethel Wedgwood (London: J. Murray, 1906); online available at: https://web.archive.org/web/20081011222823/ http://etext.lib.virginia.edu/toc/modeng/public/WedLord.html (last accessed on Jan. 15, 2021).
286 Here I draw from Joinville & Villehardouin, *Chronicles of the Crusades* (see note 264), 249.

being responsible for one of the greatest defeats any crusading army had ever experienced.

3 Charles d'Orléans: The French Dauphin as Royal Prisoner in England

We have the golden opportunity to confirm these observations also by studying the situation of the French Dauphin, Charles d'Orléans, who was taken prisoner at the end of the battle of Agincourt in 1415 and taken to England, where he tragically had to linger for twenty-five years until his ransom was finally paid, which then allowed him to return to France, though he was never to succeed to the French throne. Richard the Lionheart was captured and then kept secretly at Castle Dürnstein, which heightened the drama of his case. Charles d'Orléans was a triumphant prey for the English who felt no need to hide their prisoner who was forced to stay with them upon an oath given, even though under duress as the consequence of the military defeat. All of Europe was aware about Charles's imprisonment for more than two decades, and since he belonged to the highest echelons of French society, and this at a time of greatest political and military unrest, his case attracted greatest interest as well.[287]

Here leaving aside the complex history of the French royalty in its conflicts with the great French dukes, we only need to keep in mind that the battle of Agincourt was a great triumph for the English and their longbowmen, and a massive defeat for the French crown and especially the French nobility. Charles d'Orléans (1394–1465), though still very young in 1415, had already proven his outstanding military leadership skills as the head of the Armagnac coalition and was entrusted with taking the French army, comprising an exceptionally large number of nobles, into the battle against King Henry V. John Fox and Mary-Jo Arn summarize the personal outcome of the battle for Charles as follows:

> That he fell early in the battle points to his being in the crush of bodies and horses in the first attack, which is confirmed by that fact that he was discovered by the English (as were many others) under a pile of corpses. Though he probably did not consider himself fortunate at the time, his survival can probably be attributed to the protection his plate armor

---

[287] A. C. Spearing, "Prison, Writing, Absence: Representing the Subject in the English Poems of Charles d'Orléans," *Chaucer to Spenser: A Critical Reader*, ed. Pearsall, Derek (Oxford: Blackwell Publishing, 1999; orig. 1992), 297–311.

afforded; many others were suffocated in the crush of human and animal bodies at the battle line.²⁸⁸

Charles was a big catch, and Henry proudly paraded him along with many other prisoners throught he street of London, but he was not letting him go easily, if at all because he was more worth as a prisoner than any ransom money which the French family might be willing or able to pay. The poor prince first stayed in the Tower of London, then at Windsor Castle, and from then on was handed over from one castle to another, and this for twenty-five years, during which Charles enjoyed a rather leisurely life according to his social standing, and did not really suffer from imprisonment, as most other individuals would have to who were prisoners of war or incarcerated people who had been tried and punished for misdeeds and crimes.

In fact, Charles traveled much throughout England and even across the Channel to Normandy, constantly involved in political negotiations, many of which involved his attempts to collect the required ransom money. But unfortunately, more than two decades passed during which there were many political upheavals and much unrest on both sides of the Channel, which made it impossible for Charles to achieve his personal goal of getting released from his 'imprisonment,' that is, his lack of freedom. Of course, he was surrounded by French servants and had his own secretary; he held court, received guests, sent messen-

---

288 *Poetry of Charles d'Orléans and His Circle: A Critical Edition of BNF MS. Fr. 25458, Charles d'Orléan's Personal Manuscript*, ed. John Fox and Mary-Jo Arn. English trans. by R. Barton Palmer. Medieval and Renaissance Texts and Studies, 383 (Tempe, AZ: Arizona Center for Medieval and Renaissance Studies; Turnhout: Brepols, 2010), xxxi. For the battle itself, which has been studied from many different perspectives, see Anne Curry, *Agincourt*. Great Battles (Oxford: Oxford University Press, 2015); eadem, *The Battle of Agincourt: Sources and Interpretations*. Warfare in History (2001; Woodbridge: Boydell, 2009); *The Battle of Agincourt*, ed. Anne Curry (New Haven, CT: Yale University Press, 2015); Teresa Cole, *Henry V: The Life of the Warrior King & the Battle of Agincourt 1415* (Stroud, Gloucestershire: Amberley, 2015); Juliet R. V. Barker, *Agincourt: The King, the Campaign, the Battle* (London: Little, Brown, 2005); Michael Drayton, *The Battle of Agincourt* (Menston, Yorkshire: Scolar Press, 1972). For a good study dealing with the reception history of this famous battle, see Stephen Cooper, *Agincourt: Myth and Reality 1415–2015* (Barnsley, South Yorkshire: Pen & Sword/Praetorian Press, 2014). Much older research still deserves our attention; see, for instance, Nicholas Harris Nicolas, *History of Battle of Agincourt*. Rpt. (1832; London: Muller, 1970). Cf. also Clifford J. Rogers, "Agincourt, Battle of," *The Oxford Encyclopedia of Medieval Warfare and Military Technology*, ed. Clifford J. Rogers. Vol. 1 (Oxford: Oxford University Press, 2010), 7–10. One can often question the validity of *Wikipedia*, but concerning this battle, the respective article proves to be superior in detail, outline, descriptions, images, maps, etc., compared to some of the research published in print: https://en.wikipedia.org/wiki/Battle_of_Agincourt (last access on Jan. 15, 2021).

gers, and operated, though on English soil, as the official representative of Orléans. Yet, he was not free to go, and since he emerged as a major writer and poet of his time, we have available a large body of his texts in which he reflects upon his imprisonment and longing for his homeland, and this at rather tumultuous times.[289] As Fox and Arn observe,

> despite his best efforts, he was caught up in forces much greater than any single man could control, or even influence very much. Gloucester and his adherents feared that the return of Charles to France would result in a reunification of that country and put an end to England's hopes for wealth and dominion on the Continent.[290]

The appearance of the mystically inspired Joan of Arc who was deeply bent on liberating the dauphin achieved, despite some initial success, nothing for him; on the contrary, his situation became worse since he was guarded much more closely, and altogether it extended his imprisonment until November of 1440 when he was already forty-six and when his usefulness as a political pawn had become exhausted. His cousin, Philip the Good, duke of Burgundy (1396–1467), loaned him the money, and thus made him to one of his dependents, but he also included him into the Order of the Golden Fleece, all efforts to enhance his own political status in contrast to the French king. In the meantime, Charles had become one of the best English (!) poets of his time and was never to gain any major political role back in France, despite his own and Philip's aspirations.

Once having returned home, Charles immediately married Marie de Clèves, the daughter of Adolph I, Duke of Cleves in northern Germany, with whom he had three children; their son Louis (born in 1462) was later to ascend to the French throne in 1498 as Louis XIII. Financial, military, and political troubles deeply vexed the dauphin, but he also established a major court of letters where he could patronize many contemporary poets and artists. What matters for us, however, is only the fact that he was the perhaps most famous prisoner of his time and shared, in a way, this destiny with Richard Lionheart.[291] Charles

---

289 Although Charles d'Orléans was certainly not yet a 'Renaissance' poet, he contributed strongly to the development of autobiographical poetry; see Albrecht Classen, *Autobiographische Lyrik des europäischen Spätmittelalters. Studien zu Hugo von Montfort, Oswald von Wolkenstein, Antonio Pucci, Charles d'Orléans, Thomas Hoccleve, Michel Beheim, Hans Rosenplüt und Alfonso Alvarez de Villasandino*. Amsterdamer Publikationen zur Sprache und Literatur, 91 (Amsterdam and Atlanta, GA: Editions Rodopi, 1991), 269–345.
290 Fox and Arn, ed. *Poetry of Charles d'Orléans* (see note 288), xxxii.
291 There is much relevant scholarship on Charles d'Orléans; see, for instance, David A. Fein, *Charles d'Orléans*. Twayne's World Authors Series, 699 (Boston: Twayne, 1983); Hélène Basso,

experienced, after all, in a paradoxical fashion, both imprisonment and freedom at the same time; he was bound by his word to stay a prisoner of war, but he was kind of free to go; he was, so to speak, on a golden leash, and this for virtually a quarter of a century, living in England, acquiring complete mastery of the English language, writing superior poems in English, enjoying the cultural luxuries of an aristocratic lifestyle, enjoying companies, courtly festivals, books, music, hunting, feasts, etc., but he still longed to go home; he became almost a perennial prisoner.[292]

Charles experienced his imprisonment in rather light terms, if not to say in luxurious conditions, treated as a royal 'guest,' being entertained, participating in the public life in London and elsewhere, leading the high life of the dauphin, being served and provided with the most exquisite supplies and provisions any royalty could expect, but the duration of his enforced stay in England made it also very hard on him because he suffered from a sense of hopelessness, until Philippe le Bon, Duke of Burgundy, and especially his wife, Isabelle de Portugal, intervened on his behalf because they strongly felt, like many other contemporaries, that "a horrible injustice had been done to the duke of Orleans."[293] This finally made it possible to reach a workable compromise between the parties and thus to secure Charles's release from his imprisonment. We do not find very detailed discussions of his 'dire' experience in his poems, but there are enough comments built into his *balades* or *complaintes* which reflect the actual situation he was suffering under and which he commented on at length later in his life.[294]

One important example proves to be his "Complainte de France" (Co3, pp. 252–58), in which he voices his deep frustration about the decline of France

---

Être poète au temps de Charles d'Orléans (XVe siècle). Collection En-jeux (Avignon: Éd. Univ. d'Avignon, 2012); Daniel Poirion, *Le poète et le prince: l'évolution du lyrisme courtois de Guillaume de Machaut à Charles d'Orléans*. Publications de la Faculté des Lettres et des Sciences Humaines, 35 (Paris: Presses Universitaires de France, 1965).

292 *Charles d'Orléans in England, 1415–1440*, ed. Mary-Jo Arn (Cambridge and Rochester, NY: D.S. Brewer, 2000); see also Enid McLeod, *Charles of Orleans, Prince and Poet* (New York: Viking Press, 1970); Norma Lorre Goodrich, *Charles, Duke of Orleans: A Literary Biography* (New York: Macmillan, 1963).

293 Mary-Jo Arn, *Fortunes Stabilnes: Charles of Orleans's English Book of Love. A Critical Edition* (Binghamton, NY: Medieval & Renaissance Texts & Studies, 1994), 14.

294 Pierre Champion, "Charles d'Orléans: Prince des Lis et de la poésie," id., *Histoire poétique du quinzième siècle*. Vol. 2: *Charles d'Orléans, le pauvre Villon, Arnoul Greban, Jean Meschinor le "Banni de Liesse", Me Henri Baude, élu des finances et poète, Jean Molinet rhétoriqueur*. Bibliothèque du XVe siècle, 28 (Paris: Champion, 1923), 19; id., *Vie de Charles d'Orléans (1394–1465)* (Paris: Champion, 1911), 547.

as a kingdom. While in the past, it had enjoyed universal respect because there the greatest virtues were upheld in public, in the present time the poet can only perceive "grief mal soustenir" (v. 8) brought about by universal greed, arrogance, gluttony, and sloth, that is, some of the seven deadly sins.

The poet is, however, not completely despondent, he still harbors some hope and trusts in God for the recovery of France, and also refers to the great mythical figures of the past, Charlemagne, Roland, and Oliver (v. 57).[295] However, the French need to return to their own virtues and traditional ideals, as he perceives it. Praying to the Virgin Mary would certainly help the country to recover from its own moral and ethical decline (vv. 73–81). In order to explain and legitimize his own position, Charles then refers to his own suffering as a prisoner, sometime in the past when he composed these verses: "Car prisonier les fis, je le confesse" (v. 85; "That as a prisoner I wrote them, this I confess"). But he does not go into any details and concludes the *compainte* with expressing his ardent desire that peace and glory will return to France once again.

In the *balade* no. 114, the poet presents himself as being located at Dover, looking over the sea and longing for his home country, France, where he used to enjoy so many pleasures as a highly respected duke. His heart is filled with melancholy, as expressed by his sighs, and although this longing hurt him internally, he knows how important it is for him to ventilate these feelings (vv. 6–7). If only peace could be established between both countries, as he emphasizes, then he might be able to return home, as he expresses indirectly in the second stanza: "bonne pais" (v. 11). In fact, as he formulates it in his Envoy, "Je hé guerre, point ne la doy prisier" (v. 23; "I hate war, have no reason to esteem it" [lit.: to praise it]), and the longer the war lasts, the longer he would have to stay in England, not being able to return home. Universal peace represents the highest goal for everyone, as the poet underscores, whereas the kings and princes who continue waging their wars only repress their people's desires and act like tyrants (v. 31). We cleary perceive echoes of the same argument proposed much earlier by John of Salisbury, Marie de France, and Ulrich Bonerius.

---

295 The myth of Charlemagne was widely spread across medieval Europe; Albrecht Classen, "The Myth of Charlemagne: From the Early Middle Ages to the Late Sixteenth Century," peer-reviewed online article at http://www.charlemagne-icon.ac.uk/further-reading/articles/; or: http://www.charlemagne-icon.ac.uk/wp-content/blogs.dir/332/files/2016/01/Classen-2016-The-Myth-of-Charlemagne.pdf (last accessed on Jan. 15, 2021); for various research projects, some completed, others not yet, see https://www.charlemagne-icon.ac.uk/research-groups/ (both last accessed on Jan. 15, 2021). See now also Albrecht Classen, ""The Ambiguity of Charlemagne in Late Medieval German Literature: The De- and Reconstruction of a Mythical Figure," *Medievalia et Humanistica*, New Series, 45 (2019): 1–26.

Charles does not address 'freedom' as such, but insists that once peace would have been established, then they all would enjoy "le vray tresor de joye" (v. 50).

Charles certainly couches his deepest concern, freedom for himself and peace for the people, in allegorical and courtly terms, talking about emotions, values, ideals, dreams, and sorrows. But the autobiographical focus is never too far away, and hence also the experience in imprisonment. After his child and youth had passed, Reason intervened and forced him into prison: "Put on prison straw to grow ripe" (*balade* no. 120, v. 8). His longing for past "Largesse" (v. 10; "Generosity") is also a desire for freedom, though he does not use that term here. However, he formulates that God put him into prison so that he could grow and develop as a person. Of course, there is nothing of the banal misery of the ordinary person lingering away in a dungeon, since this is a wealthy, highly powered prisoner. But, Charles at least addresses the question why he is stuck in his situation and how he might find an explanation for his suffering, if that is the right word, offering him, curiously, a chance of transforming into a better person.

Finally, in *balade* no. 121, the poet turns more directly toward his situation in prison, determined by worry and care: "Soing et Ennnuy" (v. 6). Probably influenced by Boethius's *Consolatio de philosophiae*, here he addresses Fortune which he makes responsible for his destiny of being stuck in the English imprisonment "longuement" (v. 10). The second stanza seems to be a playful rhetorical operation with a conversation between himself and his heart, reminding the latter that most times when an individual is lingering in a prison, s/he also experiences torments and dangers (vv. 14–15), probably implying also torture, for which there would not be any recourse, no vengeance possible because the prisoner is completely at the mercy of those who have captured him. It would not even constitute a crime if he were to be treated like any other prisoner "pris en guerre" (v. 20). As we hear him lamenting many times, especially in his English poems, Fortune controls his life completely, and hence has taken away his freedom against which he cannot fight, as he expresses it movingly in "O Fortune, dost thou my deth conspyre?" (B40): "Martir am y for loue and prisonere; / allas, allas, and is this not ynow?" (1442–43).[296]

The poet then draws on the allegorical mode once again to render understandable what he had to face in prison, but the actual reality of imprisonment shines through here as well, so when Charles laments the strong feeling of melancholy, sleepless nights, sleeping during the day, being tied to chains "De Soussy et Pensement" (v. 30; "Of Worry and Deep Thought"). In the *balade* no. 122, we

---

[296] Arn, *Fortunes Stabilnes* (see note 293), 188.

are alerted to the political situation for this prisoner, insofar rumors have spread in France that he has died, but the poet, resorting to a bit of satire, insists repeatedly that Old Age has not yet caught up with him and that his own death is still far away. He thanks God "Qu'encore est vive la souris!" (v. 27; "That the mouse is still alive!"), telling his friends and relatives that it would not yet be necessary to wear black mourning clothes. Gray clothes are cheaper at any rate, and since he has not yet died, there would not be any necessity for such great expenditures.

Most curious proved to be for himself and other high-ranking prisoners that they were sometimes allowed to travel in order to conduct business, especially their personal affairs, which also entailed attempts to secure enough money to pay for the ransom. In *balade* no. 123, he appeals to Jean, Duke of Bourbon (1381–1434), who was going on one of those trips from England to France, to seek out his own wife and to appeal to her for help to secure Charles's release. Jean had also been captured during the battle of Agincourt, but despite the various attempts finding the necessary financial support, he always failed and had to return to England. He died in London in 1434.[297]

This *balade* does not go much further into details, but it certainly conveys the deep sense of loneliness, longing, and desire for freedom from this hostage situation, especially when the poet formulates in the Envoy: "'Souviengne vous du fait du prisonnier / Il ne fault ja que plus je vous en dye' ..." (v. 27; "'Remember the situation of the prisoner. / I need to tell you no more of this'").[298] Although both Charles and Jean were obviously treated very well and did not have to suffer the ordinary destiny of most other prisoners or hostages, their psychological suffering proves to be palpable in this poem which was more of an appeal for help, an indirect message to his wife, and good wishes for Jean to achieve his goal to secure his release. For the poet, the most painful feeling was the forced distance to his wife back in France: "Maugré mon vueil" (v. 14: "Against my will"). Of course, the poet completely aestheticizes his personal suffering, transforming it into the medium for his esoteric lyric verses, but this does not hide the deep sorrow and longing for the chance to return home, to see his wife again, and to be free from his imprisonment. However, as *balade* no. 125 in-

---

[297] Fox and Arn, ed., *Poetry of Charles d'Orléans* (see note 288), 884. For numerous parallel cases from the early to the late Middle Ages, see the contributions to *Medieval Hostageship, c.700-c.1500: Hostage, Captive, Prisoner of War, Guarantee, Peacemaker*, ed. Matthew Bennett and Katherine Weikert. Routledge Research in Medieval Studies, 9 (New York and London: Routledge, 2017).

[298] Adam J. Kosto, *Hostages in the Middle Ages* (Oxford: Oxford University Press, 2012); for hostages taken by the Vikings during the early Middle Ages, see Stefan Olsson, *The Hostages of the Northmen* ([Stockholm]: Stockholm University Press, 2019).

dicates, he was also longing for his wife in sexual terms and expressed both his deep frustration and the loss of his sexual prowess due to the extended separation from her: "In regard to the rabbits that you say I have loved, / I have now entirely forgotten them, for it has been several years… ." (vv. 4–6).[299] In fact, Charles delves into all kinds of fantasies about pleasant aspects of his previous life, day-dreaming, so to speak, and evoking past delights and feelings of love, which are now lost due to his long-term imprisonment (vv. 21–24).

Over and over again, the poet voices his deep desire for peace between England and France, which would provide him with the long-awaited chance to be set free again, such as in the *balades* no. 127, 128, or 129. In *balade* no. 132, which was composed in 1439, one year before Charles's release into freedom, he even resorts to the fascinating metaphor of playing tennis with Old Age, and this at a time when the poet had already reached the age of forty-five. Although his opponent knows almost too well how to return the ball, the poet draws from his hope: "Mais Espoir est mon bon amy" (v. 13), and he deftly defies Old Age (v. 20) because Fortune has held him down already for such a long time that he might be able to gain his freedom again, which is, of course, only hinted at indirectly. We may assume, however, that Charles must have spent much of his time with idle entertainment, and so we are granted here an early evidence that the sport of tennis was already practiced in the late Middle Ages.[300]

And yet, his intent was, as to be expected, always to secure enough money to pay for his ransom, as *balade* no. 135 reflects, in which he reflects on his continuous efforts to gain a loan, such as from Lombard merchants. He would even pledge his servitude to a creditor, as long as he only could regain his freedom: "Car se je suis en ma partie / Et oultre la mer franchement, / …" (vv. 17–18; "For if I'm in my own land / and across the sea in freedom, …"). We face here, in short, a whole genre of hostage or imprisonment poetry, which was quite popular in the late Middle Ages, obviously because the experience of being taken prisoner for political or military reasons was surprisingly wide-

---

[299] For a rich collection of medieval manuscript illuminations showing scenes with bunnies, see https://kulturmischmasch.com/tag/hasen/ (last accessed on Jan. 15, 2021). A most dramatic example of the sexual symbolism of the bunny can be found in the Middle High German verse narrative, "The Little Bunny Rabbit" (ca. 1300). For an English translation, see *Erotic Tales of Medieval Germany* (see note 20), 35–41.

[300] Marilyn L. Sandidge, "Gawain, Giants, and Tennis the Fifteenth Century" *Pleasure and Leisure in the Middle Ages and Early Modern Age: Cultural-Historical Perspectives on Toys, Games, and Entertainment*, ed. Albrecht Classen. Fundamentals of Medieval and Early Modern Culture, 23 (Berlin and Boston: Walter de Gruyter, 2019), 473–93. See also the discussion of tennis in other contributions, such as by Scott L. Taylor, "*Jeux Interdits:* The Rationale and Limits of Clerical and Lay Efforts to Enjoin '*Scurrilia Solatia*'" (ibid.), 529–34.

spread. Considering the enormous political, economic, and military ramifications of having a prince, a dauphin, or even a king as prisoner, it comes as little surprise that people paid great attention and closely followed the developments, at least for a short period of time, as in the case of Richard the Lionheart. If the imprisonment continued, however, over a longer period, as Charles had to endure it, if that is the right word here, the public quickly lost interest, and the individual victim had increasingly to fend for him- or herself.

4 King James I of Scotland: Another Royal Prisoner and Poet

Let us also consider the experience by King James I of Scotland (1394–1437, reigned from 1406–1437), who also had to 'endure' an extensive imprisonment. It would go much too far in the present context to examine the various factions in Scotland fighting internecine wars both amongst each other and against King Robert III. The latter was increasingly concerned about the safety of his son, James, considering that his older brother David, Duke of Rothesay, had died under suspicious circumstances while being detained by their uncle, Robert, Earl of Fife, later Duke of Albany – most likely as the result of murder. James's other brother, Robert, died young, so it was up to James to succeed his father to the throne. In 1406, he was sent by ship to the French rooyal court where he could be better protected and could be raised properly, but pirates captured the ship off Flamborough Head east of Leeds and delivered the young prince to King Henry IV of England (1367–1413), obviously for a hefty payment.

Ironically, and quite similar to Charles d'Orléans, this did not result in an imprisonment as we would normally assume. He was first kept in the Tower of London, later in Nottingham Castle and subsequently, after a second period in the Tower, at Pevensey, Kenilworth, and Windsor castles, all rather luxurious accommodations for this valuable prisoner. James actually joined the royal court, was closely supervised and educated by the King who made sure that he received a thorough training, especially in governmental and administrative affairs. Later, the Scottish (uncrowned) king even joined Henry, whom he deeply admired, on a military campaign in France (1420–1421) and who knighted him on St George's day in 1421. In February of 1424, he married Joan Beaufort, daughter of the Earl of Somerset, who himself was in French captivity for fifteen years. Already in April of that year he was released from his status as prisoner and could return to Scotland, but not without presenting hostages, for whom he seems not have paid the ransom later when he endeavored to strengthen his royal position back home. He was finally crowned king in May of 1424, but his life ended already in February of 1437 when he became the victim of an assassination in Perth as a result of the many hostile relationships that had developed following numerous political reforms and rearrangements of power structures.

During his eighteen years of absence in imprisonment, his uncle Robert Stewart, Duke of Albany, took control of most of Scotland and reigned as its governor. He withheld all money to support James, but Henry made sure that the young man held in captivity was well taken of. However, after Henry's early death in 1413, his son took over as Henry V, and he pretty much ended James's relative freedom and forced him to move to the prison in the Tower of London, where other Scottish nobles were already held under rather dire conditions, though again in relative terms, probably comparable to those Charles d'Orléans was subjected under.[301] Royal prisoners were too valuable to risk their demise or death.

James I is famous not only as the king of Scotland, as a notorious prisoner, as a significant power player in his kingdom after his release, but also as the poet of the *Kingis Quair*, a quasi-autobiographical poetic reflection upon his imprisonment, a major contribution to the genre of prison poems.[302] He dedicated it to Geoffrey Chaucer and John Gower, a tribute which clearly indicated how much he had been socialized in English culture and literature. But considering how closely he modeled his poem after the example of famous Boethius's *Consolatio de philosophiae*, with the speaker waking up and reflecting upon his lonely situation, also indicates the extent to which he had received an excellent education.[303]

---

301 Michael Brown, *James I* (East Linton, Scotland: Tuckwell Press, 1994); Alan MacQuarrie, *Medieval Scotland: Kingship and Nation* (Gloucestershire: Sutton Publishing, 2004).
302 James I of Scotland, *The Kingis Quair and Other Prison Poems*, ed. Linne R. Mooney and Mary-Jo Arn. Middle English Texts Series (Kalamazoo, MI: Medieval Institute Publications, 2005). For some critical studies, see, for example, Sally Mapstone, "Kingship and the Kingis Quair," *The Long Fifteenth Century: Essays for Douglas Gray*, ed. Helen Cooper and Sally Mapstone (Oxford: Clarendon Press, 1997), 52–69; Alessandra Petrina, *The Kingis Quair of James I of Scotland* (Padua: Unipress, 1997); Joanna Martin, *Kingship and Love in Scottish Poetry, 1424–1540* (Aldershot: Ashgate, 2008). Most authoritatively, M. H. Brown, "James I," *Oxford Dictionary of National Biography* (Oxford: Oxford University Press, 2004), online at: https://www.oxforddnb.com/view/10.1093/ref:odnb/9780198614128.001.0001/odnb-9780198614128-e-14587;jsessionid=1D02C84E35F93 A230B64898AF9EB5 A2C) (last accessed on Jan. 15, 2021).
303 *Boethius in the Middle Ages: Latin and Vernacular Traditions of the "Consolatio philosophiae"*, ed. Maarten J. F. M. Hoenen and Lodi Nauta. Studien und Texte zur Geistesgeschichte des Mittelalters, 58 (Leiden: Brill, 1997); *Vernacular Traditions of Boethius's* De Consolatione philosophiae, ed. Noel Harold Kaylor, Jr. and Philip Edward Phillips. Research in Medieval Culture (Kalamazoo, MI: Medieval Institute Publications, Western Michigan University, 2016); *Remaking Boethius: The English Language Translation Tradition of* The Consolation of Philosophy, ed. Brian Donaghey, Noel Harold Kaylorm, Philip Edward Phillips, and Paul E. Szarmach. Arizona Studies

To our surprise, we notice, however, that King James focuses primarily on Boethius's efforts to combat poverty, the sorrowful experience of exile, distress, and misfortune (v. 34), and not so much the lack of freedom. Yet, he squarely couches all his reflections in the notion of the ever-rotating wheel of fortune, which brings and takes whatever people believe they have for sure and yet then lose again (stanza 9). In James's case, in his youth, Fortune impacted him negatively, but later he recovered, all combined as a mirror of the unsteadiness of human life constantly subject to this universal mechanism (stanza 10).[304]

Subsequently, the poet develops further thoughts on this phenomenon, describing his efforts to embark on a boat and flee from the dangers threatening him in his young age. At this point, the autobiographical element enters specifically, as James then describes how his ship was captured by the pirates who took him a prisoner and turned him over to the English King Henry IV:

Upon the wawis weltering to and fro,
So infortunate was us that fremyt day
That maugré, playnly, quhethir we wold or no,
With strong hand, by forse, schortly to say,
Of inymyis takin and led away. (stanza 24)

From then on the poet lingers extensively on his experience of captivity with its depressing impact on him, wondering, in direct parallel to Boethius, what guilt he might have had for fortune to bring this upon him: "My dedely lyf, full of peyne and penance, / Saing ryght thus, 'Quhat have I gilt, to faille / My fredome in this warld and my plesance?'" (vv. 177–79). Significantly, comparing himself with all other living creatures, James bitterly laments that he alone is lacking in freedom, a remarkable statement we might not have expected from a late medieval poet: "'The bird, the beste, the fisch eke in the see, / They lyve in fredome, everich in his kynd; And I a man, and lakkith libertee!" (vv. 183–85). He has no joy left in his life (v. 205), and looking out of the prison window onto a garden with all of its greens and birds, he feels deeply forlorn and abandoned, deprived from the pleasantries of a free existence.

He also probes the religious and philosophical question as to why this captivity happened to him when he felt completely innocent. But James stays mostly within the realm of nature metaphors and does not let the more gruesome pic-

---

in the Middle Ages and Renaissance, 40 (Tempe, AZ: Arizona Center for Medieval & Renaissance Studies, 2019).
304 Elizabeth Elliot, "The Counsele of Philosophy: The *Kingis Quair* and the Medieval Reception History of the *Consolation of Philosophy* in Vernacular Literature," Ph.D. diss., University of Edinburgh, 2006.

tures of a prison cell enter his lengthy poem of 197 stanzas. Instead, the poet focuses on his lamentable state of affairs, his suffering, his sorrows, and general pain:

> And eke the goddis mercifull uirking,
> For my long pane and trewe service in lufe,
> That has me gevin halely myn asking,
> Quhich has my hert forevir sett abufe
> In perfyte joy, that nevir may remufe
> Bot onely deth, of quhome in laud and prise
> With thankfull hert I say richt in this wise (stanza 188).

Neither the philosophical dimension as pursued by Boethius nor the political aspect relevant for imprisonment as in the case of King Richard Lionheart assume center position here; instead, James develops primarily a poetic reflection on his sorrowfulness and sadness: "By twenti-fold it was in trouble more, / Bethinking me with sighing hert and sore" (vv. 1215–16), which is also not quite the same as Charles d'Orléans constant endeavors to come to terms with his melancholy. Instead, James brings to the fore of his poetic endeavor the pain, the suffering, and loneliness, and desperation of imprisonment, as he himself experienced and as many others had to sustain: "And eke I pray for all the hertis dull / That lyven here in sleuth and ignorance, / And has no curage at the rose to pull" (1296–98). There is no glorious conclusion to his ruminations as in the case of Boethius's treatise, but the poetic discourse allows him at the end to accept his condition and the embrace his life as is because he has no particular influence on it, and so he simply thanks everything that surrounds him for its own existence, though this does not return freedom to him (stanza 191). James accepts his destiny in a humble manner, expressing his thankfulness to the saints and the divine, but there is no particular transformation in his mind; his life is now that of a prisoner (stanza 193), and this is, from an emotional perspective, the reality he has to contend with.[305] As the poet states himself: "And syne throu long and trew contynuance / Of veray faith in lufe and trew service / I cum am, and forthir in this wise" (vv. 1342–44).

---

[305] *The Oxford Book of Late Medieval Verse and Prose*, ed. Douglas Gray (Oxford: Clarendon Press, 1985), 71–72. He rightly emphasizes that the *Kingis Quair* is not a philosophical tract, but a medieval allegorical poem, though it deals less with love, as Gray assumes, and more with fortune as an unchanging force of life. James was fully aware of contemporary literature and drew extensively from some of the major poets of his time, including Chaucer and Gower. See William C. Calin, "The *dit amoureux* and the Makars: An Essay on The *Kingis Quair* and *The Testament of Cresseid*," *Florilegium* 25 (2008): 217–50.

5 Oswald von Wolkenstein: A Tyrolean Poet and His Prison Experience

Yet another contemporary poet, the South-Tyrolean Oswald von Wolkenstein (1376/77–1445) had to go through the miserable experience of being imprisoned, and he was also tortured as a punishment for his recalcitrance to submit under the authority of the Tyrolean Duke Sigmund. Undaunted, Oswald later, once having been freed upon a hefty payment, utilized his own suffering as material for some of his poems.³⁰⁶ This topic has been noted already by some scholars, but it has not attracted full attention, at least outside of historical research.³⁰⁷ While Oswald's contemporary were not particularly interested in his poetry, especially not in those songs that contained novel ideas and concepts, and only rather some of his more traditional poems made their way into late fifteenth-century anthologies.³⁰⁸

We know a lot about Oswald in biographical terms, maybe more than about most of all of his contemporaries because he left behind a rich corpus of personal documents, and because he talked intensively about his own life in his more than hundred thirty poems in Middle High German (exactly: hundred thirty-two).³⁰⁹ Being only the second son in his family, his financial situation was rather difficult, and he also faced, like his entire family, constant conflicts with his territorial lord, Frederick IV, Duke of Tyrol, both over legal issues concerning the property of Castle Hauenstein and the independence of the landed gentry.³¹⁰ Oswald also tried his good luck serving the German Emperor Sigismund for some years, but later he switched his loyalty and managed, in the

---

306 *Die Lieder Oswalds von Wolkenstein*, ed. Karl Kurt Klein. 4th, fundamentally rev. ed. by Burghart Wachinger. Altdeutsche Textbibliothek, 55 (Berlin and Boston: Walter de Gruyter, 2015); *The Poems of Oswald von Wolkenstein: An English Translation of the Complete Works (1376/77–1445)*. The New Middle Ages (New York: Palgrave Macmillan, 2008).
307 See, for instance, the many valuable contributions to *Oswald von Wolkenstein*, summarizing concisely the state of art in research on this poet: *Leben – Werk – Rezeption*, ed. Ulrich Müller and Margarete Springeth (Berlin and New York: Walter de Gruyter, 2011).
308 *Untersuchungen zur Überlieferung und Rezeption spätmittelalterlicher Lieder und Spruchgedichte im 15. und 16. Jahrhundert: die "Streuüberlieferung" von Liedern und Reimpaarrede Oswalds von Wolkenstein*, ed. Hans-Dieter Mück and Dirk Joschko. Litterae 36 (Göppingen: Kümmerle, 1985).
309 *Die Lebenszeugnisse Oswalds von Wolkenstein: Edition und Kommentar*, ed. Anton Schwob, together with Karin Kranich-Hofbauer, Ute Monika Schwob, and Brigitte Spreitzer. 5 vols. (Vienna, Cologne, and Weimar: Böhlau, 1999–2013).
310 Dirk Joschko, *Oswald von Wolkenstein: Eine Monographie zu Person, Werk und Forschungsgeschichte*. Göppinger Arbeiten zur Germanistik, 396 (Göppingen: Kümmerle, 1985), 71–82.

course of time, to overcome many difficulties and challenges both locally and within the Empire. Ultimately, he gained a high status in the region of Southern Tyrol, today part of northern Italy, and both of his visual portraits in his parchment manuscripts A and B, along with the splendid tomb stone in Brixen, demonstrate clearly how much his self-awareness had grown over the course of his life.[311]

Before we turn to his imprisonment poems, it deserves to be pointed out in general that Oswald's greatest contributions to late medieval German poetry was his considerable interest in multilingualism, his focus on travel reports, his highly sexual openness (dawn songs, the use of the pastourella, marital songs), his creative modification of traditional courtly love songs, his experiments with social, political, and military issues, his emphasis on legal concerns affecting his entire class, and his strong reflections of religious feelings that considerably supersede traditional concepts, perhaps as a mirror of very common late medieval fear of death and dying.[312]

Considering Oswald's personality, his ambivalent political status at a time of major social changes, and his brash character, it is of little surprise that he quickly clashed with his neighbor, a co-owner of Castle Hauenstein, Barbara von Hauenstein, and her family, and subsequently with Duke Frederick. The specific financial and political reasons for the conflict, a rather painful and most difficult situation for our poet, do not concern us here, whereas his reflections in his verses matter critically. However, Oswald's poems are often not easy to understand without a good knowledge of the background because he tends to address very personal matters and predicates his songs intriguingly on his private affairs, such as this imprisonment brought about by betrayal of a former mistress, this Barbara. This unique feature provided Oswald's songs with a highly individual character, which we can appreciate today from a literary-historical perspective, but which made it obviously difficult for his songs to be appreciated beyond his narrow circles of friends and relatives.

In the song "Solt ich von sorgen werden greis" (Kl. 59), he bitterly refers to this young woman who was instrumentalized by his enemies to ambush him, which led to his painful imprisonment, where he was even chained. In his typically sarcastic fashion, Oswald contrasts the gold chain which he used to wear

---

[311] Anton Schwob, *Oswald von Wolkenstein: eine Biographie*. Schriftenreihe des Südtiroler Kulturinstitutes, 4. 3rd ed. (1977; Bozen: Verlagsanstalt Athesia, 1989).
[312] Jean Jost, "The Effects of the Black Death: The Plague in Fourteenth-Century Religion, Literature, and Art," *Death in the Middle Ages and Early Modern Times: The Material and Spiritual Conditions of the Culture of Death*, ed. A. Classen. Fundamentals of Medieval and Early Modern Culture, 16 (Berlin and Boston: Walter de Gruyter, 2016), 193–237.

in her honor with the iron chain to which is was then shackled: "ein eisen dreier finger brait" (10; an iron ring, three fingers wide). She employed her courtly manners ("züchten," v. 11) with regard to him, but for him this only meant a painful torture. The following stanzas continue with this strategy to utilize traditional expressions of courtly love in order to expose his mistress's evil machinations that brought him into prison and exposed him even to torture: "des ward ich hübsch aufgedrät / mit füessen an die stange" (vv. 39–40: I was nicely pulled up, with the feet attached to the iron bar). The pain must have been horrendous, but now, in his satirical poem, the poet seems to poke fun about it all, though the facetious comments only thinly hide the "smerz" (v. 43; pain) which he had to suffer. Metal shackles prevented his movement, and all this suffering he blamed on the former mistress who had now served as a bait to lure him into his enemies' ambush.

The torture caused the poet long-term consequences, forcing him after his release to use crutches, as he points out in his typically sarcastic tone of voice in "Es nahet gen der vasennacht" (Kl. 60; The Shrovetide Season is Approaching). Whereas before he had enjoyed the Shrovetide festivities without restraint together with his companions, now he has to hold back, lean on his crutches, and limp along: "seid ich muess hinken" (31; since I have to limp).[313] As is so characteristic of this fifteenth-century poet, he draws heavily from his biographical material and casts it, at the same time, in a quasi fictional context. Yet, behind the humorous remarks and the playful allusions, there is no doubt at all that Oswald reflected directly on his painful experience in prison and the physical torture he had to undergo there with which he was forced to agree to the huge payments for the other half of the castle Hauenstein which he had 'illegally' occupied when he wanted to establish his own family and estate.[314]

However, he was freed, he did not have permanent damages to his body, his reputation was not impacted negatively, and his social status actually increased subsequently. Nevertheless, here we have evidence of how much the experience in prison along with the torture deeply shaped the poet, although he seemed to react to it all after his release in 1422 with laughter and poking fun at it all through his Shrovetide poem. Nevertheless, his sarcasm remains noticeable, which would not surprise us considering the horror of the torture.

---

[313] For the relevant scholarship on this poem, see Wernfried Hofmeister in Oswald von Wolkenstein, *Sämtliche Lieder und Gedichte*. Ins Neuhochdeutsche übersetzt von Wernfried Hofmeister. Göppinger Arbeiten zur Germanistik, 511 (Göppingen: Kümmerle, 1989), 399.
[314] See already the fundamental study by Ulrich Müller, *"Dichtung" und "Wahrheit" in den Liedern Oswalds von Wolkenstein*. Göppinger Arbeiten zur Germanistik, 1 (Göppingen: Kümmerle, 1968). See also Joschko, *Oswald von Wolkenstein* (see note 310), 71–75.

Of course, every poet, every artist, or composer, and many other people who had to face prison time, or worse, responded to this situation differently, but we can be certain that the artistic expression in word, painting, or music helped profoundly to come to terms with the suffering, especially when the victim regarded himself or herself as an innocent victim, as we have already observed in terms of Boethius and many others. In order to understand Oswald's political position further, we also should keep in mind his strong opposition to the ducal court in Innsbruck and especially the courtiers there who served him completely submissively, whereas the poet proudly proclaimed in independence and freedom, as much worth as it was at the time of an impending paradigm shift toward the territorialization also in Tyrol and hence toward the supremacy of the prince.

Nevertheless, as we learn in the poem "O snöde werlt" (Kl. 11; Oh, miserable world), he despised those sycophants called (in the singular) "hofeman" (39) who happily joined the ducal service and abandoned their traditional freedom in return for a stable income: "der geit sich gar für aigen / dem herren sein umb klainen sold" (40–41; he submits himself under his lord for a little salary). Even a donkey would not lower itself as deeply and shamelessly as those courtiers do, the poet exclaims (42), especially because this service consisted of nothing but carrying out military operations, looting, pillaging, murdering, and committing arson on behalf of their lord (43–45). Gaining his favor was the only issue those courtiers cared about and thus abandoned all their sense of individual freedom, honor, and independence. Receiving a friendly word from the lord, thus being granted his favor, for instance, would be more worth than the divine promise of salvation (54).

Of course, Oswald reflected here on his experience during the severe conflict with the duke, and yet he bitterly complained about having been abandoned by all of his friends and companions. Whereas birds and animals would always protect and assist each other: "in nöten si bei ainander bleiben stan" (60; in emergencies they stay together). Undoubtedly responding to fundamental Boethian teachings and those by the Church, he realized that neither money nor honor, neither love nor any other worldly joys would last forever, and death would always await the individual at the end.[315]

A more irreverent voice addressing these issues was that by the French contemporary, François Villon (ca. 1431–1463), who existed at the margin of courtly society and yet was a member of the urban world. He was apparently involved in

---

[315] Albrecht Classen, "Oswald von Wolkenstein – a Fifteenth-Century Reader of Medieval Courtly Criticism," *Mediaevistik* 3 (1990): 27–53; Joschko, *Oswald von Wolkenstein* (see note 310), 109. See also Sieglinde Hartmann, *Altersdichtung und Selbstdarstellung bei Oswald von Wolkenstein*. Göppinger Arbeiten zur Germanistik, 288 (Göppingen: Kümmerle, 1980), 162.

numerous criminal activities, was imprisoned on several occasions, and reflected upon his experiences in many of his satirical, sarcastic, and entertaining poems. It would be worth to dedicate an entire chapter on Villon with respect to his comments on freedom and criminal justice, but this will have to be the topic of a future study.[316]

---

316 For a recent research overview, see *Villon: Hier et à jamais: Deux décennies de recherches sur François Villon*, ed. Jacqueline Cerquiglini-Toulet. Colloques, congrès et conferences sur le Moyen Âge, 28 (Paris: Honoré Champion, 2020). There are comments on his famous *Le Testament de Villon* (1461), but the issue of imprisonment does not figure here prominently.

F Crime and Imprisonment in Literary Terms

1 Wolfram von Eschenbach's *Parzival*

Crime, Imprisonment, and Evil Characters in the Courtly Romance:
The opposite perspective, that is, the reflection upon evil individuals who were imprisoned as a punishment, also finds some reverberations in medieval literary texts, well before Oswald. Wolfram von Eschenbach, for instance, discusses, even if only in passing, the crime committed by the knight Urjanz, who had tried to rape a courtly maiden.[317] While I have discussed Wolfram's *Willehalm* above in the context of slavery in its literary treatment, here the focus rests on Wolfram's *Parzival* and the appearance of evil knights. This episode is included in the long section dealing with Parzival's friend, Gâwân, who is desperately wooing his lady Orgelûse, who rejects him for a long time, treats him rather contemptuously, and shows him her cold shoulder because, as we learn later, she had been badly abused in the past, thus suffers from a trauma, and cannot trust men for a long time until Gâwân has proven, despite all odds, his superior qualities and his true love for her.

After Gâwân has treated the badly wounded knight Urjâns with some herbs and a small operation, the latter had gotten up quickly and steals his horse, forcing Gâwân to resort to a miserable animal on which he could hardly ride in an appropriate fashion. Only then does Gâwân realize who that thief really was, a knightly criminal whom he had defeated a while ago in a joust and then taken to the court of King Arthur to receive his justified punishment. Having been robbed the rank of a knight ("von schildes ambet man dich schiet," ch. 524, 24), he had been placed in a cage together with dogs for four weeks as a most humiliating punishment for his rape of a courtly maiden. Arthus had intended to get this criminal hanged, but Gâwân had pleaded for him because he himself had taken him prisoner upon his honor, and had taken him to the king: "gevangen fuort ich wider dan / für den künec disen man" (ch. 525, 29–30).

---

[317] Wolfram von Eschenbach, *Parzival*. Studienausgabe. 2nd ed. Mittelhochdeutscher Text nach der sechsten Ausgabe von Karl Lachmann. Übersetzung von Peter Knecht (Berlin and New York: Walter de Gruyter). For a solid English translation, see Wolfram von Eschenbach, *Parzival and Titurel*, trans. with Notes by Cyril Edwards (see note 29); for an excellent critical introduction, see Joachim Bumke, *Wolfram von Eschenbach*. 8th completely rev. ed. Sammlung Metzler, 36 (Stuttgart: J. B. Metzler, 2004). See now also Heiko Hartmann, *Einführung in das Werk Wolframs von Eschenbach*. Einführung Germanistik (Darmstadt: Wissenschaftliche Buchgesellschaft, 2015).

The maid had been hurt in multiple fashion; not only had Urjâns raped her, which was bad enough, but she had originally traveled to King Arthur as a messenger and thus had enjoyed a sacrosanct status, as she formulates herself (ch. 526, 2–3). Moreover, she had lost her virginity and chastity, for which she demanded revenge and justice. The king and the entire Round Table had aggreed that the death penalty would be appropriate for this rapist, but Gâwân felt obligated to plead for the convict's life because after their joust Urjâns had submitted himself to his opponent's grace, meaning that Gâwân now would lose his own honor if the opponent would have been executed (ch. 527, 26–27).

For Orgelûse, the subsequent punishment – incarceration in the dog cage for four weeks – appears as insufficient, and she vows to seek the full judgment against Urjâns (ch. 529, 4–16), threatening also physical punishment. We do not explicitly hear about future actions against this thief, who might have been killed by a new opponent whom Gâwân subsequently defeats, Lischoys Gwelljus.[318] All we need to realize here is that Wolfram presents with him the very opposite of a true knight, a rapist, liar, cheater, and thief. Orgeluse has obviously ordered his execution, but this remains in the background of the story (ch. 529, 12–16).[319] This antithetical character actually strongly profiles Gàwân in his ideal manners and abilities, but he also serves us well to understand the downside of the idyllic courtly existence since even right under Arthur's nose such horrible crime as this rape could happen. To the king's and his court's honor, of course, they undertook everything in their power to remedy the situation and to restore the maid's honor, even though she has lost her virginity for good, a catastrophic condition for this poor woman.[320] However, Urjâns was not executed because Gâwân had to spoken in his favor, but once Orgelûse has understood the entire situation and also witnessed this man's miserable behavior, she does not hesitate to get him killed.

---

318 Elke Brüggen and Joachim Bumke, "Figuren-Lexikon" (see note 240), 932.
319 Wolfgang Mohr, "Zu den epischen Hintergründen in Wolframs *Parzival*," *Mediaeval German Studies Presented to Frederick Norman*. Publications of the Institute of Germanic Studies, University of London, 8 (London: Institute of Germanic Studies, 1965), 174–87; here 178; Martin Jones, "The Significance of the Gawan Story in *Parzival*," *A Companion to Wolfram's* Parzival, ed. Will Hasty. Studies in German Literature, Linguistics, and Culture (Columbia, SC: Camden House, 1999), 37–76; here 57–58.
320 Albrecht Classen, *Sexual Violence and Rape in the Middle Ages: A Critical Discourse in Premodern German and European Literature*. Fundamentals of Medieval and Early Modern Culture, 7 (Berlin and Boston: Walter de Gruyter, 2011), 7–9, 21, 63, et passim.

2 Geoffrey Chaucer and Rape

2.1 Imprisonment and Punishment of the Evil Knight

Ca. two hundred years after Wolfram had composed his *Parzival*, Chaucer included a fairly similar situation in "The Wife of Bath's Tale," contained in his *Canterbury Tales* (ca. 1400). A knight rapes a maiden, and he is immediately charged for this severe crime, which ought to result in his execution (v. 891).[321] With just one verse, the narrator illuminates the entire legal background, confirming that "By cours of lawe, and sholde han lost his heed" (v. 892). However, in this situation, both the queen and the other courtly ladies intervene and beg the king to overturn the criminal to her. She does not necessarily want to spare his life, but she grants him a chance. If he were to find out what all women truly want, he would be free from the death penalty, and this is then the beginning of the story itself, an intricate *mise en abîme*. If he were to fail in that, as she warns him, "Yet shal I yeve thee leve for to gon" (908), and: "Thy body for to yelden in this place" (912).

Ultimately, this knight succeeds in solving this challenge, but only with the help of an ugly lady whom he must promise to marry, which is, of course, a magical trick, leading over to a happy end. We face here a fanciful treatment of crime, which turns into a significant trigger for narrative creativity, but for our purposes we can rest assured that Chaucer also, just as Wolfram long before him, reflected specifically on the tension between freedom and imprisonment, if not death penalty.

2.2 Chaucer's Knights in the Prison

We also ought to include a few comments on Chaucer's "The Knight's Tale," which focuses much on a prison, where two knights, Arcita and Palamon, linger after they have been pulled out of the pile of dead bodies following the siege and conquest of Thebes by King Theseus.[322]

---

[321] *The Riverside Chaucer*, ed. Larry D. Benson, based on *The Works of Geoffrey Chaucer*, ed. by F. N. Robinson, reissued as a paperback (1987; Oxford: Oxford University Press, 2008); here I use Geoffrey Chaucer, *The Canterbury Tales*, ed. Robert Boenig and Andrew Taylor. Sec. ed. (Peterborough, Ont.: Broadview Editions, 2012); see now John Bugbee, *God's Patients: Chaucer, Agency, and the Nature of Laws* (Notre Dame, IN: University of Notre Dame Press, 2019).
[322] Robin Stretter, "Flowers of Friendship: Amity and Tragic Desire in The Two Noble Kinsmen," *English Literary Renaissance* 47.2 (2017): 270–300. Although there is a large amount of rel-

Though badly wounded, they survive and are sent to Athens where they are placed in a prison without having any chance of ever being freed upon the payment of any ransom. As the narrator states: "to dwellen in prisoun / Perpetuelly. He nolde no raunsoun" (1023–24). It remains unclear why they receive this particularly harsh treatment, why they seem to be the only ones who had survived the slaughter, why they cannot do anything to buy their way to freedom, and what their future destiny might be: "This passeth yeer by yeer and day by day" (1033). The poet does not relate much about their suffering, does not address the boredom or the food provided for them, for instance; instead, he moves quickly to a future point in time when a love story develops, with Palamon observing the delightful Emelye picking flowers in a garden next to the prison building.[323] She is Theseus's sister-in-law and unaware of the two prisoners kept in the "chief dongeoun" (1057). Palamon, who is characterized as "woful prisoner" (1063), has the opportunity to go up to a room on the top from where he can overlook the entire city. One of the jailors has given him this little freedom (1064), but although he can breathe more freely there, he laments his destiny, stuck behind bars without any hope to be released from prison. He is at that point looking "thurgh a wyndow thikke of many a barre / Of iren greet and square as any sparre" (1075–78) and espies Emelye, whom he immediately falls in love with. His cousin Arcite experiences the same feeling as soon as he has a chance to look down into the garden, which subsequently leads to a long series of challenges pitting the two knights against each other, though both die in their effort to win the competition and thus to win Emelye's hand in marriage.

---

evant research on this tale by Chaucer, the prison itself does not seem to have attracted much attention at all. But see, for instance, John Z. Zhang, "Medieval Visual Arts and the Barred Window in Chaucer's *The Knight's Tale*," *English Language Notes* 28.3 (1991): 10–17; Peter Brown, "The Prison of Theseus and the Castle of Jalousie," *The Chaucer Review: A Journal of Medieval Studies and Literary Criticism* 26.2 (1991): 147–62. As to the sworn but fake friendship between these two knights, see Zsuzsanna Simonkay, "False Brotherhood in Chaucer's The Knight's Tale / Part 1: Sworn Brotherhood and Chaucer's Sources on Friendship," *HUSSE 11: Proceedings of the 11th Conference of the Hungarian Society for the Study of English*, ed. Veronika Ruttkay and Bálint Gárdos (Budapest: L'Harmattan, 2014), 159–71; eadem, "False Brotherhood in Chaucer's "The Knight's Tale," Part 2: Palamon and Arcite – False Friends Will Be Friends," *Heroes and Saints: Studies in Honour of Katalin Halácsy*, ed. eadem and Andrea Nagy (Budapest: Mondat, 2015), 187–202.

[323] It is a convenient convention in medieval literature having individuals gaze out of a window and espie a newcomer, a future lover, the hero of the story. The window thus proves to be a highly erotic optical medium, whether it allows a lady to look outside, or a knight, as in Chaucer's case. See Lindemann Summers, *Ogling Ladies* (see note 31), though her discussion remains much on the descriptive level. Chaucer adds the prison window as an innovative architectural piece for this purpose.

Back in the prison, however, both begin to feel great jealousy against each other since each would like to claim Emelye as their own: "Greet was the strif and long bitwix hem tweye" (1187). They have no chance, of course, still being stuck in prison without any hope. This changes one day, when Arcite is suddenly released because a duke, Perotheus, a close friend of Theseus, arrives in Athens and begs the ruler to let Arcite go without having to pay a ransom (1205–06). This happens, but on the condition that he disappears for good from any land under Theseus's control. If he ever were to be found there again, he would certainly be executed on the spot (1214–18). Again, there is no good explanation for this extreme hatred, apart from the king's old grudge against his previous opponent, King Creon of Thebes, whom he had entirely crushed. But this point does not need to be pursued further in the present context.

Ironically, because he is so deeply in love with Emelye, poor Arcite bitterly laments this development because he thus can no longer see his lady, and he would have rather stayed in his prison and enjoy the opportunity to see her from his window, than to receive his freedom but being forced to leave the country. Chaucer intended, of course, to highlight the conflict between these two cousins over their shared love with Emelye, as the second half of the tale clearly indicates (tournament to decide who would be entitled to win her hand in marriage), but we gain at least some insights into the world of imprisonment in the first part. The two knights suffer there behind bars although they are not really guilty of any crime, except that they had served under King Creon and had thus become victims of collective guilt.

Arcite offers a lengthy reflection on the vagaries of life with all of its contingency, obviously deeply informed by the philosophical teachings of Boethius,[324] and he describes himself as a miserable exile (1272)[325] and regards himself "deed" although he just gained his freedom, as if the prison had been pure paradise for him since he could enjoy the view of his beloved lady from there. Thereupon he exits very quickly, and the focus turns to Palamon, of whom we are now told that he is actually chained, since his tears which he sheds upon having un-

---

[324] John Finlayson, "The 'Knight's Tale': The Dialogue of Romance, Epic, and Philosophy," *The Chaucer Review* 27.2 (1992): 126–49.

[325] Albrecht Classen, "The Experience of Exile in Medieval German Heroic Poetry" (see note 54), 83–110; cf. the contributions to *Exil, Fremdheit und Ausgrenzung in Mittelalter und früher Neuzeit*, ed. Andreas Bihrer, Sven Limbeck and Paul G. Schmidt. Identitäten und Alteritäten, 4 (Würzburg: Ergon Verlag, 2000); see now Ricarda Wagner, *Entangled Displacements: Exile and Medieval European Literature*. Trends in Medieval Philology, 39 (Berlin and Boston: Walter de Gruyter, 2020). I could not yet consult this study because it was scheduled to appear in print not until November 2020.

derstood that Arcite had been released, make them wet: "The pure fettres on his shynes grete / Weren of his bittre salte teeres wete" (1279–80). Pitifully he laments his miserable destiny in the prison, and he can only hope that his cousin would return with an army, conquer the city, marry Emelye, and liberate him from the prison cell, certainly a woeful location (1296).

Unfortunately for Palamon, he suffers both from enduring his imprisonment and also from his jealousy, assuming that Arcite would be the lucky one to win her hand. While the gods Saturn and Juno have destroyed the city outside, Venus has destroyed him in the prison cell, feeling burning love for the lady (1528–33). This then makes the narrator pose the question who of the two men would have it worse, the one stuck in prison but being able to gaze at the lady, or the other one, freed, but being forced to stay away in a far distance from his beloved. As much as the physical constraints in the prison are painful and cause much sorrow for the lonely victim, as much can he still delight of the vision of his lady (1350–53).

While Arcite arranges to return secretly to Athens in disguise and to serve as a page for Emelye, poor Palamon lingers in prison, and this for seven years, for which the narrator has only words of great pity. In fact, we often hear the term 'martyrdom' or 'martyr' for the prisoners (e.g. 1562), through which the narrator evokes the deep sense of suffering. Nevertheless, in order to proceed with the narrative and to get out of a possible deadlock, we are told that this poor man finally manages to trick his jailor and make him fall asleep after having consumed a drink of wine, spiked with drugs: "Of nercotikes and opie of Thebes fyn" (1472). How he could get out of the locks and shackles, we are not told, but Palamon finally succeeds in fleeing, returning to Thebes where he hopes to gain help in winning Emelye's love and hand in marriage. The narrative then takes a different course, with the two cousins meeting again, and the real struggle over who might win this lady for himself begins.

3 Ulrich von Zatzikhoven and His Version of the *Lancelot* Romance

Deep Down in the Dungeon

Despite the common notion that medieval knights did nothing but fight for their honor and wooed courtly ladies, even courtly poets did not shy away from describing the suffering of their protagonists once they have been thrown into a dungeon. This is the case, for instance, in Ulrich von Zatzikhoven's *Lanzelet* (ca. 1200) where the protagonist, in the early stage of the romance, attacks a castle and is finally taken prisoner after he has hurt or even killed numerous soldiers and knights. The poet provides more details about his subsequent experience than is usual in such cases:

> Now the noble youth lay in a dungeon full of filth; it would have been most dreadful for another sort of man, who was base by nature. Day after day he was given only bread and water. He suffered greatly from the stench. He would soon have perished from this and died miserably, were it not that the lady who had rescued him often gave comfort to him.[326]

However, he is rather fortunate because the kind lady who had rescued him secretly provides him with bedding, food, and wine, and comes to visit him, giving him some personal comfort in the dreadful place. The stay in the dungeon is limited, however, because great tasks are awaiting the protagonist, as life-threatening as those might be. He clearly spells out his disgust about rotting away in the miserable location he finds himself in: "'I would rather fight a hundred knights than be left to die in all this filth'" (48).

We do not learn how the courtly lady herself can stand the terrible smell, darkness, and probably humidity, which all combined could indeed threaten the knight's life. But she has ways to bribe the guards and makes his existence down there at least partially tolerable. And she can finally convince her uncle, Linier of Limors, to release the prisoner on the condition that he fight in several terrifying adventures.

However, in order to help Lanzelet win the fights, she needs to take care of him and to prep him for a fortnight so that he can regain his previous strength. Her uncle agrees, and the first step for her is to order a bath for him and to provide him with plenty and first-rate food, "through which he soon regained his health and recovered his strength" (49). Indirectly, we thus learn that the existence in a dungeon was indeed as horrible as the word itself implies, threatening the poor prisoner's life due to lack of hygiene and sufficient food. Indeed, Lanzelet would certainly have languished for a long time without the lady's help and might have suffered a miserable death down their without her intervention on his behalf. Indirectly, we recognize her a literary echo of the account involving Willehalm and Arabel in Wolfram von Eschenbach's *Willehalm* or in his source, the *Chanson de Aliscans*.

---

326 Ulrich von Zatzikhoven, *Lanzelet: Text – Übersetzung – Kommentar*, ed. Florian Kragl (Berlin and New York: Walter de Gruyter, 2009); for an English translation, see, Lanzelet, trans. Thomas Kerth (see note 30), 47. See now Thomas Poser, *Raum in Bewegung mythische Logik und räumliche Ordnung im "Erec" und im "Lanzelet"*. Bibliotheca Germanica, 70 (Tübingen: Narr Francke Attempto, 2018).

Yet, there is another type of imprisonment which Lanzelet has to suffer from, though the outer circumstances then prove to be very pleasant and accommodating. When he is looking for adventure at the castle of Pluris, he achieves the highest accolade during a tournament and accomplishes the conditions set by the queen, who recognizes in him "the very perfection of manly excellence" (90). Both sleep with each other, and enjoy their time together, although Lanzelet has left behind his true beloved, Lady Iblis. Then, however, the queen falls passionately in love with him and wants to make sure that he will never leave her again. By assigning forty knights as his guardians who always keep a close watch on this hero, and by taking away all of his weapons, she practically imprisons him, to which he would like to object, but he has no choice: "Under these conditions he was obliged to remain there with her for nearly a year; he showed his discontent from the first until the very last" (91).

Lanzelet had certainly found her to be very attractive, at least physically, but he truly loves Iblis, so he finally employs a cunning strategy and asks the queen to reestablish the adventure which ultimately makes it possible for him to free himself from this erotic imprisonment: "He had given much in the service of fame, yet, despite all the great things he had accomplished, Lady Iblis was at no time absent from his thoughts" (92). Four of his friends from the Round Table then appear and participate in the tournament in such a way that they can all pretend to flee, and thus Lanzelet as well manages to escape, never to return to his courtly prison (102).

The personal situation of other figures also matter in our context as the knight Valerin abducts the Queen Guenevere and holds her as a captive in his castle (vv. 6563–7444). In his desperation, King Arthur calls upon the service of the magician Malduc, who agrees to help, but only if he gets under his control the knights Eric and Walwein. Arthur, not knowing any alternative, accepts, which then makes possible to seizure of Valerin's castle and the liberation of the queen. Valerin is killed, but at the same time Eric and Walwein are tortured by the magician, until Lanzelt can arrive to liberate them, after he has killed the magician.[327]

The poet does not go much into detail, and leaves most of this horrible scenario to our imagination. They are thrown into the bottom of a tower (dungeon), where they face unmentionable torments (112), which are, however, not speci-

---

[327] *Magic and Magicians in the Middle Ages and the Early Modern Time: The Occult in Pre-Modern Sciences, Medicine, Literature, Religion, and Astrology*, ed. Albrecht Classen. Fundamentals of Medieval and Early Modern Culture, 20 (Berlin and Boston: Walter de Gruyter, 2017); see already Stephen Maksymiuk, *The Court Magician in Medieval German Romance*. Mikrokosmos: Beiträge zur Literaturwissenschaft und Bedeutungsforschung, 44 (Frankfurt a. M.: Peter Lang, 1996).

fied, except that Malduc tries to starve them to death. Arthus and his court are helpless in this situation because "[w]hatever they offered to Malduc to set them free availed the lords nothing; rather, he treated them all the worse for it" (112). The two knights endure "grievous plain that was ill suited to such heroes" (113), and they "live in misery" (114).[328] Malduc has chained them in "heavy irons" (114), and they would have been beaten to death by the magician's men if Malduc's daughter had not pleaded for their lives. The narrator gives highest praise to this maiden and to all women who come to the rescue of other worthy knightly prisoners: "that they comfort eht torments of love and lighten heavy hearts with their kindness!" (114).

We face here a most interesting reflection on freedom and imprisonment, on knightly independence and the forces of love. Lanzelet is once caught in a terrible dungeon, and once in a luxurious prison, that is, in the hands of a queen who is exceedingly loves him and cannot stand the idea of losing him although he does not love her back and organizes a clever strategy to extricate himself from her captivity. Neither physical beauty nor material pleasures are sufficient for Lanzelet to abandon his true love, Iblis. Ulrich von Zatzikhoven thus projects the multiple levels of meaning of imprisonment and indicates how significant it was also for members of courtly society to guard themselves from entrapment, both concretely and metaphorically. Being thrown into a dungeon could easily lead to the victim's death, and knights are not exempted from such a destiny, as Ulrich indicates clearly.

4 Other Literary Reflections of Imprisonment

However, in many cases, such as Charles d'Orléans, captivity amounted to nothing but a restriction concerning one's mobility or the freedom to return home. One curious and yet revealing example would be the very short verse narrative "The Hazelnut Mountain" by an otherwise unknown poet called Heinrich Rafold (late thirteenth/early fourteenth century; the text is contained in a manuscript from ca. 1350).[329] A mighty Christian knight fights against Muslim forces and

---

[328] In the original: "dulten jæmerlîchen pîn, / der sölhen helden niht gezam" (7582–83); based on Ulrich von Zatzikhoven, *Lanzelet: mittelhochdeutsch / neuhochdeutsch*, trans. Wolfgang Spiewok (see note 30); online at: http://www.hs-augsburg.de/~harsch/germanica/Chronologie/12Jh/Zatzikhoven/zat_la00.html (last accessed on Jan. 15, 2021).

[329] Here I quote from my *Erotic Tales of Medieval Germany* (see note 20), 61–62. This is based on von der Hagen's edition, *Gesammtabenteuer* (1850), no. XIX, vol. 1, 441–47; now available online at: https://archive.org/details/gesammtabenteue06hagegoog/page/n13/mode/2up (last ac-

manages to capture their king, along with a band of his nobles, whom he all takes to his castle. However, out of his respect for the king's nobility, he allows him to spend his time there without being shackled, enjoying the freedom to roam around the castle as he wishes ("Niht sêre gebunden," 53; not tightly bound), while his men are taken to the dungeon. The latter fact is revealed only at the end of the story. Then, the knight travels to his own king to report about his victory, for which he is greatly rewarded. During his absence, his wife falls in love with the heathen lord, and decides to elope with him to his country. Once that affair has been confirmed, "she went down to the dungeon and liberated the prisoners, the entire heathen company, and this secretly and without anyone noticing it" (68). For the narrator, this amounts to serious treason, and he warns his audience about the lady's loss of honor, but the narrative concludes at that point and does not provide us with more information about the consequences of the elopement.[330]

---

cessed on Jan. 15, 2021). See also *Neues Gesamtabenteuer, das ist, Fr. H. von der Hagens Gesamtabenteuer, die Sammlung der mittelhochdeutschen Mären und Schwänke des 13. und 14. Jahrhunderts in neuer Auswahl*, ed. Heinrich Niewöhner. 2nd ed. by Werner Simon (1937; Dublin: Weidmann, 1967). Most recently, a new edition has appeared which offers extensive comments; *Deutsche Versnovellistik des 13. bis 15. Jahrhunderts (DVN)*, ed. Klaus Ridder and Hans-Joachim Ziegeler, together with Patrizia Barton, Reinhard Berron et al. 6 Vols. Vol. 5: German Verse-Couplet Tales from the Thirteenth to the Fifteenth Century, English trans. by Sebastian Coxon (Berlin: Schwabe Verlag, 2020), no. 71, p. 225. The text edition is in vol. 3, pp. 297–301. Despite the best efforts to uncover any information about the poet and his possible sources, much remains uncertain. It is not convincing to suggest that the knight's wife who liberates the captured heathen (Muslim) king might have been a heathen herself.

330 There is virtually no research on this short verse narrative or on the poet; see, for instance, Klaus Grubmüller, *Die Ordnung, der Witz und das Chaos: Eine Geschichte der europäischen Novellistik im Mittelalter: Fabliau – Märe – Novelle* (Tübingen: Max Niemeyer, 2006); see also Hanns Fischer, *Die deutsche Märendichtung des 15. Jahrhunderts*. Münchener Texte und Untersuchungen zur deutschen Literatur des Mittelalters, 12 (Munich: C. H. Beck, 1966); id., *Studien zur deutschen Märendichtung*. 2nd ed. by Johannes Janota (Tübingen: Max Niemeyer, 1983); *Das Märe: Die mittelhochdeutsche Versnovelle des späteren Mittelalters*, ed. Karl-Heinz Schirmer. Wege der Forschung, 558 (Darmstadt: Wissenschaftliche Buchgesellschaft, Darmstadt, 1983); Hans-Joachim Ziegeler, *Erzählen im Spätmittelalter. Mären im Kontext von Minnereden, Bispeln und Romanen*. Münchener Texte und Untersuchungen zur deutschen Literatur des Mittelalters, 87 (Munich and Zürich: Artemis, 1985); Joachim Heinzle, "Kleine Anleitung zum Gebrauch des Märenbegriffs," *Kleinere Erzählformen im Mittelalter: Paderborner Colloquium 1987*, ed. Klaus Grubmüller; Leslie Peter Johnson; Hans-Hugo Steinhoff. Schriften der Universitäts-Gesamthochschule-Paderborn, 10 (Paderborn and Munich: Schöningh, 1988), 45–48. For a solid text selection, see *Novellistik des Mittelalters: Märendichtung*, ed., trans., and commentary by Klaus Grubmüller. Bibliothek des Mittelalters, 23 (Frankfurt a.M.: Deutscher Klassiker Verlag, 1996). See now also

We notice strong parallels with the situation in Rudolf von Ems's *Der guote Gerhart*, with noble prisoners serving as highly valuable pawns in military and political terms. But while there the English lords are all chained, here in Rafold's story the king can spend his time freely, having given his pledge, or honor, not to run away. He does so, at the end, after all, with the help of the lady, but the narrator only blames her and describes her as dishonorable, whereas the Muslim king's escape receives no further comments, a typically misogynistic approach in late medieval literature.

Both here and in many other narratives, we can also recognize that prisons were not absolutely secure places from which the prisoners could not escape. Imprisonment itself was not necessarily associated with a building or a dungeon, and could also be a form of captivity predicated on one's honorable pledge not to escape until things were settled. In fact, we observe almost an infinitude of various situations where individuals are taken prisoners, become slaves, or suffer simply from the loss of freedom, all depending on the political, economic, legal, judicial, military, and economic conditions.

We would be hard pressed to identify any medieval text – literary or historical, religious or economic – where an individual would exert absolute and complete power over others, except in some extreme cases, such as the sex slave in Kaufringer's story "The Search for the Happily Married Couple," which I have discussed above already. But even there, the inn-keeper has to make sure to keep the peasant in good physical health and entertained so that he can perform well physically in satisfying his wife's sexual needs. When we consider the few available accounts about enslavement, such as by Georgius of Hungary and Johann Schiltberger, we notice that the two authors certainly lamented the loss of their freedom, but once they had adapted to their new environment and performed their duties as imposed on them by their masters, they appeared to have coped fairly well, even earned money, and felt recognized in their various roles as servants, runners, warriors, etc.

Freedom, however, was still their highest goal, as we also learn in the ninth story of the tenth day in Boccaccio's *Decameron*. The best friendship between Master Torello and the Sultan Saladin cannot compensate for his lost freedom and his continuous desire to return home as fast as possible. For that reason, Saladin's action at the end to set his old friend free and then to help him return home by magical means underscores the great value the individual already in the pre-modern age placed on this ideal (again, see above for more details).

Deutsche Versnovellistik des 13. bis 15. Jahrhunderts (DVN), ed. Klaus Ridder and Hans-Joachim Ziegeler (see note 329).

The same holds true for the story in *El Conde Lucanor* by Don Juan Manuel, which I have discussed already before.

If we return briefly from here to one of the fables by the Swiss Dominican Bonerius (*Der Edelstein*, ca. 1350), we gain significant confirmation for this subtle and yet important strand of discourse already in the Middle Ages. In that fable, "Von einem Pfâwen und einem Kranche" (no. 81; Of a Peacock and a Crane), the peacock tries to denounce the crane as being not worthy as his companion; its own physical beauty would make him extremely superior compared to the crane. The latter, however, deconstructs this argument outright and points out how quickly the peacock's feathers would be plucked, leaving it alone, naked and dirty, not being able to move away. Bodily attractiveness would not last for long, and then "undrutzes ist dîn leben vol" (v. 52; your life is filled with frustration, or dissatisfaction). The peacock can praise itself as much as it wants, but it proves to be a vain and useless strategy not worthy to be regarded seriously.

The crane, however, makes the most interesting claim that it, with its white but powerful wings and feathers, is free to fly wherever it wants: "ich vliug ûf; des hab ich gewalt / nâch mînem willen, ungezalt" (vv. 45–46; I fly up, I have the power to do so, according to my will, wherever I want to go). In contrast to the peacock, the crane prides itself of its freedom and independence: "sô bin ich stolz und wol gemuot" (v. 53; I am proud and happy in my mind). Of course, Bonerius does not address actual animals, and uses, like all other fable authors, the two birds as representatives of two types of people. While the peacock proves to be completely enamored with itself, a victim of material beauty, the crane knows fully well its own strength, power, and freedom, which it uses to go wherever it might desire. In short, this Swiss poet explicitly advocated for individual freedom, and thus he serves as a very important voice, along with that of his contemporary Boccaccio, supporting our claim that the discourse on freedom was fully underway already at that time.

It would be rather difficult to identify a more fully developed concept of freedom, apart from those few, though important, comments here and there. Often, they appear only fleetingly, and it proves to be difficult to identify here a cohesive discourse, especially since we cannot identify specific pre-modern treatises or poems extensively or entirely dedicated to the topic of freedom. But if we include as well the rise of a new narrative genre, focusing on an individual's experiences as a captive and, worse even, as a slave (Georgius of Hungary, Johann Schiltberger), we indeed grasp a significant phenomenon that needs to be considered more broadly and more in-depth in order to understand more fully the complexity of the pre-modern world.

5 Dante Alighieri, the Allegorical Prison

and His Discourse on the Political Structure: *De monarchia*

Freedom could also be perceived in a spiritual context, as we learn, for example, in Dante's *Purgatorio*, the second part of his famous *Divina Commedia* (completed ca. 1320). Having come out of Inferno, Virgil presents the pilgrim to the soul of Cato of Utica (95–46 B.C.E.) whom he encounters here although he had committed suicide in order to avoid being captured by Cesar. Virgil explains Dante's purpose and aim, and in that context also formulates: "Or ti piaccia gradir la sua venuta: / libertà va cercando, ch'è sì cara, / come sa chi per lei vita rifiuta" (70–72; May it please you to welcome his arrival, / since he's in search of liberty, which is so dear, / as he well knows who gives his life for it).[331] The religious connotations are obvious here, and yet, we should not ignore the fact that Dante explicitly elaborated on this notion, thus contributing to the overarching political discourse he was also involved in, at least in some of his other texts.[332]

In fact, if we take into consideration some of his political writings, especially his *De monarchia* from ca. 1316–1320,[333] which essentially considers the relationship between the pope and the Holy Roman emperor, but then also the role of the individual within feudal society, we observe that Dante was extensively interested in the question what constitutes freedom, where it can be developed, who holds freedom, and what is the relationship between the individual and the superior authorities, first the emperor and the pope, but then, ultimately, God Himself.[334] Whether the author favored the supreme role to be assumed by the Holy

---

[331] Dante Alighieri, *Purgatorio*, trans. Jean Hollander and Robert Hollander (New York: Anchor Books, 2003), 8–9.
[332] Romano Manescalchi, "'Purgatorio' 1 71–74: Perché non si può parlare di libertà politica," *Studi Danteschi* 78 (2013): 359–77; cf. also Inga Pierson, "Piccarda's Weakness: Reflections on Freedom, Force, and Femininity in Dante's Paradiso," *Speculum* 94.1 (2019): 68–95; Iacopo Costa, "The Will of the Emperor and Freedom in the Empire," *Dante as Political Theorist: Reading Monarchia*, ed. Maria Luisa Ardizzone (Newcastle upon Tyne: Cambridge Scholars Publishing, 2018), 98–112; Gian Carlo Garfagnini, "'Monarchia': Manifesto di libertà e responsabilità civile," *Studi Danteschi* 75 (2010): 13–23.
[333] Here I follow the reasonable suggestion of a late dating by Richard Kay, "Introduction," *Dante's Monarchia*, ed. and trans. id. (Toronto: Pontifical Institute of Medieval Studies, 1998), xv–xliii.
[334] Since this is such a 'classical' text in medieval Italian literature, little wonder that there are so many editions, translations, and critical studies. See: Dante Alighieri, *Opere minori: Rime. Vita nuova. Convivio. De vulgari eloquentia. De monarchia. Epistole. Ecloge. Questio de aqua et terra. Con il rimario*, ed. Alberto Del Monte. I classici Rizzoli (Milan: Rizzoli, 1960); see also Dante, *Monarchia*, ed. Prue Shaw. Le opere di Dante Alighieri, 5 (Florence: Casa Ed. Le lettere, 2009); Dante Alighieri, *Nuova edizione commentata delle opere di Dante*, vol. 4: *Monarchia*, ed.

Roman Emperor, specifically Henry VII, or, as Cary Nederman has claimed, leaned toward the Byzantine Emperor as the only legitimate heir to the empire, does not need to be addressed here.[335]

For Dante, like many of his predecessors and contemporaries, 'freedom' mostly entailed freedom of will, which in turn meant a spiritual freedom, and not a social or a political one, and which also entailed the danger of losing oneself to sinfulness, as manifested by the throngs of suffering sinners in *Inferno* and also in *Purgatorio*. At first, however, the author emphasizes the high importance of considering one's role in this life, which ought to be directed toward posterity and hence the question of how one can contribute to the improvement of this world for the next generations; otherwise, we would be nothing but a "destructive whirlpool, always engulfing, and never giving back what it has devoured" (Introduction). This establishes the foundation for his reflections on the role of the monarch in his relationship to the people, who need to be governed, at least somehow.

Dante leaves no doubt at all that government is an absolute necessity, as this concerns humanity at large. All things or entities have a purpose and do not exist all for themselves, and this applies to people as well, whose essential characteristic is "existence intelligent through the possible intellect" (ch. 3). Freedom, hence, as we might imagine it – even we today in the western world of the twenty-first century know only too well of our own limitations in that regard because we are social beings and mostly live within a society that is determined by laws, rules, and regulations – proves to be very much contingent on many conditions, all of which aim at the realization of the potentiality of human existence.

Dante then argues that "the proper function of the human race, taken in the aggregate, is to actualize continually the entire capacity of the possible intellect, primarily in speculation, then, through its extension and for its sake, secondarily in action" (ch. 4). This, however, would be possible only if the framework of

---

Paolo Chiesa e Andrea Tabarroni together with Diego Ellero (Rome: Salerno Editrice, 2013); Dante, *The De Monarchia of Dante Alighieri*, ed., with trans. and notes by Aurelia Henry (Boston and New York: Houghton, Mifflin, and Co., 1904); online at https://oll.libertyfund.org/titles/alighieri-de-monarchia (last accessed on Jan. 15, 2021). This online version has no clear pagination system, so I will refer to the section only where I will be quoting from. For recent critical studies, see, for instance, Dirk Lüddecke, *Das politische Denken Dantes: Überlegungen zur Argumentation der Monarchia Dante Alighieris*. Reihe politisches Denken, 3 (Neuried: Ars Una, 1999); Claude Lefort, *Dante's Modernity: An Introduction to the Monarchia* (Berlin: ICI Berlin Press, 2020); John F. Took, *Dante* (Princeton, NJ, and Oxford: Princeton University Press, 2020).

335 Cary J. Nederman, "Dante's Imperial Road Leads to ... Constantinople?: The Internal Logic of the *Monarchia*," *Theoria* 143, 62.2 (June 2015): 1–14. I am grateful to the author for sharing his article with me. He engages with much of the recent scholarship on Dante's political theory.

human existence is determined by peace and harmony, as pronounced early on in the New Testament. The promise then was not of riches or power, but peace, meaning that the individual has to accept its role within society and tolerate the others as equals. But, as Dante emphasizes, there must be a structure, with a monarch ruling over all others (ch. 5); otherwise, no order could be established, and conflicts would erupt very easily. All social entities rely on this concept, or else, anarchy would erupt, which the author implies only indirectly, but there is a clear sense about this danger underlying the entire treatise.

For Dante, the concept of the household governed by the head of the family guarantees the achievement of happiness, which can be realized only if there is structure, hence a form of hierarchy that makes possible the establishment of a community, or city. Of course, the praise of monarchy or of kingship would strike us today as completely out of date, but in essence, the idea pertains to the practical working of a political system: "there must be one king to direct and govern. If not, not only the inhabitants of the kingdom fail of their end, but the kingdom lapses into ruin, in agreement with that word of infallible truth" (ch. 5). This was not necessarily the complete consensus in the Middle Ages, as we have seen already in the case of some fables by Marie de France and Ulrich Bonerius, but monarchy as such was never really questioned, so Dante states only what was the broad *communis opinio*, especially because the political structure here on earth was then considered to be mirrored by the divine structure, with the monarch to be subject under God (ch. 7). This did not mean, of course, that all rulers were naively accepted as divinely invested; instead, chroniclers across the spectrum and throughout time voiced all kinds of opinions about the respective rulers.[336] Ultimately, the purpose would be for all people to realize that they are part of a universal whole, determined by the divine power. This does not, of course, leave much room for an individual: "the human race is the son of heaven, which is absolutely perfect in all its works. Therefore, mankind acts for the best when it follows in the footprints of heaven, as far as its distinctive nature permits" (ch. 9).

---

336 Scott L. Taylor, "Feudalism in Literature and Society," *Handbook of Medieval Culture* (see note 11), vol. 1, 465–76. For a summary of the various methodological approaches to the meaning of rulership, see now Grischa Vercamer, *Hochmittelalterliche Herrschaftspraxis im Spiegel der Geschichtsschreibung: Verstellungen von "guter" und "schlechter" Herrschaft in England, Polen und dem Reich im 12./13. Jahrhundert*. Deutsches Historisches Institut Warschau, Quellen und Studien, 37 (Wiesbaden: Harrassowitz Verlag, 2020), 11–28. This study focuses on the perception and evaluation of rulers by chroniclers, but does not address freedom or imprisonment. See my review in *Mediaevistik* 33 (forthcoming, 2021).

As all medieval and modern intellectuals would have agreed, no society can exist without the presence of justice, which is adjudicated by a judge chairing a legal court, and if there are competing princes being in conflict with each other, then they must submit under God as the ultimate arbiter. Freedom thus becomes a rather relative term for Dante, and hence also for his contemporaries. Nevertheless, just at the moment when we would think that he has turned his attention entirely to political and religious issues, the author suddenly returns to the issue of freedom, emphasizing at the beginning of ch. 12: "If the principle of freedom is explained, it will be apparent that the human race is ordered for the best when it is most free. Observe, then, those words which are on the lips of many but in the minds of few, that the basic principle of our freedom is freedom of the will." However, many individuals would be refrained in their exercise of this free will because of their appetites, desires, and hence their being subject to material conditions. Yet, freedom in spiritual terms is still attainable at least when the individual commands a higher character similar to a saint or has left this world already.

Yet, even within a political context here on earth, freedom would be possible if the supreme structure, supported by God, would liberate the individual from the political struggle and internecine strife, especially if there is a monarch who exerts clear authority: "Only if a Monarch rules can the human race exist for its own sake; only if a Monarch rules can the crooked policies8 be straightened, namely democracies, oligarchies, and tyrannies which force mankind into slavery, as he sees who goes among them, and under which kings, aristocrats called the best men, and zealots of popular liberty play at politics" (ch. 12). Of course, as the subsequent explanation immediately makes clear, Dante assumes that the Monarch would be guided by nothing but his ideals of helping all people to achieve their own happiness, granting them all the material means necessary to pursue their goal. His premise thus entails that the Monarch would operate morally correctly, looking out for the best of his subject: "Upright governments have liberty as their aim, that men may live for themselves; not citizens for the sake of the consuls, nor a people for a king, but conversely, consuls for the sake of the citizens, and a king for his people" (ch. 12). This means, for instance, that laws are not issued for their own sake, but for the people's sake so that they can live freely, securely, and safely, as long as they acknowledge, of course, the Monarch, which Dante takes as his general assumption.[337]

---

[337] Arthur P. Monahan, *From Personal Duties Towards Personal Rights: Late Medieval and Early Modern Political Thought, 1300–1600*. McGill-Queen's Studies in the History of Ideas, 17 (Montreal: McGill-Queen's University Press, 2014).

However, just as many other medieval political theorists argued (John of Salisbury, Christine de Pizan; see below), Dante claimed that the Monarch would understand his obligations and duties to serve the people as their leader, consul, governor, or king. If such an ideal position would not be realized, however, which Dante does not take into consideration, tyranny would develop, which we hear about in political treatises and literary works, such as in the anonymous *Mai und Beaflor* (late thirteenth century).[338] Perhaps, the author might have assumed a somewhat naive position when he argued: "Now it becomes clear that a Monarch is conditioned in the making of laws by his previously determined end" (ch. 12), but within this framework, he could in fact develop his own concept of freedom, also and specifically in political terms, for the individual within a community because of the supreme role and obligation by the Monarch. That ruler would be, virtually by default, an ideal character and endeavor to achieve the best for his people (ch. 12) – certainly, from a modern, cynical perspective, an absurdity, but a philosophical deduction Dante embraced as he had learned to accept it from his close studies of Aristotle's works.[339]

Insofar as Dante assumed that the Monarch would be free of personal desires, commanding already over vast resources, he would be no longer subject under the common desires and could thus observe the highest degree of justice for all, which granted his subjects all the freedom they needed, especially from lower-ranked nobility or ecclesiastics: "[A] Monarch can have no occasion for cupidity, or rather less occasion than any other men, even other princes, and cupidity is the sole corrupter of judgment and hindrance to Justice; so the Monarch is capable of the highest degree of judgment and Justice, and is therefore perfectly qualified, or especially well qualified, to rule" (ch. 13), certainly an idealistic assumption which has proven to be utterly naive throughout the subsequent centuries.

---

[338] Albrecht Classen, "The People Rise Up against the Tyrants in the Courtly World: John of Salisbury's *Policraticus*, the *Fables* by Marie de France and the Anonymous *Mai und Beaflor*," *Neohelicon* 35.1 (2008): 17–29; Mario Turchetti, *Tyrannie et tyrannicide de l'Antiquité à nos jours* (see note 161).

[339] Elisabeth von Roon-Bassermann, *Dante und Aristoteles: das Convivio und der mehrfache Schriftsinn* (Freiburg i. Br.: Herder, 1956); G. Sorensen, "The Reception of the Political Aristotle in the Late Middle Ages (from Brunetto Latini to Dante Alighieri). Hypotheses and Suggestions," *Renaissance Readings of the Corpus Aristotelicum: Proceedings of the Conference held in Copenhagen 23–25 April 1998*, ed. Marianne Pade. Renaessancestudier, 9 (Copenhagen: Museum Tusculanum Press, 2001), 9–25; Andrzej Waskiewicz, *The Idea of Political Representation and Its Paradoxes*, trans. from Polish by Agnieszka Waśkiewicz and Marilyn E. Burton. Studies in Social Sciences, Philosophy and History of Ideas, 24 (Berlin: Peter Lang, 2020).

Dante does not think that every directive, every law should emanate from the Monarch since that would be much to burdensome and impossible in practical terms. Instead, he emphasizes that local entities must have their own governments and laws, a sort of freedom in political terms. The Monarch's task would be to set the general political guidelines and framework which then would allow the administrators and governments on a lower level to carry out their duties. Whatever might perspire there would have to be subject to the global principal established by the Monarch, whom Dante identifies as a completely ideal figure looking out for all of his people, granting them all their necessary freedom, as long as they obeyed the fundamental rules issued by him. The entire system outlined here would function as projected if there would be a strong sense of a concord, i.e., a form of community to which all voluntarily contributed for the well-being of the entire system (ch. 15): "Therefore the human race for its best disposition is dependent on unity in wills. But this state of concord is impossible unless one will dominates and guides all others into unity" (ch. 15).

From here, Dante proceeds into various directions, both religious and historical, claiming the supremacy of the Roman Empire, the absolute power of God, and, still always to be kept in mind, people's freedom in individual terms within the country ruled by a Monarch. But this freedom proves to be a rather esoteric concept, though it is not completely irrelevant in our context either. While the function of the pope was to lead humankind to salvation, the emperor's responsibility was to create security and peace, and thus also a specific degree of freedom:

> And since none or few – and these with exceeding difficulty – could attain this port, were not the waves of seductive desire calmed, and mankind made free to rest in the tranquillity of peace, therefore this is the goal which he whom we call the guardian of the earth and Roman Prince should most urgently seek; then would it be possible for life on this mortal threshing-floor to pass in freedom and peace (Book III, 16).

There is a universal order holding all of humankind together, being directed by God, who in turn directs the Monarch, who in turn guarantees the individual's freedom in accordance with the natural and divine laws. Consequently, as God's mouthpiece, the Monarch had the obligation to ensure "that instruction productive of liberality and peace should be applied by the guardian of the realm, in due place and time" (ibid.).

6 Christine de Pizan: A Late Medieval Female Writer's

Perspective on Freedom and Imprisonment

Although Dante's treatise obviously met with great approval throughout the fourteenth century, the political situation in Europe was everything but peaceful and without political strife, whether in France, England, or the Holy Roman Empire. In the early fifteenth century, Christine de Pizan hence saw herself urged to address very similar issues, when she composed her *Livre de paix* (ca. 1412–1414), pleading for prudence and wisdom to occupy the minds of the ruler, and for the freedom of the individual to live his/her life in accordance with divine and worldly rules. The common good, universal happiness, and the realization of virtues constituted the principle ideas discussed in her treatise, which, however, had grown out of a great concern about the utter lack of those ideals.[340] For her, this 'freedom,' now in quotes, would be guaranteed if the ruler would be supported by counselors from many social classes, all deeply imbued with those ideals concerning justice, goodness, and virtues, and all sharing the same concept of "probity and good conscience" (80). The ruler, in turn, was supposed to be determined by a desire for justice, and be filled with a strong sense of magnanimity, generosity, and fortitude (Book II).

Christine projected a world where each estate observed its own status and contributed to the well-being of the entire country:

> The nobility, as is their duty, will devote themselves to the defense of the crown and the polity—the clergy to laws and learning, burghers to their proper business, merchants to their commerce, workers to their trades, laborers to their labor. So will everything be in its right place, without anything unreasonably encroaching upon anything else ... (95).

Most importantly, Christine reveals her central interest as being focused on the prince who ought to be, as she pleads, as virtuous as possible, and then the entire sub-structure will experience a good government where people can pursue their own path toward happiness (130). An evil prince, by contrast, would engage in many meaningless war campaigns for which he would need to secure large amounts of money, primarily through taxation: "There is no way other than inflicting many burdens and exactions on the people and heaping wrongful taxes on them" (131). Soon enough, this prince would turn to tyranny and subjugate his people: "thus the evils and persecutions that the wicked, tyrannical lord can

---

[340] Christine de Pizan, *The Book of Peace*, ed., trans., and with an intro. and commentary by Karen Green, Constant J. Mews, Janice Pinder, and Tania Van Hemelryck. Penn State Romance Studies (University Park, PA: The Pennsylvania State University Press, 2008).

contrive to take countless forms and use different means" (131). Undoubtedly, Christine's warning could have been expressed both in the eighteenth and the twentieth, if not also the twenty-first century, which indicates the degree to which for her individual freedom, not explicitly addressed here, mattered critically, as long, of course, as the ordinary people would not disturb peace and the social order. In other words, Christine is not a spokesperson for democracy, but she severely warns of the dangers when a ruler exceeds his limitations and becomes ruthless in the pursuit of his personal goal. Even though the author does not address 'freedom' in specific terms, everything in her treatise illuminates how the individual can live a good, proper, happy, and hence decent life under a fair, just, and caring ruler. Just as in the case of Dante's *Monarchia*, Christine completely subscribes to the notion of a hierarchical order, with a prince at the head of society. But within this feudal structure, she definitely demanded that this person observe fundamental rules of ethics, morality, religion, and guarantee thereby justice and peace for all.

Although certainly accepting the role of the king at the top of all estates, she strongly asserts that there should be nothing but love and friendship between the king, his advisors, and subjects:

> Let there be no false and worthless love in or around you, which, wherever it is, in the end dishonors the man who practices it and makes him despised by or hateful to wise men, so that you discover how much such falsity causes one to be utterly hated … . Let there rather be between you, those of your blood, and your good friends, such perfect love that … you want the same things and are opposed to the same things, in the end. Since this is steadfast love, it will always keep you in true friendship and concord; and united, so that everyone of you wants what the other wishes. (196)

The discourse on freedom and imprisonment, including slavery, was thus very broad already in the high and the late Middle Ages, and both Dante and Christine de Pizan, apart from many other didactic writers and philosophers, certainly harbored strong hopes that their theoretical reflections and ethical ruminations would contribute to an improved relationship between the ruler and his subjects. We do not detect here specific efforts as such to create free space for the individual, but political moves to promote a better political structure where each member of society would understand and accept his/her position and receive, in turn, adequate respect and freedom to live according to the generally recognized social, ethical, and moral norms.

Whether either one of these two authors was aware of slavery as very much in practice probably in each one's respective country, cannot be answered since they seem to pass over this entire issue in silence. Unfortunately, we cannot ignore this phenomenon, which recent historians have uncovered much more than in the past through painstaking archival research, which has yielded the startling realization that the late Middle Ages actually witnessed a considerable growth in slavery as a highly profitable business, especially after the huge human loss due to the Black Death in the middle of the fourteenth century.

What matters here, however, in light of Dante's and Christine's comments, consists of the development of ever-stronger opinions about social, political, ethical, and also material justice, which in turn could not be predicated on any kind of repressive system. Both expected the royal ruler to observe the highest ethical standards, which actually conceded much freedom to their subjects, as long as those acknowledged their king or emperor as the head of the state and as God's anointed representative here on earth, apart from the pope.

7 *Fortunatus* (anonymous, 1509)

Personal Suffering and Fear of Unjust Imprisonment
In order to test these observations and to introduce yet another literary text where some of those ideas come to the fore, let us turn to the anonymous German prose novel, *Fortunatus*, probably composed sometime in the second half of the fifteenth century, but published first in Augsburg in 1509 (no manuscripts).[341]

---

341 Quoted from *Romane des 15. und 16. Jahrhunderts* (see note 33), 385–585. For a review of the relevant research and the central topics, see Albrecht Classen, *The German Volksbuch. A Critical History of a Late-Medieval Genre*. Studies in German Language and Literature, 15 (Lewiston, NY, Queenston, and Lampeter: Edwin Mellen Press, 1995, reissued 1999), 163–83; cf. also Anne Simon, "The Fortunatus Volksbuch in the Light of Later Mediaeval Travel Literature," *Fifteenth-Century Studies* 12 (1987): 175–86; Hannes Kästner, *Fortunatus – Peregrinator mundi: Welterfahrung und Selbsterkenntnis im ersten deutschen Prosaroman der Neuzeit*. Rombach Wissenschaft – Reihe Litterae (Freiburg i. Br.: Verlag Rombach, 1990), 76–106; Albrecht Classen, "Die Welt eines spätmittelalterlichen Kaufmannsreisenden. Ein mentalitätsgeschichtliches Dokument der Frühneuzeit: *Fortunatus*," *Monatshefte* 86.1 (1994): 22–44; id., "The Crusader as Lover and Tourist: Utopian Elements in Late Medieval German Literature: From *Herzog Ernst* to *Reinfried von Braunschweig* and *Fortunatus*," *Current Topics in Medieval German Literature: Texts and Analyses (Kalamazoo Papers 2000–2006)*, ed. Sibylle Jefferis. Göppinger Arbeiten zur Germanistik, 748 (Göppingen: Kümmerle, 2008), 83–102; id., "The Encounter with the Foreign in Medieval and Early Modern German Literature: Fictionality as a Springboard for Non-Xenophobic Approaches in the Middle Ages: *Herzog Ernst*, Wolfram von Eschenbach, Konrad von Würzburg, *Die Heidin*, and *Fortunatus*," *East Meets West in the Middle Ages and Early Modern Times: Transcultural Experiences in the Premodern World*, ed. Albrecht Classen. Fundamentals of Medieval and Early Modern Culture, 14 (Berlin and Boston: Walter de Gruyter, 2013), 457–87; id., "Fremdbegegnung, Dialog, Austausch, und Staunen: Xenologische Phänomene in der deutschen Literatur des Mittelalters. Vom *Hildebrandslied* bis zum *Fortunatus*," *Mediaevistik*

The young protagonist, who originates from Cyprus, attempts to make a good career in the servants of global merchants and nobleman, but quickly faces severe problems because there is no justice and security for those who are engaged in trade in foreign countries. After various ups and downs, he makes his way to London where he finds employment with two young Cypriot merchants, who are, however, barely accustomed to the realities on the English market. They all lose their money to prostitutes and their pimps, which forces Fortunatus to look for other work, and this with a rich young Florentine merchant, Jeronimus Roberti (Jerome Robert), also in London, who apparently spends his time in bad company. In the meantime, the king had entrusted highly valuable crown jewels to a nobleman (unnamed) for safekeeping, who is murdered by another Florentine, Andreas, after both have had dinner with this Jeronimus. But the jewels are not in the nobleman's possession, which forces the murderer to flee all the way to Alexandria in Egypt.

When the king learns that the nobleman has been killed, and that the jewels are lost, he sends his charges to apprehend Jeronimus and his entire household, including Fortunatus. Once the corpse has been discovered in the privy (but not the jewels), the public gets terribly enraged and would have slain any foreign merchant, if those did not hide in their houses. Jeronimus and all his servants are tortured until they all reveal, as much as they even know, how this Andreas had murdered the nobleman and then had fled, whereas they themselves had tried to hide the corpse, as innocent they were of the crime against him.

Poor Fortunatus, who had been away in the coastal town of Sandwich to carry out charges given to him by his master, is tortured even worse than the others because he knows nothing about the entire story and cannot reveal any secrets, as much pain as they apply to him (421). The king, now totally furious about the murder and the loss of the jewels, orders that everyone, from Jeronimus down to the last servant, be executed at the gallows between Westminster Palace and the city. The two maids are buried alive underneath the gallows, whereas the men are all hanged. They are all firmly chained so that their corpses cannot fall of the gallows, as a sign of the king's wrath and a warning to all others not to replicate such crimes.[342]

---

26 (2013): 183–206; id., "Time, Space, and Travel in the Pre-Modern World: Theoretical and Historical Reflections. An Introduction," *Travel, Time, and Space in the Middle Ages and Early Modern Time: Explorations of Worldly Perceptions and Processes of Identity Formation*, ed. Albrecht Classen. Fundamentals of Medieval and Early Modern Culture, 22 (Berlin and Boston: Walter de Gruyter, 2018), 1–75; here 13 and 55–56.

342 Romedio Schmitz-Esser, *Der Leichnam im Mittelalter* (see note 45), 529–33.

Luckily, Fortunatus is recognized by an English lord in the nick of time, who yells out that this young man would be entirely innocent and should be spared since he had been away during the entire time and had not known anything about the murder. After some negotiations, the hangman actually lets the protagonist go, but he warns him to rush and to disappear from England, "wann die frauwen der gassen werden dich zu tod schlagen" (422; otherwise the women in the street will slay you). Subsequently, the royal advisors have taken the most valuable goods from Jeronimus's house, whereupon the king allows the ordinary people to ransack it entirely. This deeply frightens the other Florentine merchants, who then send a huge bribe to the king, who finally grants them the privilege to continue doing their business. However, the narrator concludes this section with the explanation that Jeronimus and his entire house had been executed because they had covered up the murder, which made them guilty, after all (422). Fortunatus emerges as an innnocent victim and is thus also granted his freedom, but only on the condition never to return to England, which he avoids, indeed, on his many subsequent travels.

Nevertheless, this temporary freedom is quickly coupled with profound challenges in his life because once he has reached the Continent and traverses a large forest in Brittany, he becomes terribly lost and is near starving to death (426–27). A bear would have almost killed him, but Fortunatus escapes from it to the top of a tree. Even though the wild animal tries to climb after him, it eventually falls down and is near dead, whereupon the young man follows it down and slays it, drinking its blood from the wound, which sustains him. This all is the negative downside of his regained freedom, leaving him alone, abandoned, outside of society, helpless, and starving. Intriguingly, he next encounters a fairy who offers him a free wish, allowing him to choose among the following list of six aspects: wisdom, wealth, physical strength, health, beauty, and a long life (430). This might help him, indeed, to regain his full independence, so he selects wealth, and the rest of the novel then follows his life in which he has limitless access to money through a magical purse.

With the help of that purse, he might indeed achieve the goal of enjoying a luxurious life, but Fortunatus has to realize quickly how much his riches quickly trigger envy in his contemporaries, especially if they are his superiors and yet lag in the same resources, such as in the case of a count who is most furious to learn that the stranger had bought horses he himself had aimed for. Fortunatus is apprehended, thrown into prison, and tortured until he 'reveals' that he had found that money in the forest, but the count insists that he as the owner of the forest would have full claim on anything coming from there, and hence also on that money (435). The narrator explicitly condemns this behavior, identifying the count's action as highway robbery (436), but the young protagonist is at least allowed to leave unharmed, though he has to promise never to return to the count's country (436), a second travel ban, which increasingly limits his freedom to traverse the world.

In a third instance which parallels these two (London and Brittany), we encounter Fortunatus in Constantinople where he operates freely with his infinite amount of money, including as a benefactor for a poor young woman whose dowry he pays for the parents. However, his inn-keeper is filled with greed and for two nights secretly enters Fortunatus's bedroom, steals all the money, but leaves the purses behind. The second time, however, Lüpoldus, Fortunatus's trusted guide, advisor, and travel companion, is awake and can prevent this by killing the thief. Even though the inn-keeper justifiably suffered his death, this situation threatens all their lives because the authorities would accuse them of murder (458–59). The parallel to the situation in London is very much present for Fortunatus; both there and here in Constantinople the foreigners do not enjoy the same freedom and privileges as the natives, and just as in London, where Jeronimus and his entire company had been executed innocently only because the murder had taken place in their house. The law is not on their side, and there is, indeed, grave danger for all of their lives, especially because the inn-keeper's friends would try their hardest to accuse them all of murder (459).

Fortunatus considers all kinds of ways how to get out of this terrible predicament, thinking even about the option to hand over the magical purse to someone whom he might trust so that that person could pay the judge a huge amount of bribery. However, he knows of the power of money and its allure, and he is only too aware that no one would then return the purse once he would have learned its true property. Once again, Fortunatus is about to despair, until Lüpoldus takes charge, throws the corpse into a well in the backyard, and orders everyone to get ready, pack their stuff, but pretend to be a jolly party. In the morning, under loud noise, they then leave the city (460–61) and travel across the border to the Ottoman Empire, where they know for sure that they will not be pursued by anyone. From there, the protagonist begins his tour throughout Europe, without facing any other significant danger, until he safely returns home to Cyprus (464).[343]

---

[343] Hans-Jürgen Bachorski, *Geld und soziale Identität im "Fortunatus": Studien zur literarischen Bewältigung frühbürgerlicher Widersprüche*. Göppinger Arbeiten zur Germanistik, 376 (Göppingen: Kümmerle, 1983); Albrecht Classen, "Die Fremden und das Fremde in der deutschen Literatur des Mittelalters: Xenologische Reflexionen: Vom *Hildebrandslied* bis zum *Fortunatus*," *Japanisch-deutsche Gespräche über Fremdheit im Mittelalter: Interkulturelle und interdisziplinäre Forschungen in Ost und West*, ed. Manshu Ide and Albrecht Classen. Stauffenburg Mediävistik, 2 (Tübingen: Stauffenburg, 2018), 141–56; Gudrun Bamberger, *Poetologie im Prosaroman: Fortu-*

Even though Fortunatus, and subsequently his two sons Ampedo and Andolosia enjoy a life of luxury and wealth, the novel quickly outlines how especially Andolosia begins to abuse the magical purse and also the wonder hat which Fortunatus had stolen from the Sultan of Cairo and which allows the one placing it on his head to travel anywhere in the world with the speed of light. After many adventures, misfortunes, sudden turns of events, and seemingly good luck, Andolosia is taken prisoner by two criminals who want to extort all of his money. Miserable Andolosia is terribly tortured until he reveals the secret of the purse, but it does not help him to regain his freedom; instead one of them murders him, which is the end of all magic. Before, Ampedo had already destroyed the travel hat out of despondence over the disappearance of his brother.

The two criminals then fight over the money purse, and one of them is mortally wounded. This then exposes their criminal activities against Andolosia, and once the king has learned the truth, both are executed by being broken on the wheel.[344] The outcome of this novel is thus loud and clear, as the narrator emphasizes himself in the epilogue, with money being identified as the root of all evil (*radix malorum*), and a severe warning to the audience not to rely on money as a means to gain individual freedom. At the same time, the novel formulates fairly strong criticism against the legal system under the various rulers. The English king obviously fails in observing justice when he has the entire company of the Florentine merchant Jeronimus executed because the murder had taken place in their house, unbeknownst to them. The emperor of Constantinople is not directly involved, but Fortunatus has valid reasons to fear that they would suffer the same destiny once the authorities would have discovered the corpse of the slain inn-keeper. There is no safety for the foreigners, and there is no security for them, despite all of their financial means.

Fortunatus enjoys considerable respect and even friendship from the ruler of Cyprus, which is his home country, and he is safe there, using his money wisely until the end of his life when he passes on the magical objects to his sons. However, one of them, the more adventurous and impetuous Andolosia, although being highly generous, experiences the same problem as his father after he

---

natus – Wickram – Faustbuch. Poetic und Episteme, (Würzburg: Königshausen & Neumann, 2018). This novel has already been discussed, of course, from many other perspectives, but the element of freedom, captivity, and punishment has not yet attracted full attention.

344 Mitchell B. Merback, *The Thief, the Cross and the Wheel: Pain and the Spectacle of Punishment in Medieval and Renaissance Europe* (Chicago and London: University of Chicago Press, 1999), 140 – 41, 153, 158 – 61, et passim. For useful images and a detailed historical survey, along with extensive references, see https://en.wikipedia.org/wiki/Breaking_wheel (last accessed on Jan. 15, 2021).

had gained the money purse from the fairy. Both then and now in Andolosia's life, his social superiors are deeply jealous of his financial means, kidnap, torture, and eventually murder him out of greed. However, they are then apprehended by the king's servants and brought to justice, but altogether, the infinite access to money represents, as both father and sons have to realize, a severe danger to the individual who finds himself threatened in his existence because hostile noblemen begrudge his material superiority and their own declassification by this nouveau-riche.[345]

Ultimately, as the narrator emphasizes at the end, if Fortunatus had chosen wisdom over money, he would have been able to enjoy a good life, would never had to fear a violent death, and would have acquired, after all, sufficient wealth to live well (580). The excessive greed for money, however, made him subject to the vagaries of life, endangered him all the time, and transformed him, who had become a rich man, to a slave of the very money he had desired so much. Granted, the notion of freedom or lack thereof is not fully expressed here, but the repeated inclusion of the motifs of imprisonment, torture, and murder speaks a clear language. True freedom is not only a matter of political, juridical, or military privileges; instead, it also entails a reasonable approach to the opportunities in the material existence and the realization of the extreme need to balance spiritual wisdom with monetary possessions.

In Fortunatus's early life, his poverty had made him completely dependent on the good-will of rich merchants or lords, until he would almost have been innocently executed for a crime which neither he nor anyone in Jeronimus's company had committed. Once he had gained the magical purse, the endless wealth made him dependent on many other factors, and he has to fear for his life all the time, knowing only too well that anyone who would find out the true origin of his money would barely hesitate to kill him, as later happens to his son Andolosia. Neither the various kings nor the Byzantine emperor offers sufficient protection, or they are the greatest danger in Fortunatus's life. Wisdom represents the essential key to open the door for the individual to escape the world of the Seven Deadly Sins here on earth, such as material temptations, envy, and

---

345 John Van Cleve, *The Problem of Wealth in the Literature of Luther's Gemany*. Studies in German Literature, Linguistics, and Culture (Columbus, SC: Camden House, 1991), 97–109. He is only partially correct in claiming that the two counts who waylay and then murder Andolosia are only motivated to commit this crime because they are angry about his public posture and jealous of his favorite position at court (107). As one of them says to the prisoner: "vnnd du wirst mir sagen / vonn wannen dir souil geltes komme; das du das gantze iar außgibest" (171–72; you will tell me where all your money is coming from which you spend throughout the year).

anger. In fact, from this perspective it seems quite likely, as Hannes Kästner has argued, that the anonymous author of *Fortunatus* might have been a Franciscan friar, such as the famous Nuremberg preacher Stephan Fridolin, author of the *Schatzbehalter* (printed in 1491).[346]

True freedom rests in the soul, as both Dante (*De monarchia*) and Christine de Pizan (*Livre de paix*), among many others, would have agreed. Certainly, Fortunatus and later his son Andolosia are able to travel wherever their interest takes them, but they move around in a world deeply determined by contingency, and this not only in abstract, philosophical terms, as Boethius or Thomas More would have formulated it.

The more money they have available for themselves, the more dangerous they live, surrounded by ever more people filled with envy and jealousy. Some of those do not even hesitate to kidnap or commit murder. Fortunatus himself is lucky enough and can escape from many dangers, but his son Andolosia does not know any bounds, uses his money excessively in public, and arouses thereby the hatred of the two counts, in whose prison he subsequently has to die a miserable death. His unabashed display of money, through which he basically is able to taunt all other members of the court apart from the king, externally a concrete indication of his material 'freedom,' thus turns into the very catalyst that robs him of this freedom and causes his death. The two criminal noblemen perceive Andolosia's behavior as an insult and a threat to their own social status: "wie da ainer genant andolosia waer / so kostlich vnd trib so grossen übermuott / vnd doch kain geborner man waere" (568; there was a man called Andolosia who lived a most splendid life to excess although he was not born into nobility). The more Andolosia succeeded in transgressing the traditional class structure of feudal society, assuming that his money would grant him that freedom, the more he encountered deadly opposition and ultimately lost all of his freedom, that is, even his own life.[347]

---

[346] Hannes Kästner, *Fortunatus – Peregrinator mundi* (see note 341), 282–92; cf. also the useful biographical and literary-historical overview online at: https://de.wikipedia.org/wiki/Stephan_Fridolin. For a digital copy, see the incunabulum held in the Library of Congress, https://www.loc.gov/resource/rbc0001.2016rosen0154/?st=gallery&c=160; Library of Congress. Lessing J. Rosenwald collection, 154 (both last accessed on Jan. 15, 2021).

[347] This is almost parallel to the account of young Helmbrecht in Wernher der Gärtner's *Helmbrecht* (ca. 1260–1280; see notes 89 and 90), who also suffers a miserable death after his attempt to rise from the peasant class to the rank of nobility/knighthood. However, he only robs other farmers and cannot rely on any magical money source. Nevertheless, Helmbrecht also believes that he could claim freedom on his own, but he does this by way of hurting mostly the members of his own social class, who therefore ultimately apprehend and lynch him to death.

Freedom thus proves to be not simply a social, legal, or political construct, but the result of complex negotiations within a larger social context. It depends heavily on a mutual acceptance of responsibilities, obligations, and privileges. While Fortunatus was still able to balance those factors quite skillfully, enjoying his personal freedom while carefully acknowledging the political power structures, Andolosia did not understand the true impact of his rather irritating public performances made possible by means of his endless, because magical, money source. As much as he believed to have gained social freedom with the help of his gold, as little did he take into consideration the social framework which did not want to grant him that freedom, which ultimately meant his violent death.

G Freedom, the Protestant Reformation, and Slavery in the New World

1 Martin Luther's Concept of Freedom

The Religious Perspective

In his *On the Freedom of a Christian* (in Latin: *De Libertate Christiana*; in German: *Von der Freiheit eines Christenmenschen*), composed in November 1520, Martin Luther developed a fundamental theory regarding the relationship between the individual and God which he predicated on the notion of freedom, as derived from a long tradition of scholastic debates about the relationship between the will and freedom (see above). This treatise was the third one he had written that year, the first, *Address to the Christian Nobility of the German Nation*, having appeared in August 1520, the second, *Prelude on the Babylonian Captivity of the Church* (October 1520), and all three together outlined the essential concepts upon which Luther then could build, together with his many fellow reformers, his new church.[348]

Luther composed this treatise in response to the papal bull, "Exsurge Domine," issued on June 15, 1520, in which the pope threatened Luther with the excommunication if he did not submit under the rule of the traditional church. Luther, addressing Pope Leo X in German, offered a detailed and theologically sophisticated response, in which he discussed, above all, the exclusive relationship between the faithful and God, and this in the framework of individual freedom in religious terms. This version was obviously intended for his German audience, while the Latin version, probably written somewhat later and expounding the basic concepts more extensively, aimed both at the pope himself and the learned, intellectual elite.

Although Luther addresses the pope with considerable respect and even humbleness, he feels no hesitation to identify the Holy See as what many of his contemporaries also viewed it: "the Church of Rome, formerly the most

---

[348] For a recent critical introduction, see Eberhard H. Pältz, "Von der Freyheyt eynisz Christen Menschen," *Kindlers Literatur Lexikon*, ed. Heinz Ludwig Arnold. 3rd, completely new ed. Vol. 10 (Stuttgart and Weimar: Metzler, 2009), 386–87. There are many editions, translations, and studies of this text; for the original German text with copies of the original prints, see https://www.freiheit2017.net/die-edition/; here I draw, for convenience's sake, from the online English translationhttps://sourcebooks.fordham.edu/mod/luther-freedomchristian.asp; see also the translation of the longer Latin version, online at: https://www.checkluther.com/wp-content/uploads/1520-Concerning-Christian-Liberty.pdf (both last accessed on Jan. 15, 2021).

holy of all churches, has become the most lawless den of thieves, the most shameless of all brothels, the very kingdom of sin, death, and hell; so that not even Antichrist, if he were to come, could devise any addition to its wickedness" (97). Only after a lengthy elaboration of the complex conditions among the flatterers and sycophants at the papal court and elsewhere, and after Luther himself has given the most praise possible to Leo, does he turn to his actual topic, the freedom of the individual Christian.

Freedom, however, quickly proves to be only a springboard for Luther's actual concern, faith and how to reflect upon it, if it is even truly present in the first place. In his endeavor to overcome a contradiction in St. Paul's letters, Luther differentiates between the material and the spiritual dimension in human beings. Whether he intended to evoke Boethius here or not, his identification as the material being as contingent carries great weight: "absolutely none among outward things, under whatever name they may be reckoned, has any weight in producing a state of justification and Christian liberty, nor, on the other hand an unjustified state and one of slavery. This can be shown by an easy course of argument" (105). The physical dimension does not grant freedom, whereas the spiritual dimension in the human being certainly does.

Simultaneously, even the most intense efforts in pursuing a whole life would not be any guarantee for the liberation of the individual from the material existence and dependency. Dismissing even meditations, prayer, a holy lifestyle, or all kinds of religious rituals, Luther then turns to the one and only source of true inspiration, Holy Scriptures: "One thing, and one alone, is necessary for life, justification, and Christian liberty; and that is the most holy word of God, the Gospel of Christ" (106), Luther's critical idea which is famously known as "scriptura sola," accompanied, of course, by "fides sola." In a way, he argued for a complete form of freedom, in material terms, pertaining to the individual in the physical context, whereas the spirit would have to follow the word of God, without any freedom, though this would certainly be most welcome to all faithful: "But, having the word, it is rich and want for nothing; since that is the word of life, of truth, of light, of peace, of justification, of salvation, of joy, of liberty, of wisdom, of virtue, of grace, of glory, and of every good thing" (106).

Luther seems to be aware of the highly problematic nature of his own teaching because he himself had launched a whole war of words with his Bible translation and interpretations, to which countless other intellectuals and theologians had responded. He tries to avoid the metaphorical bullet by highlighting rather evasively: "namely, the Gospel of God, concerning His Son, incarnate, suffering, risen, and glorified through the Spirit, the sanctifier" (106), lacking still his own authoritative translation, the September Testament from 1522. Nevertheless, he sets the tone and argues already in the affirmative that there could be only one true word which would provide the faithful with the inner freedom, the direct path to God. For him, hence, the struggle to find Christ in one's faith constitutes freedom, irrespective of what even Scripture would say, certainly almost a kind of mystical connection as the foundation of the soul's freedom: "faith alone without works justifies, sets free, and saves" (107).

Faith, and faith alone, thus constitutes for Luther the pathway to spiritual freedom, the only value of relevance for him, and this in explicit contrast to the approaches advocated by the representatives of the old Church for the salvation of the human soul. Here we grasp one of the central battle-cries of the Protestant Reformation, though this desire for freedom did not aim for political or pragmatic ends. Freedom here was understood as a spiritual liberation, which was to become a profound argument throughout the sixteenth century.[349] Of course, Luther stayed entirely clear of the political discourse on freedom and aimed exclusively at the freedom which the faithful could achieve in his/her relationship with God.

Even though most people would not be strong or competent enough to fulfill the divine laws, God would help each individual to achieve the goals if there is a firm belief in God. Abandoning the own self, or giving up one's own freedom, would thus pave the way for gaining a new form of freedom in which the soul would be supported and saved by God: "the promises of God give that which the precepts exact, and, fulfil what the law commands; so that all is of God alone, both the precepts and their fulfilment. He alone commands. He alone also fulfils" (109). Luther's concept of freedom thus deeply undermined the notion of the good Christian as the pope and his followers subscribed to, predicated on religious laws and the power of deeds (ceremonies, rituals, donations, confession, penance, etc.): "It is clear then that to a Christian man his faith suffices for everything, and that he has no need of works for justification. But if he has no

---

[349] Anja Lobenstein-Reichmann, *Freiheit bei Martin Luther: lexikographische Textanalyse als Methode historischer Semantik*. Studia linguistica Germanica, 46 (Berlin and New York: Walter de Gruyter, 1998). See now the contributions to *Luther und Erasmus über Freiheit: Rezeption und Relevanz eines gelehrten Streits*, ed. Jörg Noller and Georg Sans. Geist und Geisteswissenschaft, 4 (Freiburg i. Br.: Verlag Karl Alber, 2020). For a further discussion of freedom in Luther's thinking, especially as expressed in his treatise "De servo arbitrio," see Andrea Vestrucci, *Theology as Freedom: On Martin Luther's "De servo arbitrio"*. Dogmatik in der Moderne, 24 (Tübingen: Mohr Siebeck, 2019); see also Hartmut Schmidt, *Libertas- und Freiheitskollokationen in Luthers Traktaten "Von der Freiheit eines Christenmenschen" und "De libertate christiana"*, ed. Rudolf Bentzinger and Norbert Richard Wolf. Würzburger Beiträge zur deutschen Philologie, 11 (Mannheim: Leibniz-Institut für Deutsche Sprache (IDS), Bibliothek, 2018). Robert Kolb, *Luther's Treatise on Christian Freedom and Its Legacy*. Mapping the Tradition (Lanham, MD, Boulder, CO, New York, and London: Lexington Books / Fortress Academic, 2020).

need of works, neither has he need of the law; and, if he has no need of the law, he is certainly free from the law" (110). The key term proves to be "Christian liberty" (110), but Luther obviously did not mean this in worldly, material terms, but in spiritual terms, in opposition to the rules and regulations by the Catholic Church. To quote the crucial passage in the German: "Das ist die christliche Freiheit, der eine Glaube, der nicht macht, dass wir müßiggehen oder übeltun, sondern dass wir keines Werkes bedürfen, um Güte und Seligkeit zu erlangen" (B1r; "This is that Christian liberty, our faith, the effect of which is, not that we should be careless or lead a bad life, but that no one should need the law or works for justification and salvation").

Luther aimed for a spiritual freedom which the individual could achieve solely through faith: "Thus the believing soul, by the pledge of its faith in Christ, becomes free from all sin, fearless of death, safe from hell, and endowed with the eternal righteousness, life, and salvation of its husband Christ" (112). All that matters to gain this inner freedom would be the "faith of heart" (113), a mighty blow to the entire structure and ideology of the Catholic Church and the power and authority of the Holy See. Ironically, of course, the more Luther urges his readers to turn away from the outside dimension (works and words) and to subscribe entirely to the inner spirit (faith), the more he also advocated an external freedom insofar as the individual was thereby practically freed from the bounds imposed on him/her by the religious rules.

Luther was not caught in the illusion that his teachings would pertain to the political and material conditions of his day and age. He did not question the supreme power of kings, princes, and other authority figures, and did not ignore the fact that all people are subject to their own material existence, hence bound to die, but he insisted on the inner freedom which only the faithful would be able to achieve (115), a freedom which he regarded as the equivalent to the soul's salvation (115). The more an individual would try to rely on external efforts to achieve that salvation, the less freedom s/he would enjoy: "He himself is in servitude to all things, and all things turn out for evil to him, because he uses all things in an impious way for his own advantage. and not for the glory of God" (116). By contrast, "a Christian man is free from all things; so that he needs no works in order to be justified and saved, but receives these gifts in abundance from faith alone (116).

As we know only too well, which, however, here deserves to be repeated again, Luther's criticism aimed at the Church as an institution, at the ecclesiastics as authority figures who had imposed endless laws, rules, and regulations on the ordinary Christians and had thus robbed them of their inner freedom:

> Through this perversion of things it has happened that the knowledge of Christian grace, of faith, of liberty, and altogether of Christ, has utterly perished, and has been succeeded by an intolerable bondage to human works and laws; and, according to the Lamentations of Jeremiah, we have become the slaves of the vilest men on earth, who abuse our misery to all the disgraceful and ignominious purposes of their own will. (117)

Moreover, Luther also insisted that the new, deep, sincere, and complete faith would also provide freedom from death because the soul would no longer be beholden by that force and would be able to count on Christ's love: "For death is swallowed up in victory; not only the victory of Christ, but ours also; since by faith it becomes ours, and in it we too conquer" (118). Laying the foundation for the Protestant approach, he insists that the true Christian would not need laws or works, not even words, but only faith (119). Only the word of God would have to be trusted, but no laws or deeds, and there only would the individual faithful be able to find his/her inner freedom.

Luther did not reject good works, good words, good intentions, but he did not identify them as the solution for the individual to free him/herself from the constraints of this world. Faith alone would matter, and in that he found complete freedom. In conclusion, as he pointed out:

> Thus from faith flow forth love and joy in the Lord, and from love a cheerful, willing, free spirit, disposed to serve our neighbor voluntarily, without taking any account of gratitude or ingratitude, praise or blame, gain or loss. Its object is not to lay men under obligations, nor does it distinguish between friends and enemies, or look to gratitude or ingratitude, but most freely and willingly spends itself and its goods, whether it loses them through ingratitude, or gains good will. (127)

To be sure, however, Luther also warned explicitly those who consequently would disregard laws and customs, and this to the disadvantage and harm of society at large. The spiritual freedom would not justify lawlessness, violence, contempt of traditions and customs, or anti-social behavior (132–33). As he then concludes,

> It is not from works that we are set free by the faith of Christ, but from the belief in works, that is, from foolishly presuming to seek justification through works. Faith redeems our consciences, makes them upright and preserves them, since by it we recognise the truth that justification does not depend on our works, although good works neither can nor ought to be wanting to it. (133)

2 Bartolomé de las Casas

Early Modern Discourse on Freedom and Slavery in the American Context

For Luther, the entire debate regarding freedom, especially freedom of the will, hinged on theological questions and could thus be argued without many hindrances in a theoretical framework. Simultaneously, however, the issues raised here became a deadly consequence of probably millions of American natives who were terribly abused and killed by the Spanish and Portuguese conquistadors, apart from some other barbarous colonizers who disregarded even the most fundamental human rights and allowed their murderous instincts to come forward without any limitations. One of the most important spokespersons for the suffering native population was, of course, Bartolomé de las Casas (1484–1566), and he had quickly many urgent reasons to address the question of freedom versus slavery once he had witnessed the endless suffering of thousands and more innocent people who became victims of ruthless, greedy, brutal, and completely callous colonizers who cared only about gold and other treasures.

After he had arrived in Hispaniola as a layman, and then had joined the Dominicans, Bartolomé was appointed as the first resident Bishop of Chiapas, and the first officially appointed "Protector of the Indians." In his prolific writings, most famous among them his *Short Account of the Destruction of the Indies and Historia de Las Indias*, he chronicled the virtual genocide of the West Indies, Central and South America and tried hard to raise his voice against this crime against humanity so that he could appeal to the Spanish crown to intervene and save the indigenous people, thus saving them for the Christian Church after their conversion.

Bartolomé is too famous to be introduced here again in biographical details. All we need here is to examine his comments about the individual and fundamental rights which he claimed for people all over the world, including the native population of the Americas, as far as we can stitch them together from his many comments and observations about the actual conditions on the ground. Contemporary and modern critics have of course rightly pointed out numerous contradictions and inaccurate statements in his works, but he is universally acclaimed today as one of the first truly vocal, highly influential, though at the end also inefficient defender of freedom for all people here on earth, irrespective of their skin color, religious, language, or race.[350]

---

[350] See, for instance, the collection of articles by Mauricio Beuchot, *Los fundamentos de los derechos humanos en Bartolomé de las Casas*. Biblioteca A, 3 (Barcelona: Antropos, 1994); Josef Bordat, *Gerechtigkeit und Wohlwollen: das Völkerrechtskonzept des Bartolomé de Las Casas* (Aachen: Shaker, 2006); Daniel Castro, *Another Face of Empire: Bartolomé de Las*

Altogether, his ideas deeply influenced his posterity, although he could not prevent the continuation of the genocide in the New World, so it is quite fitting that we conclude here with an analysis of some of his arguments.[351]

When he published his book, *Brevísima relación de la destrucción de las Indias* (*The Devastation of the Indies: A Brief Account* in Seville in 1552 (originally written in 1542), Bartolomé de las Casas caused a huge stir in Spain and in many parts of the New World, exposing one of the greatest crimes in the history of humankind, almost comparable to the Holocaust. The book created a huge scandal and a public outcry, both against the colonizers and their misdeeds, and against the author himself for having exposed that group and endangering their livelihood. The right clashed with the left, as has always been the case.

His treatise was quickly translated into many European languages (into Portuguese, 1552; into French, 1579; into English, 1583; into Dutch, 1596; into German, 1597; into Latin, 1598; into Italian, 1626; each time the earliest printed version, not counting subsequent ones) and can be identified as one of the major factors for the emergence of the 'Black Legend' directed against Spain and its alleged claim on virtually all of South and Central America, with the exception of Brazil (Portuguese). In particular, the author attacked the local authorities in the New World who either supported or initiated the cruelties and murderous attacks against the indigenous population.

Once he had a chance to address the issue directly to King Charles I of Spain (Emperor Charles V of the Holy Roman Empire), his opinions finally took hold,

---

Casas, Indigenous Rights, and Ecclesiastical Imperialism. Latin America Otherwise: Language, Empires, Nations (Durham, NC: Duke University Press, 2007); Patrick Huser, *Vernunft und Herrschaft: die kanonischen Rechtsquellen als Grundlage natur- und völkerrechtlicher Argumentation im zweiten Prinzip des Traktates Principia quaedam des Bartolomé de Las Casas*. Religionsrecht im Dialog, 11 (Münster: LIT, 2011); Luis Mora Rodríguez, *Bartolomé de Las Casas: conquête, domination, souveraineté*. Fondements de la politique. Série Essais (Paris: Presses Universitaires de France, 2012).

351 Daniel R. Brunstetter, *Tensions of Modernity: las Casas and His Legacy in the French Enlightenment*. Routledge Innovations in Political Theory, 44 (London and New York: Routledge, 2014); Jesús Antona Bustos, *Los derechos humanos de los pueblos indígenas: el Az Mapu y el caso Mapuche*. Colección Cátedra Fray Bartolomé de las Casas (Temuco, Chile: Ediciones Universidad Católica de Temuco, 2014). There is a vast body of current legal, anthropological, ethic, religious, political, and philosophical literature on the rights of the indigenous people, which I cannot pursue here further. For the historical perspective, as I am pursuing here, see *Bartolomé de las Casas and the Defense of Amerindian Rights: A Brief History with Documents*, ed. edited by Lawrence A. Clayton and David M. Lantigua (Tuscaloosa, AL: The University of Alabama Press, 2020); David M. Lantigua, *Infidels and Empires in a New World Order: Early Modern Spanish Contributions to International Legal Thought*. Law and Christianity (Cambridge and New York: Cambridge University Press, 2020).

and there were numerous other co-patriots who subscribed to the same idea, trying to defend and protect the indigenous people. Critics such as Antonio de Montesinos and Juan Quevedo, Bishop of Durien, came to his support or had argued already along the same line, and finally, Charles approved that henceforth the Indians were supposed to be governed without the use of arms – a faint appeal from very distant Spain with very little impact on the local conditions, where the massive killing continued unabatedly for a long time.[352] As to be expected, Bartolomé also encountered formidable opponents, especially Juan Ginés de Sepulveda, who argued against him publicly in the famous debate of 1550 in Valladolid (though not face to face; only individually addressing the court). Even though the former gained his case, the court declined to make its finding public out of fear of reprisals, so the slaughter of the native population continued. Bartolomé resigned as bishop of Chiapas, joined the Dominican monastery San Gregorio in Valladolid, where he kept writing volumes of treatises pursuing his arguments further, making ever more enemies, but also gaining more support. He died as a truly famous man in Madrid on July 18, 1566, rightfully acclaimed as one of the greatest defenders of human rights, as much as he was certainly also hated by all those whose greed, viciousness, murderous instincts, and utter lack of humanity he had exposed so bitterly.

Irrespective of whether Bartolomé accurately described the situation on the ground, i.e., the terrible suffering of the indigenous population, or whether he dramatized it for propagandistic purposes, the basic situation would not have been much different. What concerns us here pertains only to his reflections on the fundamental human rights, irrespective of the individual's religious orientation. All modern discussions pertaining to the actual numbers of Indians who were killed by the Spaniards almost amount to the same discussion about how many Jews died in the Holocaust. Numbers do not have any significant impact on the ideas and values of freedom and justice.[353] Genocide is genocide, ir-

---

[352] Bartolomé de las Casas, *The Devastation of the Indies: A Brief Account*, trans. from the Spanish by Herma Briffault. Intro. by Bill M. Donovan (1974; Baltimore, MD, and London: The Johns Hopkins University Press, 1992). The Introduction (1–25) offers a solid commentary; but see also, particularly helpful for its extensive bibliography, among many other good websites, https://en.wikipedia.org/wiki/Bartolom%C3%A9_de_las_Casas#A_Short_Account_of_the_Destruction_of_the_Indies (last accessed on Jan. 15, 2021).

[353] Donovan, "Introduction" (see note 352); see Claude Rawson, *God, Gulliver and Genocide: Barbarism and the European Imagination, 1492–1945* (Oxford: Oxford University Press, 2001), who raises the problematic notion that all those comments about mass killing from biblical times until today have resorted to figurative speech. However, no realization of the workings of rhetorical or ideological strategies liberates us from questioning carefully the actual suffering of people. See also Roger M. Carpenter, *"Times are altered with Us": American Indians from First*

respective of how many people actually die, when the majority makes the attempt to eliminate the 'entire' population by whatever means (see the Ottoman mass murder of Armenians in 1915, a crime against humanity the Turkish government today wants to deny to wash its bloody hands).[354]

For Bartolomé, there was no doubt that the native population had every right to claim their own freedom, and for that reason he strongly opposed the tyrannical rule of the Spaniards in the New World, arguing in another account:

> They do not lose that freedom by accepting and holding Your Majesty as their supreme ruler. Rather, if they have some defects in their governance, the rule of Your Majesty would clear up, would repair those defects, and they would thus enjoy a greater liberty... . At Burgos, in a solumn consultation of certain learned men, theologians and jurists who belonged to the Council of the Catholic King, it was determined and decreed that the Indians were free peoples and should so be treated... . Take it as true, then, that the peoples and places of the New World are free. They are obligated to no one in any way for anything before they are discovered, during their discovery, today after their discovery – save only to Your Majesty, a service, an obedience, a specific kind, the kind free peoples and places owe their supreme king and Lord.[355]

Throughout his major treatise, *Brevísima relación de la destrucción de las Indias*, Bartolomé depicts the native population almost like innocent children who are "the most guileless, the most devoid of wickedness and duplicity, the most obedient and faithful to their native masters and to the Spanish Christians whom they serve" (28). The author uses a long list of descriptors to project them as pure, innocent, humble, peaceful, and loving, whereas the colonialists appear as "ravening wild beasts, wolves, tigers, or lions that had been starved for many days" (29). The author explicitly labels the indigenous as persons pos-

---

Contact to the New Republic (Chichester: Wiley Blackwell, 2015). This issue certainly opens a can of worms which cannot be the topic of our investigation. Instead, this is of central concern for historians and anthropologists.

354 Even Turkish scholars, at a high political risk at present times (2020), now acknowledge this as a historical fact; see Taner Akçam, *The Young Turks' Crime Against Humanity: The Armenian Genocide and Ethnic Cleansing in the Ottoman Empire*. Human Rights and Crimes against Humanity (Princeton, NJ: University of Princeton Press, 2012); cf. also Harry D. Harootunian, *The Unspoken as Heritage: The Armenian Genocide and Its Unaccounted Lives* (Durham, NC, and London: Duke University Press, 2019). There are, of course, also detractors, and the suffering of the Armenians has become, alas, a tool in modern-day Turkish politics, an issue that I cannot pursue here further. But see, for global perspectives, Norman M. Naimark, *Genocide: A World History* (New York and Oxford: Oxford University Press, 2017).

355 This is taken from Bartolomé's *Conclusiones sumarias sobre el remedio de los Indias*, here quoted from *Indian Freedom: The Cause of Bartolomé de las Casas, 1484–1566. A Reader*, trans. and notes by Francis Patrick Sullivan, S.J. (Kansas City, KS: Sheed & Ward, 1995), 241.

sessed with intelligence and reason, though they are, as he sees it, docile and welcoming. They quickly proved to be good Christians and received the missionaries' teachings well.

As much as Bartolomé describes the natives as completely open to their teachings, as much were they completely victimized by the conquistadors who slaughtered an infinite number of them and depopulated whole islands and regions, both in the Caribbean and in Central and South America (30). The Spaniards falsely use the argument that they were forced to pursue a 'just war,' but in reality, as the author claims, they only intended to eliminate the entire population. After having killed the leaders and the young men, they enslave everyone else: "With these infernal methods of tyranny they debase and weaken countless numbers of those pitiful Indian nations" (31). Although those Spaniards are called Christians, Bartolomé can only describe them as being completely driven by the desire to acquire gold and to become rich as quickly as possible because they want to "rise to a high estate disproportionate to their merits" (31). In the name of Christianity, they behave in the most non-Christian manner, whereas their victims receive the author's greatest empathy, although he was mostly helpless to protect them in practical terms.

The question of whether any Spaniard could actually draw from the notion of 'just war' regularly emerges throughout the treatise, obviously because this was the favorite argument legitimizing the mass murder of the indigenous population. As the author argues, however, "Only after the Spaniards had used violence against them, killing, robbing, torturing, did the Indians ever rise up against them" (32).[356] The conquistadors resorted to massacres, allegedly to eradicate all opposition, but in reality, as Bartolomé insists unequivocally, because they were cruel to the utmost and enemies of humanity (35). The author constantly presents pictures of orgies of horrifying violence, and insists that he was an eyewitness and could confirm all those cases. What he achieved in that process was that the reader was supposed to be convinced that those

---

[356] Scott L. Taylor, "The Conquest of Sodom: Symbiosis of Calumny and Canon in the *Jus Belli* from Ireland to the Indies," *War and Peace: Critical Issues in European Societies and Literature 800–1800* ed. Albrecht Classen and Nadia Margolis. Fundamentals of Medieval and Early Modern Culture, 8 (Berlin and New York: Walter de Gruyter, 2011), 81–97. He focuses more on the shift in the argument for the 'just war' against the indigenous population, first claiming that the sin of sodomy had to be eradicated, then, the threat of cannibalism. Taylor does not, however, engage with Bartolomé de las Casas. For art-historical perspectives on the topic of cannibalism in the New World, see Stephanie Leitch, *Mapping Ethnography in Early Modern Germany: New Worlds in Print Culture*. History of Text Technologies (New York: Palgrave Macmillan, 2010), 47–76.

were people like everyone else who had to suffer ghastly and most painful deaths for no apparent reason, but sadism and utter brutality.

Bartolomé never hesitates to give the rulers of the native population accolades for their virtues and manners, whether he calls King Guarionex "virtuous," "pacific," or "devotedly obedient to the Kings of Castile" (36). Yet, despite all the efforts by the Indian rulers and nobles to engage peacefully with the conquistadors, the latter consistently resorted to extreme violence and killed everyone they could put their hands on. Those who survived, were enslaved and thus certainly killed in the mines or elsewhere by being overworked and abused (e. g., 40). The author defends them all with the full force of his statements and thus identified them as human beings who deserved to be treated with fairness, kindness, and peace:

> I now want only to add that, in the matter of these unprovoked and destructive wars, and God is my witness, all these acts of wickedness I have described, as well as those I have omitted, were perpetrated against the Indians without cause, without any more cause than could give a community of good monks living together in a monastery. (40)

Bartolomé charges the Spaniards for having committed atrocities, having slaughtered the innocent, having oppressed and enslaved the conquered people, who were all completely "innocent" (42), and who thus were robbed even of their most basic human rights. Compared to any other sources studied so far, the situation in the New World appears to have been the worst for the innocent victims, since they were non-aggressive, mostly rather peaceful, and submissive, and yet were treated in the most inhumane manner possible, being butchered, burned, strangled, cut to pieces, worked to death, or killed in any other way. The author almost does not find sufficient words for all the torture committed by the Spaniards, and voices deep lament for "those unfortunate and innocent people" (43).

Wherever we look, Bartolomé has only the same story to tell, always contrasting the suffering and innocent natives with the brutal, tyrannical, cruel, and completely vicious Spaniards. In that process, he projected the victims as good people who were robbed of their freedom and their lives, they were "harmless people" (91) and deprived of all rights. Never do any of the authors who had been taken as slaves during the late Middle Ages and beyond have anything as cruel and brutal to report. Even if Bartolomé heavily exaggerated, even if only a tenth of his accounts were true, they constitute a new level of brutality and lack of humanity. While freedom on an individual and social level increasingly gained traction in late medieval political discourse, while the public debates on imprisonment and even enslavement gained in intensity, nothing of that sort could stand up to the reports by Bartolomé according to whom the conquistadors had turned into the most vile and heartless creatures one could imagine.

Certainly, in Protestant Germany, the focus of the public discourse also rested on the questions regarding the freedom of the will and the freedom of the soul, but those were really only academic issues and did not pertain to the actual suffering on the ground, as the native population in the New World had to experience. When they were enslaved, they could count this as their good fortune because they were not slowly burnt to death. However, as slaves, they were, as Bartolomé emphasizes, then abused so badly that most also died as a consequence of the hard labor and general mistreatment.

One exchange between the author and a captain-general, who had overseen one of the many raids and mass killing, deserves to be highlighted since it sheds profound light on the psychological nature of the conquistadors. Bartolomé relates that "he told me that, in truth, he had all his life lacked a mother and father and had never been treated kindly except by the Indians on the island of Trinidad" (94). Nevertheless, that captain-general himself then ordered mass killing in the most brutal fashion, betraying all of his previous promises to the Indians. Deception, treason, and betrayal were the common strategies to convey a false sense of friendliness and peace, but the outcome always was that the Spaniards either murdered the chieftains and their families or took them as captives and sold them into slavery (94–95).

The keyword which resonates throughout the entire treatise is "tyranny" or "tyrant" (99), which indicates that for Bartolomé the Spaniards (and others; in this case, Germans, 101–08) abused all the basic freedoms, betrayed their hosts, trampled on their rights, and either murdered them or sold them into slavery. Seen from the other perspective, the natives were deprived of their freedom and subjected to the worst form of imprisonment, if not burned to death or slashed to pieces.

In his defense of the indigenous population in the West Indies, Bartolomé thus developed, at least indirectly, a clear concept of basic human rights for every individual here on earth, arguing vehemently that the conquistadors broke the fundamental rules of human behavior and deserved to be called nothing but tyrants, murderers, beasts of the worst kind. Whereas Martin Luther talked about the freedom of the will to turn to God, Bartolomé argued in very practical terms for the freedom of the native population that did not deserve to be massacred and eliminated from their lands. Turning to Florida, for instance, he describes the local people as follows: "On these lands lived a population that was wise, well disposed, politically well organized" (109). By contrast, the Spaniards "perpetrated massacres with the aim of instilling and spreading terror. They afflicted, they killed the people, they took captives and compelled them to carry intolerable loads, like beasts of burden" (109).

Of course, there is always the possibility that Bartolomé exaggerated to the extreme and fell into the trap of highly sensational accounts based on horror and disgust about the unimaginable cruelty of the conquistadors. As little as this seems to be the case, however, what matters here is that he regularly projected the natives as victims, as noble and kind people, and as individuals whose lives and freedoms were taken from them in the name of a fake religious justification. Reporting about an event in the Rio de la Plata region (today Argentina and Uruguay), he relates how the miserable natives screamed out in protest: "'We came in peace to serve you, and you kill us! Our blood splattered on these walls will remain as witness to our unjust death and to your cruelty!'" (112).

Whether this would have been true or not, the author strongly makes a claim that those natives were originally free people and deserved to live their way of life without the abuse and killing they suffered at the hands of the Spaniards. Keeping in mind that Bartolomé composed this treatise with the explicit purpose to win his court case and to establish finally rules for their protection, we can understand better why the account is filled with so much brutality and gory details, through which he intended to appeal to the king's and the court's empathy and pity. In that process, however, the author succeeded in addressing all three crucial topics in one: freedom, imprisonment, and slavery.

The conquistadors did not, as he claimed throughout the treatise, respect the freedom of the natives, they freely imprisoned and enslaved them, and murdered countless others in the most brutal fashion possible. The claim of being a 'Christian' was extremely abused for personal purposes, mostly greed, sheer violence, and brutality, utter disrespect of people's individual rights, and their virtues and honors. According to Bartolomé, there was no more humanity left in those tyrants and mass murderers who claimed to defend God and the Spanish crown. Read from the opposite perspective, we face here, disregarding the heavy amount of exaggerations and gore for his argument's sake, specific arguments insisting on individual freedom, dignity, and respect also for the indigenous. The more they allegedly had suffered, the more Bartolomé insisted that they deserved to be treated with respect and as free people. The very opposite was the case, of course. In short, Bartolomé used this famous treatise to demand freedom for the natives, protection against being enslaved, and security against being murdered, either burned alive or bitten to death by trained dogs (127–29). In this respect, he was so far ahead of his contemporaries, and in his sharp criticism of people's greed, brutality, and cruelty that he actually continues to appeal to us today in our efforts to fight for the downtrodden, abused, neglected, and impoverished, and this in the time of post-capitalism.[357]

3 Marguerite de Navarre: Life as a Prison. Allegorical Reflections

Finally, one of the truly intriguing prison allegories deserves to be mentioned here once again, whereas before I touched upon it only in passing, Marguerite de Navarre's *Les Prisons* (1549; unpublished at that time). Scholars focused on the topic of the medieval or early modern prison have not yet discussed it in any significant way, but her powerful voice deserves to be listened to in our context. For her, the ultimate freedom rested, of course, in Christ and in pure spirituality:

> O Nothing, in the All you are set free,
> You dwell in peace, secure from every ill;
> Gone are your fears of prison walls and bars,
> Of outward beauty's subtle treachery;
> Possessions, honours, pleasures, all about
> You see, but such protection wraps you round
> That they can have no power over you
> Because no fragment of your flesh remains;
> That Spirit, source of your new liberty,
> Has loosed all fleshly ties and set you free. (Book 3, 3129–38)[358]

---

357 Amartya Sen, *On Ethics and Economics*. The Royer Lectures (Oxford and New York: Basil Blackwell, 1987); Martha C. Nussbaum and Amartya Sen, *The Quality of Life*. WIDER Studies in Development Economics (Oxford: Clarendon Press; New York: Oxford University Press, 1993); Amartya Sen, *Development as Freedom* (see note 1); id., *The Idea of Justice* (Cambridge, MA: Belknap Press of Harvard University Press, 2009); id., *Peace and Democratic Society*. Open Reports Series, 1 (Cambridge: Open Book Publishers, 2011). I emphasize the work by Sen so prominently, in contrast to that by John Rawls or John Harsany, not only because his views apply so well to our discussion of Bartolomé de las Casas, but also because he has received much public recognition, first in 1998 with the Nobel Memorial Prize in Economic Sciences, and now, in 2020, with the Friedenspreis des Deutschen Buchhandels, apart from numerous honorary degrees. In response, some of his studies appeared also in German translation, *Rationale Dummköpfe: Eine Kritik der Verhaltensgrundlagen der Ökonomischen Theorie*, trans. Valerie Gföhler. Was bedeutet das alles (Stuttgart: Philipp Reclam, jun., 2020); and *Elemente einer Theorie der Menschenrechte*, trans. Ute Kruse-Ebeling. Was bedeutet das alles (Stuttgart: Philipp Reclam, jun., 2020).
358 *The Prisons of Marguerite de Navarre* (see note 159), 133.

Of course, Marguerite primarily aimed at the discussion of love as the decisive force liberating the individual from the contingency of fortune, so she probably reflects in this case on her responses to Boethius's famous teachings in his *Consolatio philosophiae* (ca. 524; see above). Yet, for her, the true goal of human life was to gain freedom both in spiritual and material terms: "Alas! my Friend, what are those triple bonds, / The prison which contains all you think good? / The first is master of your heart's desires; / It is compounded of quicksilver, decked / With beauty in a myriad forms, the veil / That pity draws to hide its cruelty" (839–44). The Seven Deadly Sins, the human vices, emerge here as the bonds or fetters that keep people in their prison of material life. From a spiritual point of view, Marguerite severely challenged all laws, authorities, powers, and the legal courts and insisted on the ultimate freedom which only God can grant: "We in our ignorance, are filled with fear / Of popes and kings, our country's laws and courts, / Of torture and the gallows, prison, chains, / And often, through that fear, we hide the truth; / We must look up to where salvation lies / And then we shall not fear the punishment / That human judgement may impose on us" (1135–41).

Conclusions

There are a number of highly valuable insights that we can now draw and profit from. First, whenever we discuss the history of slavery, we must also consider the history of imprisonment and the discourse on freedom. Slaves and prisoners want to regain their freedom, whether that is a likely proposition or not. Anyone who enjoys freedom will do anything in his/her power to keep this freedom and to be safe from imprisonment, and this both in the pre-modern world and today, of course. Next, we have observed that slavery was not a phenomenon typical and exclusive of antiquity. Hannah Barker is completely correct in warning us about the amelioration theory advocated by Christian authors and about the Marxist narrative according to which only ancient societies embraced the idea of slavery, whereas medieval feudalism operated on the basis of a different economic model.

Slavery means business, and people throughout time have never felt any hesitations to make money by buying and selling human beings, and this both in Europe and in other continents. Owning slaves has always meant that those could be used to do labor without pay or could provide sexual pleasures. Medieval and early modern European travelers to the East or Northern Africa commonly reported with horror about local slave markets, but they completely ignored the slaves being sold in Venice or Genoa and kept in other parts of European societies.[359] This also means that modern historians should not identify the import of slaves to the New World – which was even advocated initially by Bartolomé de las Casas something which he later deeply regretted – as a completely new historical development. What happened was simply that the flow of slaves shifted from the Mediterranean to the Atlantic, especially because new agricultural markets opened in the Americas where slaves were highly needed. We

---

359 Barker, *That Most Precious Merchandise* (see note 119), 209–12; see also Reuven Amital, "Diplomacy and the Slave Trade in the Eastern Mediterranean: A Re-Examination of the Mamluk-Byzantine-Genoese Triangle in the Late Thirteenth Century in Light of the Existing Early Correspondence," *Oriente Moderno* 88 (2008): 349–68; Alice Rio, *Slavery after Rome, 500–1100*. Oxford Studies in Medieval European History (Oxford: Oxford University Press, 2017). See also the contributions to *The Routledge History of Slavery*, ed. Gad Heuman and Travor Burnard. The Routledge Histories (London and New York: Routledge, 2011). For slavery in the early modern period, see now Filip Batselé, *Liberty, Slavery and the Law in Early Modern Western Europe: Omnes Homines aut Liberi Sunt aut Servi*. Studies in the History of Law and Justice (Cham: Springer International Publishing, 2020); Michael Zeuske, *Handbuch Geschichte der Sklaverei: Eine Globalgeschichte von den Anfängen bis zur Gegenwart*. 2nd ed. (2013; Berlin, München, and Boston: De Gruyter – De Gruyter Oldenbourg, 2019).

could certainly also talk about a quantitative leap in the slave business, probably a significant bad mark particularly of the early modern age.

Third, both poets and chroniclers, preachers and moralists, and other writers were not loath at all to reflect on the traumatic experience of imprisonment, either having suffered through it themselves or reflecting on it through their literary fictions. This forces us to acknowledge that the institution of the prison was much more common also in the pre-modern world than we might have assumed before, especially because it often did not only serve to hold actual criminals, tried and condemned in a legal court, but also many individuals who were the unfortunate victims of war, or of piracy, and had to wait for months, years, and even decades until they were finally released. We find evidence for this tragic circumstance both in historical sources and in literary narratives and poems.

Granted, particularly the authors of the Icelandic Saga literature tended to report of many different strategies and methods to cope with crime by way of settling with material goods, or by the culprit being forced to go into exile for an extended period of time. On the Continent, however, or on the English isles, the prison was rather ubiquitous and a very effective institution for the authorities to exert their power over others, whether with legal justification or not. It would be nearly impossible to go into specifics or to carry out comparative studies contrasting Irish with Italian prisons, for instance, but it is almost self-evident that all societies, and so also those in the pre-modern world, certainly relied on prisons to lock away individuals who had egregiously transgressed the rules and laws and were hence regarded as a danger to the public.[360] However, we also would have to consider how much prisons increasingly served to enforce payments of debts, taxes, and fines, and were not simply the place where criminals were held.[361] I am afraid that this distinction holds true also for the modern-day prison where the prisoner's financial and political resources greatly influence how s/he is treated and where s/he is kept.

Finally, we have also identified a deep discourse on freedom in a variety of literary and non-literary sources from the pre-modern period. Some of the most outspoken defenders of individual freedom, virtually in the sense as we understand it today, were the authors of fables, such as Marie de France and Ulrich Bonerius. But the rebellious German poet from Southern Tyrol, Oswald von Wol-

---

360 John G. Bellamy, *Crime and Public Order in England in the Later Middle Ages*. Studies in Social History (London: Routledge and Kegan Paul; Toronto and Buffalo: University of Toronto Press, 1973); Joyce T. Cameron, *Prisons and Punishment in Scotland: From the Middle Ages to the Present* (Edinburgh: Cannongate, 1983).
361 J. Claustre, "Debt, Hatred and Force: Beginnings of Debt Prisons at the End of the Middle Ages," *Revue Historique* 10 (2007): 797–821.

kenstein, certainly also had a strong opinion in that regard, adamantly opposed to the rule by the territorial duke and the extensively strengthened institution of the princely court which threatened the freedom of the landed gentry, like Oswald. Of course, for this poet, other challengers to his freedom were both the peasants of his region, and the rising urban citizens who held the purse strings, so we could not really claim Oswald as a major spokesperson for individual freedom at large.

These four aspects do not always intersect with each other in our sources, but they have to be considered as essential aspects of the global discourse traced here. There are, as we can certainly conclude, intrinsic connections among them all, and their close examination, either together in comparison with each other or individually, depending on the conditions, intentions, or purposes of the relevant sources, makes it possible for us to gain a much deeper understanding of fundamental concerns of the pre-modern world.

Even though I have given considerable preference to literary sources here, it is obvious that the prison was a historical reality of a terrifying nature for many unfortunate individuals who had become victims of the authorities, either innocently or because they were guilty, indeed. Little wonder that we find hence many remarks on the experience in prisons and also on the high value of freedom, not to forget slavery, because all those aspects deeply impacted human lives, and could easily destroy the subjects.[362]

Not surprisingly, medieval society also knew of saints to whom people prayed and appealed when cruel rulers and tyrants took them prisoners despite their innocence. Jacobus de Voragine (1228/29–1298) thus included an account of St. Leonard who could be relied on in case of honorable people having been taken captives by a brutal and unjust prince, for instance, who wanted to receive a huge sum of ransom. For example: "Any prisoner who invoked his name saw his bonds loosened and went free with no one interfering. Such persons brought their chains and fetters to Leonard, and many stayed with him and

---

[362] *Réalités, images, écritures de la prison au Moyen Âge*, ed. Jean-Marie Fritz and Silvère Menegaldo together with Galice Pascault. Écritures (Dijon: Éditions universitaires de Dijon, 2012); Magdalena Prechsl, *Nürnberger Kriminalgeschichte: Henkerhaus, Lochgefängnis und Schuldturm*. Historische Spaziergänge, 16 (Nuremberg: Sandberg-Verlag, 2019). See also the contributions to *Crime and Punishment in the Middle Ages and Early Modern Age* (see note 10). See also the valuable primary source, *A Hangman's Diary: The Journal of Master Franz Schmidt, Public Executioner of Nuremberg, 1573–1617*, ed., with an introduction, by Albrecht Keller and translated by C. Calvert and A.W. Gruner, with an introductory essay by C. Calvert (1928; New York: Skyhorse Publishing, 2015); Gerhard Ammerer and Christoph Brandhuber, *Schwert und Galgen: Geschichte der Todesstrafe in Salzburg* (Salzburg: Verlag Anton Pustet, 2018).

served the Lord there."³⁶³ Or: "There was a man who, upon his return from a pilgrimage to Saint Leonard, was taken captive in Auvergne and locked in a cage. He pleaded with his captors, telling them that since he had done them no wrong, they ought to let him go for the love of Saint Leonard. They answered that unless he paid them a copious ransom he would not get out" (245). The commander rejected attempts by the poor pilgrim to return him to freedom, but then Leonard appeared in a dream to the commander urging him to do just that, who dismissed, however, the vision as a dream. The same happened the next night, again without success. Finally, in the third night, "Saint Leonard took the pilgrim and led him outside the fortress, and immediately the tower and half the castle collapsed and crushed many, leaving only the recalcitrant chief, whose legs were broken, to welter in his own confusion" (246). In other words, already at that time imprisonment was viewed through many different lenses; and those who were innocently subjected to it, naturally protested against their suffering vehemently, whereas society at large might have viewed it as justified, all depending on the circumstances. The parallels to our modern society are quite striking in that regard.

Significantly, as to be expected, the various legal systems with their institutionalized forms of punishment grew considerably throughout the Middle Ages, and this also triggered the emergence of the idea of freedom even within the framework of feudalism.³⁶⁴ Sadly, however, we have also to acknowledge, as indicated above numerous times, the existence of slavery throughout the Middle Ages,³⁶⁵ which constituted, however, a rather complex institution, not to be equated simply with the slaves as they existed in the early Americas. In short, the degree to which freedom and lack thereof was at play under the various social conditions mattered significantly in the pre-modern world.³⁶⁶

If we then take all these observations about pre-modern literature, history, social and economic conditions into considerations, probing the extent to which already then the notion of freedom and slavery was extensively at play, we can certainly grasp a profound sense of what mattered to the various authors,

---

363 Jacobus de Voragine, *The Golden Legend: Readings on the Saints*, trans. William Granger Ryan. Vol. II (Princeton, NJ: Princeton University Press, 1993), 244.
364 Eric Fougère, *La peine en littérature et la prison dans son histoire: solitude et servitude*. Espaces littéraires (Paris: Ed. L'Harmattan, 2001); Peter Schuster, *Verbrecher, Opfer, Heilige: eine Geschichte des Tötens 1200–1700* (see note 26); Sonja Kerth, "Gefängnis" (see note 28).
365 Janin Hunt, *Medieval Justice: Cases and Laws in France, England and Germany, 500–1500* (Jefferson, NC, and London: McFarland, 2004).
366 Geraldine Heng, *The Invention of Race in the European Middle Ages* (see note 23).

many of whom were certainly aware about the existential significance of freedom and the dire consequences of being taken prisoner or sold as a slave.

Undoubtedly, the discourse on these two diametrically opposed life conditions gained tremendously in relevance and importance since the eighteenth and nineteenth centuries, especially because of the ideological and economic fight, eventually also military struggle, over slavery (American Civil War, 1861–1865). Nevertheless, as our analysis has amply demonstrated, the issues of imprisonment and slavery were discussed intensively already in the pre-modern age, and hence the topic of freedom on an individual and communal level also mattered for numerous writers and poets.

Even though numerous scholars have correctly urged us to be careful in the use of the term 'slave,' or 'slavery,' considering the many different legal conditions of those who were unfree, we can certainly agree that medieval slaves were simply unfree and could not resist their masters' commands or orders, and could not move around freely because they were bound to their owners.[367] We might be well advised to examine closely the subtle, but maybe irrelevant difference between slavery and serfdom, which was also in the mind of some medieval writers such as Philippe de Beaumanoir, who discussed those categories in his law treatise *Coutumes de Beauvaisis* (end of the thirteenth century).[368] However, those subtleties might not be quite as fruitful for the study of the pre-modern world when many societies were still in the process of creating their own law codes and struggled to figure out the meaning of freedom, feudal bonds, serfdom, and slavery.[369] I would not want to muddle the distinction between indentured laborers and slaves, the former probably characteristic of immigration conditions in the United States and its trust territories at the end of the nineteenth and early twentieth centuries, when the immigrants had to live under a certain contract for some years before they became free. What matters here, by contrast, pertains primarily to the strong sense of loss of freedom, either through imprisonment or slavery, as we hear about it in countless historical and literary documents, some of which investigated in the present study.

---

367 Karras, *Slavery and Society in Medieval Scandinavia* (see note 215), 6–12.
368 Philippe de Beaumanoir, *Coutumes de Beauvaisis*. Texte critique publié avec une introduction, un glossaire et une table analytique par Amadée Salmon (Paris: A. Picard et fils, 1899–1900).
369 Marc Bloch, *Slavery and Serfdom in the Middle Ages: Selected Essays*. Publications of the Center for Medieval and Renaissance Studies, 8 (Berkeley, CA: University of California Press, 1975); M. L. Bush, *Serfdom and Slavery: Studies in Legal Bondage* (1996; London: Routledge, 2013). But see also the much older, yet still valuable study by John K. Ingram, *A History of Slavery and Serfdom* (London: A. and C. Black, 1895).

Freedom has always been a most precious good, even if many people in the west do not know any longer how to appreciate it fully. Opening up our perspective toward the complex discourse involving all three components as it was practiced strongly already in the pre-modern era encourages us to draw from those earlier conditions and to reflect upon those in our day and age, but then more informed and sensitized to the critical issues as explored in literary documents, philosophical treatises, law books, and chronicles. The more we can learn about imprisonment and freedom, for instance, in the Middle Ages, the more we can then appreciate and value what we are allowed to enjoy today. Nothing is written in stone: freedoms can be taken away, imprisonment can be imposed on anyone because of criminal charges, and slavery can lurk around the corner, and this also today. Personal freedom is the result of centuries of human struggle, and today often naively assumed and accepted without any thought of the long historical process that brought us to where we are now.

Also, the more we understand the discourse on those topics as practiced in the pre-modern era, the more we will be empowered to understand what our freedom really means and how precarious it is, even for those of us who live in the 'free' western world. This does not mean at all that these literary-historical and philosophical-legal reflections would suggest that we do not need prisons, any legal system to bring criminals to justice, or any laws to support and protect all members of society against violators and transgressors. On the contrary, of course, but the entire situation with prisons in past and present is highly complex and needs to be understood from many different perspectives.

The topic of slavery can only be described in negative terms, but we must also understand that it was not only a phenomenon that existed in antiquity or the early modern age (slavery in the New World) exclusively. Instead, the Middle Ages were well familiar with slavery, and the trade with slaves was a thriving business, especially in the many ports of the Mediterranean. Nevertheless, we also heard of slaves in Iceland, as the various Icelandic Sagas repeatedly confirm. A slave was not always exactly the same as all the other slaves, but complete lack of freedom was almost always the case. Slaves came from many different regions, east and west, south and north, and they were chattel and had to obey their master/s.

This book has dealt with a large number of relevant sources important for the discourse on freedom, imprisonment, and slavery. While it does not necessarily provide hard data such as statistics, and is not that ambitious to offer complete coverage in historical or geographical terms, it has unearthed the wide-ranging discourse on all three topics, which thus invites us to read many of the pre-modern texts through different lenses commonly ignored. The outcome promises us to illustrate the many different features underlying this universal discourse and connects the past much more closely with our modern times – the struggle for freedom continues certainly today as well, and we are heirs of this discourse and carry the proverbial torch on to the next generation.

As G. Siewert stated in his 1962 article, freedom is one of the fundamental aspects of human life, predicated on our will and our actions, and this in contrast to the determinism of nature. Freedom is the absence of external force and finds its expression, among other things, in spontaneity and the endless opportunity to reach a judgment on one's own. Here leaving aside theological and ethical reflections, Siewert rightly highlights that freedom is a "Selbstursächlichkeit" (primal cause) or "liber est causa sui" (freedom comes from one's self, or, the free is the cause of oneself). Without going further into the philosophical ruminations, which go as far back as to Socrates, Plato, and Aristotle, or Thomas Aquinas in the Middle Ages, and which have occupied philosophers ever since, we recognize, especially in light of the many documents examined above, how critically important the notion and experience of freedom has always been, especially when it is being lost through imprisonment and enslavement.[370]

Even within marriage, as Aquinas emphasizes at one point in his *Summa Theologiae*, both partners should treat each other equally, and especially the wife should not be kept as her husband's slave. This would explain, so Aquinas, why Eve was born from Adam's side, and not from his feet. If she had been born from his head, she would repress or even enslave her husband.[371] Instead, as this famous authority formulated, marriage should be a form of partnership between two equals – an observation which was later copied many times particularly when medieval and early modern female writers such as Christine de Pizan raised their voices to defend women's rights.

---

370 G. Siewert, "Freiheit," *Handbuch theologischer Grundbegriffe*, ed. Heinrich Fries. Vol. I (Munich: Kösel-Verlag, 1962), 392–98. The issue is here pursued further regarding the concept of freedom in biblical (G. Richter, 398–403) and theological terms (J. B. Metz, 403–14). See further Jamie Anne Spiering, "'Liber est causa sui': Thomas Aquinas and the Maxim 'The Free is the Cause of Itself'," *The Review of Metaphysics* 65.2 (2011): 351–76. For a very unusual perspective, concerning the justification of slavery by the slave owners, see Austin Choi-Fitzpatrick, *What Slaveholders Think: How Contemporary Perpetrators Rationalize What They Do* (New York: Columbia University Press, 2017).

371 "Respondeo dicendum quod conveniens fuit mulierem formari de costa viri. Primo quidem, ad significandum quod inter virum et mulierem debet esse socialis coniunctio. Neque enim mulier debet dominari in virum, et ideo non est formata de capite. Neque debet a viro despici, tanquam serviliter subiecta, et ideo non est formata de pedibus. Secundo, propter sacramentum, quia de latere Christi dormientis in cruce fluxerunt sacramenta, idest sanguis et aqua, quibus est Ecclesia instituta." Iᵃ q. 92 a. 3 co. *Summa Theologiae*, online at: http://www.unifr.ch/bkv/summa/kapitel93-3.htm (last accessed on Jan. 15, 2021).

If we ever needed any further explanation why we must study the past, especially the Middle Ages and the early modern age, then we have here available a vast storehouse of sources in which all three concepts were discussed, illuminated, and examined. The discourse contained in them continues until today and determines us in the twenty-first century deeply as well.[372] It would not be true that a major proportion of people in the pre-modern age lived in a form of slavery, and it also would not be true that most of them enjoyed a high level of freedom in the way as we define it today, at least in the western world. The situation was highly complex and diverse, and much depends for the analysis of those issues on the circumstances, the time period, the culture, and the sources through which we can examine the practice of imprisonment and enslavement, or the struggle to gain one's own freedom. Kings could just as much be taken prisoners as the ordinary soldiers, though they would have to pay a much higher ransom, which often actually saved their lives.

Women were not at all exempt or safe from becoming captives by pirates or slave traders, quite on the contrary, and as the case of the English mystic Margery Kempe (ca. 1373–after 1438) indicates, they could also be thrown into prison for many different reasons, even when many people admired and worshipped them, such as this religious citizen from Lynn (today, King's Lynn), as a truly holy person, as allegedly confirmed by her mystical visions.[373]

Although medieval society was already well structured by laws and a legal system, the case of Kempe also illustrates the degree to which arbitrary decision could be made because authorities exerted and abused their power at will. In that case, the Steward of Leicester "took two of her companions who went with her on pilgrimage – one was Thomas Marchale, aforesaid, the other a man from Wisbech – and put them in prison because of her" (151).

Curiously, however, yet not untypical of that age, a subsequent storm frightened people so much that they quickly released the prisoners the next day and questioned them as to Margery's true faith – for a paralle, though literary case, see the treatment of young Tristan by the Norwegian merchants in Gottfried von Straßburg's eponymous romance (ca. 1210). Once they had testified in the affirmative, they were let go, and the storm then subsided (151–52), a phenomenon

---

[372] Albrecht Classen, "The Amazon Rainforest of Pre-Modern Literature: Ethics, Values, and Ideals from the Past for our Future. With a Focus on Aristotle and Heinrich Kaufringer," *Humanities Open Access* 9(1).4 (2020), published on Dec. 24, 2019 (https://doi.org/10.3390/h9010004; last accessed on Jan. 15, 2021).

[373] *The Book of Margery Kempe*. Trans. by B. A. Windeatt (London: Penguin, 1985), ch. 46, pp. 148–50. See now Laura Kalas, *Margery Kempe's Spiritual Medicine: Suffering, Transformation and the Life-Course* (Cambridge: D. S. Brewer, 2020).

we might call a kind of positive outcome of an ordeal in which God spoke to the mystic's true power and identity as His own mouthpiece.³⁷⁴ Nevertheless, the danger for Margery of being executed for religious reasons was obviously very high, similarly as in the cases of Marguerite de Porète (ca. 1280–1310) and Joan of Arc (ca. 1412–1431: "For when they were both put in prison, they had told her themselves that they supposed that, if the Mayor could have his way, he would have her burnt" (152).

Youth or old age, race, or social background did not have a big impact on an individual's power to gain freedom or to hold on to that status, although collective bargaining by cities, or entire peoples, could achieve that effect. Slavery could easily affect anyone unlucky enough to be in the way of slave traders. And thus it does not come as a surprise that we find many comments in literary, philosophical, and theological texts aspiring for individual freedom, both spiritual and material, obviously because people in the pre-modern age were only too aware of the danger that they could lose their freedom and their lives under unfortunate circumstances.

We are here confronted with a highly convoluted yet meaningful topic, with all three aspects closely intertwined with the others. Individuals gain a clear understanding of freedom only once they no longer enjoy it. Imprisonment and slavery powerfully profile the deeper meaning of freedom, a form of social conditions which has been fought over since antiquity. As Alexander Demandt now formulates, freedom is a matter determined by the individual's power to establish him/herself; a matter of self-consciousness; a matter of political perspective; and a matter of social contracts. Freedom often collides with the ideal of equality, and the term 'freedom' can thus be used in many different contexts, carrying a variety of meanings. As he formulates it: "Freiheitsparole und Befreiungsrhetorik zeigen im Laufe der Jarhunderte keinerlei Abnutzungserscheinungen... . Denn Freiheit ist ein Zentralbegriff im zwischenmenschlichen Verhältnis... . Freiheit muß immer wieder neu bestimmt, immer wieder neu erfunden werden" (211; The phrase 'freedom' and the rhetoric of liberation do not demonstrate any signs of attrition in the course of centuries... . After all, 'freedom' is a central term in intrahuman relations... . Freedom must always be defined anew, it must be reinvented all the time).³⁷⁵

Even if we could not claim, finally, to have pinpointed exactly in every respect what the notion of freedom really meant for people in the pre-modern

---

[374] Peter Dinzelbacher, *Das fremde Mittelalter: Gottesurteil und Tierprozess*. 2nd, extensively expanded ed. (2006; Darmstadt: Wissenschaftliche Buchgesellschaft, 2020), 35–145. He does not, however, engage with Margery Kempe's case and that of her companions.
[375] Alexander Demandt, *Magistra Vitae* (see note 157), 211.

era, since so much depends on the circumstances, the history of mentality, and the philosophical, theological, moral, and ethical principles, we have certainly managed, I believe, to identify the range of discourses predicated on freedom and the lack thereof, which were certainly of great relevance for high and low, insiders and outsiders, young and old, and people of all races, gender, or sexual orientations, already at that time.

We also realize, through the slave narrative, that the traditional notion of a 'white Europe' in the pre-modern age needs to be critically questioned, especially since slavery actually flourished in the late Middle Ages, which created a virtually global mix of people suffering in bondage and servitude, completely lacking in freedom but living among and with the masters.[376]

Thus, altogether I like to think that this volume fits exceedingly well into our series, "Fundamentals of Medieval and Early Modern Culture." Freedom and the lack thereof, for whatever reason, constituted a critical issue in the literary, philosophical, religious, but then also political and legal domains, and this long before the eighteenth century, as previous scholars have often tended to argue. Our modern roots go much further back, so medieval perspectives prove to be highly relevant for our own discourse.

---

376 Geraldine Heng, "Early Globalities, and Its Questions, Objectives, and Methods: An Inquiry into the State of Theory and Critique," *Exemplaria* 26.2–3 (2014): 232–51; esp. 239–41.

Acknowledgment

I would like to acknowledge with gratitude the critical reading of this manuscript by my colleague Marilyn L. Sandidge, Westfield State University, MA. Similarly, I am very thankful to Fidel Fajardo-Acosta, Creighton University, Omaha, NE, for his excellent feedback on parts of this manuscript. My dear colleague and friend, Thomas Willard, University of Arizona, also read parts of this study and offered useful suggestions. I also want to express my gratitude to Laura Burlon from Walter de Gruyter for her careful copy-editing of the manuscript. All remaining mistakes are, of course, my own. Originally, this book was supposed to be nothing but the introduction to a new volume in our series "Fundamentals of Medieval and Early Modern Culture" based on a symposium to be held at the University of Arizona in May of 2020, but then COVID-19 struck, and everything was put on hold. However, I continued with my research and am very pleased with being able to present here the results of my intensive investigations throughout the entire time of the crisis.

I personally did not feel arrested, although the outside world seemed to have come to a screeching stop. The result of the global crises for me was the creation of this new monograph, which turned into a form of self-liberation from fear, governmental rules, repression, control, and lack of freedom by way of looking into the premodern world where very similar struggles were already fought and, impressively, often won. Of course, there was no remedy to protect anyone from the Black Death, for instance, except flight from one's home, but the quest for personal freedom, the fight to get out of prison, and the desperate attempt to escape from slavery already mattered critically at that time.

Obviously, there would be countless other sources, poets, or works of art and music, architectural objects, and the like to study the three topics of freedom, imprisonment, and slavery in tandem. I hope, however, that the selection presented and analyzed here has made it already very clear how important they were in the life and culture of the pre-modern period. All of them were deeply subject to the ongoing discourse, the results of innumerable fights, negotiations, agreements, debates, rules, regulations, laws, stipulations, and arrangements.[377]

---

[377] Almost serendipitously, an exhibition at the *Deutsches Hygiene-Museum Dresden*, "*Im Gefängnis – Vom Entzug der Freiheit*" held from Sept. 26, 2020 to May 31, 2021, curated by Isabel Dzierson (Dresden), Marianne Rigaud-Roy (Lyon), and Sandra Sunier (Geneva), was dedicated to the history of the prison precisely at the same time when I wrote this monograph, at that time unaware of these activities. The key statement introducing this exhibition proves to be quite revealing, and it is deeply relevant also for this study: "Jede Gesellschaft muss Recht sprechen, um die soziale Ordnung aufrecht zu erhalten. Wie und mit welchen Mitteln sie das tut, hat sich je-

This means that each case examined here proves to be both rather unique and yet also representative of society at large since it mirrors the broad and public reflections on the meaning of freedom and its opposite, imprisonment, with slavery being the extreme result of commerce and wars. The best result of this book would be if subsequent research picks up these suggestions and explores them further, adding new materials, texts, and voices. Significantly, two major conferences with parallel themes took place at virtually the same time while I researched and wrote this book, one in Tempe, Arizona State University (Feb. 7–8, 2020, "Unfreedom," still in-person), and one in Tucson, University of Arizona (Nov. 21–22, 2020, "Liberty, the Prison, and Slavery in the Pre-Modern World," online).[378]

Obviously, medievalists and early modernists have much to say about these issues that concern us very much also today. It is, unfortunately, one of the human tendencies to take other people captives and to force them to do whatever the 'owner' fancies, and this both in the past and in the present. But it is also a deeply-seated desire of practically all people in this world to aspire for freedom, to shed all forms of dependency and slavery, and to live their own lives the way they please. Of course, this very desire regularly clashes with the systematic ef-

---

doch über die Jahrhunderte geändert. Dabei sagt die Art der Bestrafung immer auch etwas über den Strafenden selbst aus – denn wir sind es, die strafen" (Every society must administer justice in order to maintain social order. The methods and means with which this is carried out, however, has changed over the centuries. In that process, the kind of punishment always tells us something about the one who metes out the punishment because it is us who punish). Online at: https://www.dhmd.de/ausstellungen/im-gefaengnis/. For a report, see Stefan Locke, "Wie sieht der Alltag im Knast aus?," *Frankfurter Allgemeine Zeitung* Oct. 7, 2020: https://www.faz.net/aktuell/feuilleton/kunst/eine-dresdner-ausstellung-ueber-das-leben-im-gefaengnis-16987475.html?printPagedArticle=true#pageIndex_3 (both last accessed on Jan. 15, 2021). The exhibition was accompanied by a catalog, *Im Gefängnis: eine gemeinsame Ausstellung von: Musée Genève, Musée des Confluences, Deutsches Hygiene-Museum Dresden*, ed. Roger Mayou (Dresden: Deutsches Hygiene-Museum Dresden, 2020). I have not yet been able to consult it for the purpose of the present study.

378 https://acmrs.asu.edu/sites/default/files/2020 – 04/Program_FinalDraft1_2020.pdf; https://aclassen.faculty.arizona.edu/content/program-nov-21-and-22-online-conference-freedom-imprisonment-and-slavery (both last accessed on Jan. 15, 2021). I am currently in the process of translating the proceedings into a volume, scheduled to be published by Lexington Books (Lanham, Boulder, etc., perhaps in 2021), with the tentative title *Incarceration and Slavery in the Middle Ages and the Early Modern Age: Cultural-Historical Investigation of the Dark Side in the Pre-Modern World*. In the introduction to that book, I focus primarily on the issue of imprisonment and review also much of the research on the history of law, the penal system, and of the medieval prison. I hope to add considerably to the main arguments in the present book, and refer the reader also to the many contributions by other scholars who significantly enrich our understanding of this topic from their individual perspectives.

forts by authorities (secular and religious) to hold on to their own power, and this on the back of millions, if not billions, of their subjects. Ironically, we are also deeply aware of the great difficulties throughout times to live peacefully with one's neighbor/s. There is, after all, no complete freedom; and every individual must live within the social confines determined by rules, regulations, laws, stipulations, and directives.

Every ship captain, general, but also every teacher, manager, supervisor, etc. knows that there has to be hierarchy, order, commands, and obedience, otherwise the organization, company, or school class would not operate. Otherwise, complete chaos and anarchy would break out and destroy human society at large. Nevertheless, both imprisonment and slavery are extreme and painful conditions, as was the case as much in the pre-modern world as it is today. By addressing these two phenomena, and by reflecting, in tandem, about the meaning of individual or collective freedom as pursued already in the Middle Ages, we are in an excellent condition to build meaningful bridges between both periods and to explain much more deeply why the modern discourse depends so much on a solid understanding of those three aspects as examined and discussed already then.[379]

I would like to dedicate this book to the countless numbers of political prisoners past and present who are innocent victims of a dictatorial system and have to suffer for their own ideals and their struggle to help their people gain freedom. There are also many prisoners who have been on death row for decades of their lives until their innocence was suddenly proven by means of modern DNA testing. This is not to say that we do not need a judicial and penal system and prisons to handle actual crimes (see above), but here I have those in mind who are guiltless and targets of horrible political persecutions in many countries on this earth. Slavery continues until today, alas, in certain parts of this world, and I can only hope that this study focused on the pre-modern conditions will at least con-

---

379 See now the contributions to *Making the Medieval Relevant: How Medieval Studies Contribute to Improving Our Understanding of the Present*, ed. Chris Jones, Conor Kostick, and Klaus Oschema. Das Mittelalter: Perspektiven mediävistischer Forschung, 6 (Berlin and Boston: Walther de Gruyter, 2020). For a critical evaluation, however, see my review to appear in *Mediaevistik* 34 (2021). Cf. also *The Middle Ages in the Modern World: Twenty-First Century Perspectives*, ed. Bettina Bildhauer and Chris Jones. Proceedings of the British Academy, 208 (Oxford: Oxford University Press, 2017). For new efforts, from a very broad interdisciplinary approach, see now the contributions to *The Relevance of The Humanities in the Twenty-First Century: Past and Present*, ed. Albrecht Classen. Special issue of *Humanities Open Access*, June 2020; online at: https://www.mdpi.com/journal/humanities/special_issues/pas_pre (last accessed on Jan. 15, 2021). Here, medievalists and modernists likewise address the same question.

tribute to the growth of our awareness about the historical, political, social, ethical, military, economic, and cultural dimensions of this topic.

Freedom has always been a most precious value and ideal, and this, of course, also in the Middle Ages and the early modern age. A very valuable, but also rather fragile concept, indeed, and we continue to struggle hard to come to terms with it. Until today, the fifty-two epigrams by Sebastian Brant in his *Freiheitstafel* (1517–1519) composed for the city hall of Strasbourg (XIII) resonate with us, maybe especially because he alerted his readers about the constant danger of losing this highly valuable ideal of freedom, which had existed already in the ancient and medieval world:

> Koenig Artus gros lob erholt
> durch taffel unnd der ehren soldt,
> das er sein Ritter stehts liesz reiszen
> zur Freyheit schirm, witwen und waiszen;
> seins gleich sind leider wenig mehr
> die der musz schuermen Freyheit sehr.[380]

> [King Artus gained great praise
> with his Round Table and the desire for honor,
> that he always let his knight go travel
> to protect freedom, widows, and orphans;
> unfortunately, there are only few of his kind left over
> who endeavor to protect freedom.]

The reason why Greece lost its freedom was that they did not fight hard enough for it; Venice enjoys its freedom, by contrast, because the city made every possible effort to maintain it. Brant's message for the citizens of Strasbourg meaningfully speaks to us until today when we think about our own freedom:

> Wer setzet wider freyheit sich
> ist ein Tyrann und wüterich,
> wenig sindt der ohn todtschlag bluth
> gefahren zu Plutonis gluth,
> nit viel uff feder wath gestorben
> sondern mit schwert und gifft verdorben.[381]

> [He who fights against freedom
> is a tyrant and a raging beast,
> there are few of them who without the blood of the death blow
> went down to Pluto's glow (i.e., hell),

---

[380] Sebastian Brant, *Narrenschiff: nebst dessen Freiheitstafel* (see note 98), 309.
[381] Brant, *Narrenschiff* (see note 98), 310.

not many of them died resting on a feather-filled mattrass,
instead they died by the sword and through poison.]

To this we can also add a brief comment by the famous Nuremberg cobbler Hans Sachs (1494–1576) who uses the term 'tyrant' or 'tyranny' to characterize the behavior of the Irish knight Morholt in his dramatic adaptation of the medieval romance of *Tristrant und Isalde* (performed first in 1553; printed in 1561), originally composed by Eilhart von Oberg. Similar to the biblical figure of Goliath, Morholt, four times as strong as all other knights, demands tribute from Cornwall, unless he might be defeated in a fight. No one dares to accept this challenge, until Tristrant learns about it and defeats, like the biblical David, his opponent. Once he has decided to face Morholt, the young man characterizes the Irish warrior as a tyrant and condemns him for his brutal strategy to repress King Marx without any legitimacy except sheer force:

So treibet er nur tiranney
Das er dein reich unter sich brecht;
Hat darzu weder fug noch recht.
Derhalb wird mir Gott thun beystant,
Weil ich kempff für das vatterlant
Und thu das auß bezwungner not.[382]

[He is practicing tyranny
trying to subjugate your country for himself,
he is not entitled to this and has no right.
Therefore, God will assist me
because I will fight for the fatherland
and do this required by necessity.]

---

382 Hans Sachs, *Tragedia mit 23 Personen von der strengen Lieb Herr Tristrant mit der schönen Königin Isalden. Faksimileausgabe nach dem ältesten Druck aus dem Jahre 1561 erschienen in Nürnberg*, ed. Danielle Buschinger and Wolfgang Spiewok. Wodan, 29. Serie 1. Texte des Mittelalters, 8 (Greifswald: Reineke-Verlag, 1993), 34. Intriguingly, the notion of freedom is here also associated with the idea of the fatherland, a political entity of abstract qualities; see Albrecht Classen, "Die Gefahren des Massenwahns aus literarhistorischer Sicht: Von Walther von der Vogelweide und Heinrich Wittenwiler zu Thomas Mann und Gustave Le Bon," *Im Clash der Identitäten: Nationalismen im literatur- und kulturgeschichtlichen Diskurs*, ed. Wolfgang Brylla and Cezary Lipiński. Andersheit – Fremdheit – Ungleichheit: Erfahrungen von Disparatheit in der deutschsprachigen Literatur, 1 (Göttingen: V&R unipress, 2020), 185–99. See also Hans Peter Herrmann, "Krieg, *Medien und Nation: zum Nationalismus in Kriegsliedern des 16. und 18. Jahrhunderts*," *"Krieg ist mein Lied": der Siebenjährige Krieg in den zeitgenössischen Medien*, ed. Wolfgang Adam and Holger Dainat, together with Ute Pott. Schriften des Gleimhauses Halberstadt, 5 (Göttingen: Wallstein-Verlag, 2007), 27–64.

Bibliography

Note: For pragmatic reasons, I have combined here primary and secondary literature. The alphabetical system will allow the reader to find the desired reference easily. When a title begins with an article (The, Der, Die, Les, El, etc.), I have used the first word, the noun or adjective, following as the key for the alphabetical arrangement. References to a wide variety of webpages are not included here and can only be found in the footnotes. Even though there is some duplication between the footnotes and this bibliography, a comprehensive collection of all references and sources here serves the purposes of scholarly research the best, especially since I have tried hard to avoid duplication within the footnotes. There, when I refer to a study cited before, I have included a back-reference, but a complete bibliography still appears to be the most appropriate documentation. The use of these almost duplicate systems will make it easier and faster for the reader to identify the sources cited either by going through the notes or by checking this bibliography. I have consulted at times articles even on Wikipedia, though only when they proved to be truly solidly researched and trustworthy, which is still not always the case. But then I always backed them up with additional secondary literature. Those online articles or sites which are not of a scholarly nature but still offer valuable information or images are not listed here. Before the manuscript went to the printer, I have checked every individual website once again to make sure that it is live and accessible.

Die abendländische Freiheit vom 10. zum 14. Jahrhundert: der Wirkungszusammenhang von Idee und Wirklichkeit im europäischen Vergleich, ed. Johannes Fried. Vorträge und Forschungen / Konstanzer Arbeitskreis für Mittelalterliche Geschichte, 39 (Sigmaringen: Thorbecke, 1991).
Acemoglu, Daron and James A. Robinson, *Economic Origins of Dictatorship and Democracy* (Cambridge: Cambridge University Press, 2009).
Acemoglu, Daron and James A. Robinson, *The Narrow Corridor: States, Societies, and the Fate of Liberty* (New York: Penguin, 2019).
Ahnert, Ruth, *The Rise of Prison Literature in the Sixteenth Century* (Cambridge: Cambridge University Press, 2013).
Akçam, Taner, *The Young Turks' Crime Against Humanity: The Armenian Genocide and Ethnic Cleansing in the Ottoman Empire*. Human Rights and Crimes against Humanity (Princeton, NJ: University of Princeton Press, 2012).
Alessandra Petrina, *The Kingis Quair of James I of Scotland* (Padua: Unipress, 1997).
Alfonso X el Sabio, *Las siete partidas (El libro del fuero de las leyes)*, intro. and ed. by José Sánchez-Arcilla Bernal (Madrid: Editorial Reus, 2004).
Aliscans, texte établi par Claude Régner. Champion classiques, 21 (Paris: Champion, 2007).
Aliscans: das altfranzösische Heldenepos nach der venezianischen Fassung M, eingeleitet und übersetzt von Fritz Peter Knapp. De Gruyter Texte (Berlin and Boston: Walter de Gruyter, 2013).
Allen, Peter L., *The Art of Love: Amatory Fiction from Ovid to the Romance of the Rose*. The Middle Ages Series (Philadelphia, PA: University of Pennsylvania Press, 1999).
Allison, Henry E., *Kant's Conception of Freedom: A Developmental and Critical Analysis* (Cambridge: Cambridge University Press, 2020).
Alltag im Spätmittelalter, ed. Harry Kühnel. 3rd ed. (1984; Graz, Vienna, and Cologne: Verlag Styria, 1984).

al-Sulūk li-Ma'rifat Duwal al-Mulūk, ed. 'Ata, Muhammad 'Abd al-Qadir (Beirut, Lebanon: Manshurat Muhammad 'Ali Baydun, Dar al-Kutub al-'Ilmiyah, 1997).

Altenbockum, Jasper von, "Die Aerosole der Freiheitsapostel," *Frankfurter Allgemeine Zeitung* Oct. 24, 2020, online at: https://www.faz.net/aktuell/politik/inland/corona-politik-die-aerosole-der-freiheitsapostel-17017176.html?premium=0x50a3320987f6d5d811c64c7 c52ed46e4 (last accessed on Jan. 15, 2021).

Althochdeutsche Literatur: Mit altniederdeutschen Textbeispielen. Auswahl mit Übertragungen und Kommentar, ed. Horst Dieter Schlosser. 2nd, rev. and expanded ed. (1998; Berlin: Erich Schmidt, 2004).

Althoff, Gerd, Hans-Werner Goetz, Ernst Schubert, *Menschen im Schatten der Kathedrale: Neuigkeiten aus dem Mittelalter* (Darmstadt: Primus Verlag, 1998).

Althoff, Gert, *Die Macht der Rituale: Symbolik und Herrschaft im Mittelalter* (Darmstadt: Primus Verlag, 2003).

Althoff, Gert, *Spielregeln der Politik im Mittelalter: Kommunikation in Frieden und Fehde* (Darmstadt: Primus Verlag, 1997).

Ambühl, Rémy, *Prisoners of War in the Hundred Years War: Ransom Culture in the Late Middle Ages* (Cambridge: Cambridge University Press, 2013).

Amital, Reuven, "Diplomacy and the Slave Trade in the Eastern Mediterranean: A Re-Examination of the Mamluk-Byzantine-Genoese Triangle in the Late Thirteenth Century in Light of the Existing Early Correspondence," *Oriente Moderno* 88 (2008): 349–68.

Ammerer, Gerhard and Christoph Brandhuber, *Schwert und Galgen: Geschichte der Todesstrafe in Salzburg* (Salzburg: Verlag Anton Pustet, 2018).

Archangeli, Alessandro, *Recreation in the Renaissance: Attitudes Towards Leisure and Pastimes in European Culture, c. 1425–1675* (Houndmills, Basingstoke, Hampshire: Palgrave Macmillan, 2003).

Archibald, Elizabeth, *Apollonius of Tyre: Medieval and Renaissance Themes and Variations. Including the text of the* Historia Apollonii Regis Tyri *with an English translation* (Cambridge: D. S. Brewer, 1991).

Arendt, Hannah, *The Life of the Mind* (New York: Jovanovich, 1978).

Arn, Mary-Jo, *Fortunes Stabilnes: Charles of Orleans's English Book of Love. A Critical Edition* (Binghamton, NY: Medieval & Renaissance Texts & Studies, 1994).

Arnold, Martin, *The Dragon: Fear and Power* (London: Reaktion Books, 2018).

Aucassin and Nicolette, trans. from the Old French by Francis William Bourdillon (London: Kegan Paul, Trench, and Trübner, 1908).

Aucassin and Nicolette: A Facing-Page Edition and Translation by Robert S. Sturges (East Lansing, MI: Michigan State University Press 2015).

Aucassin et Nicolette, ed. critique. 2nd rev. and corrected ed. by Jean Dufournet (Paris: GF-Flammarion, 1984).

Aucassin et Nicolette, trans. and photo-ill. by Katharine Margot Toohey (2017), online at: https://quemarpress.weebly.com/uploads/8/6/1/4/86149566/aucassin_and_nicolette_-_translation_by_k.m._toohey.pdf.

Aufklärung im Mittelalter? Die Verurteilung von 1277. Das Dokument des Bischofs von Paris übersetzt und erläutert von Kurt Flasch. excerpta classica, VI (Mainz: Dieterich'sche Verlagsbuchhandlung, 1989).

Authorities in the Middle Ages: Influence, Legitimacy, and Power in Medieval Society, ed. Sini Kangas, Mia Korpiola, and Tuija Aionen. Fundamentals of Medieval and Early Modern Culture, 12 (Berlin and Boston: Walter de Gruyter, 2013).

Ayerbe-Chaux, Reinaldo, *El conde Lucanor: materia tradicional y originalidad creadora*. Ensayos (Madrid: Ediciones J. Porrúa Turanzas, 1975).

Bachorski, Hans-Jürgen, *Geld und soziale Identität im "Fortunatus": Studien zur literarischen Bewältigung frühbürgerlicher Widersprüche*. Göppinger Arbeiten zur Germanistik, 376 (Göppingen: Kümmerle, 1983).

Baldwin, John W., *The Language of Sex: Five Voices from Northern France Around 1200*. The Chicago Series on Sexuality, History, and Society (Chicago and London: The University of Chicago Press, 1994).

Bamberger, Gudrun, *Poetologie im Prosaroman: Fortunatus – Wickram – Faustbuch*. Poetic und Episteme, (Würzburg: Königshausen & Neumann, 2018).

Barański, Zygmunt G., "On Dante's Trail," Italian Studies 72.1 (2017): 1–15.

Bárány, Attila, "Nicopolis, Battle of," *The Oxford Encyclopedia of Medieval Warfare and Military Technology*, ed. Clifford J. Rogers. Vol. 3 (Oxford: Oxford University Press, 2010), 57–59.

Barker, Hannah, *That Most Precious Merchandise: The Mediterranean Trade in Black Sea Slaves, 1260–1500*. The Middle Ages Series (Philadelphia, PA: University of Pennsylvania Press, 2019).

Barker, Juliet R. V., *Agincourt: The King, the Campaign, the Battle* (London: Little, Brown, 2005).

Barlett, W. B., *Richard the Lionheart: The Crusader King of England* (Stroud, Gloucestershire: Amberley Publishing, 2018).

Bartels, Larry M., "Ethnic Antagonism Erodes Republicans' Commitment to Democracy," *Proceedings of the National Academy of Sciences of the United States of America* (*PNSA*) 117.37 (2020): 22752–22759.

Bartlett, Wayne B., *The Last Crusade: The Seventh Crusade & the Final Battle for the Holy Land* (Stroud, Gloucestershire: Tempus, 2007).

Bartolomé de las Casas and the Defense of Amerindian Rights: A Brief History with Documents, ed. edited by Lawrence A. Clayton and David M. Lantigua (Tuscaloosa, AL: The University of Alabama Press, 2020).

Bartolomé de las Casas, *The Devastation of the Indies: A Brief Account*, trans. from the Spanish by Herma Briffault. Intro. by Bill M. Donovan (1974; Baltimore, MD, and London: The Johns Hopkins University Press, 1992).

Bartolomé de las Casas: *Indian Freedom: The Cause of Bartolomé de las Casas, 1484–1566. A Reader*, trans. and notes by Francis Patrick Sullivan, S.J. (Kansas City, KS: Sheed & Ward, 1995).

Baskins, Cristelle L., "Scenes from a Marriage: Hospitality and Commerce in Boccaccio's Tale of Saladin and Torello," *The Medieval Marriage Scene: Prudence, Passion, Policy*, ed. Sherry Roush, Cristelle L. Baskins, and Timothy D. Arner (Ithaca, NY, and London: Cornell University Press; 2005), 81–99.

Basso, Hélène, *Être poète au temps de Charles d'Orléans (XVe siècle)*. Collection En-jeux (Avignon: Éd. Univ. d'Avignon, 2012).

Batselé, Filip, *Liberty, Slavery and the Law in Early Modern Western Europe: Omnes Homines aut Liberi Sunt aut Servi*. Studies in the History of Law and Justice (Cham: Springer International Publishing, 2020).
The Battle of Agincourt, ed. Anne Curry (New Haven, CT: Yale University Press, 2015).
Bauer, Shane, *American Prison: A Reporter's Undercover Journey Into the Business of Punishment* (New York: Penguin, 2018).
Baum, Wilhelm, *Reichs- und Territorialgewalt (1273–1437): Königtum, Haus Österreich und Schweizer Eidgenossen im späten Mittelalter* (Vienna: Turia & Kant, 1994).
Bayley Dolson, Guy, "Imprisoned English Authors and the Consolation of Philosophy of Boethius," *The American Journal of Philology* 43.2 (1922): 168–69.
Beaumanoir, see Philipp de Beaumanoir
Becher, Matthias, "Non enim habent regem idem Antiqui Saxones … : Verfassung und Ethnogenese in Sachsen während des 8. Jahrhunderts," *Sachsen und Franken in Westfalen: Zur Komplexität der ethnischen Deutung und Abgrenzung zweier frühmittelalterlicher Stämme. Ergebnisse eines vom 22.–25. April 1997 in Paderborn durchgeführten Kolloquiums zur Vorbereitung der Ausstellung "799 Kunst und Kultur der Karolingerzeit, Karl der Große und Papst Leo III. in Paderborn"*, ed. Hans-Jürgen Hässler with Jörg Jarnut and Matthias Wemhoff. Studien zur Sachsenforschung, 12 (Oldenburg: Isensee, 1999), 1–31.
Beckmann, Gustav Adolf, *Gualter del Hum –Gaiferos – Waltharius*. Beihefte zur Zeitschrift für romanische Philologie, 359 (Berlin and New York: Walter de Gruyter, 2010).
Bede, in *Opera Historica*, vol. 2 (Cambridge, MA: Harvard University Press, 1930).
Beer, Anna, *Patriot or Traitor: The Life and Death of Sir Walter Raleg* (London: Oneworld, 2018).
Beer, Jeanette, *Villehardouin: epic historian*. Études de philologie et d'histoire, 7 (Geneva: Droz, 1968).
Bellamy, John G., *Crime and Public Order in England in the Later Middle Ages*. Studies in Social History (London: Routledge and Kegan Paul; Toronto and Buffalo: University of Toronto Press, 1973).
Bennewitz, Ingrid, "'Karl und König Artus hat er übertroffen …': Der Mythos von Richard Löwenherz in der Literatur des Mittelalters und seine Rezeption in der Neuzeit," *Richard Löwenherz, ein europäischer Herrscher im Zeitalter der Konfrontation von Christentum und Islam: Mittelalterliche Wahrnehmung und moderne Rezeption*, ed. eadem and Klaus van Eickels, together with Christine van Eickels. Bamberger interdisziplinäre Mittelalterstudien. Vorträge und Vorlesungen, 8 (Bamberg: Bamberg University Press, 2018), 149–70.
Beowulf: A Prose Translation with an Intro. by David Wright (London: Penguin, 1957)
Berg, Dieter, *Richard Löwenherz*. Gestalten des Mittelalters und der Renaissance (Darmstadt: Wissenschaftliche Buchgesellschaft, 2007).
Berndt, Sandra, *Haftautobiographik im 20. Jahrhundert: Hafterfahrungen in Tagebuchaufzeichnungen, Briefen, Gedichten, Dokumentationen und Erzähltexten* (Frankfurt a. M., Bern, and Vienna: Peter Lang, 2016).
Bernstein, Alan E., *The Formation of Hell: Death and Retribution in the Ancient and Early Christian Worlds* (London: UCL Press, 1993).

Bertelsmeier-Kierst, Christa, "Eike von Repgow: 'Sachsenspiegel'," *Klassiker des Mittelalters*, ed. Regina Toepfer. Spolia Berolinensia, 38 (Hildesheim: Weidmannsche Verlagsbuchhandlung, 2019), 59–81.

Bertolotti, Antonio, "Prigioni e prigioneri in Mantova dal secolo XIII al secolo XIX," *Bullettino ufficiale della Direzione Generale delle Carceri* 17 (1887): 51–70, 163–82; as a monograph under the same title (Rome: Mantellate, 1888).

Betti, Vanessa, *Das Zusammenspiel von Raum, Zeit und Figuren in der "Kudrun"* (Baden-Baden: Tectum Verlag, 2019).

Beuchot, Mauricio, *Los fundamentos de los derechos humanos en Bartolomé de las Casas*. Biblioteca A, 3 (Barcelona: Antropos, 1994).

Biglieri, Aníbal A., *Hacia una poética del relato didáctico: ocho estudios sobre* El conde Lucanor. North Carolina Studies in the Romance Languages and Literatures, 233 (1988; Chapel Hill, NC: North Carolina Studies in the Romance Languages and Literatures, 1989).

Bisaha, Nancy, *Creating East and West: Renaissance Humasists and the Ottoman Turks* (Philadelphia, PA: University of Philadelphia Press, 2004).

Bloch, Howard, *The Anonymous Marie de France* (Chicago and London: University of Chicago Press, 2003).

Bloch, Marc, "Servitude and Freedom," id., *Feudal Society* (1939; Chicago: University of Chicago Press, 1961), 255–74.

Bloch, Marc, *Slavery and Serfdom in the Middle Ages: Selected Essays*. Publications of the Center for Medieval and Renaissance Studies, 8 (Berkeley, CA: University of California Press, 1975).

Bloch, Marc, *La Société féodale*. Evolution de l'humanité. Synthèse collective, 3, section, 8 (Paris: A. Michel, 1968).

Blumenthal, Debra, *Enemies and Familiars: Slavery and Mastery in Fifteenth Century Valencia* (Ithaca, NY: Cornell University Press, 2009).

Boccaccio, Giovanni, *Decameron*, ed. Vittore Branca. Sixth rev. and corrected ed. (1980; Turin: Giulio Einaudi, 1987).

Boccaccio, Giovanni, *The Decameron*, trans. with an intro. and notes by G. H. McWilliam. Sec. ed. (1972; London: Penguin, 1995).

Boethius Christianus? Transformationen der "Consolatio Philosophiae" in Mittelalter und Früher Neuzeit, ed. Reinhold Glei (Berlin and New York: Walter de Gruyter, 2010).

Boethius in the Middle Ages: Latin and Vernacular Traditions of the "Consolatio philosophiae", ed. Maarten J. F. M. Hoenen and Lodi Nauta. Studien und Texte zur Geistesgeschichte des Mittelalters, 58 (Leiden: Brill, 1997).

Boethius in the Middle Ages: Latin and Vernacular Traditions of the "Consolatio philosophiae", ed. Maarten J. F. M. Hoenen and Lodi Nauta. Studien und Texte zur Geistesgeschichte des Mittelalters, 58 (Leiden: Brill, 1997).

Boethius, *Consolation of Philosophy*, trans., with intro. and notes, by Joel C. Relihan (Indianapolis, IN, and Cambridge: Hackett Publishing, 2001).

Boethius: His Life, Thought and Influence, ed. Margaret Gibson (Oxford: Basil Blackwell, 1981).

Boner, Ulrich, *Der Edelstein: Eine mittelalterliche Fabelsammlung. Zweisprachige Ausgabe: Mittelhochdeutsch – Neuhochdeutsch*, ed. Manfred Stange (Bielefeld: verlag regionalkultur, 2016).

Boner/ius, *The Fables of Ulrich Bonerius (ca. 1350): Masterwork of Late Medieval Didactic Literature*, trans. Albrecht Classen (Newcastle upon Tyle: Cambridge Scholars Publishing, 2020).

Bordat, Josef, *Gerechtigkeit und Wohlwollen: das Völkerrechtskonzept des Bartolomé de Las Casas* (Aachen: Shaker, 2006).

Bowden, Sarah, *Bridal Quest Epics in Medieval Germany. A Revisionary Approach*. Bithell Series of Dissertations, 85 (London: Modern Humanities Research Ass., 2012).

Boyd, Matthieu, "The Ring, the Sword, the Fancy Dress, and the Posthumous Child: Background to the Element of Heroic Biography in Marie de France's Yonec," *Romance Quarterly* 55.3 (2008): 205–30.

Brackert, Helmut, *Rudolf von Ems: Dichtung und Geschichte*. Germanische Bibliothek: Reihe 3. Untersuchungen und Einzeldarstellungen (Heidelberg: C. Winter, 1968).

Bradford, Broughton B., *The Legends of King Richard I, Coeur de Lion: A Study of Sources and Variations to the Year 1600*. Studies in English Literature, 25 (The Hague: Mouton, 1966).

Brandstätter, Horst, *Asperg: ein deutsches Gefängnis; der schwäbische Demokratenbuckel und seine Insassen: Pfarrer, Schreiber, Kaufleute, Lehrer, gemeines Volk und andere republikanische Brut, mit Abschweifungen über Denunzianten und Sympathisanten in alter und neuer Zeit*. Wagenbachs Taschenbücher, 46 (Berlin: Wagenbach, 1976).

Brant, Sebastian, *Das Narrenschiff: nebst dessen Freiheitstafel*, ed. Adam Walther Strobel. Bibliothek der gesammten deutschen National-Literatur von der ältesten bis auf die neuere Zeit: Abteilung 1, 17 (Quedlinburg: Basse, 1839).

Bratu, Cristian, "Je, aucteur de ce livre: Authorial Persona and Authority in French Medieval Histories and Chronicles," *Authorities in the Middle Ages: Influence, Legitimacy and Power in Medieval Society*, ed. Sini Kangas, Mia Korpiola, and Tuija Ainonen. Fundamentals of Medieval and Early Modern Culture, 12 (Berlin and Boston: Walter de Gruyter, 2013), 183–204.

Bridbury, A. R., "The Black Death," *Economic History Review*, 2nd Ser. 26 (1973): 557–92.

Brodman, James William, *Ransoming Captives in Crusader Spain: The Order of Merced on the Christian-Islamic Frontier*. The Middle Ages Series (Philadelphia, PA: University of Pennsylvania Press, 1986).

Brown, M. H., "James I," *Oxford Dictionary of National Biography* (Oxford: Oxford University Press, 2004), online at: https://www.oxforddnb.com/view/10.1093/ref:odnb/ 9780198614128.001.0001/odnb-9780198614128-e-14587;jsessionid= 1D02C84E35F93 A230B64898AF9EB5 A2C (last accessed on Jan. 15, 2021).

Brown, Michael, *James I* (East Linton, Scotland: Tuckwell Press, 1994); Alan MacQuarrie, *Medieval Scotland: Kingship and Nation* (Gloucestershire: Sutton Publishing, 2004).

Brown, Peter, "The Prison of Theseus and the Castle of Jalousie," *The Chaucer Review: A Journal of Medieval Studies and Literary Criticism* 26.2 (1991): 147–62.

Brucker, Charles, "Marie de France and the Fable Tradition," *A Companion to Marie de France*, ed. Logan E. Whalen. Brill's Companions to the Christian Tradition, 27 (Leiden and Boston, MA: Brill, 2011), 187–208.

Brüggen, Elke and Joachim Bumke, "Figuren-Lexikon," *Wolfram von Eschenbach: Ein Handbuch*, ed. Joachim Heinzle. Vol. II: *Figuren-Lexikon, Beschreibendes Verzeichnis der Handschriften, Bibliographien, Register und Abbildungen* (Berlin and Boston: Walter de Gruyter, 2011), 919–20.

Brunner, Karl and Gerhard Jaritz, *Landherr, Bauer, Ackerknecht: der Bauer im Mittelalter: Klischee und Wirklichkeit* (Vienna: Böhlau, 1985).

Brunstetter, Daniel R., *Tensions of Modernity: las Casas and His Legacy in the French Enlightenment*. Routledge Innovations in Political Theory, 44 (London and New York: Routledge, 2014).

Bugbee, John, *God's Patients: Chaucer, Agency, and the Nature of Laws* (Notre Dame, IN: University of Notre Dame Press, 2019).

Bulang, Tobias, *Enzyklopädische Dichtungen: Fallstudien zu Wissen und Literatur in Spätmittelalter und früher Neuzeit*. Deutsche Literatur, 2 (Berlin: Akademie-Verlag, 2011).

Bumke, Joachim, *Wolfram von Eschenbach*. 8th completely rev. ed. Sammlung Metzler, 36 (Stuttgart: J. B. Metzler, 2004).

Burger, Daniel, "In den Turm geworfen: Gefängnisse und Folterkammern auf Burgen im Mittelalter und in der frühen Neuzeit," *Burgenbau im späten Mittelalter*, vol. II. Ed. Wartburg-Gesellschaft zur Erforschung von Burgen und Schlössern in Verbindung mit dem Germanischen Nationalmuseum. Forschungen zu Burgen und Schlössern, 12 (Berlin and Munich: Deutscher Kunstverlag, 2009), 221–36.

Burgoyne, Jonathan, *Reading the Exemplum Right: Fixing the Meaning of* El Conde Lucanor. North Carolina Studies in the Romance Languages and Literatures, 289 (Chapel Hill, NC: North Carolina Studies in the Romance Languages and Literatures, 2007).

Burrichter, Brigitte, "Thibaut de Chapagne: Lyrik im Gefängnis der Liebe," *Formen der Selbstthematisierung in der vormodernen Lyrik*. Hrsg. von Dorothea Klein in Verbindung mit Thomas Baier, Brigitte Burrichter, Michael Erler und Isabel Karremann. Spolia Berolinensia: Beiträge zur Literatur- und Kulturgeschichte des Mittelalters und der Neuzeit, 39 (Hildesheim: Weidmannsche Verlagsbuchhandlung, 2020), 79–99.

Bush, M. L., *Serfdom and Slavery: Studies in Legal Bondage* (1996; London: Routledge, 2013).

Busk, Larry Alan, *Democracy in Spite of the Demos: Fom Arendt to the Frankfurt School* (London and New York: Rowman & Littlefield International, 2020).

Bustos, Jesús Antona, *Los derechos humanos de los pueblos indígenas: el Az Mapu y el caso Mapuche*. Colección Cátedra Fray Bartolomé de las Casas (Temuco, Chile: Ediciones Universidad Católica de Temuco, 2014).

Byock, Jesse L., *Viking Age Iceland* (London: Penguin, 2001).

Calin, William C., "The *dit amoureux* and the Makars: An Essay on The *Kingis Quair* and *The Testament of Cresseid*," *Florilegium* 25 (2008): 217–50.

The Cambridge Companion to Boethius, ed. John Marenbon (Cambridge: Cambridge University Press, 2009).

The Cambridge Companion to Dante's Commedia, ed. Zygmunt G. Barański and Simon A. Gilson (Cambridge: Cambridge University Press, 2019).

The Cambridge Companion to the African American Slave Narrative, ed. Audrey A. Fisch (Cambridge: Cambridge University Press, 2007).

The Cambridge Companion to the First Amendment and Religious Liberty, ed. Michael D. Breidenbach and Owen Anderson (Cambridge: Cambridge University Press, 2019).

The Cambridge Companion to Thomas More, ed. George M. Logan. Cambridge Companions to Religion (Cambridge and New York: Cambridge University Press, 2011).

Cameron, Joyce T., *Prisons and Punishment in Scotland: From the Middle Ages to the Present* (Edinburgh: Cannongate, 1983).

Campagna, Norbert, *Staatliche Macht und menschliche Freiheit: Das Staatsdenken Bertrand de Jouvenels*. Staatsdiskurse, 35 (Stuttgart: Franz Steiner Verlag, 2020).
Campbell, Bradley and Jason Manning, *The Rise of Victimhood Culture: Microaggressions, Safe Spaces, and the New Culture Wars* (Cham: Springer International Publishing, 2018).
Captivating Subjects: Writing Confinement, Citizenship, and Nationhood in the Nineteenth Century, ed. Julia M. Wright and Jason Haslam (Toronto: University of Toronto Press, 2005).
Caravale, Mario, *Magna carta libertatum* (Bologna: Il mulino, 2020).
Carpenter, Roger M., *"Times are altered with Us": American Indians from First Contact to the New Republic* (Chichester: Wiley Blackwell, 2015).
Carruthers, Elspeth Jane, "Christianization and Colonization on the Medieval South Baltic Frontier," Ph.D. diss., Princeton University, 1999.
Cartlidge, Neil, *Medieval Marriage: Literary Approaches, 1100–1300* (Cambridge: D. S. Brewer, 1997).
Caspar, Cyril L., 'New Perspectives of the Early Modern Afterlife: The Last Pilgrimage in the Poetry of John Donne and Sir Walter Raleigh," *Death in the Middle Ages and Early Modern Times: The Material and Spiritual Conditions of the Culture of Death*, ed. A. Classen. Fundamentals of Medieval and Early Modern Culture, 16 (Berlin and Boston: Walter de Gruyter, 2016), 433–56.
Castro, Daniel, *Another Face of Empire: Bartolomé de Las Casas, Indigenous Rights, and Ecclesiastical Imperialism*. Latin America Otherwise: Language, Empires, Nations (Durham, NC: Duke University Press, 2007).
Caviness, Madeline H. and Charles G. Nelson, *Women and Jews in the Sachsenspiegel Picture-Books* (Turnhout: Brepols, 2018).
Challenges to Authority and the Recognition of Rights: From Magna Carta to Modernity, ed. Catharine MacMillan and Charlotte Smith (Cambridge: Cambridge University Press, 2018).
Champion, Pierre, "Charles d'Orléans: Prince des Lis et de la poésie," id., *Histoire poétique du quinzième siècle*. Vol. 2: *Charles d'Orléans, le pauvre Villon, Arnoul Greban, Jean Meschinor le "Banni de Liesse", Me Henri Baude, élu des finances et poète, Jean Molinet rhétoriqueur*. Bibliothèque du XVe siècle, 28 (Paris: Champion, 1923).
Champion, Pierre, *Vie de Charles d'Orléans (1394–1465)* (Paris: Champion, 1911).
Charles d'Orléans in England, 1415–1440, ed. Mary-Jo Arn (Cambridge and Rochester, NY: D.S. Brewer, 2000).
Charles d'Orléans: *Poetry of Charles d'Orléans and His Circle: A Critical Edition of BNF MS. Fr. 25458, Charles d'Orléan's Personal Manuscript*, ed. John Fox and Mary-Jo Arn. English trans. by R. Barton Palmer. Medieval and Renaissance Texts and Studies, 383 (Tempe, AZ: Arizona Center for Medieval and Renaissance Studies; Turnhout: Brepols, 2010).
Chaucer, Geoffrey: *The Canterbury Tales*, ed. Robert Boenig and Andrew Taylor. Sec. ed. (Peterborough, Ont.: Broadview Editions, 2012).
Chaucer, Geoffrey: *The Riverside Chaucer*, ed. Larry D. Benson, based on *The Works of Geoffrey Chaucer*, ed. by F. N. Robinson, reissued as a paperback (1987; Oxford: Oxford University Press, 2008).
Cherchi, Paolo, *Andreas and the Ambiguity of Courtly Love* (Toronto: University of Toronto Press, 2016).

Choi-Fitzpatrick, Austin, *What Slaveholders Think: How Contemporary Perpetrators Rationalize What They Do* (New York: Columbia University Press, 2017).

Christian Spirituality: The Essential Guide to the Most Influential Spiritual Writings of the Christian Tradition, ed. Frank N. Magill and Ian P. McGreal (San Francisco, CA: Harper & Row, 1988).

Christine de Pizan, *The Book of Peace*, ed., trans., and with an intro. and commentary by Karen Green, Constant J. Mews, Janice Pinder, and Tania Van Hemelryck. Penn State Romance Studies (University Park, PA: The Pennsylvania State University Press, 2008).

Christoph, Siegfried, "The Language and Culture of Joy," *Words of Love and Love of Words in the Middle Ages and the Renaissance*, ed. Albrecht Classen. Medieval and Renaissance Texts and Studies, 347 (Tempe: Arizona Center for Medieval and Renaissance Studies, 2008), 319–33.

Chronicle of the Third Crusade, a Translation of Itinerarium Peregrinorum et Gesta Regis Ricardi, trans. Helen J. Nicholson. Crusade Texts in Translation, 3 (Aldershot: Ashgate, 1997).

Clark Walter, Katherine, *The Profession of Widowhood: Widows, Pastoral Care, and Medieval Models of Holiness* (Washington, DC: Catholic University of America Press, 2018).

Classen, Albrecht, "Aucassin et Nicolette," *Encyclopedia of Medieval Literature*, ed. Jay Ruud (New York: Facts on File, 2005), 44–46.

Classen, Albrecht, *Autobiographische Lyrik des europäischen Spätmittelalters. Studien zu Hugo von Montfort, Oswald von Wolkenstein, Antonio Pucci, Charles d'Orléans, Thomas Hoccleve, Michel Beheim, Hans Rosenplüt und Alfonso Alvarez de Villasandino*. Amsterdamer Publikationen zur Sprache und Literatur, 91 (Amsterdam and Atlanta, GA: Editions Rodopi, 1991).

Classen, Albrecht, "Boethius' 'De consolatione philosophiae'. Eine 'explication du texte'," *Jahrbuch für internationale Germanistik* XXXII.2 (2000): 44–61.

Classen, Albrecht, "Das Paradox der widersprüchlichen Urteilsprechung und Weltwahrnehmung: göttliches vs. menschliches Recht in Heinrich Kaufringers 'Die unschuldige Mörderin' – mit paneuropäischen Ausblicken und einer neuen Quellenspur ('La femme du roi de Portugal')," *Neuphilologische Mitteilungen* CXX.II (2019): 7–28.

Classen, Albrecht, "Dialectics and Courtly Love: Abelard and Heloise, Andreas Capellanus, and the *Carmina Burana*," *Journal of Medieval Latin* 23 (2013): 161–83.

Classen, Albrecht, "Die Fremden und das Fremde in der deutschen Literatur des Mittelalters: Xenologische Reflexionen: Vom *Hildebrandslied* bis zum *Fortunatus*," *Japanisch-deutsche Gespräche über Fremdheit im Mittelalter: Interkulturelle und interdisziplinäre Forschungen in Ost und West*, ed. Manshu Ide and Albrecht Classen. Stauffenburg Mediävistik, 2 (Tübingen: Stauffenburg, 2018), 141–56.

Classen, Albrecht, "Die Gefahren des Massenwahns aus literarhistorischer Sicht: Von Walther von der Vogelweide und Heinrich Wittenwiler zu Thomas Mann und Gustave Le Bon," *Im Clash der Identitäten: Nationalismen im literatur- und kulturgeschichtlichen Diskurs*, ed. Wolfgang Brylla and Cezary Lipiński. Andersheit – Fremdheit – Ungleichheit: Erfahrungen von Disparatheit in der deutschsprachigen Literatur, 1 (Göttingen: V&R unipress, 2020), 185–99.

Classen, Albrecht, "Die iberische Halbinsel im frühen Mittelalter: Ausgangspunkt für interkulturelle Kontakte zwischen den Ottonen und den andalusischen Muslimen.

Kulturhistorische Betrachtungen aus literarischer (Hrotsvit von Gandersheim) und chronikalischer Sicht (Johannes von Gorze," *arcadia* 53.2 (2018): 397–418.

Classen, Albrecht, "Die Welt eines spätmittelalterlichen Kaufmannsreisenden. Ein mentalitätsgeschichtliches Dokument der Frühneuzeit: *Fortunatus*," *Monatshefte* 86.1 (1994): 22–44.

Classen, Albrecht, "Eine einsame Stimme für den Frieden im Mittelalter: Der erstaunliche Fall von *Kudrun*," *Thalloris* 1 (2016): 69–90.

Classen, Albrecht, "Epistemology at the Courts: The Discussion of Love by Andreas Capellanus and Juan Ruiz," *Neuphilologische Mitteilungen* CIII.3 (2002): 341–62.

Classen, Albrecht, "Fremdbegegnung, Dialog, Austausch, und Staunen: Xenologische Phänomene in der deutschen Literatur des Mittelalters. Vom *Hildebrandslied* bis zum *Fortunatus*," *Mediaevistik* 26 (2013): 183–206.

Classen, Albrecht, "Friendship in the Heroic Epics: Rüedegêr in the *Nibelungenlied*," *Friendship in the Middle Ages*, ed. Albrecht Classen and Marilyn Sandidge. Fundamentals of Medieval and Early Modern Culture, 6 (Berlin and New York: Walter de Gruyter, 2010), 429–43.

Classen, Albrecht, Albrecht Classen, "Die Gefahren des Massenwahns aus literarhistorischer Sicht: Von Walther von der Vogelweide und Heinrich Wittenwiler zu Thomas Mann und Gustave Le Bon," *Im Clash der Identitäten: Nationalismen im literatur- und kulturgeschichtlichen Diskurs*, ed. Wolfgang Brylla and Cezary Lipiński. Andersheit – Fremdheit – Ungleichheit: Erfahrungen von Disparateit in der deutschsprachigen Literatur, 1 (Göttingen: V&R unipress, 2020), 185–99.

Classen, Albrecht, "Global Travel in the Late Middle Ages: The Eyewitness Account of Johann Schiltberger," *Medieval History Journal* 23.1 (2020): 1–28.

Classen, Albrecht, "Happiness in the Middle Ages? Hartmann von Aue and Marie de France," *Neohelicon* XXV.2 (1998): 247–74.

Classen, Albrecht, "Hunde als Freunde und Begleiter in der deutschen Literatur vom Mittelalter bis zur Gegenwart: Reaktion auf den 'Animal Turn' aus motivgeschichtlicher Sicht," *Etudes Germaniques* 73.4 (2018): 441–66.

Classen, Albrecht, "Life Writing as a Slave in Turkish Hands: Georgius of Hungary's Reflections About His Existence in the Turkish World," *Neohelicon* 39.1 (2012): 55–72.

Classen, Albrecht, "Love, Marriage, and Sexual Transgressions in Heinrich Kaufringer's Verse Narratives (ca. 1400)," *Discourses on Love, Marriage, and Transgression in Medieval and Early Modern Literature*, ed. Albrecht Classen. Medieval and Renaissance Texts and Studies, 278 (Tempe, AZ: Arizona Center for Medieval and Renaissance Studies, 2004 [appeared in 2005]), 289–312.

Classen, Albrecht, "Magic in the Middle Ages and the Early Modern Age – Literature, Science, Religion, Philosophy, Music, and Art: An Introduction," *Magic and Magicians in the Middle Ages and the Early Modern Time: The Occult in Pre-Modern Sciences, Medicine, Literature, Religion, and Astrology*, ed. Albrecht Classen. Fundamentals of Medieval and Early Modern Culture, 20 (Berlin and New York: Walter de Gruyter, 2017), 1–108.

Classen, Albrecht, "Medieval Transculturality in the Mediterranean from a Literary-Historical Perspective: The Case of Rudolf von Ems's *Der guote Gêrhart* (ca. 1220–ca. 1250)," *Journal of Transcultural Medieval Studies* 5.1 (2018): 133–60.

Classen, Albrecht, "Mord, Totschlag, Vergewaltigung, Unterdrückung und Sexualität. Liebe und Gewalt in der Welt von Heinrich Kaufringer," *Daphnis* 29.1–2 (2000): 3–36.

Classen, Albrecht, "Objects of Memory as Hermeneutic Media in Medieval German Literature: Hartmann von Aue's *Gregorius*, Wolfram von Eschenbach's Parzival, Thüring von Ringoltingen's *Melusine*, and *Fortunatus*," *Amsterdamer Beiträge zur älteren Germanistik* 65 (2009): 159–82.

Classen, Albrecht, "Oswald von Wolkenstein – a Fifteenth-Century Reader of Medieval Courtly Criticism," *Mediaevistik* 3 (1990): 27–53.

Classen, Albrecht, "Sarcasm in Medieval German Literature: From the *Hildebrandslied* to *Fortunatus*. The Dark Side of Human Behavior," *Words that Tear the Flesh: Essays on Sarcasm in Medieval and Early Modern Literature and Cultures*, ed. Alan Baragona and Elizabeth L. Rambo. Fundamentals of Medieval and Early Modern Culture, 21 (Berlin and Boston: Walter de Gruyter, 2018), 249–69.

Classen, Albrecht, "Sebastian Brant," *Literary Encyclopedia*, online (2021); https://www.li tencyc.com/php/speople.php?rec=true&UID=11830.

Classen, Albrecht, "The Agency of Wives in High Medieval German Courtly Romances and Late Medieval Verse Narratives: From Hartmann von Aue to Heinrich Kaufringer," *Quidditas* 39 (2018): 25–53, online at: https://humanities.byu.edu/rmmra/pdfs/39.pdf (last accessed on Jan. 15, 2021).

Classen, Albrecht, "The Amazon Rainforest of Pre-Modern Literature: Ethics, Values, and Ideals from the Past for our Future. With a Focus on Aristotle and Heinrich Kaufringer," *Humanities Open Access* 9(1).4 (2020), published on Dec. 24, 2019, online at: https://doi.org/10.3390/h9010004 (last accessed on Jan. 15, 2021).

Classen, Albrecht, "The Ambiguity of Charlemagne in Late Medieval German Literature: The De- and Reconstruction of a Mythical Figure," *Medievalia et Humanistica*, New Series, 45 (2019): 1–26.

Classen, Albrecht, "The Crusader as Lover and Tourist: Utopian Elements in Late Medieval German Literature: From *Herzog Ernst* to *Reinfried von Braunschweig* and *Fortunatus*," *Current Topics in Medieval German Literature: Texts and Analyses (Kalamazoo Papers 2000–2006)*, ed. Sibylle Jefferis. Göppinger Arbeiten zur Germanistik, 748 (Göppingen: Kümmerle, 2008), 83–102.

Classen, Albrecht, "The Encounter with the Foreign in Medieval and Early Modern German Literature: Fictionality as a Springboard for Non-Xenophobic Approaches in the Middle Ages: *Herzog Ernst*, Wolfram von Eschenbach, Konrad von Würzburg, *Die Heidin*, and *Fortunatus*," *East Meets West in the Middle Ages and Early Modern Times: Transcultural Experiences in the Premodern World*, ed. Albrecht Classen. Fundamentals of Medieval and Early Modern Culture, 14 (Berlin and Boston: Walter de Gruyter, 2013), 457–87.

Classen, Albrecht, "The Erotic and the Quest for Happiness in the Middle Ages. What Everybody Aspires to and Hardly Anyone Truly Achieves," *Eroticism in the Middle Ages and the Renaissance: Magic, Marriage, and Midwifery*, ed. Ian Moulton. Arizona Studies in the Middle Ages and the Renaissance, 39 (Tempe, AZ, and Turnhout, Belgium: Brepols, 2016), 1–33.

Classen, Albrecht, "The Experience of Exile in Medieval German Heroic Poetry," *Medieval German Textrelations: Translations, Editions, and Studies (Kalamazoo Paper 2010–2011)*, ed. by Sibylle Jefferis. Göppinger Arbeiten zur Germanistik, 765 (Göppingen: Kümmerle, 2012), 83–110.

Classen, Albrecht, "The People Rise Up against the Tyrants in the Courtly World: John of Salisbury's *Policraticus*, the *Fables* by Marie de France and the Anonymous *Mai und Beaflor*," *Neohelicon* 35.1 (2008): 17–29.

Classen, Albrecht, "The Topic of Imprisonment in Medieval German Literature: With an Emphasis on Johann Schiltberger's Account About his 30-Year Enslavement in the East," *Studia Neophilologica* (2020), online at: https://www.tandfonline.com/doi/full/10.1080/00393274.2020.1755362 (last accessed on Jan. 15, 2021).

Classen, Albrecht, "The World of the Turks Described by an Eye-Witness: Georgius de Hungaria's Dialectical Discourse about the Foreign World of the Ottoman Empire," *Journal of Early Modern History* 7.3–4 (2003): 257–79.

Classen, Albrecht, "Time, Space, and Travel in the Pre-Modern World: Theoretical and Historical Reflections. An Introduction," *Travel, Time, and Space in the Middle Ages and Early Modern Time: Explorations of Worldly Perceptions and Processes of Identity Formation*, ed. Albrecht Classen. Fundamentals of Medieval and Early Modern Culture, 22 (Berlin and Boston: Walter de Gruyter, 2018), 1–75.

Classen, Albrecht, "*Tractatus de moribus, condictionibus et nequicia Turcorum*," *Christian-Muslim Relations: A Bibiographical History*. Vol. VII: *Central and Eastern Europe, Asia, Africa and South America (1500–1600)*, ed. David Thomas and John Chesworth (Leiden and Boston: Brill, 2015), 36–40, online at: http://dx.doi.org/10.1163/2451–9537_cmrii_COM_24643 (last accessed on Jan. 15, 2021).

Classen, Albrecht, "Treason: Legal, Ethical, and Political Issues in the Middle Ages: With an Emphasis on Medieval Heroic Poetry," *Journal of Philosophy and Ethics* 1.4 (2019): 13–29; https://www.sryahwapublications.com/journal-of-philosophy-and-ethics/pdf/v1-i4/2.pdf.

Classen, Albrecht, "Widows: Their Social and Religious Functions According to Medieval German Literature, with Special Emphasis on Erhart Gross's *Witwenbuch* (1446)," *Fifteenth-Century Studies* 28 (2003): 65–79.

Classen, Albrecht, "Witwen in der Literatur des deutschen Mittelalters: Neue Perspektiven auf ein vernachlässigtes Thema," *Etudes Germaniques* 57.2 (2002): 197–232.

Classen, Albrecht, *Der Liebes- und Ehediskurs vom hohen Mittelalter bis zum frühen 17. Jahrhundert*. Volksliedstudien, 5 (Münster, New York, Munich, and Berlin: Waxmann, 2005), 32–72.

Classen, Albrecht, *Prostitution in Medieval and Early Modern Literature: The Dark Side of Sex and Love in the Premodern Era*. Studies in Medieval Literature (Lanham, MA, Boulder, CO, et al.: Lexington Books, 2019).

Classen, Albrecht, *Reading Medieval European Women Writers: Strong Literary Witnesses from the Past* (Frankfurt a. M.: Peter Lang, 2016).

Classen, Albrecht, *Religious Toleration in the Middle Ages and Early Modern Age: An Anthology of Literary, Theological, and Philosophical Texts* (Berlin: Peter Lang, 2020).

Classen, Albrecht, *Sexual Violence and Rape in the Middle Ages: A Critical Discourse in Premodern German and European Literature*. Fundamentals of Medieval and Early Modern Culture, 7 (Berlin and Boston: Walter de Gruyter, 2011).

Classen, Albrecht, *The German Volksbuch. A Critical History of a Late-Medieval Genre*. Studies in German Language and Literature, 15 (Lewiston, NY, Queenston, Ont., and Lampeter, Wales: Edwin Mellen Press, 1995, reissued 1999).

Classen, Albrecht, *Toleration and Tolerance in Medieval and Early Modern European Literature*. Routledge Studies in Medieval Literature and Culture, 8 (New York and London: Routledge, 2018).

Classen, Albrecht, *Verzweiflung und Hoffnung. Die Suche nach der kommunikativen Gemeinschaft in der deutschen Literatur des Mittelalters*. Beihefte zur Mediaevistik, 1 (Frankfurt a. M., Berlin, et al.: Peter Lang, 2002).

Classen, Albrecht, *Water in Medieval Literature: An Ecocritical Reading*. Ecocritical Theory and Practice (Lanham, MD, Boulder, CO, et al.: Lexington Books, 2018).

Claustre, J., "Debt, Hatred and Force: Beginnings of Debt Prisons at the End of the Middle Ages," *Revue Historique* 10 (2007): 797–821.

Clifford R. Backman, *The Worlds of Medieval Europe* (New York and Oxford: Oxford University Press, 2003).

Cohen, Jeffrey Jerome and Karl Steel, "Race, Travel, Time, Heritage," *Postmedieval: A Journal of Medieval Cultural Studies* 6.1 (2015): 98–110.

Cole, Teresa, *Henry V: The Life of the Warrior King & the Battle of Agincourt 1415* (Stroud, Gloucestershire: Amberley, 2015).

A Companion to Hrotsvit of Gandersheim: Contextual and Interpretive Approaches, ed. Phyllis R. Brown and Stephen L. Wailes (Leiden and Boston: Brill, 2012).

A Companion to Malory, ed. Elizabeth Archibald. Arthurian Studies, 37 (Cambridge: D. S. Brewer, 1996).

A Companion to the Premodern Apocalypse, ed. Michael A. Ryan. Brill's Companions to the Christian Tradition (Leiden and Boston: Brill, 2016).

The Concept of Freedom in Judaism, Christianity and Islam, ed. Georges Tamer and Ursula Männle. Key Concepts in Interreligious Discourses, 3 (Berlin and Boston: Walter de Gruyter, 2019).

Constable, Olivia Remie, "Muslim Spain and Mediterranean Slavery: The Medieval Slave Trade as an Aspect of Muslim-Christian Relations," *Christendom and Its Discontents: Exclusion, Persecution, and Rebellion, 1000–1500*, ed. Scott L. Waugh, and Peter D. Diehl (Cambridge: Cambridge University Press, 1996), 264–84.

Cooper, Stephen, *Agincourt: Myth and Reality 1415–2015* (Barnsley, South Yorkshire: Pen & Sword/Praetorian Press, 2014).

Costa, Iacopo, "The Will of the Emperor and Freedom in the Empire," *Dante as Political Theorist: Reading Monarchia*, ed. Maria Luisa Ardizzone (Newcastle upon Tyne: Cambridge Scholars Publishing, 2018), 98–112.

Crabb, Ann, *The Strozzi of Florence: Widowhood and Family Solidarity in the Renaissance* (Ann Arbor, MI: University of Michigan Press, 2000).

Çrakman, Aslı, *From the "Terror of the World" to the "Sick Man of Europe": European Images of Ottoman Empire and Society from the Sixteenth Century to the Nineteenth*. Studies in Modern European History, 43. (2002; New York, Washington, DC, Baltimore, et al.: Peter Lang, 2005).

Crime and Punishment in the Middle Ages and Early Modern Age: Mental-Historical Investigations of Basic Human Problems and Social Responses, ed. Albrecht Classen and Connie Scarborough. Fundamentals of Medieval and Early Modern Culture, 11 (Berlin and Boston: Walter de Gruyter, 2012).

Criticising the Ruler in Pre-Modern Societies – Possibilities, Chances, and Methods, ed. Karina Kellermann, Alheydis Plassmann, and Christian Schwermann. Macht und Herrschaft, 6 (Göttingen: Bonn University Press/V&R unipress, 2019).

Crowley, Roger, *Der Fall von Akkon: Der letzte Kampf um das Heilige Land*, trans. from the English by Norbert Juraschitz (2019; Darmstadt: Theiss, 2019).

The Crusade of Frederick Barbarossa: The History of the Expedition of the Emperor Frederick and Related Texts. Crusade Texts in Translation, 19 (London: Taylor and Francis, 2016).

Culture Wars: An Encyclopedia of Issues, Viewpoints, and Voices, ed. Roger Chapman (Armonk, NY, and London: M.E. Sharpe, 2010).

Curry, Anne, *Agincourt*. Great Battles (Oxford: Oxford University Press, 2015).

Curry, Anne, *The Battle of Agincourt: Sources and Interpretations*. Warfare in History (2001; Woodbridge: Boydell, 2009).

d'Avray, David, *Medieval Marriage: Symbolism and Society*. D. L. d'Avray (Oxford: Oxford University Press, 2005).

d'Orbigny, Robert, *Le conte de Floire et Blanchefleur: nouvelle édition critique du texte du manuscrit A (Paris, BNF, fr.375)*. Publié, traduit, présenté et annoté par Jean-Luc Leclanche. Champion Classiques. Série "Moyen Âge", 2 (Paris: Champion Classiques, 2003).

Dagenais, John and Margaret R. Greer in their introductory article to a guest-edited volume, "Decolonizing the Middle Ages: Introduction," *Journal of Medieval and Early Modern Studies* 30.3 (Fall 2000): 431–48.

Dante Alighieri, *Monarchia*, ed. Prue Shaw. Le opere di Dante Alighieri, 5 (Florence: Casa Ed. Le lettere, 2009).

Dante Alighieri, *Nuova edizione commentata delle opere di Dante*, vol. 4: *Monarchia*, ed. Paolo Chiesa e Andrea Tabarroni together with Diego Ellero (Rome: Salerno Editrice, 2013).

Dante Alighieri, *Opere minori: Rime. Vita nuova. Convivio. De vulgari eloquentia. De monarchia. Epistole. Ecloge. Questio de aqua et terra. Con il rimario*, ed. Alberto Del Monte. I classici Rizzoli (Milan: Rizzoli, 1960).

Dante Alighieri, *Purgatorio*, trans. Jean Hollander and Robert Hollander (New York: Anchor Books, 2003).

Dante Alighieri, *The De Monarchia of Dante Alighieri*, ed., with trans. and notes by Aurelia Henry (Boston and New York: Houghton, Mifflin, and Co., 1904).

Dante Alighieri, *The Divine Comedy*. Vol. I: *Inferno*, trans. with an intro., notes, and commentary by Mark Musa (London: Penguin, 1971).

Dante Worlds: Echoes, Places, Questions, ed. Peter Caravetta. Circolarità mediterranee, 2 (Rome and Bristol, CT: "L'Erma" di Bretschneider, 2019).

Davies, Brian L., *Warfare, State and Society on the Black Sea Steppe*. Warfare and History (London and New York: Routledge, 2007).

Davis, Robert C., *Christian Slaves, Muslim Masters: White Slavery in the Mediterranean, the Barbary Coast, and Italy, 1500–1800* (New York: Palgrave Macmillan, 2003).

De Lucia, Lori "The Space between Borno and Palermo: Slavery and Its Boundaries in the Late Medieval Saharan-Mediterranean Region," *Rethinking Medieval Margins and Marginality*, ed. Zimo, Anne E., Tiffany D. Vann Sprecher, Kathryn Reyerson, and Debra Blumenthal. Studies in Medieval History and Culture (London and New York: Routledge, 2020), 11–25.

De Wolf, Philippe, "La critique de l'amour courtois dans la littérature médiévale: Le 'De amore' d'André le Chapelain et 'Aucassin et Nicolette' (fin du XIIe-début du XIIIe siècle)," Ph.D. Université libre de Bruxelles, 2010.

Demandt, Alexander, *Magistra Vitae: Essays zum Lehrgehalt der Geschichte*. Historica Minora, 4 (Vienna, Cologne, and Weimar: Böhlau, 2020).

Demontis, Luca, *Enrico di Castiglia senatore di Roma (1267–1268): diplomazia, guerra e propaganda tra il comune di "popolo" e la corte papale*. Medioevo, 28 (Rome: Antonianum, 2017)

DeNardis, Laura, *The Internet in Everything: Freedom and Security in a World With No Off Switch* (New Haven, CT: Yale University Press, 2020).

Denter, Tom, "Freiheit," *Lexikon der Geisteswissenschaften: Sachbegriffe – Disziplinen – Personen* (Vienna, Cologne, and Weimar: Böhlau, 2011), 207–19.

Deutsche Versnovellistik des 13. bis 15. Jahrhunderts (DVN), ed. Klaus Ridder and Hans-Joachim Ziegeler, together with Patrizia Barton, Reinhard Berron et al. 6 Vols. Vol. 5: German Verse-Couplet Tales from the Thirteenth to the Fifteenth Century, English trans. by Sebastian Coxon (Berlin: Schwabe Verlag, 2020).

Di-Crescenzo, Lisa and Sally Fisher, "Exile and Imprisonment in Medieval and Early Modern Europe," *Parergon* 34.2 (2017): 1–23.

Dietrichs Flucht, ed. Elisabeth Lienert and Gertrud Beck. Texte und Studien zur mittelhochdeutschen Heldenepik, 1 (Tübingen: Max Niemeyer, 2003).

Digitalisierung und Demokratie: Ethische Perspektiven, ed. Petra Grimm and Oliver Zöllner. Medienethik, 18 (Stuttgart: Franz Steiner Verlag, 2020).

Dinzelbacher, Peter, *Das fremde Mittelalter: Gottesurteil und Tierprozess*. 2nd, extensively expanded ed. (2006; Darmstadt: Wissenschaftliche Buchgesellschaft, 2020).

Dinzelbacher, Peter, *Himmel, Hölle, Heilige: Visionen und Kunst im Mittelalter* (Darmstadt: Primus Verlag, 2002).

Dinzelbacher, Peter, *Lebenswelten des Mittelalters 1000–1500*. Bachmanns Basiswissen, 1 (Badenweiler: Wissenschaftlicher Verlag Bachmann, 2010).

Dopsch, Heinz, *Die Länder und das Reich: der Ostalpenraum im Hochmittelalter*. Österreichs Geschichte 1122–1278 (Vienna: Ueberreuter, 1999).

Drachenblut & Heldenmut, ed. Stefanie Knöll (Regensburg: Steiner + Schnell, 2019).

Drayton, Michael, *The Battle of Agincourt* (Menston, Yorkshire: Scolar Press, 1972).

Driessen, Christoph, *Geschichte der Niederlande: von der Seemacht zum Trendland*. 2nd. expanded ed. (2009; Regensburg: Verlag Friedrich Pustet, 2016).

Duchhardt, Heinz and Horst Lademacher, "Das Heilige Römische Reich und die Republik der Vereinigten Niederlande: Ausgangslage einer Beziehung bis 1648," *Kaufleute und Fürsten: Außenpolitik und politisch-kulturelle Perzeption im Spiegel niederländischdeutscher Beziehungen 1648–1748*, ed. Helmut Gabel and Volker. Niederlande-Studien, 18 (Münster, Munich, et al.: LIT, 1998), 11–38.

Dunbabin, Jean, *Captivity and Imprisonment in Medieval Europe, 1000–1300*. Medieval Culture and Society (Houndmills, Basingstoke, Hampshire; New York: Palgrave Macmillan, 2002).

Dybaś, Bogusłse, "Probleme der Mehrsprachigkeit bei Martin Gruneweg," *Mehrsprachigkeit in Ostmitteleuropa (1400–1700): Kommunikative Praktiken und Verfahren in gemischtsprachigen Städten und Verbänden*, ed. Hans-Jürgen Bömelburg and Norbert

Kersken. Tagungen zur Ostmitteleuropaforschung, 37 (Marburg: Verlag Herder-Institut, 2020), 207–19.

Dybel, Katarzyna, *Etre heureux au Moyen Age: d'apres le roman arthurien en prose du XIIIe siècle*. Synthema, 2 (Louvain, Paris, and Dudley, MA: Peeters, 2004).

Eala frya Fresena: die friesische Freiheit im Mittelalter, Ostfriesische Landschaft, ed. Monika van Lengen. Preparation of the ms. by Uda von der Nahmer and Nicolaus Hippen (Aurich: Ostfriesische Landschaftliche Verlags- und Vertriebsgesellschaft, 2003).

Eisner, Martin, "The Tale of Ferondo's Purgatory (III.8)," *The Decameron Third Day in Perspective*, ed. Francesco Ciabattoni and Pier Massimo Forni (Toronto: University of Toronto Press, 2014), 150–69.

El Hamel, Chouki, *Black Morocco: A History of Slavery, Race, and Islam*. African Studies (Cambridge: Cambridge University Press, 2013).

The Elder Edda: A Book of Viking Lore, trans. with intro. and notes by Andy Orchard (London: Penguin, 2011).

Elior, Rachel, *Jewish Mysticism: The Infinite Expression of Freedom*, trans. Yudith Nave and Arthur B. Millman. The Littman Library of Jewish Civilization (Oxford and Portland, OR: Littman Library of Jewish Civilization, 2007).

Elliot, Elizabeth, "The Counsele of Philosophy: The *Kingis Quair* and the Medieval Reception History of the *Consolation of Philosophy* in Vernacular Literature," Ph.D. diss., University of Edinburgh, 2006.

Endorfer: *Die Korrespondenz der Augsburger Patrizierfamilie Endorfer, 1621–1627: Briefe aus Italien und Frankreich im Zeitalter des Dreißigjährigen Krieges*, ed. Mark Häberlein, Hans-Jörg Künast, and Irmgard Schwanke. Documenta Augustana, 21 (Augsburg: Wißner, 2011).

Epstein, Steven A., *Speaking of Slavery: Color, Ethnicity and Human Bondage in Italy*. Conjunctions of Religion & Power in the Medieval Past (Ithaca, NY, and London: Cornell University Press, 2001).

Erotic Tales of Medieval Germany. Selected and trans. by Albrecht Classen. Medieval and Renaissance Texts and Studies, 328. Rev. and expanded sec. ed. (2007; Tempe: Arizona Center for Medieval and Renaissance Studies, 2009).

Ertzdorff, Xenja von, *Rudolf von Ems: Untersuchungen zum höfischen Roman im 13. Jahrhundert* (Munich: Fink, 1967).

Ethics, Politics and Justice in Dante, ed. Giulia Gaimari (London: UCL Press, 2019).

Eurasian Slavery, Ransom and Abolition in World History, 1200–1860, ed. Christoph Witzenrath (Farnham, Surrey, and Burlington, VT: Ashgate, 2015).

Europa und die Türken in der Renaissance, ed. Bodo Guthmüller and Wilhelm Kühlmann. Frühe Neuzeit, 54 (Tübingen: Niemeyer, 2000).

Europäische Mentalitätsgeschichte: Hauptthemen in Einzeldarstellungen, ed. Peter Dinzelbacher. 2nd rev. and expanded ed. Kröner's Taschenausgabe, 469 (1993; Stuttgart: Alfred Kröner Verlag, 2008).

Exil, Fremdheit und Ausgrenzung in Mittelalter und früher Neuzeit, ed. Andreas Bihrer, Sven Limbeck and Paul G. Schmidt. Identitäten und Alteritäten, 4 (Würzburg: Ergon Verlag, 2000).

Exile in the Middle Ages: Selected Proceedings from the International Medieval Congress, University of Leeds, 8–11 July 2002, ed. Laura Napran and E. van Houts. International Medieval Research, 13 (Turnhout: Brepols, 2004).

Fabbri, Lorenzo, "Da Firenze a Ferrara: Gli Strozzi tra Casa d'Este e antichi legami di sangue", *Alla corte degli Estensi: Filosofa, arte e cultura a Ferrara nei secoli XV e XVI. Atti del Convegno internazionale di studi, 5–7 marzo 1992*, ed. Marco Bertozzi (Ferrara: Università di Ferrara, 1994), 91–108.

Fabbri, Lorenzo, "The Memory of Exiled Families: The Case of the Strozzi," *Art, Memory and Family in Renaissance Florence*, ed. Giovanni Ciappelli and Patricia Lee Rubin (Cambridge: Cambridge University Press, 2000), 253–61.

The Fabliaux: A New Verse Translation, trans. Nathaniel E. Dubin. Intro. R. Howard Bloch (New York and London: W. W. Norton, 2013).

Fahlbusch, F. B., "Freie Städte," *Lexikon des Mittelalters*, Vol. IV (Munich and Zürich: Artemis, 1989), 895–96.

Faidutti, Bernard, *Copernic, Kepler et Galilée face aux pouvoirs: les scientifiques et la politique*. Acteurs de la science, 363 (Paris: L'Harmattan, 2010).

Fajardo-Acosta, Fidel, *Courtly Seductions, Modern Subjections: Troubadour Literature and the Medieval Construction of the Modern World*. Medieval and Renaissance Texts and Studies, 376 (Tempe, AZ: Arizona Center for Medieval and Renaissance Studies, 2010).

Fanon, Frantz, *Peau noire, masques blancs*. Collection points, 26 (Paris: Éd. du Seuil, 1975).

Die faröischen Lieder der Nibelungensage. Vol. 1: *Regin Smiður/Regin der Schmied*, ed. Klaus Fuss. Göppinger Arbeiten zur Germanistik, 427 (Göppingen: Kümmerle, 1985).

Fehling, Detlev, "Die Eingesperrte (Inclusa) und der verkleidete Jüngling (Iuvenis femina). Neues zur Traditionsgeschichte zweier antiker Komödienmotive nebst einem Beitrag zur Geschichte des ›Sindbad‹-Zyklus, " *Mittellateinisches Jahrbuch* 21 (1986): 186–207.

Fein, David A., *Charles d'Orléans*. Twayne's World Authors Series, 699 (Boston: Twayne, 1983).

Ferme, Valerio C., "Torello and the Saladin (X, 9): Notes on Panfilo, Day X, and the Ending Tale of the Decameron," *Medievalia et Humanistica: Studies in Medieval and Renaissance Culture* 35 (2009), 33–55.

Ferme, Valerio, *Women, Enjoyment, and the Defense of Virtue in Boccaccio's* Decameron. The New Middle Ages (New York: Palgrave Macmillan, 2015).

Fernández-Armesto, Felipe, *Before Columbus: Exploration and Colonisation from the Mediterranean to the Atlantic 1229–1492*. New Studies in Medieval History (Basingstoke: Macmillan, 1987).

Field, P. J. C., *The Life and Times of Sir Thomas Malory*. Arthurian Studies, 29 (Cambridge: D. S. Brewer, 1993).

Fierro, Maribel, *'Abd al-Rahman III: The First Cordoban Caliph* (Oxford: Oneworld, 2005).

Findon, Joanne, "Supernatural Lovers, Liminal Women, and the Female Journey," *Florilegium* 30 (2013): 27–52.

Finlayson, John, "The 'Knight's Tale': The Dialogue of Romance, Epic, and Philosophy," *The Chaucer Review* 27.2 (1992): 126–49.

Fischer, Hanns, *Die deutsche Märendichtung des 15. Jahrhunderts*. Münchener Texte und Untersuchungen zur deutschen Literatur des Mittelalters, 12 (Munich: C. H. Beck, 1966).

Fischer, Hanns, *Studien zur deutschen Märendichtung*. 2nd ed. by Johannes Janota (Tübingen: Max Niemeyer, 1983).

Fischer, Robert-Tarek, *Richard I. Löwenherz: Ikone des Mittelalters*. 2nd rev. ed. (2006; Vienna: Böhlau, 2019).

Fitzmaurice-Kelly, James, *The Life of Miguel de Cervantes Saavedra*. Rpt. (1892; Norderstedt: Hansebooks GmbH, 2017).

Flatt, Tyler, "The Book of Friends: Hagen and Heroic Traditions in the 'Waltharius'," *Journal of English and Germanic Philology* 1154 (2016): 463–85.

Fleck, Konrad, see Christine Putzo

Flierman, Robert, *Saxon Identities, AD 150–900* (London: Bloomsbury, 2017).

Flori, Jean, *Richard Coeur de Lion: le roi-chevalier*. Biographie Payot (Paris: Payot & Rivages, 1999).

Fludernik, Monika, *Metaphors of Confinement: The Prison in Fact, Fiction, and Fantasy* (Oxford: Oxford University Press, 2019).

Foehr-Janssens, Yasmina, *Le temps des fables: Le Roman des sept sages ou l'autre voie du roman*. Nouvelle bibliothèque du moyen âge, 27 (Paris: Champion, 1994).

Foerster, Anne, *Die Witwe des Königs: zu Vorstellung, Anspruch und Performanz im englischen und deutschen Hochmittelalter*. Mittelalter-Forschungen, 57 (Ostfildern: Jan Thorbecke Verlag, 2018).

Forms of Servitude in Northern and Central Europe: Decline, Resistance, and Expansion, ed. Paul H. Freedman. Medieval Texts and Cultures of Northern Europe, 9 (Turnhout: Brepols, 2005).

Foster Baxendale, Susannah, "Exile in Practice: The Alberti Family in and out of Florence, 1401–1428," *Renaissance Quarterly* 44.4 (1991): 720–56.

Fougère, Eric, *La peine en littérature et la prison dans son histoire: solitude et servitude*. Espaces littéraires (Paris: Ed. L'Harmattan, 2001).

Frankfurt, Harry G., "Alternate Possibilities and Moral Responsibility," *Journal of Philosophy* 66.23 (1969): 829–39.

Franklin, H. Bruce, *The Victim as Criminal and Artist: Literature from the American Prison* (New York: Oxford University Press, 1978).

Frantz Fanon's 'Black Skin, White Masks': New Interdisciplinary Essays, ed. Maxim Silverman (Baltimore, MD: Project Muse, 2018).

Freed, John B., *Frederick Barbarossa: The Prince and The Myth* (New Haven, CT, and London: Yale University Press, 2016).

Freedom and Authority: Scotland c.1050 – c.1650; Historical and Historiographical Essays presented to Grant G. Simpson, ed. Terry Brotherstone (East Linton, Scotland: Tuckwell, 2000).

Freedom as a Key Category in Origen and in Modern Philosophy and Theology, ed. Alfons Fürst. Adamantiana, 14 (Münster i. W.: Aschendorff, 2019).

Freedom: A Philosophical Anthology, ed. Ian Carter, Matthew H. Kramer, and Hillel Steiner (Malden, MA: Blackwell Publishing, 2007).

Freiheit im Mittelalter am Beispiel der Stadt, ed. Dagmar Klose and Marco Ladewig. Perspektiven historischen Denkens und Lernens, 4 (Potsdam: Universitäts-Verlag, 2009).

Freiheit und Gerechtigkeit als Herausforderung der Humanwissenschaften = Freedom and Justice as a Challenge of the Humanities, ed. Mira Miladinović and Dean Komel (Bern, Berlin, and Vienna: Peter Lang, 2018).

Freiheit und Unfreiheit: mittelalterliche und frühneuzeitliche Facetten eines zeitlosen Problems, ed. Kurt Andermann and Gabriel Zeilinger.Kraichtaler Kolloquium: Kraichtaler Kolloquien, 7 (Epfendorf: Bibliotheca-Academica-Verlag, 2010).

Freund, Stephan, "fride unde reht sint sere wunt: Eike von Repgow, das Reich und Europa in der ersten Hälfte des 13. Jahrhunderts, *Sachsen und Anhalt: Jahrbuch der Landesgeschichtlichen Forschungsstelle für die Provinz Sachsen und für Anhalt-Weimar* 26 (2014): 121–41.

Fried, Johannes, ed., see *Die abendländische Freiheit vom 10. zum 14. Jahrhundert.*

Friedrich, Udo, *Menschentier und Tiermensch: Diskurse der Grenzziehung und Grenzüberschreitung im Mittelalter* (Göttingen: Vandenhoeck & Ruprecht, 2009).

Friedrichs Freyherrn von der Trenck Kaiserl. Königl. Obristwachtmeisters Samlung vermischter Gedichte, welche in seinem zehnjährigen Gefängnis in Magdeburg geschrieben wurden (Frankfurt a. M. and Leipzig: n.p., 1767).

Fynn-Paul, Jeffrey, "Empire, Monotheism and Slavery in the Greater Mediterranean Region from Antiquity to the Modern Era," *Past and Present* 205 (November 2009): 3–40.

Ganz, Margery, "Paying the Price for Political Failure: Florentine Women in the Aftermath of 1466," *Rinascimento* 34 (1994): 237–57.

Garcés, Maria Antonia, *Cervantes in Algiers: A Captive's Tale* (Nashville, TN: Vanderbilt University Press, 2002).

Gardiner, Eileen, "Hell, Purgatory, and Heaven," *Handbook of Medieval Culture: Fundamental Aspects and Conditions of the European Middle Ages*, ed. Albrecht Classen. Vol. 1 (Berlin and Boston: Walter de Gruyter, 2015), 653–73.

Garfagnini, Gian Carlo, "'Monarchia': Manifesto di libertà e responsabilità civile," *Studi Danteschi* 75 (2010): 13–23.

Geltner, Guy, Coping in Medieval Prisons," *Continuity and Change* 23.1 (2008): 151–72

Geltner, Guy, *The Medieval Prison: A Social History* (Princeton, NJ: Princeton University Press, 2008).

Guy Geltner, "Medieval Prisons: Between Myth and Reality, Hell and Purgatory," *History Compass* 4 (2006), https://doi.org/10.1111/j.1478-0542.2006.00319.x

Georgius de Hungarica: *Chronica unnd Beschreibung der Türckey. Mit eyner Vorrhed D. Martini Lutheri. Unveränderter Nachdruck der Ausgabe Nürnberg 1530 sowie fünf weiterer "Türkendrucke" des 15. und 16. Jahrhunderts.* Mit einer Einführung von Carl Göllner. Schriften zur Landeskunde Siebenbürgens, 6 (Cologne and Vienna: Böhlau, 1983).

Georgius de Hungarica, *Tractatus de Moribus, Condictionibus et Nequicia Turcorum. Traktat über die Sitten, die Lebensverhältnisse und die Arglist der Türken.* Nach der Erstausgabe von 1481 herausgegeben, übersetzt und eingeleitet von Reinhard Klockow. Schriften zur Landeskunde Siebenbürgens, 15 (Cologne, Weimar, and Vienna: Böhlau, 1994).

Gephart, Irmgard, *Der Zorn der Nibelungen: Rivalität und Rache im "Nibelungenlied"* (Cologne, Weimar, and Vienna: Böhlau, 2005).

Gerdes, Udo, "'Sieben weise Meister' (Zyklische Rahmenerzählung orientalischer Herkunft)," *Die deutsche Literatur des Mittelalters: Verfasserlexikon*, ed Burghart Wachinger et al. 2nd completely rev. ed. Vol. 8 (Berlin and New York: Walter de Gruyter, 1992), col. 1174–89.

Ghidoni, Andrea, "Narrazioni eroopoietiche mediolatine: 'punteggiature' nell'evoluzione delle letterature profano-volgari," *Mittellateinisches Jahrbuch* 53.3 (2018): 399–422.

Gibbons, Katy, *English Catholic Exiles in Late Sixteenth-Century Paris* (Rochester, NY: Boydell, 2011).

Giese, Simone, "Johannes Messenius, ein schwedischer Gelehrter im Konflikt mit überkommenen Traditionen," *Frühneuzeitliche Universitätskulturen: Kulturhistorische Perspektiven auf die Hochschulen in Europa*, ed. Barbara Krug-Richter and Ruth E. Mohrmann. Beihefte zum Archiv für Kulturgeschichte (Cologne: Böhlau, 2009), 223–44.

Gillingham, John, *Die Gefangenschaft des englischen Königs Richard I. als Wendepunkt in der mittelalterlichen deutschen Geschichte*, trans. from the English by Helmut Schlieger. Schriftenreihe zur Geschichte und Baukunst des Trifels, 4 (Annweiler: Freundeskreis für mittelalterliche Geschichte und höfische Kultur auf Burg Trifels e.V., 2018).

Glück: The New World Book of Happiness, mit den neuesten Erkenntnissen aus der Glücksforschung, ed. Leo Bormans and Sofia Blind (Cologne: DuMont, 2017).

Goheen, Jutta, *Mensch und Moral im Mittelalter: Geschichte und Fiktion in Hugo von Trimbergs 'Der Renner'* (Darmstadt: Wissenschaftliche Buchgesellschaft, 1990).

Goldberg, Eric, "Popular Revolt, Dynastic Politics, and Aristocratic Factionalism in the Early Middle Ages: The Saxon Stellinga Reconsidered," *Speculum* 70 (1995): 467–501.

Göllner, Carl, *Tvrcica: Die europäischen Türkendrucke des XVI. Jahrhunderts*. 2 vols. (Bucharest: Editura Academiei; Berlin: Akademie-Verlag, 1961).

Gomez, Michael A., *African Dominion: A New History of Empire in Early and Medieval West Africa* (Princeton, NJ, and London: Princeton University Press, 2018).

Goodrich, Norma Lorre, *Charles, Duke of Orleans: A Literary Biography* (New York: Macmillan, 1963).

Goodwin, Godfrey, *The Janissaries* (London: Saqi Books, 1994).

Görich, Knut, "Verletzte Ehre: König Richard Löwenherz als Gefangener Kaiser Heinrichs VI.," *Historisches Jahrbuch* 123 (2003): 65–91.

Gotsch, Kara and Vinay Basti, "Capitalizing on Mass Incarceration: U.S. Growth in Private Prisons," Aug. 2, 2018, online at: https://www.sentencingproject.org/wp-content/uploads/2018/07/Capitalizing-on-Mass-Incarceration.pdf (last accessed on Jan. 15, 2021).

Grabois, Aryeh, *The Illustrated Encyclopedia of Medieval Civilization* (London: Octopus Books; Jerusalem: The Jerusalem Publishing House, 1980).

Graf, Tobias, *The Sultan's Renegades: Christian-European Converts to Islam and the Making of the Ottoman Elite, 1575–1610* (Oxford: Oxford University Press, 2017).

Grand, Roger, "La prison et la notion d'emprisonnement dans l'ancien droit," *Revue historique de droit français et étranger*, 4th ser., 19–20/1–2 (1940–1941): 58–87.

The Great Prisoners: The First Anthology of Literature Written in Prison, selected and ed. Isidore Abramowitz (New York: Dutton, 1946).

Gregory, Heather, "The Return of the Native: Filippo Strozzi and Medicean Politics," *Renaissance Quarterly* 38.1 (1985): 1–21.

Grell, Ole Peter, *Calvinist Exiles in Tudor and Stuart England* (London: Routledge, 1996).

Grettir's Saga, trans. Denton Fox and Hermann Palsson (1977; Toronto, Buffalo, and London: University of Toronto Press, 2002).

Grettir's Saga, trans. G. A. Hight (s.l: s.p., 1914); online at: https://www.sagadb.org/grettis_saga.en2 (last accessed on Jan 15, 2021).

Grévin, Benoît, *Rhétorique du pouvoir médiéval: les lettres de Pierre de la Vigne et la formation du langage politique européen, XIIIe–XVe siècle*. Bibliothèque des écoles françaises d'Athènes et de Rome, 339 (Rome: École française de Rome, 2008).

Grieser, Heike, *Sklaverei im spätantiken und frühmittelalterlichen Gallien: (5.–7. Jh.): das Zeugnis der christlichen Quellen*. Forschungen zur antiken Sklaverei, 28 (Stuttgart: Steiner, 1997).

Grieve, Patricia E., *Floire and Blancheflor and the European Romance*. Cambridge Studies in Medieval Literature, 32 (Cambridge: Cambridge University Press, 1997).

Grillmeier, A., "Höllenabstieg Christi, Höllenfahrt Christi," *Lexikon für Theologie und Kirche*. 2nd completely rev. ed. by Josef Höfer and Karl Rahner. Vol. 5 (Freiburg i. Br.: Herder, 1960), cols. 450–55.

Grimm, Dieter, *Sovereignty: The Origin and Future of a Political and Legal Concept*. Columbia Studies in Political Thought / Political History (New York: Columbia University Press, 2015).

Gross, J., "Trinitarier, -innen," *Lexikon des Mittelalters*. Vol. VIII (Munich: Lexma Verlag, 1997), 1009–11.

Gruber, Joachim, *Boethius: eine Einführung*. Standorte in Antike und Christentum, 2 (Stuttgart: Anton Hiersemann, 2011).

Gruber, Joachim, *Kommentar zu Boethius De Consolatione Philosophiae*. Texte und Kommentare – eine altertumswissenschaftliche Reihe, 9 (Berlin and New York: Walter de Gruyter, 1978).

Grubmüller, Klaus, "Boner," *Die deutsche Literatur des Mittelalters: Verfasserlexikon*, 2nd, completely revised ed. by Kurt Ruh et al. Vol. I (Berlin and New York: Walter de Gruyter, 1978), cols. 947–52.

Grubmüller, Klaus, *Die Ordnung, der Witz und das Chaos: Eine Geschichte der europäischen Novellistik im Mittelalter: Fabliau – Märe – Novelle* (Tübingen: Max Niemeyer, 2006).

Grubmüller, Klaus, *Meister Esopus: Untersuchungen zu Geschichte und Funktion der Fabel im Mittelalter*. Münchener Texte und Untersuchungen zur deutschen Literatur des Mittelalters, 56 (Zürich and Munich: Artemis, 1977).

Gruneweg, Martin: *Die Aufzeichnungen des Dominikaners Martin Gruneweg (1562 – ca. 1618) über seine Familie in Danzig, seine Handelsreisen in Osteuropa und sein Klosterleben in Polen*, ed. Almut Bues. 4 vols. Quellen und Studien / Deutsches Historisches Institut Warschau, 19.1–4 (Wiesbaden: Harrassowitz, 2008).

Guillaume et Willehalm: les épopées françaises et l'oeuvre de Wolfram von Eschenbach: actes du colloque de 12 et 13 janvier 1985, ed. Danielle Buschinger. Göppinger Arbeiten zur Germanistik, 421 (Göppingen: Kümmerle, 1985).

Habermas, Jürgen, *Auch eine Geschichte der Philosophie*. Vol. 1: *Die okzidentale Konstellation von Glauben und Wissen*. Vol. 2: *Vernünftige Freiheit. Spuren des Diskurses über Glauben und Wissen* (Frankfurt a. M.: Suhrkamp, 2019).

Hamilton Baker, John, *The Reinvention of Magna Carta 1216–1616* (Cambridge: Cambridge University Press, 2017).

Hammacher, Klaus, *Die Frage nach der Freiheit* (Baden-Baden: Nomos, 2015).

Hammer, Carl I., *A Large-Scale Slave Society of the Early Middle Ages: Slaves and Their Families in Early Medieval Bavaria* (Aldershot: Ashgate, 2002).

Hammer, Michael M., *Gemeine Dirnen und gute Fräulein: Frauenhäuser im spätmittelalterlichen Österreich*. Beihefte zur Mediaevistik, 25 (Berlin: Peter Lang, 2019).

Handbook of Medieval Culture: Fundamental Aspects and Conditions of the European Middle Ages, ed. Albrecht Classen. 3 vols. (Berlin and Boston: Walter de Gruyter, 2015).

Handbook on Prisons, ed. Yvonne Jewkes, Ben Crewe, and Jamie Bennett. Sec. ed. (London and New York: Routledge, 2016).

Händl, Claudia, "Il 'Waltharius' – un poema eroico germanico in lengua latina?," *Il ruolo delle lingue e delle letterature germaniche nella formazione dell'Europa medievale*, ed. Dagmar Gottschall (Lecce: Milella, 2018), 119--1.

Hangman's A Diary: The Journal of Master Franz Schmidt, Public Executioner of Nuremberg, 1573–1617, ed., with an introduction, by Albrecht Keller and translated by C. Calvert and A.W. Gruner, with an introductory essay by C. Calvert (1928; New York: Skyhorse Publishing, 2015).

Harding, Alan, "Political Liberty in the Middle Ages," *Speculum* 55.3 (1980): 423–43.

Hardyment, Christina, *Malory: The Life and Times of King Arthur's Chronicler* (London: HarperCollins, 2005).

Harootunian, Harry D., *The Unspoken as Heritage: The Armenian Genocide and Its Unaccounted Lives* (Durham, NC, and London: Duke University Press, 2019).

Harper, Kyle, *Slavery in the Late Roman Wworld, AD 275–425* (Cambridge: Cambridge University Press, 2011).

Harrison, Dick, *Sveriges historia medeltiden* (Stockholm: Liber, 2002).

Hartmann von Aue, *Iwein*. 4., überarbeitete Auflage. Text der siebenten Ausgabe von G. F. Benecke, K. Lachmann und L. Wolff. Übersetzt und Nachwort von Thomas Cramer (Berlin and New York: Walter de Gruyter, 2001).

Hartmann von Aue, *The Complete Works of Hartmann von Aue*, trans. with commentary by Frank Tobin, Kim Vivian, and Richard H. Lawson. Arthurian Romances, Tales, and Lyric Poetry (University Park, PA: The Pennsylvania State University Press, 2001).

Hartmann, Heiko, *Einführung in das Werk Wolframs von Eschenbach*. Einführung Germanistik (Darmstadt: Wissenschaftliche Buchgesellschaft, 2015).

Hartmann, Sieglinde, *Altersdichtung und Selbstdarstellung bei Oswald von Wolkenstein*. Göppinger Arbeiten zur Germanistik, 288 (Göppingen: Kümmerle, 1980),

Heebøll-Holm, Thomas K., ""Piratical Slave-Raiding – The Demise of a Viking Practice in High Medieval Denmark," *Scandinavian Journal of History* June 4 (2020), online at: https://www.tandfonline.com/doi/full/10.1080/03468755.2020.1748106 (last accessed on Jan. 15, 2021).

Heers, Jacques, *L'esilio, la vita politica e la società nel medioevo* (Naples: Liguori, 1997).

Heinrich, Peter, *Mensch und freier Wille bei Luther und Erasmus: Ein Brennpunkt reformatorischer Auseinandersetzung – Unter besonderer Berücksichtigung der Anthropologie* (Nordhausen: Traugott Bautz, 2003).

Heinzle, Joachim, "Kleine Anleitung zum Gebrauch des Märenbegriffs," *Kleinere Erzählformen im Mittelalter: Paderborner Colloquium 1987*, ed. Klaus Grubmüller; Leslie Peter Johnson; Hans-Hugo Steinhoff. Schriften der Universitäts-Gesamthochschule-Paderborn, 10 (Paderborn and Munich: Schöningh, 1988), 45–48.

Heinzle, Joachim, *Einführung in die mittelhochdeutsche Dietrichepik*. de Gruyter Studienbuch (Berlin and New York: Walter de Gruyter, 1999).

Hélary, Xavier, *La dernière croisade: Saint Louis à Tunis (1270)* (Paris: Perrin, 2016).

Hemmie, Dagmar M. H., *Ungeordnete Unzucht: Prostitution im Hanseraum (12.–16. Jahrhundert): Lübeck – Bergen – Helsingør* (Cologne, Weimar, and Vienna, 2007).

Heng, Geraldine, "Early Globalities, and Its Questions, Objectives, and Methods: An Inquiry into the State of Theory and Critique," *Exemplaria* 26.2–3 (2014): 232–51.

Heng, Geraldine, *The Invention of Race in the European Middle Ages* (New York and Cambridge: Cambridge University Press, 2018).

Hennings, Thordis, *Französische Heldenepik im deutschen Sprachraum: Die Rezeption der Chansons de geste im 12. und 13. Jahrhundert – Überblick und Fallstudien – .* Beiträge zur älteren Literaturgeschichte (Heidelberg: Universitätsverlag Winter, 2009).

Hensler, Ines, *Ritter und Sarrazin; zur Beziehung von Fremd und Eigen in der hochmittelalterlichen Tradition der "Chansons de geste": Struktur und Funktion des Sarrrazin-Bildes.* Beihefte zum Archiv für Kulturgeschichte, 62 (Cologne, Weimar, and Vienna: Böhlau, 2006).

Herrmann, Hans Peter, "Krieg, *Medien und Nation: zum Nationalismus in Kriegsliedern des 16. und 18. Jahrhunderts*," *"Krieg ist mein Lied": der Siebenjährige Krieg in den zeitgenössischen Medien*, ed. Wolfgang Adam and Holger Dainat, together with Ute Pott. Schriften des Gleimhauses Halberstadt, 5 (Göttingen: Wallstein-Verlag, 2007), 27–64.

Hermits and Anchorites in England, 1200–1550, selected sources trans. and annotated by E. A. Jones (Manchester: Manchester University Press, 2019).

Hershenzon, Daniel, *The Captive Sea: Slavery, Communication, and Commerce in Early Modern Spain and the Mediterranean* (Philadelphia, PA: University of Pennsylvania Press, 2018).

Himmel, Hölle, Fegefeuer: das Jenseits im Mittelalter, ed. Peter Jezler (Zürich: Verlag Neue Zürcher Zeitung, 1994).

Hippel, R. von, "Beiträge zur Geschichte der Freiheitsstrafe," *Zeitschrift für die gesamte Strafrechtswissenschaften* 18 (1898): 419–94, 609–66

Hiscock, Andrew, "Walter Ralegh and the Arts of Memory," *Literature Compass* 4.4 (2007): 1030–58.

Historia Apollonii regis Tyri: A Fourteenth-Century Version of a Late Antique Romance. Ed. from Vatican City, Biblioteca Apostolica Vaticana, MS Vaticanus latinus 1961, by William Robins. Toronto Medieval Latin Texts (Toronto: Pontifical Institute of Mediaeval Studies, 2019).

Historia Apollonii regis Tyri: The Middle English "Kynge Appolyn of Thyre", Historia Apollonii regis Tyri with a parallel text of the Medieval French "La cronicque et hystoire de Appollin, roy de Thir": La cronicque et hystoire de Appollin, roy de Thir, trans. Robert Copland, edited from the text published by Wynkyn de Worde (1510) by Stephen Morrison with Jean-Jacques Vincensini (Heidelberg: Universitätsverlag Winter, 2020).

Die Historia von den Sieben weisen Meistern und dem Kaiser Diocletianus, ed. Ralf-Henning Steinmetz. Altdeutsche Textbibliothek, 116 (Tübingen: Max Niemeyer, 2002).

Hoffmann, Hartmut, "Kirche und Sklaverei im frühen Mittelalter," *Deutsches Archiv für Erforschung des Mittelalters* 42 (1986): 1–24.

Hofman, Rijcklof, "Inwardness and Individualization in the Late Medieval Low Countries: An Introduction," *Inwardness, Individualization, and Religious Agency in the Late Medieval Low Countries: Studies in the Devotio Moderna and Its Contexts*, ed. Rijcklof Hofman, Charles Caspers, Peter Nissen, et al. Medieval Church Studies, 43 (Turnhout: Brepols, 2020), 1–34.

Hofmeister, Wernfried, in Oswald von Wolkenstein, *Sämtliche Lieder und Gedichte*. Ins Neuhochdeutsche übersetzt von Wernfried Hofmeister. Göppinger Arbeiten zur Germanistik, 511 (Göppingen: Kümmerle, 1989), 193–237.

Holt, James C., *Magna Carta*. 2nd ed. (Cambridge and New York: Cambridge University Press, 1992).
Howard, A. E. Dick, *Magna Carta: Text and Commentary*. Revised Edition (1964; Charlottesville, VA: University Press of Virginia, 1998).
Hoyer, Wolfram, OP, "Volumus ut carceres fiant: Medieval Dominican Legislation on Detention and Imprisonment," *Making and Breaking the Rules: Discussion, Implementation, and Consequences of Dominican Legislation*, ed. Cornelia Linde. Studies of the German Historical Institute London (Oxford: Oxford University Press, 2018), 323–48.
Hrotsvit of Gandersheim, *A Florilegium of Her Works*, trans. Katharina M. Wilson. The Library of Medieval Women (Woodbridge, Suffolk: S. S. Brewer, 1998).
Hrotsvit von Gandersheim, *Opera omnia*, ed. Walter Berschin. Bibliotheca scriptorum Graecorum et Romanorum Teubneriana (Leipzig: B. G. Teubner, 2013).
Hrotsvithae Opera, ed. H. Homeyer (Munich, Paderborn, and Vienna: Ferdinand Schöningh, 1970).
Hugo von Trimberg, *Der Renner*, ed. Gustav Ehrismann. With an epilogue and additions by Günther Schweikle. Deutsche Neudrucke. Reihe: Texte des Mittelalters (1908; Berlin: Walter de Gruyter, 1970).
Hunt, Janin, *Medieval Justice: Cases and Laws in France, England and Germany, 500–1500* (Jefferson, NC, and London: McFarland, 2004).
Huser, Patrick, *Vernunft und Herrschaft: die kanonischen Rechtsquellen als Grundlage natur- und völkerrechtlicher Argumentation im zweiten Prinzip des Traktates Principia quaedam des Bartolomé de Las Casas*. Religionsrecht im Dialog, 11 (Münster: LIT, 2011).
Ibn Arabshah, Ahmad, *Tamerlane: The Life of the Great Amir*, trans. J. H. Sanders (1936; London and New York: I. B. Tauris, 2018).
Im Gefängnis: eine gemeinsame Ausstellung von: Musée Genève, Musée des Confluences, Deutsches Hygiene-Museum Dresden, ed. Roger Mayou (Dresden: Deutsches Hygiene-Museum Dresden, 2020).
Imagining the Medieval Afterlife, ed. Richard Matthew Pollard (Cambridge: Cambridge University Press, 2020).
In Quest of Marie de France: A Twelfth-Century Poet, ed. Chantal A. Maréchal (Lewiston, NY, Lampeter, Wales, and Queenston, Ont.: Edwin Mellon Press, 1992).
Ingham, Mary Elizabeth, *Ethics and Freedom: An Historical-Critical Investigation of Scotist Ethical Thought* (Lanham, MD: University Press of America, 1989).
Ingram, John K., *A History of Slavery and Serfdom* (London: A. and C. Black, 1895).
Internal Colonization in Medieval Europe, ed. Felipe Fernández-Armesto. The Expansion of Latin Europe, 1000–1500, 2 (Aldershot: Ashgate, 2008).
Inwardness, Individualization, and Religious Agency in the Late Medieval Low Countries: Studies in the Devotio Moderna and Its Contexts, ed. Rijcklof Hofman, Charles Caspers, Peter Nissen, et al. Medieval Church Studies, 43 (Turnhout: Brepols, 2020).
Irsigler, Franz, "Freiheit und Unfreiheit im Mittelalter: Formen und Wege sozialer Mobilität," *Miscellanea Franz Irsigler: Festgabe zum 65. Geburtstag*, ed. Volker Henn, Rudolf Holbach, Rudolf, Michel Pauly, and Wolfgang Schmid (Trier: Porta Alba Verlag, 2006), 133–52.
Isenmann, Eberhard, *Die deutsche Stadt im Mittelalter: 1150–1550; Stadtgestalt, Recht, Verfassung, Stadtregiment, Kirche, Gesellschaft, Wirtschaft*. 2nd ed. (2012; Cologne, Weimar, and Vienna: Böhlau, 2014).

Israel, Uwe, "Masse und Stadt: die Bewältigung großer Menschenmengen im Mittelalter am Beispiel von Nürnberg," *Concilium medii aevi: Zeitschrift für Geschichte, Kunst und Kultur des Mittelalters und der Frühen Neuzeit* 15 (2012): 151–83.

Jacobus de Voragine, *The Golden Legend: Readings on the Saints*, trans. William Granger Ryan. Vol. II (Princeton, NJ: Princeton University Press, 1993).

Jaeger, C. Stephen, *Ennobling Love: In Search of a Lost Sensibility*. The Middle Ages Series (Philadelphia, PA: University of Pennsylvania Press, 1999).

Jafarzadeh, Shahram and Mohhamad Bagher Beheshti, "Importance of Freedom in Humanities Developing," *Procedia: Social and Behavioral Sciences* 31 (2012): 323–32.

Jahner, Jennifer, *Literature and Law in the Era of Magna Carta*. Oxford Studies in Medieval Literature and Culture (Oxford: Oxford University Press, 2019).

James I of Scotland, *The Kingis Quair and Other Prison Poems*, ed. Linne R. Mooney and Mary-Jo Arn. Middle English Texts Series (Kalamazoo, MI: Medieval Institute Publications, 2005).

Janota, Johannes, *Orientierung durch volkssprachige Schriftlichkeit (1280/90–1380/90)*. Geschichte der deutschen Literatur von den Anfängen bis zum Beginn der Neuzeit, III: *Vom späten Mittelalter zum Beginn der Neuzeit* (Tübingen: Max Niemeyer, 2004).

Janssen, Geert H., *The Dutch Revolt and Catholic Exile in Reformation Europe* (Cambridge: Cambridge University Press, 2014).

Jarvis, Brian, *Cruel and Unusual: Punishment and US Culture* (London and Sterling, VA: Pluto Press, 2004).

Jaspert, Nikolas, "Gefangenenloskauf in der Krone Aragón und die Anfänge des Mercedarierordens: Institutionelle Diversität, religiöse Kontexte, mediterrane Verflechtungen," *Gefangenenloskauf im Mittelmeerraum: Ein interreligiöser Vergleich: Akten der Tagung vom 19. bis 21. September 2013 an der Universität Paderborn*, Heike Grieser and Nicole Priesching. Sklaverei – Knechtschaft – Zwangsarbeit, 13 (Hildesheim, Zürich, and New York: Georg Olms Verlag, 2015), 99–121.

Jean d'Arras, *Melusine; or, the Noble History of Lusignan*, trans. and with an intro. by Donald Maddox and Sara Sturm-Maddox (University Park, PA: The Pennsylvania State University Press, 2012).

Joinville: *The Memoirs of the Lord of Joinville: A New English Version* (*Vie de Saint Louis*), by von Ethel Wedgwood (London: J. Murray, 1906).

Jones, Martin, "The Significance of the Gawan Story in *Parzival*," *A Companion to Wolfram's Parzival*, ed. Will Hasty. Studies in German Literature, Linguistics, and Culture (Columbia, SC: Camden House, 1999), 37–76.

Jordan, William Chester, *From Servitude to Freedom: Manumission in the Senonais in the Thirteenth Century*. The Middle Ages Series (Philadelphia, PA: University of Pennsylvania Press, 2016).

Jordan, William Chester, *Louis IX and the Challenge of the Crusade: A Study in Rulership* (Princeton, NJ: Princeton University Press, 1979).

Joschko, Dirk, *Oswald von Wolkenstein: Eine Monographie zu Person, Werk und Forschungsgeschichte*. Göppinger Arbeiten zur Germanistik, 396 (Göppingen: Kümmerle, 1985).

Jost, Jean, "The Effects of the Black Death: The Plague in Fourteenth-Century Religion, Literature, and Art," *Death in the Middle Ages and Early Modern Times: The Material and Spiritual Conditions of the Culture of Death*, ed. A. Classen. Fundamentals of Medieval and Early Modern Culture, 16 (Berlin and Boston: Walter de Gruyter, 2016).

Jowett, Caroline, *The History of Newgate Prison* (Bamsley: Pen & Sword History, 2017).

Juan Manuel, *El Conde Lucanor: A Collection of Mediaeval Spanish Stories*. Ed. with an Intro., trans. and notes by John England (Warminster: Aris & Phillips, 1987).

Jütte, Daniel, "Interfaith Encounters between Jews and Christians in the Early Modern Period and Beyond: Toward a Framework," *American Historical Review* 118.2 (2013): 378–400.

Kaeuper, Richard W., *Medieval Chivalry*. Cambridge Medieval Textbooks (Cambridge: Cambridge University Press, 2016).

Kalas, Laura, *Margery Kempe's Spiritual Medicine: Suffering, Transformation and the Life-Course* (Cambridge: D. S. Brewer, 2020).

Kamp, Norbert, "Enrico di Castiglia," *Dizionario Biografico degli Italiani* 42 (1993); online at: https://www.treccani.it/enciclopedia/enrico-di-castiglia_%28Dizionario-Biografico%29/

Kaplan, M. Lindsay, *Figuring Racism in Medieval Christianity* (New York: Oxford University Press, 2019).

Karras, Ruth Mazo, "Slavery," *Medieval Scandinavia: An Encyclopedia*, ed. Phillip Pulsiano (New York and London: Garland, 1993), 598–99.

Karras, Ruth Mazo, *Slavery and Society in Medieval Scandinavia*. Yale Historical Publications, 135 (New Haven, CT: Yale University Press, 1988).

Kästner, Hannes, *Fortunatus – Peregrinator mundi: Welterfahrung und Selbsterkenntnis im ersten deutschen Prosaroman der Neuzeit*. Rombach Wissenschaft – Reihe Litterae (Freiburg i. Br.: Verlag Rombach, 1990).

Kaufringer, Heinrich, *Werke*, ed. Paul Sappler. Vol. 1: *Text* (Tübingen: Max Niemeyer, 1972).

Kaufringer, Heinrich: Albrecht Classen, *Love, Life, and Lust in Heinrich Kaufringer's Verse Narratives*. Medieval and Renaissance Texts and Studies, 467. MRTS Texts for Teaching, 9 (Tempe: Arizona Center for Medieval and Renaissance Studies, 2014; rev. and expanded 2nd ed., 2019).

Kauth, Jean-Marie, "Barred Windows and Uncaged Birds: The Enclosure of Woman in Chrétien de Troyes and Marie de France," *Medieval Feminist Forum* 46.2 (2010): 34–67.

Kay, Richard, "Introduction," *Dante's Monarchia*, ed. and trans. id. (Toronto: Pontifical Institute of Medieval Studies, 1998), xv–xliii.

Keen, Maurice Hugh, *Chivalry* (New Haven, CT: Yale University Press, 1984).

Kelly, Gary, *Newgate Narratives: General Introduction and Newgate Documents*. Newgate Narratives, 1 (London: Routledge, 2017).

Kelly, Gordon P., *A History of Exile in the Roman Republic* (Cambridge: Cambridge University Press, 2006).

Kempe, Margery: *The Book of Margery Kempe*. Trans. by B. A. Windeatt (London: Penguin, 1985)

Kern, Iso, *Der gute Weg des Handelns: Versuch einer Ethik für die heutige Zeit* (Basel: Schwabe Verlag, 2020).

Kerth, Sonja, "Gefängnis, Orte der Gefangenschaft," *Literarische Orte in deutschsprachigen Erzählungen des Mittelalters: ein Handbuch*, ed. Tilo Renz, Monika Hanauska, and Mathias Herweg (Berlin and Boston: Walter de Gruyter, 2018), 190–98.

Khanmohamadi, Shirin Azizeh, *In Light of Another's Word: European Ethnography in the Middle Ages*. The Middle Ages Series (Philadelphia, PA: University of Pennsylvania Press, 2013).

Kim, Dorothy, "Introduction to Literature Compass Special Cluster: Critical Race and the Middle Ages," *Literature Compass* 16.9–10 (2019): 1–16.
Kinkade, Richard P., *Dawn of a Dynasty: The Life and Times of Infante Manuel of Castile*. Toronto Iberic, 46 (Toronto: University of Toronto Press, 2020).
Kinoshita, Sharon and Jason Jacobs, "Ports of Call: Boccaccio's Alatiel in the Medieval Mediterranean," *Journal of Medieval and Early Modern Studies* 37.1 (2007): 163–95.
Kinoshita, Sharon and Peggy McCracken, *Marie de France: A Critical Companion*. Gallica, 24 (Cambridge: D. S. Brewer, 2012).
Diu Klage, mittelhochdeutsch – neuhochdeutsch. Einleitung, Übersetzung, Kommentar und Anmerkungen von Albrecht Classen. Göppinger Arbeiten zur Germanistik, 647 (Göppingen: Kümmerle, 1997).
Diu Klage, The Lament of the Nibelungen (Div Chlage), trans. and with an intro. by Winder McConnell. Studies in German Literature, Linguistics, and Culture (Columbia, SC: Camden House, 1994).
Klein, Uta, *Gefangenenliteratur: Sprechen, Schreiben, Lesen in deutschen Gefängnissen* (Hagen: Padligur, 1988).
Kleine Welten: Ländliche Gesellschaften im Karolingerreich, ed. Thomas Kohl, Steffen Petzold, and Bernhard Zeller. Vorträge und Forschungen, 87 (Ostfildern: Jan Thorbecke, 2019).
Kluge, Paul, *Friesische Freiheit und die Reformation in Ost-Friesland* (Schortens: Heiber GmbH Druck & Verlag, 2015).
Knaeble, Susanne, "Im Zustand der Liminalität – Die Braut als Zentrum narrativer Verhandlungen von Gewalt, Sippenbindung und Herrschaft in der Kudrun," *Genus und generatio. Rollenerwartungen und Rollenerfüllungen im Spannungsfeld der Geschlechter und Generationen in Antike und Mittelalter*, ed. Hartwin Brandt, Anika M. Auer, and Johannes Brehm. Bamberger historische Studien, 6 (Bamberg: University of Bamberg Press, 2011), 295–314.
Knape, Joachim, *Dichtung, Recht und Freiheit. Studien zu Leben und Werk Sebastian Brants 1457–1521*. Saecvla Spiritalia, 23 (Baden-Baden: Koerner, 1991).
Knape, Joachim, "Sebastian Brant," *Deutsche Dichter der frühen Neuzeit (1450–1600): Ihr Leben und Werk*, ed. Stephan Füssel (Berlin: Erich Schmidt Verlag, 1993), 156–72.
Knapp, Fritz Peter, *Rennewart: Studien zu Gehalt und Gestalt des "Willehalm" Wolframs von Eschenbach*. Dissertationen der Universität Wien, 45 (Vienna: Verlag Notring, 1970).
Knighton, Rachel, *Writing the Prison in African Literature*. Race and Resistance Across Borders in the Long Twentieth Century, 5 (Oxford, Bern, Berlin, et al.: Peter Lang, 2019).
Koebler, Gerhard, *Althochdeutsches Wörterbuch*, 6th ed. (2014), online at: http://www.koeblergerhard.de/ahd/ahd_r.html
Kolb, Herbert, "Über den Ursprung der Unfreiheit: Eine Quaestio im "Sachsenspiegel," *Zeitschrift für deutsches Altertum* 103 (1974): 289–311.
Kolb, Robert, *Luther's Treatise on Christian Freedom and Its Legacy*. Mapping the Tradition (Lanham, MD, Boulder, CO, New York, and London: Lexington Books / Fortress Academic, 2020).
Kollektive Freiheitsvorstellungen im frühneuzeitlichen Europa: (1400–1850), ed. Georg Schmidt, Martin van Gelderen, and Christopher Snigula. Jenaer Beiträge zur Geschichte, 8 (Frankfurt a. M., Berlin, Bern, et al.: Peter Lang, 2006).

König Rother: Mittelhochdeutscher Text und neuhochdeutsche Übersetzung von Peter K. Stein. Ed. Ingrid Bennewitz together with Beatrix Koll and Ruth Weichselbaumer (Stuttgart: Philipp Reclam jun., 2000).

Korpela, Jukka, *Slaves from the North: Finns and Karelians in the East European Slave Trade, 900–1600*. Studies in Gobal Slavery, 5 (2018; Leiden and Boston: Brill, 2019).

Korte, Petra, *Die antike Unterwelt im christlichen Mittelalter: Kommentierung – Dichtung – philosophischer Diskurs / Autoren*. Tradition – Reform – Innovation, 16 (Frankfurt a. M.: Peter Lang, 2012).

Kosto, Adam J., *Hostages in the Middle Ages* (Oxford: Oxford University Press, 2012).

Krafft, Hans-Ulrich: *H. U. Krafft: Ein schwäbischer Kaufmann in türkischer Gefangenschaft: Reisen und Gefangenschaft Hans Ulrich Kraffts*, ed. Klaus Schubring. Schwäbische Lebensläufe (Heidenheim: Heidenheimer Verlags-Anstalt, 1970).

Krafft, Hans-Ulrich: *Reisen und Gefangenschaft Hans Ulrich Kraffts, aus der Originalhandschrift herausgegeben* von Dr. L. D. Haszlett. Bibliothek des Litterarischen Vereins, LXI (Stuttgart: Litterarischer Verein, 1861).

Krohn, Rüdiger, "'Richardes lob gemêret wart mit hôher werdekeit': Der Löwenherz-Mythos in Mittelalter und Neuzeit," *Herrscher, Helden, Heilige*, ed. Ulrich Müller and Werner Wunderlich. Mittelalter Mythen, 1 (St. Gall: UVK-Fachverlag für Wissenschaft und Studium, 1996), 133–53.

Kropp, Claus and Thomas Meier, "Entwurf einer Archäologie der Grundherrschaft im älteren Mittelalter," *Beiträge zur Mittelalterarchäologie in Österreich* 26 (2010): 97–114.

Krugman, Paul, "When Libertarianism Goes Bad: Liberty Doesn't Mean Freedom to Infect Other People," *The New York Times* Oct. 22, 2020, https://www.nytimes.com/2020/10/22/opinion/coronavirus-masks.html.

Kruse, Britta-Juliane, *Witwen: Kulturgeschichte eines Standes in Spätmittelalter und Früher Neuzeit* (Berlin and New York: Walter de Gruyter, 2007).

Kudrun, trans. by Winder McConnell. Medieval Texts and Translations (Columbia, SC: Camden House, 1992).

Kudrun. Nach der Ausgabe von Karl Bartsch herausgegeben von Karl Stackmann. Altdeutsche Textbibliothek, 115 (Tübingen: Max Niemeyer, 2000).

Kuhnau, Petra, *Masse und Macht in der Geschichte: zur Konzeption anthropologischer Konstanten in Elias Canettis Werk "Masse und Macht"*. Epistemata. Reihe Literaturwissenschaft, 195 (Würzburg: Königshausen & Neumann, 1996).

Kyriazēs-Gubelēs, Dēmētrios L., *Magna Carta: Palladium der Freiheiten oder Feudales Stabilimentum*. Schriften zur Verfassungsgeschichte, 36 (Berlin: Duncker & Humblot, 1984).

La notion de liberté au Moyen Age: Islam, Byzance, Occident. Penn-Paris-Dumbarton Oaks colloquia IV; session des 12–15 octobre 1982 [Mandelieu-La Napoule]: The Concept of Freedom in the Middle Ages Islam, Byzantium and the West, ed. George Makdisi (Paris: Les Belles Lettres, 1985).

Laïd, Baptiste, *L'élaboration du recueil de fables de Marie de France: " Trover " des fables au XIIe siècle*. Nouvelle bibliothèque du moyen âge, 128 (Paris: Honoré Champion éditeur, 2020).

Lambert, Malcolm, *Medieval Heresy: Popular Movements from the Gregorian Reform to the Reformation* (1977; Malden, MA, Oxford, and Carlton, Victoria, Australia: Blackwell Publishing, 2002).

The Lament, see *Diu Klage*
Land, Lords and Peasants: Peasants' Right to Control Land in the Middle Ages and the Early Modern Period. Norway, Scandinavia and the Alpine Region, ed. Tore Iversen. Trondheim Studies in History, 52 (Trondheim: Department of History and Classical Studies, 2005).
Lantigua, David M., *Infidels and Empires in a New World Order: Early Modern Spanish Contributions to International Legal Thought*. Law and Christianity (Cambridge and New York: Cambridge University Press, 2020).
Larne, John, *Marco Polo and the Discovery of the World* (New Haven, CT: Yale University Press, 1999).
Larsson, Lars-Olof, *Engelbrekt Engelbrektsson och 1430-talets svenska uppror* (Stockholm: Norstedt, 1984).
Lawler, Peter Augustine and Richard Reinsch, "Freedom and the Human Person," *National Affairs* 44 (2020), online at: https://www.nationalaffairs.com/publications/detail/freedom-and-the-human-person (last accessed on Jan. 15, 2021).
Lawn, Elizabeth, *"Gefangenschaft": Aspekt und Symbol sozialer Bindung im Mittelalter, dargestellt an chronikalischen und poetischen Quellen*. Europäische Hochschulschriften, Reihe: 1, 214 (Frankfurt a. M.; Peter Lang, 1977).
Lebec, S., "Sklave," *Lexikon des Mittelalters*, ed. Norbert Angermann. Vol. VII (Munich: Lexma Verlag, 1990), 1977–80.
Lectures de "El Conde Lucanor" de Don Juan Manuel, ed. César García de Lucas and Alexandra Oddo-Bonnet. Didact Espagnol (Rennes: Presses universitaires de Rennes, 2014).
Leding, Okko, *Die Freiheit der Friesen im Mittelalter und ihr Bund mit den Versammlungen beim Upstallsbom* (1878; Walluf bei Wiesbaden: Sändig, 1973).
Lefort, Claude, *Dante's Modernity: An Introduction to the Monarchia* (Berlin: ICI Berlin Press, 2020).
Lehr, Peter, *Pirates: A New History, from Vikings to Somali Raiders* (New Haven, CT, and London: Yale University Press, 2019).
Leitch, Stephanie, *Mapping Ethnography in Early Modern Germany: New Worlds in Print Culture*. History of Text Technologies (New York: Palgrave Macmillan, 2010).
Lessenich, Stephan, *Grenzen der Demokratie: Teilhabe als Verteilungsproblem* (Stuttgart: Philipp Reclam jun., 2019).
Lewis, Katherine J., *Kingship and Maculinity in Late Medieval England* (London and New York: Routledge, 2013).
Liberté e(s)t choix: Verhandlungen von Freiheit in der französischen Literatur, ed. Sieglinde Borvitz and Yasmin Temelli. Studienreihe Romania (StR), 34 (Berlin: Erich Schmidt Verlag, 2019).
Liberty and the Ecological Crisis: Freedom on a Finite Planet, ed. Christopher Orr, Kaitlin Kish, and Bruce Jennings. Routledge Explorations in Environmental Studies (London and New York: Routledge, 2020).
The Liberty Reader, ed. and intro. David Miller (1991; Edinburgh: Edinburgh University Press, 2006).
Das Lied vom Hürnen Seyfrid, ed. Maike Claußnitzer and Kassandra Sperl. Relectiones (Stuttgart: S. Hirzel Verlag, 2019).

Liedl, Gottfried, *Granada. Ein europäisches Emirat an der Schwelle zur Neuzeit. Islamische Renaissancen*, 2. Die Levante – frühe Ansätze der Globalisierung. Vom 5. Jahrhundert bis zur Neuzeit, 3 (Vienna: LIT Verlag, 2020).

Liedl, Gottfried, *Dokumente der Araber in Spanien: Zur Geschichte der spanisch-arabischen Renaissance in* Granada. Vol. 2 (Vienna: Turia and Kant, 1993).

Liendo, Elizabeth, "The Wound that Bleeds: Violence and Feminization: Violence and Feminization in the Lais of Marie de France," *Neophilologus* 104 (2020): 19–32

Lienert, Elisabeth, *Die ›historische‹ Dietrichepik: Untersuchungen zu ›Dietrichs Flucht‹, ›Rabenschlacht‹ und ›Alpharts Tod‹*. Texte und Studien zur mittelhochdeutschen Heldenepik, 5 (Berlin and New York: Walter de Gruyter, 2010).

Lindemann Summers, Sandra, *Ogling Ladies: Scopophilia in Medieval German Literature* (Gainesville, Tallahassee, et al.: University Press of Florida, 2013).

Linebaugh, Peter, *The Magna Carta Manifesto: Liberties and Commons for All* (Berkeley, CA: University of California Press, 2009).

Lobenstein-Reichmann, Anja, *Freiheit bei Martin Luther: lexikographische Textanalyse als Methode historischer Semantik*. Studia linguistica Germanica, 46 (Berlin and New York: Walter de Gruyter, 1998).

Locke, Stefan, "Wie sieht der Alltag im Knast aus?," *Frankfurter Allgemeine Zeitung* Oct. 7, 2020: https://www.faz.net/aktuell/feuilleton/kunst/eine-dresdner-ausstellung-ueber-das-leben-im-gefaengnis-16987475.html?printPagedArticle=true#pageIndex_3.

Lofmark, Carl, *Rennewart in Wolfram's Willehalm: A Study of Wolfram von Eschenbach and His Sources*. Anglica Germanica, 2 (Cambridge: Cambridge University Press, 1972).

Lohrmann, Klaus, *Die Babenberger und ihre Nachbarn* (Vienna, Cologne, and Weimar: Böhlau, 2020).

Lück, Heiner, *Der Sachsenspiegel: Das berühmteste deutsche Rechtsbuch des Mittelalters* (Darmstadt: Lambert Schneider Verlag/Wissenschaftliche Buchgesellschaft, 2018).

Lüddecke, Dirk, *Das politische Denken Dantes: Überlegungen zur Argumentation der Monarchia Dante Alighieris*. Reihe politisches Denken, 3 (Neuried: Ars Una, 1999).

Luther und Erasmus über Freiheit: Rezeption und Relevanz eines gelehrten Streits, ed. Jörg Noller and Georg Sans. Geist und Geisteswissenschaft, 4 (Freiburg i. Br.: Verlag Karl Alber, 2020).

MacLean, Simon, "'Waltharius': Treasure, Revenge and Kingship in the Ottonian Wild West," *Emotion, Violence, Vengeance and Law in the Middle Ages: Essays in Honour of William Ian Miller*, ed. Kate Gilbert and Stephen D. White. Medieval Law and Its Practice, 24 (Leiden and Boston: Brill, 2018), 225–51.

MacQuarrie, Alan, *Medieval Scotland: Kingship and Nation* (Gloucestershire: Sutton Publishing, 2004).

Madden, Thomas F., *The Concise History of the Crusades*. 3rd ed. (1999; Lanham, MD: Rowman & Littlefield Publishers, 2013).

Das Märe: Die mittelhochdeutsche Versnovelle des späteren Mittelalters, ed. Karl-Heinz Schirmer. Wege der Forschung, 558 (Darmstadt: Wissenschaftliche Buchgesellschaft, 1983).

Magic and Magicians in the Middle Ages and the Early Modern Time: The Occult in Pre-Modern Sciences, Medicine, Literature, Religion, and Astrology, ed. Albrecht Classen. Fundamentals of Medieval and Early Modern Culture, 20 (Berlin and Boston: Walter de Gruyter, 2017).

Magna carta libertatum, ed. Mario Caravale. Introduzioni. Diritto (Bologna: Il mulino, 2018).

Magna Carta: Law, Liberty, Legacy, ed. Claire Breay and Julian Harrison (London: The British Library, 2015).

Magnus von Reichersberg, *Chronicon*, ed. Wilhelm Wattenbach. Monumenta Germaniae Historica, Scriptores, 17 (Hanover: Hahn, 1861).

Maier, Bruno, *Ein Königshaus aus der Schweiz: die Habsburger, der Aargau und die Eidgenossenschaft im Mittelalter* (Baden: Hier + Jetzt, Verlag für Kultur und Geschichte, 2008).

Making the Medieval Relevant: How Medieval Studies Contribute to Improving Our Understanding of the Present, ed. Chris Jones, Conor Kostick, and Klaus Oschema. Das Mittelalter: Perspektiven mediävistischer Forschung, 6 (Berlin and Boston: Walther de Gruyter, 2020).

Maksymiuk, Stephen, *The Court Magician in Medieval German Romance*. Mikrokosmos: Beiträge zur Literaturwissenschaft und Bedeutungsforschung, 44 (Frankfurt a. M.: Peter Lang, 1996).

Malm, Mike, "Rudolf von Ems," *Deutsches Literatur-Lexikon: Das Mittelalter*, ed. Wolfgang Achnitz. Vol. 5: *Epik (Vers – Strophe – Prosa) und Kleinformen* (Berlin and Boston: Walter de Gruyter, 2013), 393–408.

Malory, Thomas, Sir, *Le Morte d'Arthur*, ed. Janet Cowen. 2 vols. (1969; Harmondsworth, Middlesex: Penguin, 1979).

Manescalchi, Romano, "'Purgatorio' 1 71–74: Perché non si può parlare di libertà politica," *Studi Danteschi* 78 (2013): 359–77.

Mangini, Angelo M., "Il purgatorio di Ferondo, e quello di Forese: L'intertestualità dantesca in Decameron III.8 e la questione dei suffragi," *Lettere Italiane* 69.1 (2017): 59–82.

Mantik, Schicksal und Freiheit im Mittelalter, ed. Loris Sturlese. Technical ed. Katrin Bauer. Archiv für Kulturgeschichte, Beihefte zum Archiv für Kulturgeschichte, 70 (Cologne, Weimar, and Vienna: Böhlau, 2011).

Manuel, see Juan Manuel

Mapstone, Sally, "Kingship and the Kingis Quair," *The Long Fifteenth Century: Essays for Douglas Gray*, ed. Helen Cooper and Sally Mapstone (Oxford: Clarendon Press, 1997), 52–69.

Mapstone, Sally, "Kingship and the Kingis Quair," *The Long Fifteenth Century: Essays for Douglas Gray*, ed. Helen Cooper and Sally Mapstone (Oxford: Clarendon Press, 1997), 52–69.

Marenbon, John, *Boethius* (Oxford: Oxford University Press, 2004).

Marguerite de Navarre, *Les Prisons*, ed. and commentary by Simone Glasson. Textes littéraires français, 260 (Geneva: Droz, 1978).

Marguerite de Navarre, *Les prisons: A French and English Edition*, ed. Claire Lynch Wade. American University Studies. Ser. 2: Romance Languages and Literature, 99 (New York, Bern, et al.: Peter Lang, 1989).

Marguerite de Navarre: *The Prisons of Marguerite de Navarre: An English Verse Translation*, trans. Hilda Dale (Reading, United Kingdom: Whiteknights Press, 1989).

Marie de France, *Die Lais*. Übersetzt, mit einer Einleitung, einer Bibliographie sowie Anmerkungen versehen von Dietmar Rieger. Klassische Texte des romanischen Mittelalters, 19 (Munich: Wilhelm Fink, 1980).

Marie de France, *Fables*, ed. and trans. Harriet Spiegel. Medieval Academy Reprints for Teaching (Toronto, Buffalo, and London: University of Toronto Press, 1994).
Marie de France, *Lais: Guigemar, Bisclavret, Lanval, Yonec, Laüstic, Chievrefoil*. Altfranzösisch/Deutsch, ed. Philipp Jeserich (Stuttgart: Philipp Reclam jun., 2015).
Marie de France, *Lais: texte original en ancien français; manuscrit Harley 978 du British Museum*, ed. Nathalie Desgrugillers-Billard (Clermont-Ferrand: Éd. Paleo, 2007).
Marie de France: *Les lais de Marie de France*, ed. Jean Rychner. Les classiques français du Moyen Âge (Paris: Champion, 1978).
Marie de France: *The Lais of Marie de France: Text and Translation*, ed. and trans. by Claire M. Waters (Peterborough, Ont.: Broadview, 2018).
Martin, Joanna, *Kingship and Love in Scottish Poetry, 1424 – 1540* (Aldershot: Ashgate, 2008).
Martin, Molly A., *Castles and Space in Malory's Morte Darthur*. Arthurian Studies, 89 (Cambridge: D. S. Brewer, 2019).
Martines, Lauro, "Political Conflict in the Italian City-States," *Government and Opposition* 3.1 (1968): 69 – 91.
Martínez, Alberto A., *Burned Alive: Giordano Bruno, Galileo and the Inquisition* (London: Reaktion Books, 2018).
Mas i Forners, Antoni, *Esclaus i catalans: Esclavitud i segregació a Mallorca durant els segles XIV i XV*. Trafalempa, 1 (Palma, Mallorca: Lleonard Muntaner, 2005).
Massimo, Pier, *Adventures in Speech: Rhetoric and Narration in Boccaccio' Decameron*. Middle Ages Series (Philadelphia, PA: University of Pennsylvania Press, 1996).
Mazzotta, Giuseppe, *The World at Play in Boccaccio's Decameron* (Princeton, NJ: Princeton University Press, 1986).
McConnell, Winder, *The Epic of Kudrun: A Critical Commentary*. Göppinger Arbeiten zur Germanistik, 463 (Göppingen: Kümmerle, 1988).
McCrory, Donald P., *No Ordinary Man: The Life and Times of Miguel de Cervantes* (London: Peter Owen, 2005).
McInerny, Ralph, "Boethius," *Medieval Philosophers*, ed. Jermiah Hackett. Dictionary of Literary Biography, 115 (Detroit and London: Gale Research, 1992), 110 – 17.
McLeod, Enid, *Charles of Orleans, Prince and Poet* (New York: Viking Press, 1970).
McMunn, Meradith Tilbury, "Roman de Kanor: Édition critiqued'un texte en prose du XIIIe siècle," Ph.D. diss., Storrs, University of Connecticut, 1978.
Medieval Anchorites in Their Communities, ed. Cate Gunn and Liz Herbert McAvoy. Studies in the History of Medieval Religion (Woodbridge, Suffolk: D. S. Brewer, 2017).
Medieval Hostageship, c.700-c.1500: Hostage, Captive, Prisoner of War, Guarantee, Peacemaker, ed. Matthew Bennett and Katherine Weikert. Routledge Research in Medieval Studies, 9 (New York and London: Routledge, 2017).
Medieval London Widows, 1300 – 1500, ed. Caroline M. Barron and Anne F. Sutton (London and Rio Grande, OH: The Hambledon Press, 1994).
Meister Eckhart und die Freiheit, ed. Christine Büchner and Freimut Löser, together with Janina Franzke. Meister-Eckhart-Jahrbuch, 12 (Stuttgart: Verlag W. Kohlhammer, 2018).
Merback, Mitchell B., *The Thief, the Cross and the Wheel: Pain and the Spectacle of Punishment in Medieval and Renaissance Europe* (Chicago and London: University of Chicago Press, 1999).
Merchants, Pirates, and Smugglers: Criminalization, Economics, and the Transformation of the Maritime World (1200–1600), ed. Thomas Heebøll-Holm, Philipp Höhn, and Gregor

Rohmann. Discourses of Weakness and Resource Regimes, 6 (Frankfurt a. M. and New York: Campus, 2019).
Michael Brown, *James I* (East Linton, Scotland: Tuckwell Press, 1994).
Mickel, Emanuel J. Jr., "Guigemar's Ebony Boat," *Cultura Neolatina* 37 (1977): 9–15.
Middendorf, Wolf, *Menschenraub, Flugzeugentführungen, Geiselnahme, Kidnapping: historische und moderne Erscheinungsformen* (Bielefeld: Gieseking, 1972).
The Middle Ages in the Modern World: Twenty-First Century Perspectives, ed. Bettina Bildhauer and Chris Jones. Proceedings of the British Academy, 208 (Oxford: Oxford University Press, 2017).
Miller, David, *Richard the Lionheart: The Mighty Crusader* (London: Weidenfeld & Nicolson, 2003).
Miller, Gregory J., *The Turks and Islam in Reformation Germany*. Routledge Research in Early Modern History (New York and London: Routledge, 2017).
Miller, William Ian, *Bloodtaking and Peacemaking: Feud, Law, and Society in Saga Iceland* (Chicago: University of Chicago Press, 1990).
Millet, Victor, *Germanische Heldendichtung im Mittelalter: Eine Einführung*. de Gruyter Studienbuch (Berlin and New York: Walter de Gruyter, 2008).
Misch, Jürgen, *Das christliche Sklavenland: Menschenhandel im frühen Mittelalter bis zur Neuzeit* (Berlin: Rhombos-Verlag, 2015).
Mitchell, Mark T., *The Limits of Liberalism: Tradition, Liberalism, and the Crisis of Freedom* (Notre Dame, IN: University of Notre Dame Press, 2018).
Mohr, Wolfgang, "Zu den epischen Hintergründen in Wolframs *Parzival*," *Mediaeval German Studies Presented to Frederick Norman*. Publications of the Institute of Germanic Studies, University of London, 8 (London: Institute of Germanic Studies, 1965), 174–87.
Monahan, Arthur P., *From Personal Duties Towards Personal Rights: Late Medieval and Early Modern Political Thought, 1300–1600*. McGill-Queen's Studies in the History of Ideas, 17 (Montreal: McGill-Queen's University Press, 2014).
Monson, Don A., *Andreas Capellanus, Scholasticism, & the Courtly Tradition* (Washington, DC: The Catholic University of America Press, 2005).
Mora Rodríguez, Luis, *Bartolomé de Las Casas: conquête, domination, souveraineté*. Fondements de la politique. Série Essais (Paris: Presses Universitaires de France, 2012).
More, Thomas, *A Dialogue of Comfort Against Tribulation* (New York: Dover Publications, 2016).
Morewitz, Stephen, *Kidnapping and Violence: New Research and Clinical Perspectives*. SpringerNature, 4116 (New York: Springer New York, 2019).
Morris, Colin, "Geoffroy de Villehardouin and the Conquest of Constantinople," *History. The Journal of the Historical Society* 53.177 (1968): 24–34.
Müller, Jan-Dirk, *Spielregeln für den Untergang: Die Welt des Nibelungenliedes* (Tübingen: Max Niemeyer, 1998).
Müller, Johannes, *Exile Memories and the Dutch Revolt: The Narrated Diaspora, 1550–1750*. Studies in Medieval and Reformation Traditions, 199 (Leiden and Boston: Brill, 2016).
Müller, Ulrich, *"Dichtung" und "Wahrheit" in den Liedern Oswalds von Wolkenstein*. Göppinger Arbeiten zur Germanistik, 1 (Göppingen: Kümmerle, 1968).
Mummey, Kevin, "Women and Chains: Women, Slavery, and Community in Late Fourteenth-Century Mallorca," Ph.D. diss., University of Minnesota, 2013.

Mummey, Kevin, "Women, Slavery, and the Notarial Process in Late Fourteenth-Century Mallorca," *Rethinking Medieval Margins and Marginality*, ed. Anne E. Zimo, Tiffany D. Vann Sprecher, Kathryn Reyerson, and Debra Blumenthal. Studies in Medieval History and Culture (London and New York: Routledge, 2020), 110–28.

Muslimische Sklaverei: ein "vergessenes" Verbrechen. Die muslimische Sklaverei, ed. Manfred Pittioni. Muslimische Sklaverei, 1 (Berlin and Münster: LIT, 2018).

Mystik, Recht und Freiheit: religiöse Erfahrung und kirchliche Institutionen im Spätmittelalter, ed. Dietmar Mieth and Britta Müller-Schauenburg (Stuttgart: Kohlhammer, 2012).

Naimark, Norman M., *Genocide: A World History* (New York and Oxford: Oxford University Press, 2017).

Narrating Law and Laws of Narration in Medieval Scandinavia, ed. Roland Scheel. Ergänzungsbände zum Reallexikon der Germanischen Altertumskunde, 117 (Berlin and Boston: Walter de Gruyter, 2020).

Nederman, Cary J., "Dante's Imperial Road Leads to ... Constantinople?: The Internal Logic of the *Monarchia*," *Theoria* 143, 62.2 (June 2015): 1–14.

Neményi, Géza von, *Kommentar zu den Götterliedern der Edda*. Vol. 3: *Die Vanenlieder Skirnisfor, Grógaldr, Fjolsvinnsmál, Rígsþula, Hynduljóð: Textausgabe nach der korrigierten Übersetzung von Karl Simrock mit ausführlicher Einleitung (im Teil 1) und Kommentierung zu den Liedstrophen aus heidnischer Sicht*. Reihe altheidnische Schriften (Holdenstedt: Kersken-Canbaz-Verlag, 2014).

Neues Gesamtabenteuer, das ist, Fr. H. von der Hagens Gesamtabenteuer, die Sammlung der mittelhochdeutschen Mären und Schwänke des 13. und 14. Jahrhunderts in neuer Auswahl, ed. Heinrich Niewöhner. 2nd ed. by Werner Simon (1937; Dublin: Weidmann, 1967).

A New Companion to Malory, ed. Megan G. Leitch and Cory James Rushton. Arthurian Studies, 87 (Cambridge: D. S. Brewer, 2019).

Niall, Christie, *Muslims and Crusaders: Christianity's Wars in the Middle East, 1095–1382, From the Islamic Sources*. Sec. ed. (Abingdon, Oxon, and New York: Routledge, 2020).

Das Nibelungenlied: Mittelhochdeutsch / Neuhochdeutsche. Nach der Handschrift B herausgegeben von Ursula Schulze. Ins Neuhochdeutsche übersetzt und kommentiert von Siegfried Grosse (Stuttgart: Philipp Reclam jun., [2010]).

The Nibelungenlied, trans. A. T. Hatto (1965; London: Penguin, 1969).

Nicolas, Nicholas Harris, *History of Battle of Agincourt*. Rpt. (1832; London: Muller, 1970).

Nicolle, David, *Nicopolis 1396: The Last Crusade*. Campaign Series (London: Osprey Publishing, 1999).

Nicolle, David, *The Janissaries*. 11th ed. Elite Series, 58 (1995; London: Osprey Publishing, 2008).

Nicolle, David, *The Third Crusade 1191: Richard the Lionheart and the Battle for Jerusalem*. Osprey Campaign, 161 (Oxford: Ospre, 2005).

Nieser, Florian, *Die Lesbarkeit von Helden: uneindeutige Zeichen in der "Bataille d'Aliscans" und im "Willehalm" Wolframs von Eschenbach* (Stuttgart: J. B. Metzler, 2018).

Nigel H Jones, *Tower: An Epic History of the Tower of London* (London: Hutchinson, 2011).

Niiranen, Susanna, "From Prison to Print: Johannes Messenius' *Scondia illustrata* as a Co-Product of Early Modern Prison Writing," *Transmission of Knowledge in the Late Middle Ages and the Renaissance*, ed. Outi Merisalo, Miika Kuha, and Susanna Niiranen. Bibliologia, 53 (Turnhout: Brepols, 2019), 153–65.

Njal's Saga, trans. with intro. and notes by Robert Cook (London: Penguin, 1997).
Northern Revolts: Medieval and Early Modern Peasant Unrest in the Nordic Countries, ed. Kimmo Katajala. Studia Fennica. Historica, 8 (Helsinki: Finnish Literature Society, 2001).
Novellistik des Mittelalters: Märendichtung, ed., trans., and commentary by Klaus Grubmüller. Bibliothek des Mittelalters, 23 (Frankfurt a. M.: Deutscher Klassiker Verlag, 1996).
Nussbaum, Martha C. and Amartya Sen, *The Quality of Life*. WIDER Studies in Development Economics (Oxford: Clarendon Press; New York: Oxford University Press, 1993).
O'Connell Davidson, Julia, *Modern Slavery: The Margins of Freedom* (Basingstoke, Hampshire, and New York: Palgrave Mcmillan, 2015).
Oberman, Heiko A., "Europa afflicta: The Reformation of the Refugees," *Archiv für Reformationsgeschichte* 83 (1992): 91–111.
Ochoa, Rolando, *Intimate Crimes: Kidnapping, Gangs, and Trust in Mexico City*. Clarendon Studies in Criminology (Oxford: Oxford University Press, 2019).
Oexle, Otto Gerhard, "Die funktionale Dreiteilung als Deutungsschema der sozialen Wirklichkeit in der ständischen Gesellschaft des Mittelalters," *Ständische Gesellschaft und soziale Mobilität*, ed. Winfried Schulze (Munich: R. Oldenbourg, 1988), 19–51.
Olberg-Haverkate, Gabriele, *Die Textsorte Rechtsbücher*. Germanistische Arbeiten zu Sprache und Kulturgeschichte, 55 (Frankfurt a. M.: Peter Lang, 2018).
Olsson, Stefan, *The Hostages of the Northmen* ([Stockholm]: Stockholm University Press, 2019).
Ordering Medieval Society: Perspectives on Intellectual and Practical Modes of Shaping Social Relations, ed. Bernhard Jussen. Trans. by Pamela Selwyn. The Middle Ages Series (Philadelphia, PA: University of Pennsylvania Press, 2001).
Oswald von Wolkenstein: *Die Lebenszeugnisse Oswalds von Wolkenstein: Edition und Kommentar*, ed. Anton Schwob, together with Karin Kranich-Hofbauer, Ute Monika Schwob, and Brigitte Spreitzer. 5 vols. (Vienna, Cologne, and Weimar: Böhlau, 1999–2013).
Oswald von Wolkenstein: *Die Lieder Oswalds von Wolkenstein*, ed. Karl Kurt Klein. 4th, fundamentally rev. ed. by Burghart Wachinger. Altdeutsche Textbibliothek, 55 (Berlin and Boston: Walter de Gruyter, 2015).
Oswald von Wolkenstein: Leben – Werk – Rezeption, ed. Ulrich Müller and Margarete Springeth (Berlin and New York: Walter de Gruyter, 2011).
Oswald von Wolkenstein: *The Poems of Oswald von Wolkenstein: An English Translation of the Complete Works (1376/77–1445)*, by Albrecht Classen. The New Middle Ages (New York: Palgrave Macmillan, 2008).
Ott, N(orbert) H., "Sieben weise Meister," *Lexikon des Mittelalters*, Vol. VII (Munich: Lexma Verlag, 1995), col. 1836–39.
Otto von Freising: Bischof Otto von Freising und Rahewin, *Die Taten Friedrichs oder richtiger Cronica*, ed. Franz-Josef Schmale, trans. Adolf Schmidt (Darmstadt: Wissenschaftliche Buchgesellschaft, 2000).
Ottonis de Sancto Blasio chronica: Ad librum septem chronici Ottonis Frisingensis continuatae historiae appendix Chronica, ed. Adolf Hofmeister. Monumenta Germaniae Historica, 1.7. Scriptores, rer. Germ., 47 (Hanover and Leipzig: Hahn, 1912).
The Oxford Book of Late Medieval Verse and Prose, ed. Douglas Gray (Oxford: Clarendon Press, 1985).

The Oxford Dictionary of the Middle Ages, ed. Robert E. Bjork, 4 vols. (Oxford: Oxford University Press, 2010).

The Oxford Handbook of the African American Slave Narrative, ed. John Ernest (Oxford: Oxford University Press, 2014).

The Oxford History of the Prison: The Practice of Punishment in Western Society, ed. Norval Morris and David J. Rothman (New York: Oxford University Press, 1995).

Page, Jamie, "Masculinity and Prostitution in Late Medieval German Literature," *Speculum* 94.3 (2019): 739–73.

Page, R. I., *Chronicles of the Vikings: Records, Memorials and Myths* (Toronto and Buffalo, NY: University of Toronto Press, 1995), 58–76.

Pálsson, Herrman, *Oral Tradition and Saga Writing* (Vienna: Fassbaender, 1999).

Pältz, Eberhard H., "Von der Freyheyt eynisz Christen Menschen," *Kindlers Literatur Lexikon*, ed. Heinz Ludwig Arnold. 3rd, completely new ed. Vol. 10 (Stuttgart and Weimar: Metzler, 2009), 386–87.

Panayotakis, Stelios, *'The Story of Apollonius, King of Tyre': A Commentary*. Texte und Kommentare, 38 (Berlin and Boston: Walter de Gruyter, 2012).

Parnell, Geoffrey, *The Tower of London: Past and Present* (Stroud, Gloucestershire: Sutton Publishing, 2009).

Patterson, Olleander, "The Ancient and Medieval Origin of Freedom," *The Problem of Evil: Slavery, Freedom, and the Ambiguities of American Reform*, ed. Steven Mintz and John Stauffer (Amherst and Boston, MA: University of Massachusetts Press, 2007), 31–61.

Pensom, Roger, *Aucassin et Nicolete: The Poetry of Gender and Growing Up in the French Middle Ages* (Bern, Berlin, et al.: Peter Lang, 1999).

Perez, J. L., "Mercedarier," *Lexikon für Theologie und Kirche*, ed. Josef Höfer and Karl Rahner. Vol. 7 (Feiburg i. Br.: Herder, 1962), 304–05.

Pesch, O. H., "Freiheit. III," *Historisches Wörterbuch der Philosophie*, ed. Joachim Ritter. Vol. 2 (Darmstadt: Wissenschaftliche Buchgesellschaft, 1972), 1083–88.

Pesch, O., "Freiheit, Freie: Philosophische und Theologische," *Lexikon des Mittelalters*, ed. Robert-Henri Bautie, vol. 4 (Munich and Zürich: Artemis, 1995), 899–901.

Petrácek, Tomás, *Power and Exploitation in the Czech Lands in the 10th–12th Centuries: A Central European Perspective*. East Central and Eastern Europe in the Middle Ages, 40 (Leiden: Brill, 2017).

Petrina, Alessandra, *The Kingis Quair of James I of Scotland* (Padua: Unipress, 1997).

Phelpstead, Carl, *An Introduction to the Sagas of Icelanders* (Gainesville, Tallahassee, et al., FL: University Press of Florida, 2020).

Philippe de Beaumanoir, *Coutumes de Beauvaisis*. Texte critique publié avec une introduction, un glossaire et une table analytique par Amadée Salmon (Paris: A. Picard et fils, 1899–1900).

Phillips, Jonathan, *The Life and Legend of the Sultan Saladin* (London: The Bodley Head, 2019).

Phillips, Kim M., *Before Orientalism: Asian Peoples and Cultures in European Travel Writing, 1245–1510*. The Middle Ages Series (Philadelphia, PA: University of Pennsylvania Press, 2013).

Phillips, Philip Edward, "Boethius, the Prisoner, and *The Consolation of Philosophy*," *Prison Narratives from Boethius to Zana*, ed. id. (New York: Palgrave Macmillan, 2014), 11–33.

Phillips, William D., *Slavery in Medieval and Early Modern Iberia*. The Middle Ages Series (Philadelphia, PA: University of Pennsylvania Press, 2014).
Pick, Lucy K., *Her Father's Daughter: Gender, Power, and Religion in the Early Spanish Kingdoms* (Ithaca, NY, and London: Cornell University Press, 2017).
Pierson, Inga, "Piccarda's Weakness: Reflections on Freedom, Force, and Femininity in Dante's Paradiso," *Speculum* 94.1 (2019): 68–95.
Piracy and Captivity in the Mediterranean, 1550–1810, ed. Mario Klarer. Routledge Research in Early Modern History (Abingdon, Oxon: Routledge, 2019).
Piracy in the Early Modern Era: An Anthology of Sources, ed. and trans., with an intro. by Kris Lane and Arne Bialuschewski (Indianapolis, IN, and Cambridge: Hackett, 2019).
Pisarek, Janin, "Mehr als nur die Liebe zum Wassergeist: Das Motiv der 'gestörten Mahrtenehe' in europäischen Volkserzählungen," *Märchenspiegel. Zeitschrift für internationale Märchenforschung und Märchenpflege* 27.1 (2016): 3–8.
Plotke, Seraina, "Polydimensionale Parodie: Verfahren literarischer Verkehrung im 'Helmbrecht' Wernhers des Gärtners," *Parodie und Verkehrung: Formen und Funktionen spielerischer Verfremdung und spöttischer Verzerrung in Texten des Mittelalters und der Frühen Neuzeit*, ed. eadem and Stefan Seeber. Encomia Deutsch, 3 (Göttingen: V&R unipress, 2017), 73–88.
Poe, Edgar Allan, *The Selected Writings of Edgar Allan Poe: Authoritative Texts, Backgrounds and Contexts, Criticism*, selected and ed. by Gary R. Thompson (New York: Norton, 2004).
Pohl, Walter, *Die Welt der Babenberger: Schleier, Kreuz und Schwert*, ed. Brigitte Vacha (Graz: Verlag Styria, 1995).
Poirion, Daniel, *Le poète et le prince: l'évolution du lyrisme courtois de Guillaume de Machaut à Charles d'Orléans*. Publications de la Faculté des Lettres et des Sciences Humaines, 35 (Paris: Presses Universitaires de France, 1965).
Pollmann, Judith, *Catholic Identity and the Revolt of the Netherlands, 1520–1635* (Oxford: Oxford University Press, 2011).
Poole, Austin Lane, *From Domesday Book to Magna Carta 1087–1216*. 2nd ed. (1951; Oxford: Oxford University Press, 1993).
Poser, Thomas, *Raum in Bewegung mythische Logik und räumliche Ordnung im "Erec" und im "Lanzelet"*. Bibliotheca Germanica, 70 (Tübingen: Narr Francke Attempto, 2018).
Powell, James M., *Albertanus of Brescia: The Pursuit of Happiness in the Early Thirteenth Century*. The Middle Ages Series (Philadelphia, PA: University of Pennsylvania Press, 1992).
Prechsl, Magdalena, *Nürnberger Kriminalgeschichte: Henkerhaus, Lochgefängnis und Schuldturm*. Historische Spaziergänge, 16 (Nuremberg: Sandberg-Verlag, 2019).
Price, Byron Eugene and John Charles Morris, *Prison Privatization: The Many Facets of a Controversial Industry* (Westport, CT: ABC-CLIO, 2012).
Price, Neil, *Children of Ash and Elm: A History of the Vikings* (New York: Basic Books, 2020), 141–46, 150–54.
Prison Narratives from Boethius to Zana, ed. Philip Edward Phillips (New York, NY: Palgrave Macmillan, 2014).
Public Execution in England, 1573 – 1868, ed. Leigh Yetter. 10 vols. (London: Pickering & Chatto, 2009-2010).

Putzo, Christine, *Konrad Fleck: 'Flore und Blanscheflur': Text und Untersuchungen*. Münchener Texte und Untersuchungen zur deutschen Literatur des Mittelalters, 143 (Berlin and Boston: Walter de Gruyter, 2015).

Raaflaub, Kurt, "freedom in the ancient world," *The Oxford Companion to Classical Civilization*, ed. Simon Hornblower and Antony Spawforth (Oxford: Oxford University Press, 1998; published online, 2003 at: https://www.oxfordreference.com/view/10.1093/acref/9780198601654.001.0001/acref-9780198601654-e-276 (last accessed on Jan. 15, 2021).

Race and Liberty in America, ed. Jonathan J. Bean (Lexington, KY: Kentucky University Press, 2009).

Rădulescu, Adrian, *Ovid in Exile: Ovidiu la Pontul Euxin* (Las Vegas, NV: Vita Histria, 2019).

Raffield, Ben, "The Slave Markets of the Viking World: Comparative Perspectives on an 'Invisible Archaeology'," *Slavery & Abolition* 40.4 (2019): 682–705.

Rapp, Catherine Teresa, *Burgher and Peasant in the Works of Thomasin von Zirclaria, Freidank, and Hugo von Trimberg*. The Catholic University of America Studies in German, 7 Rpt. (1936; New York: AMS Press, 1970).

Rawson, Claude, *God, Gulliver and Genocide: Barbarism and the European Imagination, 1492–1945* (Oxford: Oxford University Press, 2001).

Reading the Middle Ages: Sources from Europe, Byzantium, and the Islamic World, ed. Barbara H. Rosenwein (Peterborough, Ont.: Broadview Press, 2006).

Réalités, images, écritures de la prison au Moyen Âge, ed. Jean-Marie Fritz and Silvère Menegaldo together with Galice Pascault. Écritures (Dijon: Éditions universitaires de Dijon, 2012).

Rebschloe, Timo, *Der Drache in der mittelalterlichen Literatur Europas*. Beiträge zur älteren Literaturgeschichte (Heidelberg: Universitätsverlag Winter, 2014).

Reitz, Dirk, *Die Kreuzzüge Ludwigs IX. von Frankreich 1248/1270*. Neue Aspekte der europäischen Mittelalterforschung, 3 (Münster: LIT, 2005).

The Relevance of The Humanities in the Twenty-First Century: Past and Present, ed. Albrecht Classen. Special issue of *Humanities Open Access*, June 2020; online at: https://www.mdpi.com/journal/humanities/special_issues/pas_pre.

Remaking Boethius: The English Language Translation Tradition of The Consolation of Philosophy, ed. Brian Donaghey, Noel Harold Kaylorm, Philip Edward Phillips, and Paul E. Szarmach. Arizona Studies in the Middle Ages and Renaissance, 40 (Tempe, AZ: Arizona Center for Medieval & Renaissance Studies, 2019).

Reston, James, *Warriors of God: Richard the Lionheart and Saladin in the Third Crusade* (New York: Doubleday, 2001).

Revelations of the Medieval World, ed. Georges Duby, trans. Arthur Goldhammer. A History of Private Life, II (1985; Cambridge, MA, and London: The Belknap Press of Harvard University Press, 1988).

Reyerson, Kathryn, "Pirates as Marginals in the Medieval Mediterranean World," *Rethinking Medieval Margins and Marginality*, ed. Anne E. Zimo, Tiffany D. Vann Sprecher, Kathryn Reyerson, and Debra Blumenthal. Studies in Medieval History and Culture (London and New York: Routledge, 2020), 186–203.

Reynolds, Susan, *Kingdoms and Communities in Western Europe, 900–1300*. 2nd ed. (1984; Oxford: Oxford University Press, 1997).

Rheinheimer, Martin, *Der fremde Sohn: Hark Olufs' Wiederkehr aus der Sklaverei.* Nordfriesische Quellen und Studien, 3 (Wachholtz: Neumünster 2001).
Ricciardelli, Fabrizio, *The Politics of Exclusion in Early Renaissance Florence* (Turnhout: Brepols, 2007).
Richard Coeur de Lion in History and Myth, ed. Janet L. Nelson. King's College London Medieval Studies, 7 (London: King's College, Centre for Late Antique and Medieval Studies, 1992).
Richthofen, Karl von, *Untersuchungen über friesische Rechtsgeschichte* (Berlin: Hertz, 1880).
Rieken, Bernd, *"Nordsee ist Mordsee": Sturmfluten und ihre Bedeutung für die Mentalitätsgeschichte der Friesen.* Veröffentlichungen des Nordfriisk Instituut: Abhandlungen und Vorträge zur Geschichte Ostfrieslands, 186 (Münster and New York: Waxmann, 2005).
Rio, Alice, *Slavery after Rome, 500–1100.* Oxford Studies in Medieval European History (Oxford: Oxford University Press, 2017).
Roberta, Davidson, "Prison and Knightly Identity in Sir Thomas Malory's Morte Darthur," *Arthuriana* 14.2 (2004): 54–63.
Rodriguez, Jarbel, *Captives and Their Saviors in the Medieval Crown of Aragon* (Washington, DC: Catholic University of America Press, 1900).
Rodriguez, Jarbel, *Captives and Their Saviors in the Medieval Crown of Aragon* (Washington, DC: The Catholic University of America Press, 2007).
Rogers, Clifford J., "Agincourt, Battle of," *The Oxford Encyclopedia of Medieval Warfare and Military Technology*, ed. Clifford J. Rogers. Vol. 1 (Oxford: Oxford University Press, 2010), 7–10.
Roll, Carsten, "Vom 'asega' zum 'redjeven': Zur Verfassungsgeschichte Frieslands im Mittelalter," *Concilium Medii Aevi* 13 (2010): 187–221.
Le Roman de Cassidorus, ed. Joseph Palermo. Société des Anciens Textes Français, 1 and 2 (Paris: Picard 1963–1964).
Le Roman de Helcanus. Édition d'un texte en prose du XIIIe siècle par Henri Niedzielski. Textes Littéraires Françaises, 418 (Geneva: Droz 1966).
Le Roman des Sept Sages de Rome. A Critical Edition of the Two Verse Redactions of a Twelfth-Century Romance, ed. Mary B. Speer. The Edward C. Armstrong Monographs on Medieval Literature, 4 (Lexington, KY: French Forum Publisher, 1989).
The Romance of Floire and Blanchefleur: A French Idyllic Poem of the Twelfth Century, trans. Merton Jerome Hubert. University of North Carolina Studies in the Romance Languages and Literatures, 63 (Chapel Hill, NC: The University of North Carolina Press, 1966).
Romane des 15. und 16. Jahrhunderts: Nach den Erstdrucken mit sämtlichen Holzschnitten, ed. Jan-Dirk Müller. Bibliothek der Frühen Neuzeit, 1 (Frankfurt a. M.: Deutscher Klassiker Verlag, 1990).
Römer, Zdenka Janeković, *The Frame of Freedom: The Nobility of Dubrovnik Between the Middle Ages and Humanism.* Studies in the History of Dubrovnik, 5 (Zagreb and Dubrovnik: Hrvatska akademija znanosti i umjetnosti, 2015).
Roon-Bassermann, Elisabeth von, *Dante und Aristoteles: das Convivio und der mehrfache Schriftsinn* (Freiburg i. Br.: Herder, 1956).
Ros, William L. L. F. de, *Memorials of the Tower of London* (1866; Norderstedt: Hansebooks GmbH, 2018).

Rothschild, Judith R., *Narrative Technique in the Lais of Marie de France: Themes and Variations*. North Carolina Studies in the Romance Languages and Literatures, 1 (Chapel Hill, NC: U.N.C. Dept. of Romance Languages, 1974).
The Routledge Companion to Free Will, ed. Kevin Timpe, Meghan Griffith, and Neil Levy. Routledge Pilosophy Companions (New York and London: Routledge, 2017).
The Routledge History of Slavery, ed. Gad Heuman and Travor Burnard. The Routledge Histories (London and New York: Routledge, 2011).
Rudolf von Ems, *Der guote Gêrhart*, ed. John A. Asher. Altdeutsche Textbibliothek, 56. 3rd ed. (1971; Tübingen: Max Niemeyer, 2013).
Rudolf von Ems: Albrecht Classen, *An English Translation of Rudolf von Ems's* Der guote Gêrhart (Newcastle upon Tyne: Cambridge Scholars Press, 2016).
Rudolf von Ems, *Zennin gēruharuto: Ōkō kishitachi shimintachi*, trans. Hirao Kōzō (Tōkyō: Keiō Gijuku Daigaku Shuppankai, 2005).
Rudolf, Hans Ulrich, *Grundherrschaft und Freiheit im Mittelalter* (Düsseldorf: Schwann, 1976).
Ruge, Nicolaus, "Schiltberger, Hans," *Deutsches Literaturlexikon: Das Mittelalter*, ed. Wolfgang Achnitz. Vol. 3: *Reiseberichte und Geschichtsdichtung* (Berlin and Boston: Walter de Gruyter, 2012), 594–96.
Sabaté, Flocel, *Medieval Urban Identity: Health, Economy and Regulation* (Newcastle upon Tyne: Cambridge Scholars Press, 2015).
Sachs, Hans, *Tragedia mit 23 Personen von der strengen Lieb Herr Tristrant mit der schönen Königin Isalden. Faksimileausgabe nach dem ältesten Druck aus dem Jahre 1561 erschienen in Nürnberg*, ed. Danielle Buschinger and Wolfgang Spiewok. Wodan, 29. Serie 1. Texte des Mittelalters, 8 (Greifswald: Reineke-Verlag, 1993).
Sachsenspiegel: The Saxon Mirror: A Sachsenspiegel *of the Fourteenth Century*, trans. Maria Dobozy. The Middle Ages Series (Philadelphia, PA: University of Pennsylvania Press, 1999).
The Saga of the People of Laxardal and Bolli Bollason's Tale, trans. Keneva Kunz, ed. with an intro. by Bergljót S. Kristjánsdóttir (London: Penguin, 1997).
Salicrú i Lluch, Roser, "L'esclau com a inversió? Aprofitament, assalariament i rendibilitat del treball esclau en l'entorn català tardomedieval," *Recerques: història, economia, cultura* 52–53 (2006): 49–85.
Samaké, Abdoulaye, *Liebesträume in der deutsch-, französisch- und italienischsprachigen Erzählliteratur des 12. bis 15. Jahrhunderts*. Traum – Wissen – Erzählen, 6 (Paderborn: Wilhelm Fink Verlag, 2020).
Sandidge, Marilyn L., "Gawain, Giants, and Tennis the Fifteenth Century," *Pleasure and Leisure in the Middle Ages and Early Modern Age: Cultural-Historical Perspectives on Toys, Games, and Entertainment*, ed. Albrecht Classen. Fundamentals of Medieval and Early Modern Culture, 23 (Berlin and Boston: Walter de Gruyter, 2019), 473–93.
Sanna, Simonetta, *Nazi-Täterinnen in der deutschen Literatur: die Herausforderung des Bösen*. Signaturen der Gewalt, 1 (Frankfurt a. M., Bern, Brussels, et al.: Peter Lang, 2017).
Sawyer, P. H., *Kings and Vikings: Scandinavia and Europe AD 700–1100* (New York and London: Routledge, 2002).
Sawyer, Wendy and Peter Wagner, "Mass Incarceration: The Whole Pie 2020," online report at: https://www.prisonpolicy.org/reports/pie2020.html.
Saxon Mirror, see *Sachsenspiegel*

Schaller, H. M., "Petrus de Vinea," *Lexikon des* Mittelalters, Vol. VI (Munich: Artemis, 1993), 1987–88.

Schiltberger, Johann, *The Bondage and Travels of Johann Schiltberger, a Native of Bavaria, in Europe, Asia, and Africa 1396–1427*, trans. from the Heidelberg ms. ed. in 1859 by Karl Friedrich Neumann by J. Buchan Telfer. With notes by P. Bruun and a preface, introduction and notes by the translator and editor (London: Hakluyt Society, 1897).

Schiltberger, Johannes, *Als Sklave im Osmanischen Reich und bei den Tataren: 1394–1427*, ed. Ulrich Schlemmer. Alte abenteuerliche Reiseberichte (Wiesbaden: Ed. Erdmann, 2008).

Schiltberger, Johannes: *Johann Schiltbergers Irrfahrt durch den Orient: Der aufsehenerregende Bericht einer Reise, die 1394 begann und erst nach über 30 Jahren ein Ende fand*. Aus dem Mittelhochdeutschen übertragen und herausgegeben von Markus Tremmel. Bayerische Abenteuer (Taufkirchen: Via Verbis Bavarica, 2000).

Schmale, Franz-Josef, *Die Chronik Ottos von St. Blasien und die Marbacher Annalen*. Ausgewählte Quellen zur deutschen Geschichte des Mittelalters, 18, a (Darmstadt: Wissenschaftliche Buchgesellschaft, 1998).

Schmidt, Hartmut, *Libertas- und Freiheitskollokationen in Luthers Traktaten "Von der Freiheit eines Christenmenschen" und "De libertate christiana"*, ed. Rudolf Bentzinger and Norbert Richard Wolf. Würzburger Beiträge zur deutschen Philologie, 11 (Mannheim: Leibniz-Institut für Deutsche Sprache (IDS), Bibliothek, 2018).

Schmidt, Joachim, *Herrschaft durch Schrecken und Liebe: Vorstellungen und Begründungen im Mittelalter*. Orbis mediaevalis, 17 (Göttingen: V&R unipress, 2019).

Schmitt, Christoph, "Mann auf der Suche nach der verlorenen Frau (AaTh 400)," *Enzyklopädie des Märchens*, ed. Rolf Wilhelm Brednich. Vol. 9 (Berlin and New York: Walter de Gruyter, 1999), cols. 195–210.

Schmitz, Florian, *Der Orient in Diskursen des Mittelalters und im "Willehalm" Wolframs von Eschenbach*. Kultur, Wissenschaft, Literatur: Beiträge zur Mittelalterforschung, 32 (Berlin: Peter Lang, 2018).

Schmitz-Esser, Romedio, *Der Leichnam im Mittelalter: Einbalsamierung, Verbrennung und die kulturelle Konstruktion des toten Körpers*. Mittelalter-Forschungen, 48. Sec. unchanged ed. (2014; Ostfildern: Jan Thorbecke Verlag, 2016) (this will soon [2021] appear in an English translation by Albrecht Classen and Carolyn Radtke)

Schneider, Martin, *Kampf, Streit und Konkurrenz: Wettkämpfe als Erzählformen der Pluralisierung in Mären*. Aventiuren, 15 (Göttingen: V&R unipress, 2020).

Scholz, Luca, *Borders and Freedom of Movement in the Holy Roman Empire* (Oxford: Oxford University Press, 2020).

Schott, C., "Freiheit, Freie (Rechtsgesch[ichte])," *Lexikon des Mittelalters*, ed. Robert-Henri Bautie, vol. 4 (Munich and Zürich: Artemis, 1988), 896–99.

Schulz, Armin, "Spaltungsphantasmen – Erzählen von der "gestörten Mahrtenehe"," *Wolfram-Studien* 18 (2004): 233–62.

Schulz, Knut, *"Denn sie lieben die Freiheit so sehr ...": Kommunale Aufstände und Enstehung des europäischen Bürgertums im Hochmittelalter* (Darmstadt: Wissenschaftliche Buchgesellschaft, 1992).

Schumacher, Meinolf, "Toleranz, Kaufmannsgeist und Heiligkeit im Kulturkontakt mit den 'Heiden'. Die mittelhochdeutsche Erzählung "Der guote Gêrhart" von Rudolf von Ems," *Zeitschrift für interkulturelle Germanistik* 1.1 (2010): 49–58.

Schupp, Volker and Hans Szklenar, *Ywain auf Schloß Rodenegg: Eine Bildgeschichte nach dem 'Iwein' Hartmanns von Aue* (Sigmaringen: Jan Thorbecke, 1996).
Schuster, Peter, *Verbrecher, Opfer, Heilige: eine Geschichte des Tötens 1200 – 1700* (Stuttgart: Klett-Cotta, 2015).
Schütze, Paul, *Die Entstehung des Rechtssatzes: Stadtluft macht frei*. Historische Studien, 36 (Berlin: Ebering, 1903).
Schwob, Anton, *Oswald von Wolkenstein: eine Biographie*. Schriftenreihe des Südtiroler Kulturinstitutes, 4. 3rd ed. (1977; Bozen: Verlagsanstalt Athesia, 1989).
Schwob, Anton: "'Toleranz' im Türkentraktat des Georg von Ungarn: Eine Infragestellung," "*swer sînen vriunt behaltet, daz ist lobelîch*": *Festschrift für András Vizkelety zum 70. Geburtstag*, ed. Márta Nagy and László Jónácsik, together with Edit Madas and Gábor Sarbak (Piliscsaba and Budapest: Katholische Péter-Pázmány-Universität, Philosophische Fakultät, 2001), 253–59.
Scott, Jamie S., *Christians and Tyrants: The Prison Testimonies of Boethius, Thomas More, and Dietrich Bonhoeffer*. Toronto Studies in Religion, 19 (New York, Washington, DC, Baltimore, MD, et al.: Peter Lang, 1995).
Scott, Tom, *The Swiss and Their Neighbours, 1460–1560: Between Accommodation and Aggression* (Oxford: Oxford University Press, 2017).
Seeraub im Mittelmeerraum: Piraterie, Korsarentum und maritime Gewalt von der Antike bis zur Neuzeit, ed. Nikolas Jaspert and Sebastian Kolditz. Mittelmeerstudien, 3 (Munich and Paderborn: Wilhelm Fink and Ferdinand Schöningh, 2013).
Sela, Ron, *The Legendary Biographies of Tamerlane: Islam and Heroic Apocrypha in Central Asia*. Trans. Clements R. Markham. Cambridge Studies in Islamic Civilization (Cambridge: Cambridge University Press, 2011).
Sen, Amartya, *Development as Freedom* (Oxford: Oxford University Press, 1999).
Sen, Amartya, *Elemente einer Theorie der Menschenrechte*, trans. Ute Kruse-Ebeling. Was bedeutet das alles (Stuttgart: Philipp Reclam, jun., 2020).
Sen, Amartya, *On Ethics and Economics*. The Royer Lectures (Oxford and New York: Basil Blackwell, 1987).
Sen, Amartya, *Peace and Democratic Society*. Open Reports Series, 1 (Cambridge: Open Book Publishers, 2011).
Sen, Amartya, *Rationale Dummköpfe: Eine Kritik der Verhaltensgrundlagen der Ökonomischen Theorie*, trans. Valerie Gföhler. Was bedeutet das alles (Stuttgart: Philipp Reclam, jun., 2020).
Sen, Amartya, *The Idea of Justice* (Cambridge, MA: Belknap Press of Harvard University Press, 2009).
Sertl, Brigitte, *Carceri e invenzioni: italienische Schriftsteller in Gefangenschaft*. Abhandlungen zur Sprache und Literatur, 79 (Bonn: Romanistischer Verlag, 1995).
Seth, Vanita, "The Origins of Racism: A Critique of the History of Ideas," *History & Theory* 59.3 (2020): 343–68.
The Seventh Crusade, 1244–1254: Sources and Documents, ed. Peter Jackson. Crusade Texts in Translation, 16 (Aldershot: Ashgate, 2007).
Shaw, Christine, *The Politics of Exile in Renaissance Italy* (Cambridge: Cambridge University Press, 2000).
Siebert, Barbara, *Rezeption und Produktion: Bezugssysteme in der "Kudrun"*. Göppinger Arbeiten zur Germanistik, 491 (Göppingen: Kümmerle, 1988).

Siewert, G., "Freiheit," *Handbuch theologischer Grundbegriffe*, ed. Heinrich Fries. Vol. I (Munich: Kösel-Verlag, 1962), 392–98.

Simon, Anne, "The Fortunatus Volksbuch in the Light of Later Mediaeval Travel Literature," *Fifteenth-Century Studies* 12 (1987): 175–86.

Simonkay, Zsuzsanna, "False Brotherhood in Chaucer's The Knight's Tale / Part 1: Sworn Brotherhood and Chaucer's Sources on Friendship," *HUSSE 11: Proceedings of the 11th Conference of the Hungarian Society for the Study of English*, ed. Veronika Ruttkay and Bálint Gárdos (Budapest: L'Harmattan, 2014), 159–71.

Simonkay, Zsuzsanna, "False Brotherhood in Chaucer's "The Knight's Tale," Part 2: Palamon and Arcite – False Friends Will Be Friends," *Heroes and Saints: Studies in Honour of Katalin Halácsy*, ed. eadem and Andrea Nagy (Budapest: Mondat, 2015), 187–202.

Skenazi, Cynthia, "Les Prisons' Poetics of Conversion," *A Companion to Marguerite de Navarre*, ed. Gary Ferguson, Gary and Mary B. McKinley. Brill's Companions to the Christian Tradition, 42 (Leiden: Brill, 2013), 211–35.

Skinner, Quentin, *Foundations of Modern Political Thought*. 2 vols. (Cambridge and New York: Cambridge University Press, 1978).

Sklaverei in der Vormoderne: Beispiele aus außereuropäischen Gesellschaften, ed. Stephan Conermann. Dhau, 2 (St. Ingbert: Röhrig Universitätsverlag, 2017).

Skyum-Nielsen, Niels, "Nordic Slavery in an International Context," *Medieval Scandinavia* 11 (1978–1979): 126–48.

The Slave Narrative, ed. Kimberly Drake. Critical Insights (Ipswich, MA: Grey House Publ./ Salem Press, 2014).

Slavery and the Slave Trade in the Eastern Mediterranean (c. 1000–1500 CE), ed. Reuven Amitai and Christoph Cluse. Mediterranean Nexus 1100–1700, 5 (Turnhout: Brepols, 2017).

Slavery's Capitalism: A New History of American Economic Development, ed. Sven Beckert and Seth Rockman. Early American Studies (Philadelphia: University of Pennsylvania Press, 2016).

Slaves and Slave Agency in the Ottoman Empire, ed. Stephan Conermann and Gül Şen. Ottoman Studies / Osmanistische Studien, 7 (Göttingen: V&R Unipress, 2020).

Slocum, Kay, *Medieval Civilization* (Belmont, CA: Thomson Wadsworth, 2005).

Sobanet, Andrew, *Jail Sentences: Representing Prison in Twentieth-Century French Fiction*. Stages (Lincoln, NE: University of Nebraska Press, 2008).

Sobers-Khan, Nur, *Slaves Without Shackles: Forced Labour and Manumission in the Galata Court Registers, 1560–1572*. Studien zur Sprache, Kultur und Geschichte der Türkvölker, 20 (Berlin: Schwarz, 2014).

Social Norms in Medieval Scandinavia, ed. Jakub Morawiec, Aleksandra Jochymek, and Grzegorz Bartusik. Beyond Medieval Europe (Leeds: Arc Humanities Press, 2019).

Sohmer Tai, Emily, "Restitution and the Definition of a Pirate: The Case of Sologrus De Nigro," *Mediterranean Historical Review* 19 (2004): 34–70.

Sohmer Tai, Emily, "The Legal Status of Piracy in Medieval Europe," *History Compass* 10.11 (2012): 838–51.

Sommerfeld, Martin Philipp, *Staatensouveränität und ius cogens; eine Untersuchung zu Ursprung und Zukunftsfähigkeit der beiden Konzepte im Völkerrecht. State Sovereignty and ius cogens*. Beiträge zum ausländischen öffentlichen Recht und Völkerrecht, 287 (Berlin: Springer, 2019).

Sorensen, G., "The Reception of the Political Aristotle in the Late Middle Ages (from Brunetto Latini to Dante Alighieri). Hypotheses and Suggestions," *Renaissance Readings of the Corpus Aristotelicum: Proceedings of the Conference held in Copenhagen 23–25 April 1998*, ed. Marianne Pade. Renaessancestudier, 9 (Copenhagen: Museum Tusculanum Press, 2001), 9–25.

La sottrazione internazionale di minori da parte di un genitore: studi e documenti sul "kidnapping" internazionale, ed. Franco Mosconi. Pubblicazioni della Università di Pavia: Studi nelle scienze giuridiche e sociali. Nuova serie, 53 (Padua: CEDAM, 1988).

Spaemann, R., "Freiheit, IV," *Historisches Wörterbuch der Philosophie*, ed. Joachim Ritter. Vol. 2 (Darmstadt: Wissenschaftliche Buchgesellschaft, 1972), 1088–98.

Spearing, A. C., "Prison, Writing, Absence: Representing the Subject in the English Poems of Charles d'Orléans," *Chaucer to Spenser: A Critical Reader*, ed. Pearsall, Derek (Oxford: Blackwell Publishing, 1999; orig. 1992), 297–311.

Spiering, Jamie Anne, "'Liber est causa sui': Thomas Aquinas and the Maxim 'The Free is the Cause of Itself'," *The Review of Metaphysics* 65.2 (2011): 351–76.

Ständische Gesellschaft und soziale Mobilität, ed. Winfried Schulze (Munich: R. Oldenbourg, 1988).

Starn, Randolph, *Contrary Commonwealth: The Theme of Exile in Medieval and Renaissance Italy* (Berkeley, CA: University of California Press, 1982).

The State and Its Limits: The Economic and Politics of Freedom for the III Millennium – Essays in Honor of Prince Hans-Adam II of Liechtenstein, ed. Kurt R. Leube (Triesen: van Eck Verlag, 2020).

Stede, Marga, *Schreiben in der Krise: die Texte des Heinrich Kaufringers*. Literatur, Imagination, Realität, 5 (Trier: Wissenschaftlicher Verlag Trier, 1993).

Steensen, Thomas, *Die Friesen* (Kiel and Hamburg: Wachholtz, 2020).

Steffen, Uwe, *Drachenkampf: Der Mythos vom Bösen*. Buchreihe Symbole. 2nd ed. (1984; Stuttgart: Kreuz-Verlag, 1989).

Steinhöwel, Heinrich: Tina Terrahe, *Heinrich Steinhöwels* Apollonius: *Edition und Studien*. Frühe Neuzeit, 179 (Berlin and Boston: Walter de Gruyter, 2013).

Steinwascher, Gerd, "Städtische Freiheit und gräfliche Residenz Oldenburg im späten Mittelalter und im Zeitalter der Reformation," *Oldenburg: Stadtgeschichte in Bildern und Texten. Vom Heidenwall zur Wissenschaftsstadt*, ed. Udo Elerd (Oldenburg: Isensee, 2009), 33–44.

Strauss, Paul, *In Hope of Heaven: English Recusant Prison Writings of the Sixteenth Century*. American University Studies. Series IV, English Language and Literature, 166 (New York: Peter Lang, 1995).

Stretter, Robin, "Flowers of Friendship: Amity and Tragic Desire in The Two Noble Kinsmen," *English Literary Renaissance* 47.2 (2017): 270–300.

Der Stricker, *Erzählungen, Fabeln, Reden. Mittelhochdeutsch / Neuhochdeutsch*, ed., trans., and commentary by Otfrid Ehrismann (Stuttgart: Philipp Reclam jun., 1992).

Stuard, Susan Mosher. "Ancillary Evidence for the Decline of Medieval Slavery," *Past & Present* 149 (1995): 3–28.

Sturges, Robert Stuart, "Race, Sex, Slavery: Reading Fanon with Aucassin et Nicolette," *Postmedieval* 6 (2015/16): 12–22.

Symes, Carol, "The Middle Ages Between Nationalism and Colonialism," *French Historical Studies* 34.1 (2011): 37–46.

Taylor, Scott L., "Feudalism in Literature and Society," *Handbook of Medieval Culture: Fundamental Aspects and Conditions of the European Middle Ages*, ed. Albrecht Classen (Berlin and Boston: Walter de Gruyter, 2015), vol. 1, 465–76.

Taylor, Scott L., "*Jeux Interdits*: The Rationale and Limits of Clerical and Lay Efforts to Enjoin '*Scurrilia Solatia*'," *Pleasure and Leisure in the Middle Ages and Early Modern Age: Cultural-Historical Perspectives on Toys, Games, and Entertainment*, ed. Albrecht Classen. Fundamentals of Medieval and Early Modern Culture, 23 (Berlin and Boston: Walter de Gruyter, 2019), 529–34.

Taylor, Scott L., "Law in the Middle Ages," *Handbook of Medieval Studies: Terms – Methods – Trends*, ed. Albrecht Classen. Vol. 2 (Berlin and New York: Walter de Gruyter, 2010), 771–88.

Taylor, Scott L., "The Conquest of Sodom: Symbiosis of Calumny and Canon in the *Jus Belli* from Ireland to the Indies," *War and Peace: Critical Issues in European Societies and Literature 800–1800* ed. Albrecht Classen and Nadia Margolis. Fundamentals of Medieval and Early Modern Culture, 8 (Berlin and New York: Walter de Gruyter, 2011), 81–97.

Tears, Sighs and Laughter: Expressions of Emotions in the Middle Ages, ed. Per Förnegård, Erika Kihlman, Mia Åkestam, and Gunnel Engwall. KVHAA konferenser, 92 (Stockholm: Kungl. Vitterhets Historie och Antikvitets Akademien, 2017).

Terpstra, Nicholas, *Religious Refugees in the Early Modern World: An Alternative History of the Reformation* (Cambridge: Cambridge University Press, 2015).

Terrahe, see Steinhöwel

Thomas, Arvind, *Piers Plowman and the Reinvention of Church Law in the Late Middle Ages* (Toronto: University of Toronto Press, 2019).

Thompson, Faith, *Magna Carta – Its Role in The Making of The English Constitution 1300–1629* (Minneapolis, MN: University of Minnesota Press, 1948).

Toch, Michael, "Wirtschaft und Verfolgung: die Bedeutung der Ökonomie für die Kreuzzugspogrome des 11. und 12. Jahrhunderts. Mit einem Anhang zum Sklavenhandel der Juden," *Juden und Christen zur Zeit der Kreuzzüge*, ed. Alfred Haverkamp. Vorträge und Forschungen. Konstanzer Arbeitskreis für Mittelalterliche Geschichte, 47 (Sigmaringen: Jan Thorbeckek, 1999), 253–85.

Took, John F., *Dante* (Princeton, NJ, and Oxford: Princeton University Press, 2020).

Tornau, Christian, "Saint Augustine," *The Stanford Encyclopedia of Philosophy* (Summer 2020 edition), ed. Edward N. Zalta, 2020, online at: https://plato.stanford.edu/archives/sum2020/entries/augustine/ (last accessed on Jan. 15, 2021).

Torres, Margarita, *Enrique de Castilla* (Barcelona: Plaza & Janés, 2003).

Treadgold, Donald W., *Freedom: A History* (New York: New York University Press, 1990).

Treason: Medieval and Early Modern Adultery, Betrayal, and Shame, ed. Larissa Tracy. Explorations in Medieval Culture, 10 (Leiden and Boston: Brill, 2019).

Troutt Powell, Eve M., *Tell This in My Memory: Stories of Enslavement from Egypt, Sudan, and the Ottoman Empire*. History, Middle East Studies (Stanford, CA: Stanford University Press, 2012).

Truitt, E. R., *Medieval Robots: Mechanism, Magic, Nature, and Art*. The Middle Ages Series (Philadelphia, PA: University of Pennsylvania Press, 2015).

Turchetti, Mario, *Tyrannie et tyrannicide de l'Antiquité à nos jours*. Bibliothèque de la Renaissance, 11 (Paris: Classiques Garnier, 2013).

Turner, Ralph V. and Richard R. Heiser, *The Reign of Richard Lionheart: Ruler of the Angevin Empire, 1189–1199*. The Medieval World (Harlow, Munich, et al.: Longman, 2000).
Turner, Ralph, *Magna Carta* (London: Taylor and Francis, 2016).
Turning, Patricia, *Municipal Officials, Their Public, and the Negotiation of Justice in Medieval Languedoc: Fear not the Madness of the Raging Mob*. Later Medieval Europe, 10 (Leiden and Boston: Brill, 2012).
Two Thousand Years of Solitude: Exile After Ovid, ed. Jennifer Ingleheart. Classical Presences (Oxford: Oxford University Press, 2011).
Tyrannentötung: eine Textsammlung, ed. Wilhelm Baum (Munich: Herbert Utz Verlag, 2017).
Ulrich von Zatzikhoven, *Lanzelet*, trans. by Thomas Kerth, with additional notes by Kenneth G. T. Webster and Roger Sherman Loomis. Records of Western Civilization (New York: Columbia University Press, 2004).
Ulrich von Zatzikhoven, *Lanzelet: Mittelhochdeutsch/Neuhochdeutsch* von Wolfgang Spiewok. Wodan, 71. Texte des Mittelalters, 16 (Greifswald: Reineke-Verlag, 1997).
Ulrich von Zatzikhoven, *Lanzelet: Text – Übersetzung – Kommentar*, ed. Florian Kragl (Berlin and New York: Walter de Gruyter, 2009).
Umana "cosa è aver compassione degli afflitti": raccontare, consolare, curare nella narrative europea da Boccaccio al Seicento. Special issue of *Levia Gravia: quaderno annuale di letteratura italiana* (Alessandria: Ed. dell' Orso, 2015).
Unfreiheit und Sexualität von der Antike bis zur Gegenwart, ed. Josef Fischer und Melanie Ulz, together with Marcel Simonis. Sklaverei – Knechtschaft – Zwangsarbeit, 6 (Hildesheim and New York: Olms, 2010).
Untersuchungen zur Überlieferung und Rezeption spätmittelalterlicher Lieder und Spruchgedichte im 15. und 16. Jahrhundert: die "Streuüberlieferung" von Liedern und Reimpaarrede Oswalds von Wolkenstein, ed. Hans-Dieter Mück and Dirk Joschko. Litterae 36 (Göppingen: Kümmerle, 1985).
Upon My Husband's Death: Widows in the Literature and Histories of Medieval Europe, ed. Louise Mirrer. Studies in Medieval and Early Modern Civilization (Ann Arbor, MI: The University of Michigan Press, 1992).
Urban Liberties and Citizenship from the Middle Ages Up To Now: actes du colloque 2009 de la Commission Internationale pour l'Histoire des Villes = Städtische Freiheiten und bürgerliche Partizipation vom Mittelalter bis heute, ed. Michel Pauly and Alexander Lee. Beiträge zur Landes- und Kulturgeschichte, 9 (Trier: Porta-Alba Verlag, 2015).
Urban Space in the Middle Ages and Early Modern Times, ed. Albrecht Classen. Fundamentals of Medieval and Early Modern Culture, 4 (Berlin and New York: Walter de Gruyter, 2009).
Van Cleve, John, *The Problem of Wealth in the Literature of Luther's Gemany*. Studies in German Literature, Linguistics, and Culture (Columbus, SC: Camden House, 1991).
van der Linden, David, *Experiencing Exile: Huguenot Refugees in the Dutch Republic, 1680–1700* (London: Routledge, 2015).
Vaquer Bennàssar, Onofre, *L'Esclavitud a Mallorca, 1448–1500* (Palma, Mallorca: IEB, 1997).
Vaucher, Daniel, *Sklaverei in Norm und Praxis: Die frühchristlichen Kirchenordnungen*. 2nd ed. Sklaverei – Knechtschaft – Zwangsarbeit, 18 (2017; Hildesheim, Zürich, and New York: Olms / Weidmann, 2020).
Vercamer, Grischa, *Hochmittelalterliche Herrschaftspraxis im Spiegel der Geschichtsschreibung: Verstellungen von "guter" und "schlechter" Herrschaft in*

England, Polen und dem Reich im 12./13. Jahrhundert. Deutsches Historisches Institut Warschau, Quellen und Studien, 37 (Wiesbaden: Harrassowitz Verlag, 2020).

Verlinden, Charles, *L'esclavage dans l'Europe medieval*. 2 vols. Rijksuniversiteit te Gent; Werken uitgegeven door de Faculteit van de Letteren en Wijsbegeerte, 119e aflevering, 162 (Bruges: "De Tempel", 1955).

Verlinden, Charles, *Slavenhandel en economische ontwikkeling in Midden-, Oost- en Noord-Europa gedurende de hoge middeleeuwen*. Mededelingen van de Koninklijke Academie voor Wetenschappen, Letteren en Schone Kunsten van België, Klasse der Letteren, 41.2 (Brussel: Paleis der Academiën, 1979).

Verlinden, Charles, *The Beginnings of Modern Colonization: Eleven Essays with an Introduction* (Ithaca, NY, and London: Cornell University Press, 1970).

Vernacular Traditions of Boethius's De Consolatione philosophiae, ed. Noel Harold Kaylor, Jr. and Philip Edward Phillips. Research in Medieval Culture (Kalamazoo, MI: Medieval Institute Publications, Western Michigan University, 2016).

Verräter: Geschichte eines Deutungsmusters, ed. André Kritscher (Vienna, Cologne, and Weimar, 2019).

Verschleppt, Verkauft, Versklavt: deutschsprachige Sklavenberichte aus Nordafrika (1550–1800). Edition und Kommentar, ed. Mario Klarer (Vienna: Böhlau, 2019).

Vestrucci, Andrea, *Theology as Freedom: On Martin Luther's "De servo arbitrio"*. Dogmatik in der Moderne, 24 (Tübingen: Mohr Siebeck, 2019).

Vetter, Angila, *Textgeschichte(n): Retextualisierungsstrategien und Sinnproduktion in Sammlungsverbünden: der "Willehalm" in kontextueller Lektüre*. Philologische Studien und Quellen, 269 (Berlin: Erich Schmidt Verlag, 2018).

Vettori, Alessandro, *Dante's Prayerful Pilgrimage: Typologies of Prayer in the Comedy*. Medieval and Renaissance Authors and Texts, 22 (Leiden and Boston: Brill, 2019).

Villon: Hier et à jamais: Deux décennies de recherches sur François Villon, ed. Jacqueline Cerquiglini-Toulet. Colloques, congrès et conferences sur le Moyen Âge, 28 (Paris: Honoré Champion, 2020).

Volfing, Gerhard, *Von Akkon nach Dürnstein: Herzog Leopold V. und König Richard Löwenherz* (Salzburg: Östereichischer Milizverlag Salzburg, 2016).

Vollmann-Profe, Gisela, "Kudrun – eine kühle Heldin: Überlegungen zu einer problematischen Gestalt," *Blütezeit: Festschrift für L. Peter Johson zum 70. Geburtstag*, ed. Mark Chinca, Joachim Heinzle, and Christopher Young (Tübingen: Max Niemeyer Verlag, 2000), 231–44.

Vossen, Rüdiger, "Drachen und mythische Schlangen im Kulturvergleich: Drachen von Ostasien bis Westeuropa seit dem 4. Jahrtausend v. Chr.," *Auf Drachenspuren: Ein Buch zum Drachenprojekt des Hamburgischen Museums für Völkerkunde*, ed. Bernd Schmelz and Rüdiger Vossen (Bonn: Holos-Verlag, 1995), 10–24.

Wagner, Ricarda, *Entangled Displacements: Exile and Medieval European Literature*. Trends in Medieval Philology, 39 (Berlin and Boston: Walter de Gruyter, 2020).

Wailes, Stephen L., *Studien zur Kleindichtung des Stricker*. Philologische Studien und Quellen, 104 (Berlin: Erich Schmidt Verlag, 1981).

Walliczek, Wolfgang, "Rudolf von Ems," *Die deutsche Literatur des Mittelalters: Verfasserlexikon*. 2nd, completely rev. and expanded ed. by Kurt Ruh et al. Vol. 8 (Berlin and New York: Walter de Gruyter, 1992), col. 322–345.

Walliczek, Wolfgang, *Rudolf von Ems, 'Der guote Gêrhart'*. Münchener Texte und Untersuchungen zur deutschen Literatur des Mittelalters, 46 (Munich: C. H. Beck, 1973).
Waltharius, ed., trans., and intro. by Abram Ring. Dallas Medieval Texts and Translations, 22 (Leuven, Paris, and Bristol, CT: Peeters, 2016).
Wandhoff, Haiko, *Ekphrasis: Kunstbeschreibungen und virtuelle Räume in der Literatur des Mittelalters*. Trends in Medieval Philology, 3 (Berlin and New York: Walter de Gruyter, 2003).
Wandycz, Piotr S., *The Price of Freedom: A History of East Central Europe from the Middle Ages to the Present*. History/Soviet Studies (London and New York: Routledge, 1992).
Waskiewicz, Andrzej, *The Idea of Political Representation and Its Paradoxes*, trans. from Polish by Agnieszka Waśkiewicz and Marilyn E. Burton. Studies in Social Sciences, Philosophy and History of Ideas, 24 (Berlin: Peter Lang, 2020).
Weißweiler, Jens, *Gewaltentwürfe in der epischen Literatur des 12. Jahrhunderts: zur narrativen Verortung von Gewalt im "König Rother" und im "Straßburger Alexander"*. Germanistische Literaturwissenschaft, 12 (Baden-Baden: Ergon Verlag, 2019).
Wenninger, Markus J., "*Iudei et ceteri ...*: Bemerkungen zur rechtlichen, sozialen und wirtschaftlichen Stellung der Juden in karolingischer und ottonischer Zeit," *Aschkenas* 30.2 (2020): 217–44.
Werner, Ernst, *Stadtluft macht frei: Frühscholastik und bürgerliche Emanzipation in der ersten Hälfte des 12. Jahrhunderts*. Sitzungsberichte der Sächsischen Akademie der Wissenschaften zu Leipzig, Philologisch-Historische Klasse, 118.5 (Berlin: Akademie-Verlag, 1976).
Wernher der Gärtner, *Helmbrecht. Mittelhochdeutsch / Neuhochdeutsch*, ed., trans., and commentary by Fritz Tschirch (1974; Stuttgart: Philipp Reclam jun.,1991).
Wernher der Gärtner: 'Helmbrecht': Die Beiträge des Helmbrecht-Symposions in Burghausen 2001, ed. Theodor Nolte and Tobias Schneider (Stuttgart: S. Hirzel Verlag, 2001).
Whalen, Brett Edward, *The Two Powers: The Papacy, the Empire, and the Struggle for Sovereignty in the Thirteenth Century* (Philadelphia, PA: University of Pennsylvania Press, 2019).
Whalen, Logan E., "A Medieval Book-Burning: Objet d'art as Narrative Device in the Lai of Guigemar," *Neophilologus* 80.2 (1996): 205–11.
Whitaker, Cord J., *Black Metaphors: How Modern Racism Emerged from Medieval Race-Thinking*. The Middle Ages Series (Philadelphia, PA: University of Pennsylvania Press, 2019).
Whitteridge, Gweneth, "The Identity of Sir Thomas Malory, Knight-Prisoner," *The Review of English Studies* 24.95 (1973): 257–65.
Wilde-Stockmeyer, Marlis, *Sklaverei auf Island: Untersuchungen zur rechtlich-sozialen Situation und literarischen Darstellung der Sklaven im skandinavischen Mittelalter*. Skandinavistische Arbeiten, 5 (Heidelberg: Universitätsverlag Winter, 1978).
Wilson, David, *Pain and Retribution: A Short History of British Prisons 1066 to the Present* (London: Reaktion Books, 2014).
Die Wirklichkeit der konkreten Freiheit: G. W. F. Hegels Lehre vom Staat als ausgeführter Idee der Sittlichkeit, ed. Michael Städtler. Staatsdiskurse, 37 (Stuttgart: Franz Steiner Verlag, 2020).
Wohlgschaft, Hermann, *Schuld und Versöhnung: das Letzte Gericht und die größere Hoffnung* (Würzburg: Echter, 2019).

Wolf, Alois, *Die Saga von der Njálsbrenna und die Frage nach dem Epos im europäischen Mittelalter*. Beiträge zur Nordischen Philologie, 53 (Tübingen: A. Francke Verlag, 2014).
Wolfram von Eschenbach, *Parzival* and *Titurel*, trans. with Notes by Cyril Edwards (Oxford: Oxford University Press, 2006).
Wolfram von Eschenbach, *Parzival*. Studienausgabe. 2nd ed. Mittelhochdeutscher Text nach der sechsten Ausgabe von Karl Lachmann. Übersetzung von Peter Knecht (Berlin and New York: Walter de Gruyter).
Wolfram von Eschenbach, *Willehalm*, trans. Marion E. Gibbs and Sidney M. Johnson (London: Penguin, 1984).
Wolfram von Eschenbach, *Willehalm: nach der Handschrift 857 der Stiftsbibliothek St. Gallen*, mittelhochdeutscher Text, Übersetzung, Kommentar; mit den Miniaturen aus der Wolfenbütteler Handschrift, ed. Joachim Heinzle. Mit einem Aufsatz von Peter und Dorothea Diemer. Bibliothek des Mittelalters, 9 (Frankfurt a.M.: Deutscher Klassiker Verlag, 1991).
Wolframs "Willehalm": Fifteen Essays, ed. Martin H. Jones and Timothy McFarland. Studies in German Literature, Linguistics, and Culture (Rochester, NY: Camden House, 2002).
Wolverton, Lisa, "Why Kings?," *Rethinking Medieval Margins and Marginality*, ed. Anne E. Zimo, Tiffany D. Vann Sprecher, Kathryn Reyerson, and Debra Blumenthal. Studies in Medieval History and Culture (London and New York: Routledge, 2020), 91–106.
Woman Defamed and Woman Defended: An Anthology of Medieval Texts, ed. Alcuin Blamires with Karen Pratt and C. W. Marx (Oxford: Clarendon Press, 1992).
The Work of Work: Servitude, Slavery, and Labor in Medieval England, ed. Allen J. Frantzen (Glasgow: Cruithne Press, 1994).
Wunderlich, Werner, *Der "ritterliche" Kaufmann: literatursoziologische Studien zu Rudolf von Ems' "Der guote Gêrhart"*. Scriptor-Hochschulschriften / Literaturwissenschaft, 7 (Kronberg/Ts.: Scriptor-Verlag, 1975).
Wyatt, David, *Slaves and Warriors in Medieval Britain and Ireland, 800–1200*. The Northern World, 45 (Leiden and Boston: Brill, 2009).
Young, Christopher, *Narrativische Perspektiven in Wolframs "Willehalm": Figuren, Erzähler, Sinngebungsprozeß*. Untersuchungen zur deutschen Literaturgeschichte, 104 (Tübingen: Max Niemeyer, 2000).
Zeldenrust, Lydia, *The Mélusine Romance in Medieval Europe: Translation, Circulation, and Material Contexts*. Studies in Medieval Romance (Cambridge: Cambridge University Press, 2020).
Zeune, Joachim, "Verliese, Gefängnisse und Folterkammern," *Burgen in Mitteleuropa. Ein Handbuch*. Vol. 1: *Bauformen und Entwicklung*, ed. Deutsche Burgenvereinigung and Horst Wolfgang Böhme (Stuttgart: Theiss, 1999), 314–15.
Zeuske, Michael, *Handbuch Geschichte der Sklaverei: Eine Globalgeschichte von den Anfängen bis zur Gegenwart*. 2nd ed. (2013; Berlin, München, and Boston: Walter De Gruyter – De Gruyter Oldenbourg, 2019).
Zhang, John Z., "Medieval Visual Arts and the Barred Window in Chaucer's *The Knight's Tale*," *English Language Notes* 28.3 (1991): 10–17.
Ziegeler, Hans-Joachim, *Erzählen im Spätmittelalter. Mären im Kontext von Minnereden, Bispeln und Romanen*. Münchener Texte und Untersuchungen zur deutschen Literatur des Mittelalters, 87 (Munich and Zürich: Artemis, 1985).

Zilfi, Madeline C., *Women and Slavery in the Late Ottoman Empire: The Design of Difference.* Cambridge Studies in Islamic Civilization (Cambridge: Cambridge University Press, 2010).

Zim, Rivkah, *The Consolations of Writing: Literary Strategies of Resistance from Boethius to Primo Levi* (Princeton, NJ: Princeton University Press, 2014).

Ziolkowski, Jan, "Fighting Words: Wordplay and Swordplay in the 'Waltharius'," *Germanic Texts and Latin Models: Medieval Reconstructions*, ed. K. E. Olsen, A. Harbus, and T. Hofstra. Mediaevalia Groningana, 2 (Leuven, Paris, and Stirling, VA: Peeters, 2001), 9–51.

Ziolkowski, Jan M., "Waltharius," *The Virgil Encyclopedia*, ed. id. and Richard F. Thomas. Vol. 3 (New York: Wiley, 2014), online at: https://doi.org/10.1002/9781118351352.wbve2221 (last accessed on Jan. 15, 2021).

Zöller, Sonja, *Kaiser, Kaufmann und die Macht des Geldes: Gerhard Unmaze von Köln als Finanzier der Reichspolitik und der "Gute Gerhard" des Rudolf von Ems.* Forschungen zur Geschichte der älteren deutschen Literatur, 16 (Munich: Wilhelm Fink Verlag, 1993).

Zwierlein, Otto, "Das Waltharius-Epos und seine lateinischen Vorbilder," *Antike und Abendland* 16 (1970): 153–84.

Index

Note: Although the apparatus to this study offers a wide range of additional discussions about related issues and relevant research, I have not drawn key words from there for this index. However, the reader is encouraged to utilize this index as a gateway toward the wider issues addressed there.

Abd al-Rahmān III, Caliph   12
Abelard, Peter   17, 39, 42, 113
Act of Abjuration   13
Adolph I, Duke of Cleves   184
Aegidius Romanus   97
Alfonso X of Castile   55, 171
Aliscans   143–145
Alpharts Tod   33
Alphonse de Poitiers   180
Andreas Capellanus   113
Anselm of Canterbury   42
Apollonius of Tyre   134, 138, 148–52, 154, 168
Aquinas, Thomas   42, 95, 248
Aristotle   93, 215, 248
Attila the Hun   97
Aucassin et Nicolette   20, 134, 138, 146, 148
Augustine, St., Bishop of Hippo   2, 96, 100

Baibars al-Bunduqdari   180
Barbara von Hauenstein   195
Bartolomé de las Casas   232–236, 240, 242
Beaufort, Joan   190
Beowulf   59, 67f.
Berlin Wall   13
Bernard of Clairvaux   17, 42
Bertram de Born (the Elder)   179
Bey of Constantine   84
Blondel, minstrel   178f.
Boccaccio   33, 87, 115, 120, 123f., 137, 168f., 171, 173f., 209f.
Boethius   29f., 32, 37f., 42, 65, 86–92, 94, 96, 99f., 179, 187, 191–193, 197, 203, 225, 228, 241
Bogdan   27f.
Boleyn, Anne, Queen   29

Bonerius, Ulrich   13f., 59–65, 186, 210, 213, 243
Bonhoeffer, Dietrich   29, 37
Brant, Sebastian   15, 56, 255
Brinhild   157
Brooke, Henry   31
Bunyan, John   37

Campanella, Tommaso   37
Capone, Alphonse Gabriel   37f.
Cassou, Jean   37
Cato of Utica   211
Chanson de Aliscans   205
Chanson de Roland   59, 103, 109
Charlemagne, Emperor   57, 96, 179, 186
Charles d'Anjou   180
Charles d'Orléans   182–185, 188, 190f., 193, 207
Charles V, Emperor   233
Chaucer, Geoffrey   46, 182, 191, 193, 201–203
Christine de Pizan   215, 217f., 225, 248
Cobham, Lord   31
Conrad, Priest   103
Czech Lands   13, 58

Daniel, Arnaut   27, 37, 67, 114, 160, 165, 179, 185, 232f.
Dante Alighieri   86, 211f., 215
Das Lied vom Hürnen Seyfrid   156f., 159
David, Duke of Rothesay   6, 13, 19, 31, 35, 68, 71, 76, 81, 119, 176, 179, 184, 190, 233, 256
Der Stricker   22
Descartes, René   1f., 95
Devotio moderna   16f.
Dietrichs Flucht   33
Diu Klage   156

Duns Scotus 42
Dutch Republic 12, 35

Edward I, King 100
Edward IV, King 23
Eike von Repgow 53, 55
Eilhart von Oberg 256
Ekkehard I of St. Gall, monk 103
Elisabeth of Schönau 17
Elizabeth I, Queen 30
Endorfer, Friedrich 32
Engelbert of Admont 97
Ensslin, Gudrun 37
Epicureans 93
Erasmus of Rotterdam 43
Eric of Pomerania, King 47
exile 32–36, 64, 105f., 109, 132, 157, 192, 203, 243

Fakhr-ad-Din Yusuf, Emir 180
Faris ad-Din Aktai 180
Fichte, Johann Gottlieb 96
Fitzwalter, Robert 101
Fleck, Konrad 20, 139, 141
Floire and Blanchefleur 138f., 146
Formulary of Marculf 97
Fortunatus 24, 52, 219–226
Frank, Ann 30, 37, 45, 57, 104f., 167, 181
Frankfurt, Harry G. 9, 11f., 24, 37, 40, 44, 53, 66, 86, 108, 111, 143, 162, 206, 208, 253
Frederick I Barbarossa, Emperor 169
Frederick II, Emperor 30, 97
Frederick IV, Duke of Tyrol 194
Fridolin, Stephan 225
Frisia 58f., 84

Galilei, Galileo 11
Geoffrey de Villehardouin 166
Geoffrey of Fontaines 97
Georgius of Hungary 70, 74, 76, 84, 209f.
Gospel of Nicodemus 88
Gottfried von Strassburg 117, 249
Gower, John 191, 193
Gramsci, Antonio 37
Gregory the Great 96
Grettir's Saga 126, 132f.

Grettis saga Ásmandarsonar 132
Gruneweg, Martin 27f.
Guantanamo Bay 38
Guarionex, King 237
Guiraut de Borneil 179

Harald, King 57
Hartmann von Aue 24, 45, 111, 122f.
Henry IV, King 190, 192
Henry of Castile the Senator 174
Henry of Ghent 97
Henry V, King 182f., 191
Henry VI, Emperor 37, 175, 177
Henry VII, King 212
Henry VIII, King 29, 37
Hess, Rudolph 37
Higden, Ranulf 179
"Hildebrandslied" 33, 108f.
Hildegard of Bingen 17
Historia septem sapientum 115
Hitler, Adolf 38
Hrotsvit of Gandersheim 11f.
Hugh de Morville 178
Hugo von Trimberg 46, 48–50
Huguenots 34

Iceland 15, 17, 41, 56–58, 60, 105, 126, 130f., 247
Isidor of Seville 96
Islendingasôgur 128

Jacobus de Voragine 157, 244f.
James I of England, King 30–31
James I of Scotland, King 190f.
Japanese-Americans (internment camps) 10
Jean, Duke of Bourbon 19, 25, 38, 111, 115, 134, 139, 148, 178, 185, 188, 195, 211, 244
Jean d'Arras 24f.
Johanitza, King 166, 168
John, King 5, 15, 20, 31, 60, 76, 78, 88, 98, 100f., 113, 161, 169, 172, 177, 182f., 201–203, 212, 224, 234, 240, 243, 246
John of Salisbury 186, 215
Joinville 166, 181
Juan Ginés de Sepulveda 234
Juan Manuel, Don 171–173, 210

Index — **309**

Kaufringer, Heinrich   121–123, 209, 249
Kempe, Margery   249 f.
kidnapping   4, 94, 134, 138
König Rother   110, 152
Krafft, Hans Ulrich   8, 26 f., 71
Kudrun   105, 152–156

Landnámabó   57, 128
Latini, Brunetto   97, 215
Law of Uppland   128
Laxdæla Saga   130, 134
Lebuinus, St.   57
Leo X, Pope   227
Leonard, Saint   244 f.
Leopold V, Duke of Austria   174, 177
Levi, Primo   37 f.
Lombardus, Peter   42
Louis IX, King   180 f.
Louis the Pious, Emperor   96
Louis VIII of France, King   101
Louis XIII, King   184
Louis XIV   34, 98
Ludgate prison   31
Luis de León, Fray   37
Luther, Martin   43, 76, 80, 95, 224, 227–232, 238

Magna Carta   98, 100–102
Malory, Thomas   23, 174
Mandela, Nelson   37
Marco Polo   19 f., 73
Marcus Aurelius, Emperor   95
Marguerite de Navarre   95, 240
Marguerite de Porète   39, 250
Marie de Clèves   184
Marie de France   20, 59–62, 110–112, 115, 118 f., 136, 186, 213, 215, 243
Marshalsea Prison   23
Marsilio of Padua   97
Meister Eckhart   17
Melchior Manlich Trade Company   26
Messenius, Johannes   11
Migerditz   27 f.
Miguel de Cervantes   37, 83
Mill, John Stuart   6, 40, 56, 58, 79, 108, 179
Montesinos, Antonio de   234

More, Thomas   29 f., 37, 61 f., 78, 88, 95, 167, 225

Neville, Richard   23
Newgate prison   31
Nibelungenlied   20, 35 f., 91, 103, 107, 110, 156, 159
Njál's Saga   6, 125 f., 128–130

Odorico da Pordenone   73
Olufs, Harck   84 f.
Order of Merced   10
Order of the Trinitarians   10
Ortnit   33
Oswald   152, 194–197, 199, 244
Oswald von Wolkenstein   14, 184, 194–197, 244
Otto I, Emperor   12
Otto von Freising   176
Ovid   32 f., 110, 112 f.

Philip II, King   13, 174
Philip the Good, Duke   184
Philippe de Beaumanoir   246
Pietro della Vigna   30
Plato   93, 95, 248
Poe, Edgar Allan   103, 123, 139
El Poema de Mío Cid   59
Poland   58, 73
Pommerania   15
Pound, Ezra   37

Quevedo, Juan   234

Rabenschlacht   33
racism   5, 16
Radulph of Coggeshall   176
Rafold, Heinrich   207, 209
Rahewin   176
Raleigh, Walter   30 f.
Ratushinskaya, Irina   37
Regin Smiður   157
Remigio dei Girolami   97
Richard I Lionheart, King   174–80, 182, 190, 193
Richard of Devizes   177
Rígsþula   128 f.

Robert, Earl of Fife   9, 57, 96, 100, 126, 134, 139, 148, 165, 176, 190 f., 201, 211, 220, 229
Robert of Melun   42
Roger of Howden   176
Rolan, Marie-Jeanne   37
Roman de Cassidorus   115
Le Roman des Sept Sages de Rome   115
Rudolf von Ems   10, 160–162, 165, 171, 173, 209
Ruodlieb   103
Rustichello da Pisa   19

Sachs, Hans   55, 57, 256
Saladin   168–176, 209
Salman und Morolf   24
Schiltberger, Johann   70–74, 76 f., 84, 209 f.
Scotus, John Duns   97
Shakespeare, William   148
Siete Partidas   55
Sigmund, Duke of Tyrol   194
Simonsson, Tomas, Bishop   47
Socrates   90, 95, 248
Solzhenitsyn, Alexander   39
"Song of Engelbrekt"   47
Steinhöwel, Heinrich   151
Stewart, Robert, Duke of Albany   191
Stoics   93
Stuart, Arabella   30, 34, 134
Switzerland   15, 56

Tamerlane   73

Tempier, Etienne   43
The Pipe Roll   55
Thibaut de Champagne   66
Thirty Years' War   13
Thomas Marchale   249
Thorgilsson, Arí   57
Thüring von Ringoltingen   24 f.
Þiðrekssaga   103
Tower   29–32, 37, 183, 190 f.
"Türkendrucke"   76
tyranny   3, 45, 96, 215, 217, 236, 238, 256

Ulrich von Zazikhoven   21

Viaticum   118
Vidal, Peire   179
Villon, François   14, 185, 197 f.
Vlad II, Duke   77
Völsunga Saga   156

Waldere   103
Waltharius   103–105, 107–110, 143, 148
Wernher der Gardenære   51 f.
Wilde, Oscar   37, 126, 132
William of Occam   97
William of St. Thierry   17
William von Newburgh   176
Winterbach, Mayer   26
Wolfdietrich D   24
Wolfram von Eschenbach   20, 24, 46, 143–146, 163, 199, 205, 219